Also in the Variorum Collected Studies Series

BENEDICTA WARD
Signs and Wonders:
Saints, Miracles and Prayer from the 4th Century to the 14th

CYRILLE VOGEL
En rémission des péchés:
Recherches sur les systèmes pénitentiels dans l'Eglise latine

VICTOR SAXER
Pères saints et culte chrétien dans l'Eglise des premiers siècles

CHARLES MUNIER
Autorité épiscopale et sollicitude pastorale (IIe–VIe siècles)

R. A. MARKUS
From Augustine to Gregory the Great:
History and Christianity in late antiquity

R. A. MARKUS
Sacred and Secular:
Studies on Augustine and Latin Christianity

BRIGITTE BEDOS-REZAK
Form and Order in Medieval France:
Studies in social and quantitative sigillography

MARJORIE CHIBNALL
Piety, Power and History in Medieval England and Normandy

GILES CONSTABLE
Culture and Spirituality in Medieval Europe

JACQUES DUBOIS
Aspects de la vie monastique en France au Moyen Âge

ROSAMOND McKITTERICK
Books, Scribes and Learning in the Frankish Kingdoms, 6th–9th Centuries

ROGER E. REYNOLDS
Clerics in the Early Middle Ages: Hierarchy and Image

ROGER E. REYNOLDS
Clerical Orders in the Early Middle Ages: Duties and Ordination

VARIORUM COLLECTED STUDIES SERIES

Word, Image and Experience

Giselle de Nie

Giselle de Nie

Word, Image and Experience

Dynamics of Miracle and Self-Perception in Sixth-Century Gaul

ASHGATE
VARIORUM

Published in the Variorum Collected Studies Series by

Ashgate Publishing Limited
Gower House, Croft Road,
Aldershot, Hampshire GU11 3HR
Great Britain

Ashgate Publishing Company
Suite 420, 101 Cherry Street,
Burlington, Vermont 05401–5600
USA

Ashgate website: http://www.ashgate.com

ISBN 0–86078–933–0

British Library Cataloguing-in-Publication Data
Nie, Giselle de
Word, Image and Experience : Dynamics of Miracle and Self-Perception in Sixth-Century Gaul. – (Variorum Collected Studies Series: CS771).
1. Gregory, Saint, Bishop of Tours 2. Miracles 3. Image (Theology) 4. Identity (Psychology) – France – History – To 1500 5. Miracles in Literature 6. France – Church History – To 987
I. Title
231.7'3'0944'09021

US Library of Congress Cataloging-in-Publication Data
Nie, Giselle de.
Word, Image, and Experience: Dynamics of Miracle and Self-Perception in Sixth-Century Gaul / Giselle de Nie.
p. cm. – (Variorum Collected Studies Series: CS771).
Includes bibliographical references and index.
1. Miracles – History of Doctrines – Early Church, ca. 30–600. 2. Self – Religious Aspects – Christianity – History of Doctrines – Early Church, 30–600. 3. Gregory, Saint, Bishop of Tours, 538–594. 4. Fortunatus, Venantius Honorius Clementianus, ca. 540–ca. 600. 5. Gaul – Church History. I. Title. II. Collected Studies: CS771.

BT97.3.N54 2003
231.7'3'094409021–dc21 2003045230

The paper used in this publication meets the minimum requirements of the American National Standard for Information Sciences – Permanence of Paper for Printed Library Materials, ANSI Z39.48–1984. ∞ ™

Printed and bound in Great Britain by TJ International Ltd, Padstow, Cornwall

VARIORUM COLLECTED STUDIES SERIES CS771

CONTENTS

Introduction: Visions of the Heart ix

Acknowledgements xiv

SELF-PERCEPTION: A PERMEABLE VESSEL

I Is a Woman a Human Being?
Precept, Prejudice and Practice in Sixth-Century Gaul 1–26
First Published in Dutch as 'Is een vrouw een mens? Voorschrift, vooroordeel en praktijk in zesde-eeuws Gallië', in Het raadsel vrouwengeschiedenis, ed. F. de Haan et al. Tiende Jaarboek voor Vrouwengeschiedenis 10. Nijmegen, 1989, pp. 51–74

II The Body, Fluidity and Personal Identity
in the World View of Gregory of Tours 1–13
First published in French as 'Le corps, la fluidité et l'identité personnelle dans la vision du monde de Grégoire de Tours', in Aevum inter utrumque. Mélanges offerts à Gabriel Sanders, ed. M. van Uytfanghe and R. Demeulenaere. Instrumenta Patristica 23. Steenbrugge, 1991, pp. 75–87

III *Contagium* and Images of Self in
Late Sixth-Century Gaul 247–261
Purity and Holiness. The Heritage of Leviticus, ed. M.J.H.M. Poorthuis and J. Schwartz. Jewish and Christian Perspectives Series 2. Leiden, 2000

IV Images of Invisible Dynamics: Self and Non-Self in
Sixth-Century Saints' Lives 52–64
Studia Patristica 35, ed. M.F. Wiles and E.J. Yarnold. Leuven, 2001

SYMBOLIC ACTION: MIRACLE – OR MAGIC?

V Caesarius of Arles and Gregory of Tours: Two Sixth-Century Gallic Bishops and 'Christian Magic' 170–196
Cultural Identity and Cultural Integration: Ireland and Europe in the Early Middle Ages, ed. D. Edel. Dublin, 1995

ICONIC ALCHEMY: THE DYNAMIC OF IMAGES

VI A Broken Lamp or the Effluence of Holy Power? Common Sense and Belief-Reality in Gregory of Tours' Own Experience 269–279
Mediävistik 3. Frankfurt am Main, 1990

VII Seeing and Believing in the Early Middle Ages: A Preliminary Investigation 67–76
The Pictured Word. Word and Image Interactions 2, ed. M. Heusser et al. Studies in Comparative Literature 12. Amsterdam, 1998

VIII Gregory of Tours' Smile: Spiritual Reality, Imagination and Earthly Events in the "Histories" 68–95
Historiographie im frühen Mittelalter, ed. A. Scharer and G. Scheibelreiter. Veröffentlichungen des Instituts für Österreichische Geschichtsforschung 32. Wien, 1994

IX History and Miracle: Gregory's Use of Metaphor 261–279
The World of Gregory of Tours, ed. K. Mitchell and I. Wood. Cultures, Beliefs and Traditions 8. Leiden, 2002

X The Poet as Visionary: Venantius Fortunatus's "New Mantle" for Saint Martin 49–83
Cassiodorus 3. Catanzaro, 1997

XI Iconic Alchemy: Imaging Miracles in Late Sixth-Century Gaul 158–166
Studia Patristica 30, ed. E.A. Livingstone. Leuven, 1997

XII Word, Image and Experience in the Early Medieval Miracle Story 97–122
Language and Beyond. Actuality and Virtuality in the Relations between Word, Image and Sound, ed. P. Joret and A. Remael. Studies in Comparative Literature 17. Amsterdam, 1998

XIII Fatherly and Motherly Curing in Sixth-Century Gaul: Saint Radegund's *Mysterium* 53–86
Women and Miracle Stories. A Multidisciplinary Exploration, ed. A.-M. Korte. Numen Book Series. Studies in the History of Religions 88. Leiden, 2001

XIV Poetics of Wonder: Dream-Consciousness and Transformational Dynamics in Sixth-Century Miracle Stories 1–17
First published in German as 'Eine Poetik des Wunders: bildhaftes Bewusstsein und Verwandlungsdynamik in den Wundererzählungen des späten sechsten Jahrhunderts', in Mirakel im Mittelalter: Konzeptionen, Erscheinungsformen, Deutungen, ed. M. Heinzelmann, K. Herbers and D.R. Bauer. Beiträge zur Hagiographie 3. Stuttgart 2002, pp. 135–150

THE MIRACLE IN LANGUAGE

XV The 'Power' of What is Said in the Book: Word, Script and Sign in Gregory of Tours 1–27
First published in Dutch as 'De "kracht" van wat in het boek gezegd wordt: Woord, schrift en teken in zesde-eeuws Gallië', in Oraliteit en Schriftcultuur, ed. R.E.V. Stuip and C. Vellekoop. Utrechtse Bijdragen tot de Mediëvistiek 12. Hilversum, 1993, pp. 63–88

XVI Text, Symbol and 'Oral Culture' in the Sixth-Century Church: The Miracle Story 115–133
Mediävistik 9. Frankfurt am Main, 1997

XVII The Language in Miracle – The Miracle in Language: Words and the Word according to Gregory of Tours 1–29
First published in German as 'Die Sprache im Wunder – das Wunder in der Sprache. Menschenwort und Logos bei Gregor von Tours', in Mitteilungen des Instituts für Österreichische Geschichtsforschung 103. Wien, 1995, pp. 1–25

Index 1–4

This volume contains xiv + 374 pages

PUBLISHER'S NOTE

The articles in this volume, as in all others in the Collected Studies Series, have not been given a new, continuous pagination. In order to avoid confusion, and to facilitate their use where these same studies have been referred to elsewhere, the original pagination has been maintained wherever possible.

Each article has been given a Roman numeral in order of appearance, as listed in the Contents. This number is repeated on each page and quoted in the index entries.

INTRODUCTION

Visions of the heart

A little more than a hundred years ago, miracle stories in medieval sources were sometimes simply omitted as useless in printed editions. In the past decades, however, stories about saints and their miracles have finally been receiving the attention they deserve as serious testimonies of human experience. Scrutinized at first only for historical facts, and then also for implicit evidence of larger social relationships, now their most baffling aspect – their seemingly impenetrable thought world and mind-set – is increasingly being explored.

For the irrational notions and acts involved in medieval miracles, which historians in the Enlightenment tradition had dismissed as naive benightedness and rank superstition, appear in a different light when they are compared to modern cultural anthropologists' assessment of similar behaviour in certain oral societies today. In addition, recent psychological research and practice in the field of imagination have revealed a great deal about the workings of the human mind and affects that had not been known before. Finally, even in the abstruse field of theoretical physics, dynamics are being discovered that resemble those of a mechanistic universe less than they resemble what used to be regarded as the 'outrageously improbable' ones of miracle.

What is happening, it seems to me, is that – thanks to pioneers such as Carl Gustav Jung, Ernst Cassirer, Mircea Eliade and Gaston Bachelard (to name only a few) – the dynamic properties of images and imagery are being rediscovered: as visualized representations of patterns of affective energy, they are not only vectors of meaning but can also be transformers of consciousness. And the reality value of their non-rational, non-materialist – as it were 'dreamlike' or 'poetic' – interrelations is also being re-assessed: they manifest precisely the kind of leaping dynamics which early medieval sources attribute to miracles. The essays collected here attempt to approach an understanding of the sixth-century experience of miracles by examining the latter's imagistic contours and dynamics as these are mentioned, or hinted at, in the sources. Because each was designed to present its theoretical argument independently, the reader will find that there is a certain unavoidable overlap between them in this respect.

From this troubled period in Gaul, in which an inadequately ordered society of warring Frankish kings had replaced the political structure and civilization of the late Roman Empire, a substantial corpus of writings has survived of only two authors: bishop Gregory of Tours (539–594) and the poet Venantius Fortunatus, in later life bishop of Poitiers (540–c.604). Their perceptions of miracles – and their renderings of the human self-awareness through which miracles are perceived and happen – are analyzed as attempts to adjust the early Christian tradition so as to make sense of, and protect themselves in, their highly insecure environment. An in-depth comparison with some of the above-mentioned modern observations of the workings of images and symbols makes these stories look much less naive than they have so long seemed to be: they now appear to point to a forgotten world in ourselves which is still there for us to re-discover.

Since the fourth century – but possibly dating back as far as the Origen in the third – seeing and interpreting events and ideas in terms of images that were regarded as representing autonomous, powerful patterns of spiritual reality had been gaining ground in Christian circles. The great increase of dreams and visions that determined personal action – the best-known of these is, of course, the emperor Constantine's vision and/or dream – shows that this experience of images was an intimate as well as decisive one. In order to experience God's speaking to mankind through these images, Christian monks followed Origen in exploring the hidden meanings in the Bible through meditating on the associations and implications of its imagery – a consciousness-transforming practice that later became mandatory for all Catholic clergy.

The later fourth century, however, also saw a sudden increase of attention to miracles: Augustine's original overlooking of them and his later active endorsement are well-known. He came to regard a contemporary miracle, too, as making visible a message from God. This privileging of a visible image as the vector of a pattern of truth that could not be rigorously defined or circumscribed, and that extended into the divine realm, came to Gregory of Tours through Church tradition. However, whereas Augustine, the former rhetor, had regarded biblical images primarily as linguistic phenomena, Gregory clearly experiences religious imagery as standing for power patterns directly inherent in and determining all of happening reality: in his perception, then, the intra- and extra-mental spheres tend to coalesce.

Accordingly, the dominant fact in the self-awareness that emerges from Gregory and Fortunatus's – usually unintentional – descriptions of 'self' is the absence of a delimited interior space, of a clear boundary between 'self', or one's interior thoughts and feelings, and the visible (or invisible) 'outside' world. This must also be closely connected with the notion of the omnipresence of good and evil powers inhering in or passing through objects as well as bodies and minds – obviously, a core notion in the contemporary view of miracle. Not surprisingly, this permeability was experienced as dangerous. Fortunatus spells out with dynamic images what Gregory only suggests; for the real (that is: heavenly) self: firm groundedness, immobility, dissociation from the unruly body and the pernicious world, resting in the spirit in heaven; and for the experience of alienation from this true self: emptiness, falling into an abyss, turbulence, whirling, being engulfed, evanescence, dissolution into nothingness. Protection, firmness and permanence were therefore sought in the identification with the powerful heavenly Christ, who suffused and thereby transformed the human self-awareness by coming to live in the ascetic body and heart as in a vessel or temple. The image of the individual human consciousness or self, then, was essentially that of an unsubstantial, empty and extremely permeable container.

When we compare our authors' mostly indirect descriptions of the human self-awareness with that of Augustine as it appears in his *Confessions* – a book which does not seem to have reached western Europe in their time – the contrast is stunning. Whereas Augustine analyses emotions and inclinations as phenomena produced by the individual human consciousness, Gregory and Fortunatus tend to describe these as invading powers coming from without. Good power is to be kept in and evil power out through correct behaviour and meditation upon biblical models, accompanied by acts of symbolic ritual. And whereas the Church Father talks to an intimate God as the deepest layer of self in the language of the Psalms, they speak – instead – to the heavenly saint Martin as a client would address a powerful patron at the court of a divine and kingly Christ who is too august to access directly. It is now the more recognizably human saint who is prayed to for guidance, protection and healing.

Gregory and Fortunatus's descriptions of symbolic action in the context of miracle to keep evil spirits away and call upon the good power of saints raise the question in how far they may – unwittingly – have been indulging in a manipulation that could be designated as "Christian magic". I have argued that the difference between miracle and magic is that the traditional (biblical) purpose of the former includes the transformation of the heart – something which is not at issue in magic. The use of symbols in religious gestures has tended to be misunderstood among historians. As has become ever clearer in the past century – but east Asian Buddhist monks have known this for centuries –, instead of being "empty forms", the dynamic patterns inherent in images and symbols, when meditatively or ritually internalized, appear to activate congruent interior psychic dynamisms of which few people are consciously aware. Western psychologists and anthropologists now tell us that such an internalization can function as a silencer of the common-sense, verbalizing mind and opener of an interior dimension of consciousness that, as in poetry and dreams, becomes aware of its movements through images. In other words, symbols and images become springboards from which a subject may leap into a poetic or dreamlike dimension of experience which cannot be accessed through reasoning.

The more specific question of how the visualization of such images can affect mind and body during the process of miracle is probably the most baffling one. And here too we must look to sister disciplines for help. What psychologists show us with examples from their guided imagery therapies, and anthropologists with their observations on the enactment of symbols in healing rituals, is that the affective visualization of an image induces in the human subject a spontaneous inner mimicking of the dynamic pattern which it makes visible. Powerful symbols tend to be those involving so-called liminal situations, in which the subject is experiencing a transgression of the limits of everyday life: as in death and birth. Thus, visualizing the dynamic pattern of a seed dying to live precipitates an affective replication of this death-as-rebirth. This experience presences the image as an autonomous reality: it is sensed to be actively present outside the person as well as inside the heart, for – as in meditation – the boundary between the intra- and extramental spheres tends to dissolve.

Field observation among present-day oral societies has shown that enacting such symbols through elaborate ritual can dissolve knots of pent-up, debilitating tensions and thereby release new energy that heals the mind and body. I would like to acknowledge here my special debt to the illuminating insights of Professor René Devisch of the University of Louvain.[1] A well-known American surgeon ascribes the healing effect, upon cancer patients, of meditational visualizations of vitalizing images to the hypothalamus' translation of these images' inherent dynamic pattern into a congruent message to the body's autonomous systems.[2] But a modern faith healer's description of her practice reveals that, there too, the meditative

[1] As in R. Devisch, *Weaving the Threads of Life. The Khita Gyn-Eco-Logical Healing Cult Among the Yaka* (Chicago–London 1993), *passim.*

[2] B.S. Siegel, *Love, Medicine and Miracles* (New York 1986), pp. 66–69.

visualization of the affected body part as at that moment actually being healed, or as already perfectly well, played a central role in precipitating a cure.[3] This leap from a meditationally or ritually internalized vitalizing image to the healing of the body – as well as, more widely, that from the image of a spiritual reality to an empowering perception of its sensory concretization – is the essence of the mysterious dynamism which I have designated as 'iconic alchemy' in Gregory and Fortunatus's miracle stories.

Although Gregory never mentions Augustine, the reason which he gives for his writing about the miracles which he saw or which came to his attention shows how relatively close he is to the Church Father, and how far from us. Essentially, it is this: speaking or writing about holy subjects is becoming part of God's speaking to mankind through Christ, the divine Word, who is actively present in such human words. Carried by them into what may be arid, barren human hearts, he there continues his Creation: causing a faith to sprout that transforms and heals. But Gregory also tell us that just seeing a miracle happen at a saint's shrine – and thus, by implication, actually seeing Christ at work – will produce a similar result in the perceiver. In contrast to Augustine, however, for Gregory significant words in the religious sphere (especially holy names, but also words about a saint's deeds of holy power) are not only formal elements of language. As in dream-consciousness, the individual words themselves are the manifestation in sound (or written letters) of the actual presence of their specific referents, with their full, active power. Depending upon the spiritual state of the person concerned, pronouncing, hearing or touching them can therefore precipitate instant healing or debilitation.

What we see, then, in the interweaves of events and imagery which Gregory and Fortunatus describe for us as "miracles to be embraced in delight"[4] may be visions of forgotten, or as yet unfathomed, enabling and transformational potentialities of the human heart.

GISELLE DE NIE

Halle-Heide,
January 2003

---

[3] A. Sanford, *The Healing Light* (New York 1947), *passim*.

[4] Venantius Fortunatus, *De virtutibus sancti Hilarii* 21, ed. B. Krusch, Monumenta Germaniae Historica, Auctores Antiquissimi 4.2: *delectabiliter amplectanda miracula.*

ACKNOWLEDGEMENTS

Grateful acknowledgement is made to the following persons, editors publishers and institutions for their kind permission to reprint the articles included in this volume: SUN Uitgevers B.V. (I); the editors of *Instrumenta Patristica* (II); Brill NV (III, IX and XIII);the editors of *Studia Patristica* (IV and XI); Four Courts Press (V); Verlag Peter Lang (VI and XVI); Editions Rodopi B.V. (VII and XII); R. Oldenbourg Verlag (VIII and XVII); Rubettino Editore Srl (X); Franz Steiner Verlag (XIV); Uitgeverij Verloren (XV).

Is a Woman a Human Being? Precept, Prejudice and Practice in Sixth-Century Gaul[1]

In the sixth-century Frankish kingdom of Gaul, the private interests of large aristocratic families confronted the more centralizing policies of a rudimentary monarchy and of what was in fact a federation of bishops representing the Church. In these conditions, wherever royal or ecclesiastical officials were unable to enforce their authority, personal influence or private armed bands decided matters. In recent years more information has become available about the position of women in this society. Not allowed to carry arms, and excluded from ecclesiastical as well as political office, they could enjoy protection and exercise power only through their own and adopted families or through the patronage of ecclesiastical authorities.[2]

---

[1] This is a revised version of G. de Nie, "Is een vrouw een mens? Het beeld van de vrouw in de verhalen van Gregorius van Tours", in: L. van Tongerloo and E. Hattinga van 't Sant (ed.), *Convivium. Opstellen aangeboden aan J. M. van Winter* (Hilversum 1988), pp. 37–63. With thanks to Verloren Publishers, Hilversum. Author's translation of "Is een vrouw een mens? Voorschrift, vooroordeel en praktijk in zesde-eeuws Gallië", in: F. de Haan et al. (ed.), *Het raadsel vrouwengeschiedenis*, Jaarboek voor Vrouwengeschiedenis 10 (Nijmegen 1989), pp. 51–74.

[2] J.A. McNamara and S. Wemple, "The power of women through the family in medieval Europe: 500–1100", in: M.S. Hartmann and L. Banner (ed.), *Clio's Consciousness Raised. New Perspectives on the History of Women* (New York 1974), pp. 103–118, here pp. 103–109; J.A. McNamara and S. Wemple, "Sanctity and power: the dual pursuit of medieval women", in: R. Bridenthal and C. Koonz (ed.), *Becoming Visible. Women in European History* (Boston 1977), pp. 90–118, here pp. 96–98; J.L. Nelson, "Queens as Jezebels: the careers of Brunhild and Balthild in Merovingian history", in: D. Baker (ed.), *Medieval Women*, Studies in Church History, Subsidia 1 (Oxford 1978), pp. 31–77; J.T. Sschulenburg, "Sexism and the celestial gyneceum – from 500 to 1200", *Journal of Medieval History* 4 (1978), pp. 117–133, here pp. 119–121; J.A. McNamara, "A legacy of miracles: hagiography and nunneries in Merovingian Gaul", in: J. Kirschner and S.F. Wemple (ed.), *Women of the Medieval World. Essays in Honor of John H. Mundy* (London 1985), pp. 36–52; S. Mosher Stuard ed., *Women in medieval History and Historiography* (Philadelphia 1987); J.A. Nichols and L.T. Shank (ed.), *Medieval Religious Women*, 2 vols., Cistercian Studies 71 and 72 (Kalamazoo, Mich. 1984 and 1987).

The American historian Suzanne Wemple is one of the feminist historians subscribing to the above view. In her study of women in early medieval Frankish society she shows that they were discriminated against in many ways. The fact that there nevertheless was, in the sixth century, a slow increase in the legal possibilities of economical independence for women is explained by pointing to the policies of the Frankish kings. The latter used this strategy in an attempt to diminish the power of important families by breaking up their concentrations of landed power.[3] Consequently, some women were able exercise a certain political and economic influence.

Alongside the continuing general social and political discrimination of women, however, Wemple claims that there was in this period also an increased hostility to women in the Church.[4] The evidence adduced for this assertion is that of prescriptive sources: it includes conciliar decrees such as the abolishment of the female diaconate – and thereby of all female ordination – and the gradual delimitation, and later prohibition, of clerical marriage that ousted women from pastoral activities. As an example of the mentality behind this Wemple notes that a council at Tours in 567, refers to non-related women who – contrary to Church law – functioned as clerical housekeepers as "serpents".[5] In addition, certain ecclesiastical rulings prohibiting women from touching consecrated objects are said to point to the reason for the official distrust of these women: they would have been regarded as a threat to the "ritual purity" of the clergy. Wemple infers from this that women were therefore regarded as *by nature* impure beings who would "pollute" by their touch alone.[6] This view of women, she claims, was to have been a generally accepted one in the Franco-Gallic Church of this period, and to have played an important role in its contemporary attempt to establish the rule of male dominance in ecclesiastical affairs.[7]

---

[3] S.F. Wemple, *Women in Frankish Society. Marriage and the Cloister 500–900* (Philadelphia 1981), pp. 29–31, 38–50, and especially 49.

[4] *Ibid.*, pp. 127–141.

[5] Council of Tours (567), canon 10, in: C. de Clercq (ed.), *Concilia Galliae 511–695* Corpus Christianorum, Series Latina [CCSL] 148a (Turnhout 1963), pp. 179–180. See also canon 13 of this council: "[...] *ut nec* [...] *famularum propinqua contagione polluantur*." The "pollution" indicated here must be that of the sexual desire aroused by familiar contacts.

[6] Wemple, *Women*, p. 130: "there was nothing else she could do to counter the argument that the mere touch of her hands was polluting"; p. 136; and p. 139: "During the sixth century [...] the very nature of women [...] was held to be a threat to the ritual purity of the church."

[7] *Ibid.*, pp. 127 and 139.

But does the evidence confirm this? To begin with, the specific prohibitions to which Wemple points as proofs of a generally held view of the "impurity" of women occur only once in the conciliar legislation of the sixth-century Frankish kingdom, and they are the product of a diocesan synod which, as such, could have had only local authority.[8] In addition, as we shall see below, the wording of these rulings is not unambiguous. Further, although Wemple herself infers from the repeated occurrence of certain prohibitions that these will not have had the intended effect (and thus in fact point to the opposite situation), she does not integrate this into her overall view. Finally, one might well wonder whether church council rulings alone can give an accurate representation of the general ecclesiastical view of women in this period. Brian Brennan showed in 1985, for instance, that the narrative sources and poetry of the period present a positive appreciation of the status and duties of bishops' wives which is not found in contemporary conciliar decrees.[9]

Conciliar rulings alone, then, do not give us the whole picture. Fortunately, we also have a narrative source: the stories of the aristocratic Gallo-Roman Gregory. As bishop of Tours (573–594), he held one of the most important Church positions in the kingdom, and was a member of the ecclesiastical hierarchy that produced the conciliar decrees. Can the extreme misogyny to which Wemple points be found in his description of the actual practices in his time? His report of an incident in a synod addresses the core of the issue:

> [...] One of the bishops at this synod [in Mâcon in 585] asserted that a woman cannot be called a human being (*homo*). But after he had been corrected by the other bishops he gave up this opinion. For the holy book of the Old Testament clearly teaches [the opposite] saying that, in the beginning, when God created the human being (*homo*), "He created them masculine and feminine, and called their name Adam", that is: earth being (*homo terrenus*); thus both man and woman have this name: each is said to be a human being (*homo*). But our Lord Jesus Christ is for this reason also called the Son of Man, that is, the son of the

---

[8] *Ibid.*, p. 141: "A synod held at Auxerre [...] asserted that women by nature were impure." The acts of the synod of Auxerre (561/605) in: de Clercq, *Concilia*, pp. 264–272.

[9] Wemple, *Women*, p. 134: "no doubt that ecclesiastical sanctions were defied by both clergy and their wives". On p. 141, however, she speaks of a sixth-century ecclesiastical "campaign against women for polluting the sacraments and seducing the clergy". In this period it was not unusual for a married layman to be elected bishop when his children were grown; the couple was then expected to live in chastity: B. Brennan, "'*Episcopae*': bishops' wives viewed in sixth-century Gaul", *Church History* 54 (1985), pp. 311–323.

> Virgin, who is a woman. For when he was about to change water into wine, he said: "What have I to do with you woman?" etc. The matter was put to rest with many additional testimonies.[10]

This bishop was persuaded by semantic arguments, but the background of his question was probably theological.[11] For the early Christian view of woman as it was developed by the Church Fathers contained a fundamental ambivalence that derived primarily from statements in the letters attributed to the apostle Paul.

In Jesus' Jewish, Hellenistic and Roman environment, his treatment of men and women as equals had been exceptional. A reflection of this new view of women is found in the Pauline words that would continue to work as a ferment in the Christian community: "you are all sons of God through your belief in Christ Jesus. [...] There is no Jew or Greek, no slave or free, no male or female: for you are all one in Christ Jesus."[12] Alongside these liberating words, however, there are a number of statements that reflect the established values of late antique society, in which women were treated as morally and intellectually inferior beings and therefore unfit for public office. Paul makes a well-known double comparison:

> let women be subjected to their husbands as they are to the Lord, for man is the head of woman as Christ is the head of the Church; it is He who saves his body. Just as the Church is subject to Christ, women are subject to their husbands in everything.[13]

---

[10] Gregorius Turonensis, *Historiae libri decem* [*Hist.*] 8.20, in: R. Buchner (ed. and tr.), *Gregor von Tours. Zehn Bücher Geschichten.* 2 vols., Ausgewählte Quellen zur deutschen Geschichte des Mittelalters, Freiherr von Stein-Gedächtnisausgabe, 2 and 3 (Darmstadt 1967), p. 188; this edition is based on that of B. Krusch and W. Levison, MGH SSrM 1.1, editio altera (Hannover 1951). Bible references (Vulgate): Genesis 5:2 ; John 2:4.

[11] Cf. G. Kurth, *Études franques*, vol. 1 (Paris–Brussels 1919), pp. 161–167.

[12] Galatians 3:26, 28 (this and subsequent biblical quotations are my own translation from the Vulgate). On this theme see, for instance, J.A. Brundage, *Law, Sex and Society in Medieval Europe* (Chicago–London 1987), pp. 10–61; C.F. Parvey, "The theology and leadership of women in the New Testament", in: R.R. Ruether (ed.), *Religion and Sexism. Images of Woman in the Jewish and Christian Tradition* (New York 1974), pp. 117–149; R. Rader, *Breaking Boundaries. Male-female Friendship in Early Christian Communities* (Ramsey, N.J. 1983), p. 40.

[13] Ephesians 5:22–24. Cf., for instance, R.R. Ruether, "Misogynism and virginal feminism in the Fathers of the Church", in: idem, *Religion*, pp. 150–183; D. S. Bailey, *The Man-Woman Relation in Christian Thought* (London 1959), pp. 63–68; G.H. Tavard, *Women in Christian Tradition* (Notre Dame–London 1973), pp. 59, 105; Brundage, *Law*, pp. 60–65.

In symbolical terms, then, man corresponds to Christ and to the head, and woman to the Church and the body. Somewhat later, the apostle makes this explicit in what might appear to be an invidious comparison: "in this way men ought to love their wives as they love their own bodies."[14] And when he says elsewhere that women, "while praying and prophesying" should cover their heads, he gives the following reason: "for [man] is the image and the glory (*imago et gloria*) of God, but woman is the glory of man. [...]. Man was not created for woman, but woman for man."[15]

Given this tradition, it is hardly surprising that some could wonder if a being who was not created in God's image, and who was to be treated as a subjected body devoid of reason, was indeed fully human. Such doubts, moreover, are likely to have been further fueled by the rise in post-apostolic times of an as yet insufficiently explained negative obsession with the body and sexuality that continued into the early Middle Ages.[16] In the fourth century, the apostle Paul's advice to await the imminent end of the world in chastity[17] was viewed through this lens. This and the related notion that the liberation of the spirit from its enslavement to the body was a condition for its union with God now inspired large numbers of men and women to withdraw from the world as hermits or in monasteries; but it was also the reason for the papal policy requiring celibacy of the clergy.[18] Total sexual renunciation and withdrawal from secular affairs, then, was praised as the most perfect life.[19]

---

[14] Ephesians 5:28.

[15] 1 Corinthians 11: 7, 9.

[16] See, for instance, Brundage, *Law*, pp. 62–76; S. Laeuchli, *Power and Sexuality. The Emergence of Canon Law at the Synod of Elvira* (Philadelphia 1972); A. Rousselle, *Porneia. De la maîtrise du corps à la privation sensorielle: IIe–IVe siècle de l'ère chrétienne* (Paris 1983); and especially P. Brown, *The Body and Society. Men, Women and Sexual Renunciation in Early Christianity* (New York 1988).

[17] 1 Corinthians 7:8.

[18] Romans 8:5–11 is one of the central statements cited in support of this. About clerical celibacy see: R. Gryson, *Les origines du célibat ecclésiastique du premier au septième siècle*, Recherches et synthèses, Section d'histoire 11 (Gembloux 1970). Divergent views about this subject in: Laeuchli, *Power*, *passim*, and J.P. Audet, *Mariage et célibat dans le service de l'église. Histoire et orientations* (Paris 1967).

[19] P. Brown, "Late Antiquity", in: P. Veyne (ed.), *A History of Private Life*, vol. 1: *From Pagan Rome to Byzantium* (Cambridge, Mass.–London 1987), pp. 235–311, here p. 263; and P. Brown, "The notion of virginity in the early Church", in: B. McGinn (ed.), *Christian Spirituality. Origins to the Twelfth Century*, World Spirituality 16 (New York 1987), pp. 427–443.

The increased emphasis upon the importance of total sexual renunciation threatened to devalue the ontological status of woman still further. Her being symbolically associated with the body devoid of reason could turn her, in masculine eyes, into the embodiment of the temptation to indulge in sexual feelings and actions. And, as such, woman in general tended to be degraded into a – if possible, to be avoided – threat to man. From the fourth century, such notions, already present in the first letter to Timothy, appear more and more frequently in Church literature and legislation.[20] Amidst what appears in fact to have been an increasing male anxiety about contacts with women there was, however, no mention of woman as a being *by nature impure*.

But what about other kinds of sources? Gregory of Tours' *Histories* (*Historiae*), *The Lives of the Fathers* (*Vita patrum*) and his seven books of collected miracles[21] are about the only narrative source for about political, ecclesiastical and daily life in sixth-century Gaul. They are written in an ostensibly simple but very lively style, and in a no longer classical Latin that, because it approached the spoken language of the period, is likely to have been generally understood. The aim of his writings was to transmit the truths of the Christian faith, as illustrated through the events of daily life, not only to his contemporaries, but also to future generations. As a natural story-teller, however, Gregory usually presents his message indirectly. I have taken the fact that he here and there directly addresses his contemporaries – for instance, warning the powerful – as a reason to assume that his stories would have been recognizable to them as not too far removed from the facts of everyday life. Do these show that the Apostle's and the Church Fathers' above-mentioned notions and precepts were being enacted in everyday practice?

In what follows, I shall investigate Gregory's stories for traces of hostility to women or its opposite. The following questions will be asked: how do the concepts of "purity" and "pollution" relate to women in his

---

[20] 1 Timothy 2:14. On Church literature and legislation: Ruether, "Misogynism", pp. 157–158; and Wemple, *Women*, pp. 22–23. The fullest discussion of Church literature on this subject is Brown, *Body*.

[21] All of these were revised and corrected by him near the end of his life. Alongside the *Historiae* (see n. 10), there are: *In gloria martyrum* (*Glor. mart.*), *De virtutibus sancti Juliani* (*Virt. Jul.*), *De virtutibus sancti Martini* (*Virt. Mart.*), *In gloria confessorum* (*Glor. conf.*), *De vita patrum* (*Vit. patr.*), in: B. Krusch (ed.), *Gregorii episcopi Turonensis Libri octo miraculorum*, in: W. Arndt and B. Krusch (ed.), *Gregorii episcopi Turonensis Opera*, MGH SSrM 1.2 (Hannover 1885), pp. 451–820.

stories? To what extent does he regard woman as an "inferior" being? Is she less intelligent or wise than a man? And finally: is it necessary for her to put aside her femininity in order to be equal to a man? Before investigating Gregory's view of women and pollution, however, it is necessary to take a closer look at the Gallic conciliar legislation on women in connection with ritual impurity which led Wemple to her conclusion.

Woman, "purity" and "pollution" in the Gallic councils

As we saw, the late fourth-century popes had implemented the increasing emphasis upon the life of the spirit by initiating the requirement of sexual renunciation for the western clergy.[22] The first mention of this in Gaul is found in the middle of the fifth century, and it recurs thereafter in ever stricter formulations. Canon 1 of the council of Tours in 461 speaks of: "purity not only of the heart but also of the body (*non solum cordis verum etiam corporis purita[s]*)", and about "the polluted (*coinquinati*)" whose "mind and conscience is polluted (*polluta est eorum mens et conscientia*)".[23]

In a letter of Pope Innocent I, included in the acts of the council of Agde in 506, we find the most explicit and clear statement about "purity".[24] The pope, referring to a decree about clerical celibacy of his predecessor Siricius, reminds his readers that the Old Testament priests had been required to abstain from sexual relations during their period of Temple service, because God had said: "be holy for I am holy". Further, the pope continues, if even laymen, upon the advice of Paul, abstain to be able to pray, how much more should priests do so, whose office it is to pray constantly and to celebrate masses. How can anyone who is "contaminated by carnal concupiscence (*contaminatus [...] carnali concupiscentia*)", the pope asks, think that his prayers will be heard? Later, he quotes Paul: "Those who are in the flesh cannot please God. You, however, are not in the flesh but in the Spirit." What we see in the pope's words is that sensuality – and not woman – pollutes a person in body, spirit and conscience and makes him unfit for prayer and liturgy. For, as appears in a canon of the council of Clermont in 535, this pollution is transmitted through physical contact:

---

[22] Gryson, *Célibat*, p. 190; Audet, *Mariage*, p. 133; Tavard, *Woman*, p. 119.

[23] Council of Orange (441), can. 21 and 22; Council of Tours (461), can. 10 and 11, in: C. Munier (ed.), *Concilia Galliae A..314–A.506*, CCSL 148 (Turnhout 1963), pp. 84, 143–144. Cf. Titus 1:15 and Gryson, *Célibat*, 194–195.

[24] Council of Agde (506), can. 9, in: Munier, *Concilia*, pp. 196–199. Biblical references: Leviticus 11:44, 1 Corinthians 7:5, Romans 8:8–9. Cf. Audet, *Mariage*, pp. 114, 128–134, and Brundage, *Law*, p. 111.

> Liturgical vessels (*ministeria divina*) may not be used to decorate weddings because they will be polluted by the touch of sinners and the shows of worldly sensuality (*improborum tactu et pompa saecularis luxuriae polluuntur*), and would therefore seem to be unworthy (*videantur indigna*) for the celebration of the holy mysteries.[25]

It is only in the acts of a diocesan synod held in Auxerre at some time between 561 and 605, however, that there are specific prohibitions concerning the touching of consecrated objects by women. Is this when they are "impure" during menstruation and after having given birth through their contact with blood, as in the purity rules of the book of Leviticus?[26] Although a letter of Pope Gregory I, mentioning this specific rule, shows that it was not forgotten in this period, there is not a single mention of it in the acts of the Gallic councils. Nowhere is "impurity" or "pollution" explicitly and without more ado associated with *the nature of* women.[27] Nor do the prohibitions of Auxerre mention such a notion; they stipulate:

> 36. A woman is not allowed to receive the Eucharist with an uncovered hand (*nudam manum*).
> 37. A woman is not allowed to touch the cloth that covers the Eucharist with her hand.[28]

These are the rulings that lead Wemple to postulate a subjacent notion of a woman's intrinsic, *natural* impurity. They appear to be unambiguous: evidently, men *were* allowed to do this. A comparison with an earlier prohibition of the same synod might indeed seem to indicate that women

[25] Council of Clermont (535), can. 8, in: de Clercq, *Concilia*, p. 107.

[26] Leviticus 15:19–24 and 12:1–8.

[27] Pope Gregory is of the opinion that a menstruating woman should be admitted to communion if she so desires; if she wishes to abstain from communion at these times, however, she is to be commended: *Gregorii I Papae Registrum Epistolarum* II.xi.56a (ed. P. Ewald and L.M. Hartmann, MGH Epistolae 2 [Berlin 1899], pp. 339–340); cited in Wemple, *Women*, p. 22, n. 56. In Gaul, bishop Caesarius of Arles (503–543), had forbidden marital relations with a menstruating woman in one of his sermons; he based this on Ezekiel 18:6, which designates her condition as her "monthly impurity". Caesarius omits this term, however. He also does not say that a woman in this condition cannot receive communion, whereas he does prohibit communion to men who have had a seminal emission: even though it may have been involuntary, they must first perform a penitential action (*Sancti Caesarii Arelatensis episcopi Sermones*, vol. 1, 44.5–7, ed. G. Morin, CCSL 103 [Turnhout 1953], pp. 197–199).

[28] De Clercq, *Concilia*, p. 269.

must have been associated with an intrinsic impurity such as that, again as in Leviticus, would inhere in a corpse:

> 12. It is forbidden to give the Eucharist to the dead or to kiss them, and to wrap their bodies in liturgical cloths.[29]

Immediately after this, however, follow two prohibitions for the clergy:

> 13. It is forbidden for a deacon to drape liturgical cloths around his shoulders.
> [....]
> 19. It is forbidden for a priest, deacon or subdeacon to celebrate masses or be in the church during masses after they have eaten or drunk anything.[30]

Then come repetitions of the celibacy rulings for the clergy, as well as restrictions concerning the marriages of laymen. It is only thereafter – significantly, in a series of rules for the behaviour of the clergy – that the prohibitions for women appear. As well as, somewhat further another, not unambiguous, precept for them:

> 42. Every woman should have her *dominicalis* with her when she comes to communion. If she does not have this, she will not receive communion until the next Sunday.[31]

The term *dominicalis* probably refers to a cloth or veil for the covering of the head which the apostle Paul had commanded women to wear in the church.[32]

Although the terms "purity" and "pollution" are not mentioned in these rulings, could these notions nevertheless, as Wemple assumes, have been taken for granted in the precepts for the covering of the hand, the prohibition of touching the Eucharistic cloth and the command to wear a head-covering? Are they part of an implicit symbolic system, in which "pure" is aligned with male, and "impure" with female, sexuality, body and death? And would this regional synod, then, indeed have connected being a

---

[29] *Ibid.*, p. 267. Cf. Leviticus 21:1. That even the dead body of a priest "pollutes" these cloths appears from a ruling of an earlier council of Clermont (535), can. 7 (de Clercq, *Concilia*, p. 107).

[30] De Clercq, *Concilia*, p. 267.

[31] *Ibid.*, p. 270.

[32] 1 Corinthians 11:5–6. *Dominicalis* as veil: A. Blaise, *Dictionnaire latin-français des auteurs chrétiens* (Turnhout 1954), p. 209.

woman with (sexual) carnality, an association which the popes and larger ecclesiastical councils might have consciously avoided making explicit?

There are some obscurities. As we have seen, the apostle Paul had not connected wearing a veil with impurity, but with not being created according to God's image. And, considering their placement among behavioral rules for the clergy, might not the covering of a woman's hand and her veil while receiving the Eucharist be a practical protection for the priest against involuntary sensual arousal? Furthermore, it is not impossible that the latter rule, as well as the prohibition for women to touch the cloth covering the Eucharist, may point instead to the participation of women in the liturgy – something that pope Gelasius I had mentioned in the late fifth century as an existing, evil practice, and had forbidden.[33] Does the just-reviewed legislation of Auxerre thus perhaps point to the fact that, in the second half of the sixth century, women threatened to acquire a certain influence in the ecclesiastical affairs of this diocese? And was the sharp confrontation with the above-mentioned symbolic system perhaps a last resort to enforce clerical discipline at the local level? The other acts of this synod indeed indicate that there was a great deal of highly undesirable and illegal contact between clergy – and even monks – and women. The scarcity of evidence, however, does not permit us to gain a clearer picture of the situation in Auxerre at this time and of the exact meaning of these precepts in it, and certainly not to base broad conclusions upon it. Also because they were, as already indicated, no more than a unique and local phenomenon.

Wemple's only other concrete evidence for her claim derives from the tribal law code of the Baiuwarii in southern Germany; also because this code was written up only centuries later, it cannot count as evidence for sixth-century Gaul.[34] In this law, deacons and priests are again forbidden to have anyone other than close female relatives as housekeepers, for non-related women would seduce them. Thereby, the priests would be "polluted" when celebrating mass, and this would cause disasters to come upon the people – a threat that also occurs in Leviticus. Carefully read, however, the law does not say or imply here that it is woman, by nature "impure", who

---

[33] Gelasius I, *Epistola* 9.26, ed. J.P. Migne, Patrologia Latina [PL] 59 (Paris 1862), col. 55D.

[34] *Lex Baiuwariorum* 1.12, ed. E.L. de Schwind, MGH Legum Sectio 1. 5.2 (Hannover 1926), pp. 284–285; cited in Wemple, *Women*, p. 136, n. 59. Cf. Leviticus 26:14–25. Bailey, *Man-woman*, p. 68, n. 11, shows that the decree of the fourth-century council of Laodicea forbidding women to approach the altar was repeated in the Frankish kingdom in 797 and 816; this, by itself, cannot be held to prove, however, that the prohibition had been effective there in the intervening period.

"pollutes" the priest and through him the sacrament. It is the priest who is polluted by the sexual contact. For if he lives together with his mother or sister, and is occasionally affectionately touched by them (something one might reasonably assume), he is evidently not "polluted"! It seems to me that Wemple does not sufficiently differentiate here between the touch of a woman as such and the erotically charged touch in sexual relations. This text too, then, does not confirm her characterization of the general view of the Merovingian church as: "the mere touch of [a woman's] hands was polluting".[35]

"A fetid touch"? Gregory's testimony

Can traces of the above view be found in Gregory's stories? When he mentions large-scale disasters – one of the main components of his *Historiae* – he never connects them with offences against ritual purity, or lets others do so. The calamities are punishments for sin in general – internecine strife, civil war, the plundering of churches, not living according to the Christian commandment of brotherly love – or they are signs of the imminent end of the world.[36]

Nor do we find indications that women, only because they are women, are forbidden to touch holy objects, whether with or without covering their hands. Quite the contrary. Everywhere we come upon women – and men – touching a saint's tomb, often also an altar: washing it, or carefully collecting the dust upon it for healing purposes. Gregory advises everyone who wants to be cured by the saint to touch the cloth hanging over the tomb reverently. Only once does he let a devout lady, a widowed queen, say that she feels "unworthy (*indigna*)" to approach the tomb/altar.[37] Character-

---

[35] Wemple, *Women*, p.130; cf. p. 132.

[36] See on this: G. de Nie, *Views from a Many-Windowed Tower. Studies of Imagination in the Works of Gregory of Tours*, Studies in classical antiquity 7 (Amsterdam 1987), pp. 27–69.

[37] Touch: for instance in *Virt. Mart.* 2.1, 10 and 54, and 3. *prol.*; *Glor. conf.* 25. "Unworthy": *Virt. Mart.* 1.12. This statement could point to knowledge of an older or earlier (?) ruling about this (see n. 33). The source that Wemple gives for this prohibition (*Women*, p. 140, n. 77), to show that it would also have in effect in the Latin Church – Gelasius I, *Epistola* 9.26 – says only that women are forbidden to "serve (*ministrare*)" the altar: they may not (help) celebrate mass. This ruling, then, has nothing to do with the approaching of the altar in other contexts. That the latter is indeed allowed is shown by the acts of the council of Tours in 567 (in which, as we saw, the term "serpents" occurs): while lay folk are not allowed to stand close to the altar during the liturgy in general, "laymen and

istically, however, he lets us see in the story that follows that the contrary is true: her piety – prayer, vigils, alms, humility – are rewarded by the occurrence of a miraculous cure in her presence. Since her prayer has been heard, she too, as a woman, must therefore have been pure in heart.

Nevertheless, there are a few stories in which Gregory at first sight appears to be saying that a woman's touch, as such, pollutes. Bishop Eparchius of Clermont, he tells us, was "a man of very holy and pious life". One night, however, he entered the church to pray and found it full of evil spirits. A women laden with jewels (a sign of social elevation) sat like a prince on the bishop's throne. He called out to her:

> "Cursed whore! Is it not enough for you to contaminate the whole world with your various pollutions (*pollutionibus infecire*)? Must you also pollute the seat consecrated to the Lord by the fetid touch of your sitting on it (*fetida sessionis tuae accessione coinquinas*)? Get out of the house of God, so that it will not be still further polluted (*polluatur*) by you!"
>
> She answered: "Because you call me a whore, I shall arrange many temptations for you through the desire for women." And after she had said this, she vanished like smoke. And the bishop was indeed tempted through the movement of his body by desire, but, protecting himself with the sign of the Cross, the Enemy could not hurt him.[38]

Here, a female apparition "pollutes" the church by her presence and the consecrated seat by sitting on it. The book of Leviticus rules that a man who touches a menstruating woman or an object upon which she sits by this becomes impure.[39] But this specific pollution is not mentioned in Gregory's story: the contamination seems to be of a more general kind. The notion that the contact with blood pollutes does occur several times in Gregory's stories, but not in connection with women.[40] And, in any case, the woman in this story is not a human being but an apparition that vanishes like smoke. She is a phantom: the visualized embodiment of diabolic sexual desire, and it is the latter that "pollutes". The use of the term "whore" and the reference to her genitals, too, appear to indicate that it cannot be woman in general who is envisaged here.

---

women, as is the custom, have access to the Holy of Holies for prayer and for the receiving of communion" (Council of Tours [567], can. 4, in: de Clercq, *Concilia*, p. 178).

[38] *Hist.* 2.21. Something similar also in *Virt. Mart.* 2.45.

[39] Leviticus 15:19–20.

[40] *Hist.* 5.32, 7.29, 9.12, and *Virt. Mart.* 2.45.

Apart from what was probably clerical sexual licence, is it possible that bishop Eparchius also felt threatened in the discharge of his duties by the power of certain aristocratic ladies? Gregory shows us elsewhere that, in Clermont, such a fear could be well-founded.[41] At the same time, this vision shows how easy it was in that period for a man to project his fear of a temporary possession by sexual desire upon women. There is, nevertheless, one passage in Gregory's writings which, taken by itself, might be understood to confirm Wemple's view. When Gregory writes about two wayward bishops that "they did not lack women with whom they polluted themselves (*cum quibus polluerentur*)",[42] one could read the statement as an expression of the above-mentioned fear – but also as an indication of woman's intrinsic impurity. The latter interpretation, however, would not fit into the views he expresses everywhere else in his writings. For in his synopsis of the story of Creation, he – in contrast to the author of the first letter to Timothy – does not blame Eve for the original sin; he writes: "deluded by the ruse of the serpent, they violated the divine commands and were expelled from the abode of the angels".[43] The same is evident in his characterization of Adam as reflecting the "image (*tipus*)" of Christ and of Eve as reflecting that of "the immaculate virgin, the Church, redeemed by His blood, purified by the water [of baptism], 'without stain or wrinkle'".[44]

In many other passages, too, it is evident that it is not woman herself who is "dirty", but lust (*luxuriae coenum*).[45] Thus he speaks of "the contagion of lust (*voluptatis contagio*)", and even of "the contamination of the worldly life through the bond of marriage (*per copulam nuptialem contagi[um]... mundan[um]*)".[46] This state of contamination is almost certainly the equivalent of being polluted – a state that could be transferred to others and to objects through contact. This may be inferred from a passage in which Gregory compares leprosy – in Leviticus: a state of impurity – with sensuality (*lurida lepra luxuriae*) and in which he warns married couples that children conceived on a Saturday night (before attending mass on

---

[41] *Hist.* 3.2. Cf. I. Wood, "The ecclesiastical politics of Merovingian Clermont", in: P. Wormald *et al.* (ed.), *Ideal and Reality in Frankish and Anglo-Saxon Society* (Oxford 1983), pp. 34–57, here p. 43.

[42] *Hist.* 5.20. Cf. Revelation 14:4, and see Bailey, *Man-woman*, p. 12.

[43] *Hist.* 1.1. Cf. 1 Timothy 2:14: "Adam was not seduced; the woman, however, was seduced into a violation".

[44] Ephesians 5:27.

[45] *Vit. patr.* 15. *prol.*

[46] *Glor. conf.* 32; *Vit. patr.* 16.1.

Sunday morning) will suffer from leprosy as well as other diseases.[47] In another story, Gregory gives as the reason that the Eucharist would not remain in the hands of an adulterous deacon, the fact that this man "polluted in his conscience (*pollutus erat in conscientia*)".[48] Only when we – meaning all: men and women – know that we are pure (*mund[i]*), Gregory writes at the beginning of this story, may we approach the altar to receive the Eucharist.

But there is still another story in which Gregory lets someone say something from which one might conclude that the touch of a woman pollutes.[49] When his laundress, a consecrated virgin, bore a child, the people of Tours accused their bishop Brictius, shouting: "Our reverence for your holy office has concealed your sensuality (*luxuria*) long enough! God does not want us to be polluted (*pollui*) any longer by kissing your unworthy (*indignas*) hands!" To prove his innocence, the bishop publicly carried glowing coals under his clothes to saint Martin's tomb, where they were shown to be undamaged. The bishop then said to the crowd: "Just as you see this vestment undamaged by the fire, so is my body unpolluted by the touch of coitus with a woman (*a tactu muliebris coiti est inpollutum*)". Gregory's formulation is precise here: not the touch of a woman, but the touch of coitus with a woman. It is the erotically charged touch and not that of a woman as such that is the source of pollution. Both the consecrated virgin and the bishop would have been "polluted" by a sensual touch or by giving in to feelings of sensual desire.

The same distinction between woman as a person on the one hand and sensuality in feeling and act on the other is made when Gregory lets a plundering, but evidently still relatively pious, soldier seize the relics of a saint from a burning church without even being scorched.[50] Once outside the church, he felt his body suddenly cramping, and "thereby he understood that he was unworthy to carry the relics any further. He chose from his booty, which included prisoners, a small, pure (*impolluta*) girl, hung the casket around her neck and thus reached home safely". This must have been a girl who had not yet reached puberty, and thus would not yet have been polluted by sexual desire. However, showing that, in his view, adult women too could be "pure", Gregory elsewhere speaks of the "chaste purity

---

[47] Leviticus 13:44–46; *Virt. Mart.* 2.60, 2.24.
[48] *Glor. mart.* 85.
[49] *Hist.* 2.1.
[50] *Glor. mart.* 30.

(*puritatis castita[s]*)" of a pious noble lady, and in another story he refers to a nun as "a most pure virgin (*virgo purissima*)".[51]

He does know about saints who do not want to see women, but of all those he mentions, only three belong to this category.[52] His story about one of these, Lupicinus, makes clear that he does not share their attitude. Whereas the latter studiously avoided all women, his brother Romanus, although he too was a hermit, is described by Gregory as "such a simple man (*simplex*) that such a thought did not enter his mind", and accordingly he cured women as well as men, and gave them spiritual advice.[53] Eventually, he let himself be buried outside the monastery so that women – who were forbidden to enter the monastery – would be able to find health and help at his tomb.[54] Gregory's tone here betrays his sympathy for this hermit's compassionate concern. What we see in all the above, then, is that the supposition that the Merovingian church regarded women as by nature impure is not confirmed by Gregory's stories about the facts of everyday life.

In her well-known book *Purity and Danger*, Mary Douglas describes the enactment of purity rules as a symbolic system that makes a group cohere. Ritual fear concerning the boundaries and apertures of the body is interpreted by her as anxiety about the survival and unity of the group concerned. In a society with two conflicting value systems, however, purity rules could also be used to reinforce the cohesion of one of these against the other.[55] The Gallic episcopate's enforcing clerical discipline and securing its monopoly of spiritual power against secular competition through purity rules would be an example of the latter. As we saw, the fundamental ambivalence in the tradition of Christian thought about the nature of woman as such also tended to be expressed in terms of symbols, but those of purity or its opposite are not among these. And Gregory's own attitude shows no trace of this ambivalence. Does this mean that he held a more generous view?

---

[51] *Glor. conf.* 75 and *Vit. patr.* 6.7. Gregory's descriptions of the chaste married love of two pure persons (*Glor. conf.* 75) indicates that, in apparent contrast to present-day views, he does not regard affectionate physical contact between them as necessarily sensual.

[52] *Glor. mart.* 103; *Glor. conf.* 26; and *Vit. patr.* 1.2: Lupicinus.

[53] We see in other stories that being touched by saints – in dreams or in physical reality – is a recurring motif in cures. Cf. de Nie, *Views*, pp. 247–249.

[54] *Vit. patr.* 1.2 and 6.

[55] M. Douglas, *Purity and Danger, An Analysis of the Concepts of Pollution and Taboo* (London 1966; 1985) pp. 41, 115, 124; cf. Tavard, *Woman*, pp. 31–77.

"The inferior sex"?

There are many examples, in his *Histories*, of the general notion of the inequality between men and women in secular and ecclesiastical law being translated into practice. But Gregory also shows, as Wemple too emphasizes,[56] that an energetic woman, especially if she belonged to a noble family, could exercise an influence, either through the informal means of her marriage and children, or through her patronage (especially through gifts) of ecclesiastical leaders. In this manner, she could also gain a certain freedom of movement. One example is queen Clotild, who let her parents' murder be avenged by her sons.[57] But Gregory also shows us women acting on their own, and they are not better or worse than men. On the one hand, there is a lady like Radegund, already during her life regarded as a saint, who managed – through her contacts with the court and with the Church – to acquire a fragment of the Holy Cross for her convent in Poitiers. On the other, we see a vixen like the former slave Fredegund: if we are to believe Gregory, she administered poison and sent unnamed agents on a whole slew of murderous missions.[58]

In a dramatic story about the queen-mother Brunhild we see again how Gregory uses his role as narrator to show, indirectly, how misplaced the prejudice against women as inferior beings really is. Lupus, duke of Champagne and one of queen's men, had for some time been persecuted and robbed by the magnates Ursio and Bertefred; at last, the latter approached Lupus openly with an army; but

> [w]hen queen Brunhild heard this, she was grieved that her man was being threatened unjustly. Girding herself like a man (*praecingens se viriliter*),[59] she threw herself between the hostile armies and shouted, "Don't carry out this evil deed, O men. Don't persecute an innocent man! Don't let a battle take place that will destroy a whole region on account of one man!"
>
> When she had said this, Ursio replied: "Get out of our way, woman. Let it be sufficient for you to hold the kingdom under a man; now your son reigns, and his government is maintained not by your but by our protection (*tuitio*). Get

---

[56] Wemple, *Women*, pp. 51–70. Cf. Nelson, "Queens", pp. 31–77.

[57] *Hist*. 3.6.

[58] Holy Cross: *Glor. mart.* 5. Fredegund's murderous missions: *Hist.* 7.7, 14, and 20; 8.29, 31, 41 and 44; 9.3 and 38; 10.18.

[59] This must be metaphor: in Frankish society, women as such were unarmed and not trained to use weapons.

> yourself out of here so that you won't be trodden into the dust by the hooves of our horses!"
>
> After they had talked back and forth like this for a very long time, however, the queen's effort achieved the aversion of the battle.[60]

This fearless, resolute and eloquent queen achieves peace through persuasion. Because Gregory, whose region was frequently devastated by war, often pleads for peace, we may assume that he admired Brunhild's deed. In this case, she needed to act in a so-to-speak "manly" way; nevertheless, she succeeded not by force but by means of words, perhaps even through a certain charm. For Gregory describes her at her wedding as "beautiful to look at (*venusta aspectu*), [...] prudent in her advice (*prudens in consilio*), and charming in conversation (*blanda colloquio*)".[61]

The words reported of Ursio, however, show that Gregory was definitely aware of the general prejudice against women. The same is evident when he lets a king say that he would be held to be "a weak woman (*mulier infirma*)" if he did not avenge his brother's murder.[62] When this king subsequently foregoes revenge because Gregory has convinced him that his brother had been slain as a punishment by God for his sins, he is described as strong and prudent – thus as the opposite of "a weak [unarmed?] woman". Gregory here sets the ecclesiastical view over against the sex-specific rules of behaviour in a society dominated by blood feuds: leave punishment to God; by acting according to this insight instead of resorting to the force of weapons, one would exhibit true strength.

In one passage, Gregory himself nevertheless appears to connect women with weakness. After relating how a girl who stole something in the marketplace was later discovered through the cooperation of a saint, Gregory presents the moral of the story in a tirade against greed:

> What are you doing, wretched avarice? Why do you succumb to the desire for others' goods, O feminine instead of masculine mind (*mens feminea, non virilis*)? Why do you pierce the firm cuirass of your mind with a small arrow of greed? Why do you, O man (*homo*) collect talents of ruddy gold when you will burn with them in hell?[63]

---

[60] *Hist.* 6.4.

[61] *Ibid.* 4.27.

[62] *Ibid.* 9.19.

[63] *Glor. mart.* 57.

Here, I suggest, the adjectives "feminine" and "masculine" can be understood to point to moral qualities qualified by a general opposition: physical weakness and unarmed vulnerability versus armoured, armed strength. As we saw, others in this period – such as Ursio – could apply this common metaphor to living women. Seeing, however, that Gregory, in his story of the thievish girl, addresses mankind in general (*homo*), and that the next story is about a male thief, it seems to me that he is not saying here that women are by nature morally weaker than men. The fact that Gregory also does not regard avarice as a typical "female" vice is evident in several stories in which he lets wives return estates to the Church which their husbands had unlawfully seized.[64]

In this period, moral strength and courage were usually represented by images from exclusively male activities: athletics and war.[65] A description of a strong-minded woman, therefore, would tend to represent her as one who acts "manfully", an image that also occurs in the writings of the Church Fathers. And Gregory uses it in the prologue to his *Life of Saint Monegund*, one of the very first biographies of a holy woman in Gaul. He speaks there of Christ,

> who, according to the continuous gift of his teaching, exhorts us to live according to the examples of his saints; and who gives us as examples not only men, but also even the inferior sex (*sed etiam ipsum inferiorem sexum*), that fights not feebly, but in a manly manner (*non segniter sed viriliter agonizantem*); and who not only receives men – who are accustomed to fight (*legitime decertantibus*) – but even (*verum etiam*) women who sweat in these battles (*praeliis*) with good results, into his starry kingdom.[66]

Here again, Gregory introduces a prejudice – the "inferior sex" – and subsequently shows that it does not conform to reality. Although neither the ecclesiastical nor the secular hierarchy in the Gaul of his period was prepared to allow an office or place of honour to a woman, he seems to be saying that such a place is nevertheless achievable for every woman who is prepared to fight for it. The battle he is speaking of is, of course, that of the spirit against the flesh.[67] Here, he explicitly and emphatically argues for the equality of men and women in this contest.

---

[64] *Virt. Jul.* 8 and 14. Twice, however, he also reports that someone's wife objects to her husband's extreme generosity: *Hist.* 1.11 and *Glor. conf.* 108.

[65] For instance: *Vit. patr.* 13.*prol.*: *athleta Christi*; *ibid.* 1.1: *milites Christi*.

[66] *Ibid.* 19.*prol.*

[67] As, for instance, in *Hist.* 5.*prol.* and *Glor. mart.* 105.

That this equality is not always completely evident is because he now and then also directs the readers' attention to the humility with which a pious lady carries out her duties. Queen Radegund exhibited humility (*humilitas*) in her monastic life in that she placed herself under the authority of a younger abbess.[68] Of the widowed queen Clotild, whom he qualifies as "pure (*pura*)" and very generous, he says that "it seemed as though she served assiduously not as queen but as God's own maid-servant (*ancilla*) [...] and her humility (*humilitas*) lifted her up to grace".[69] Significantly, however, humility is expected not only of women but also of men. Immediately after a story in which a lady (*matrona*) is cured while she is "serving (*deserviens*) the blessed poor", Gregory tells one about a blind man. He was cured after he had for many years "ministered to the poor as a servant (*famulus*)".[70] And although Gregory often describes bishops as acting in an authoritarian manner, he also describes especially them and abbots as humble,[71] thus showing in his stories that the Christian ideal of humility should be and was practiced by men as well as by women. By explicitly confronting the generally held prejudices of his time, then, he shows himself to be a defender of the spiritual and moral equality of man and woman – an equality not only in theory but also in practice.

Woman's advice: "listen to the voice of Sarah"

Does Gregory, like the apostle Paul and some of the Church Fathers, imply or say that men are more intelligent beings than women? One might infer this from passages such the one in which he compares a noble lady who came to saint Martin's church to contemplate his miracles to the queen of Sheba, who came to listen to the wisdom of Solomon.[72] But a saint residing in heaven is, of course, not the same as an ordinary, earthly man. Moreover, miracles operated by female saints, which Gregory also reports, can also count as wisdom. And in his stories, it is often an earthly woman who comes with good advice in a problematic situation. As we saw, he writes

---

[68] *Hist.* 9.39.

[69] *Ibid.* 3.18.

[70] *Virt. Mart.* 2.22, 23; cf. 3.56.

[71] *Vit. patr.* 6.4, 8.2, 9.1, 11.1, 16.1, 20.2. But this is probably not only a specifically Christian virtue. Within the secular and ecclesiastical élite of a hierarchically ordered society modest behaviour can be a condition for acquiring the benevolence and enlisting the support of others: C.S. Jaeger, *The Origins of Courtliness. Civilizing Trends and the Formation of Courtly Ideals 939–1210* (Philadelphia 1987), pp. 40–42.

[72] *Virt. Mart.* 1.12; *Vit. patr.* 19.*prol.*

that queen Brunhild was "prudent in her advice"; furthermore, the momentous conversion of king Clovis is attributed to the efforts of his wife Clotild.[73] And when the husband of Nicetius of Lyon's future mother tells her that he has been elected bishop of Geneva and that the king has already given his permission, she says to him:

> "Forget about this matter, dearest husband, and don't seek to acquire the episcopate of this city: for I have conceived from you a bishop whom I carry in my womb."
>
> And the wise man, when he had heard his wife's words, acquiesced in this, remembering what the divine voice had once commanded the blessed Abraham, the origin of our faith, saying: "Listen to Sarah's voice and to all that she shall say to you".[74]

That a wife is sometimes knows better how to act in accordance with ecclesiastical law than her husband is also evident, as we have seen, in a number clearly didactic stories about returned church estates.

It seems reasonable to assume that Gregory's attitude toward women would correspond at least to some degree with his kind of relationship with his mother. The prologue to Gregory's *Miracles of Saint Martin* shows how great his admiration for her is. There he lets her appear in his dream or vision (in this period, these are not distinguished) and, as mouthpiece for God, give him the command to record the saint's miracles. While he is seeing, in the dream-vision, many people being cured, she says (either in the vision or standing by him while he is seeing it): "Why do you keep putting off writing about what you see?" And he answers her (as his mother, and thus in a tone of familiarity): "You know very well that I am uneducated in letters. I am so stupid and unlettered that I don't dare to write about such admirable miracles." After this, he lets her say: "Don't you know that someone like you, who is able to speak in a way that the people can understand, will because of this be much better understood? Therefore don't hesitate and get to work! It would be a crime if you remain silent." Although, in this period, it is a common sign of modesty to mention the person who asked the author for a particular piece of writing, Gregory is, as far as I know, the only one who lets his mother appear in this way.[75] In

---

[73] *Hist.* 4.27; 2.28–30.

[74] Genesis 21:12; *Vit. patr.* 8.1.

[75] See G. Strunk, *Kunst und Glaube in der lateinischen Heiligenlegende. Zu ihrem Selbstverständnis in den Prologen*, Medium Aevum 12 (Munich 1970), pp. 13–57.

addition, if she appears as a dream figure, she would be the only one in his stories who is not either a dead saint or other heavenly being. In other dream-visions, male and female saints appear to give advice. One remarkable story is that of the Virgin Mary appearing to a desperate architect to tell him how he can lift massive pillars for her church by means of pulleys.[76]

However, it is not only holy or aristocratic women but also pious, living unknown or simple women – as well as pious men – who appear in Gregory's stories as advice-givers to men, even when these are bishops and saints. When there was a deadlock among the collected prelates and the people about the choice of a new bishop for the city of Clermont, an unnamed veiled nun resolved the conflict:

> [...] audaciously, she entered the meeting, and said: "Listen to me, bishops of God! Know that the one whom you are thinking of electing to the episcopate is not pleasing to God. Behold, the Lord himself will today provide a bishop [...] and send someone here who will govern this church."
>
> And while all wondered at these words, suddenly Rusticus, a priest in the diocese of Clermont, entered the hall. When she had seen him, the nun cried: "He is the one whom the Lord chose! [....] Let him be consecrated bishop!"
>
> When she had said this, all the people laid aside their strife and shouted that he was worthy and just.[77]

Not every woman would have been heard here. The fact that she was seen to be a nun and, as such, leading a respected, pious life, must have been the reason that the bishops accepted her vision as one from God.

In the next story Gregory, with an undertone of irony, lets a poor old woman remind two religious heroes to conduct themselves in a "manly" way. When the hermits Romanus and Lupicinus felt they could not continue their chosen exile in the wilderness because the Devil kept throwing stones at them, they returned to an inhabited region, and asked a poor old woman if they might spend the night in her hut. When she asked where these "soldiers of Christ (*milites Christi*)" came from, they told her their story "with some embarrassment". Thereupon she said to them:

---

[76] *Glor. mart.* 8; cf. *Glor. conf.* 18. On dreams and visions in Gregory see de Nie, *Views*, pp. 213–293.

[77] *Hist.* 2.13. Cf. *ibid.* 8.33, *Virt. Jul.* 14.

"O men of God, you ought to fight in a manly way (*viriliter*) against the wiles of the Devil, and not fear his hostilities, for he is very often overcome by the friends of God! [....]"

[Through these words,] they were pierced to the heart and, withdrawing a little way from the woman, said to each other: "Woe to us, for we have sinned against God by going back upon our decision! Behold, now we are being reproved by a woman for our lack of resolve (*ignavia*)! And what kind of life would we have if we don't return to the place from where the rage of the Enemy expelled us?"[78]

Gregory points out the foibles of everyone, including bishops and (future) saints. And wisdom and prudent advice may be found also among women, even in the most humble ones.

"As a man among men"?

We have seen that, in Gregory's view, a woman could participate alongside men as an equal in the war of the spirit against the flesh. One way in which a woman might do this is shown in his brief biography of Pappola. Because her parents opposed her decision for the religious life, she fled from home and disguised herself as a man in order to be admitted into a male monastery. Gregory tells us that she lived there for thirty years, unrecognized, "as a man among men".[79] Pappola's "masculinization" was necessary because she entered a male monastery. How are other strong-minded women described who conduct themselves as the equals of men? Do they shed their "feminine" characteristics? And what are these characteristics anyway: outside the opposition strong/weak, does Gregory mention other stereotypes? When speaking about women, does he, for instance, highlight the quality of charm more than when speaking of men?

In goodness and wickedness, purity and sensuality, heroism and piety, wilfulness and cruelty, the women whom Gregory describes are not different from men.[80] We have seen that Brunhild was described as "beautiful to behold (*venusta aspectu)*" and "pleasant in conversation (*blanda*

[78] *Vit. patr.* 1.1.

[79] *Glor. conf.* 16. Cf. on this theme and the combining of masculine and feminine qualities: Rader, *Boundaries*, pp. 81–83, and Tavard, *Woman*, p. 32.

[80] Other strong personalities are, for instance, Deoteria (*Hist.* 3.22), Susanna (*Hist.* 4.36), Magnatrude (*Hist.* 8.39, 10.5), Rauching's wife (*Hist.* 9.5), Ingotrude (*Hist.* 9.33), Gundetrude (*Virt. Mart.* 2.9), Georgia (*Glor. conf.* 33), Simplicius' wife (*Glor. conf.* 75), and Pelagia (*Glor. conf.* 102). See also: Nelson, "Queens".

colloquio)".[81] Alongside Brunhild's portrait, however, we have a description of the entrancing beauty of a male saint: Julian. Gregory tells us what he looked like when he appeared in a dream to a crippled woman:

> It is said that she used to describe the appearance of the man who had talked to her. She said that he was tall of stature, wearing a shining robe, of exceeding elegance (*elegantia nimium*), with a smiling face, and blond hair mixed with white; that he moved with grace, had a pleasant voice as well as a most charming manner of speaking (*allocutione blandissimum*), and that the whiteness of his skin glowed more than that of lilies [...]".[82]

This description of aristocratic masculine charm is much more detailed than any description in Gregory's writings of its feminine counterpart. And when we look at with whom he associates loving care (*caritas; diligere*) and amiability (*dulcissima voluntas; lorica dulcedinis; suavis colloquio et blandus affectu*), these turn out to be: men![83] More precisely: male saints. In this image, the Christian ideal of brotherly love appears to have merged with the well-known *dulcedo* ideal of the late antique aristocratic cults of personality and friendship.[84] What we see is that the image of the ideal male saint largely covers that of the ideal man in this period: a beautiful appearance and an amiable personality.

Likewise, Brunhild, who combined intelligence with honourable behaviour, education, personal grace and visible beauty, is clearly regarded as a most admirable woman. The matron Deoteria, who became king Theudebert's wife, is described as "extremely prudent and wise (*utilis valde et sapiens*)" and "beautiful (*speciosa*)".[85] Clotild, king Clovis' wife, is also said to have been "elegant and wise (*elegans atque sapiens*)".[86] And

---

[81] *Hist.* 4.27.

[82] *Virt. Jul.* 9.

[83] *Hist.* 2.36, 4.36, 5.5, 7.1; *Vit. patr.* 1.4; 2.2; 4.1; 5.*prol.*; 6.2, 6 and 7; 7.1; 8.2; 9.1; 11.2; 14.2; 16.1 and 18.1.

[84] This cult is elegantly represented in the poetry of Gregory's friend Venantius Fortunatus. See: R. Koebner, *Venantius Fortunatus. Seine Persönlichkeit und seine Stellung in der geistigen Kultur des Merowinger-reiches*, Beiträge zur Kulturgeschichte des Mittelalters und der Renaissance 22 (Leipzig–Berlin 1915), pp. 31–37; and Jaeger, *Origins*, pp. 43–46, especially p. 43: "There is a broad complex of virtues [...] whose focus is the amicability of the courtier". The most recent overview of Fortunatus' career is that of B. Brennan, "The career of Venantius Fortunatus", *Traditio* 41 (1985), pp. 49–78.

[85] *Hist.* 3.22.

[86] *Ibid.* 2.28.

Gregory's mother, too, is spoken of as a noble and wise lady.[87] However, the saintly lady whom Gregory describes most fully, and whom he probably admired the most, is Radegund, the energetic and compassionate former queen who became a nun in Poitiers. At her funeral, Gregory tells his readers, he could hardly stop his tears. Describing her appearance as the sixty-year old lady lay on the bier, he says: "her holy face shone so brightly that its beauty outdid that of lilies and roses".[88] A nun later writes about him that he had said, upon this occasion, that it seemed to him "as though he saw, in the appearance of a human being, the face of an angel, shining as a rose and a lily", and that he stood there, trembling, "as though he were in the presence of the holy Mother of the Lord".[89]

In the face, then, of a dead lady for whom he evidently had a deep reverence and affection (they appear to have been in frequent communication), Gregory sees a heavenly woman who is also a mother. When he reports what the grieving nuns cried out at her funeral, we hear echoes of experiences of "light", beauty and spiritual motherhood. It is in this context of motherly care, too, that we encounter words such as "tender (*blandus*)" and "sweet (*dulcis*)" in connection with women: the expression "mother's tendernesses (*matris blanditiae*)" reveals a whole world.[90]

But it is not only women who behave in this way with children. Contrary to what might be expected on the grounds of what we know about the prescriptions of Roman educational discipline, Gregory lets us see that men too could be caring and tender: his uncle Nicetius, later bishop of Lyon, asked him when he was eight years old (and had probably just lost his father) to come into bed with him, and "took [him] in his arms with the tenderness of fatherly love (*paternae dilectionis dulcedine*)".[91] A number of times Gregory also lets us see men lovingly raising children which are not their own. For instance, when he tells us how his uncle Gallus was raised by bishop Quintianus, he writes: "He raised him in spiritual sweetness (*in dulcedine spiritali*) as a heavenly father."[92] It is not unlikely that his uncle's

---

87 She is mentioned in: *Ibid.* 5.5; *Glor. mart.* 50, 85; *Virt. Mart.* 1.*prol.* and 35, 3.10 and 60; *Glor. conf. 39*; *Vit. patr.* 2.2 and 7.2.

88 *Glor. conf.* 104. About Radegund see: B. Brennan, "St. Radegund and the early development of her cult at Poitiers", *Journal of Religious History* 13 (1985), pp. 340–354.

89 Baudonivia, *Vita sanctae Radegundis* 23, ed. B. Krusch, MGH SSrM 2 (Hannover 1888), pp. 377–395, here pp. 392–393).

90 *Virt. Mart.* 2.38, 3.16; *Vit. patr.* 2.2 and 4; 8.1; 9.1.

91 *Vit. patr.* 8.2.

92 *Vit. patr.* 6.2. Other examples of men's care for children not their own in, for instance: *ibid.* 6.7 and 9.1.

education reminded Gregory of his own by Avitus, later bishop of Clermont. This would also explain his well-known identification with the parents' or others' care for children who had died in an epidemic. He writes about this: "And we lost the sweet little ones so dear to us (*dulcis et caros nobis infantulos*), whom we had nurtured in our company, carried in our arms, fed with our own hand and raised with attentive care".[93] Roman educational manuals for fathers and their families prescribe the opposite behaviour.[94] What Gregory says here appears to be something he has personally experienced, either in his own life or in that of parents whom he knew well. In his stories we get a glimpse of a daily reality which, as concerns "masculine" and "feminine" behaviour, does not accord with the picture presented by such prescriptive sources as the acts of councils, secular laws, pastoral treatises, and medical textbooks. Gregory's picture of this daily reality is sometimes much grimmer, but often also much warmer.

Gregory: woman as a human being

To review what we have found: ideas about the "impurity" of (menstruating) women and prohibitions concerning the latter are nowhere explicitly referred to in sixth-century Gallic conciliar acts. Repeatedly, however, we find mention of the notion that sexual desire "pollutes", that is: makes unfit for approaching the holy. And that ecclesiastical authorities sometimes projected their own "impure" sexual desire upon women. The only substantial narrative source of this period – Gregory of Tours' writings – show, however, that this kind of projection cannot have been a general phenomenon: for there is no trace of it in the author himself. He did not, for instance, associate his horror at "the pallid leprosy of sexual desire", which he recognized also in himself,[95] with his thoughts about and feelings for women. In his stories, a woman is in every way just as fully human as a man.

What Gregory wants to show us is that a woman, notwithstanding her inferior social position and her limited possibilities in the ecclesiastical sphere, could now and then create a more or less equal position for herself through energetic and wise action, and especially through reverence toward the Church and its saints. She is not inferior: not less intelligent, more lustful, or morally weaker than a man, and she has, in principle, the same

[93] *Hist.* 5.34.
[94] See on this: Rousselle, *Porneia*, pp. 65–84.
[95] *Virt. Mart.* 2.60.

possibilities as a man for effective action and for becoming a saint and, as such, performing miracles. When a woman is pious and prudent, she gives wise advice, to which a man ought to listen. Humility, furthermore, is expected of both men and women. And amiability is not an exclusively "feminine" virtue but turns out to be at least as important for the ideal aristocratic man – also as a saint. Tender care of children, the sick and the poor thus appears in descriptions of men as well as of women.

In short, Gregory does not think in terms of "masculine" and "feminine" codes of behaviour. Although he recognizes the existence of contemporary prejudices about female inferiority in prescriptive sources as well as in daily practice, he shows in his stories that they do not do justice to reality. The sympathy and admiration for women that is evident there appear to be grounded in an affective ideal and in his own experience: his writings exhibit no trace of the deep ambivalence about women in the Church Fathers. It is possible that he was an exception. But if Gregory, as a member of the clerical hierarchy that drew up and promulgated the rulings of the sixth-century Gallic councils, had the ideas he did and ventilated them, the whole Merovingian Church at this time cannot have been permeated by misogyny. Gregory's friend, Venantius Fortunatus, too, did not look down upon women: he is best known for his fervent admiration and intimate friendship with the saintly Radegund.[96] I would not be surprised if more testimonies were to be found in this period of a tradition sympathetic to women. To investigate ideas about women in the early medieval Church, therefore, an examination of the prescriptive sources alone is not enough. Narrative sources such as the *Histories* and hagiographical works of Gregory of Tours can bring to light a reality that remains concealed there.

---

[96] Cf. Venantius Fortunatus, *Vita sanctae Radegundis*, ed. B. Krusch, MGH AA 4.2 (Berlin 1885), and book 8 of his *Carmina*, ed. F. Leo, MGH AA 4.1 (Berlin 1881).

II

The Body, Fluidity and Personal Identity in the World View of Gregory of Tours*

In the course of a dinner conversation with King Guntram about his recently assassinated brother Chilperic, bishop Gregory of Tours, the historian of sixth-century Gaul, has the king say:

> [...] I saw a dream-vision (*vidi ... visionem*) which announced his death. For three bishops led him into my sight, bound by chains [...]. Two of these said, 'Unfasten him, we pray, and permit him to go after he has been chastised.'
>
> But Bishop Tetricus replied bitterly: 'No! He will be burned by fire (*concremabitur*) for his crimes!'
>
> And while they appeared to be exchanging many words about this for a long time, I noticed at some distance a cauldron boiling furiously (*fervere vehementer*) above a fire. Then, while I wept, they seized Chilperic, broke his bones, and threw him into the cauldron. At once, he was so completely dissolved and liquified (*dissolutus ac liquefactus est*) in the seething, steaming liquid (*inter undarum vapores*) that not the least trace of him remained.[1]

---

* English version of "Le corps, la fluidité et l'identité personelle dans la vision du monde de Grégoire de Tours", *Aevum inter utrumque. Mélanges offerts à Gabriel Sanders*, Instrumenta Patristica 23 (Steenbrugge/The Hague 1991), pp. 75–88.

[1] Gregorius Turonensis, *Historiae* [*Hist.*] 8.5. Almost exactly the same happens in Gregory's *In gloria martyrum* [*Glor. mart.*] 9: a Jewish father who had wished to burn his little son alive for having taken the Christian Eucharist was himself thrown into the oven and "so completely consumed by the fire that hardly any trace of his bones remained (*ita totum ignis absorbuit, ut vix de ossibus eius parvum quodammodo relinqueretur indicium*)". The editions of Gregory's works used are: B. Krusch and W. Levison (ed.), *Gregorii Turonensis libri Historiarum X*, Monumenta Germaniae Historica, Scriptores rerum Merovingicarum [MGH SSrM] 1.1, editio altera (Berlin 1951); and B. Krusch (ed.), *Libri octo miraculorum*, in: W. Arndt and B. Krusch (ed.), *Gregorii Turonensis opera*, MGH SSrM 1.2 (Hannover 1885), pp. 451–820.

Complete dissolution into nothingness in a turbulent fluid is evidently the most humiliating fate a man can suffer, a condign punishment for Gregory's favourite villain, whom he elsewhere grimly designates as "the Nero and Herod of our times".[2] Accordingly, as we shall see, the highest honour which his heroes – the saints – can hope for is that their sanctity will be confirmed to the living community by the fact that their dead bodies are seen not to decay. However, wholeness of the *living* body, or cures, are also the subject of by far the most of Gregory's many tales of miracle. What is he expressing with all these images of the body?

In addition, however, he is interested in the body's discharges: they abound in his reports of miraculous cures. And his visceral hatred of heretics appears in his repeatedly associating them with excrements. Although, no doubt out of modesty, he does not mention sexual fluids, they probably play a not inconsiderable role in his anxiety-ridden view of this aspect of human life. But there is also another kind of liquidity in his stories: a *fluidum* between spiritual powers, man and material objects – they appear to permeate and merge into each other. For Gregory, the existence of this all-pervasive fluidity is so much taken for granted that, in contrast to the body's disintegration and its discharges, he does not conceptualize it as such.[3] It does appear indirectly, however, in the dynamics that become visible in his stories.

Did the decomposition and dissolution of the human body perhaps have a deeper significance for him, one that he could not put into words?[4] And

---

[2] *Hist.* 6.46.

[3] Gregory held "(a)n archaic view of reality, structured by not-quite-expressible 'dream' relations between immediately-experienced symbolic images rather than by the discursive logic of concepts [...], in which sensory perception, deliberate imagination and waking dreams often overlap and coalesce [...].": G. de Nie, *Views from a many-windowed tower. Studies of imagination in the works of Gregory of Tours*, Studies in Classical Antiquity 7 (Amsterdam 1978), p. 210; see also pp. 287–290.

[4] In a recent article, J.-M. Matthieu points to "une honte de la nature humaine" in the Greek Fathers of the fourth century: "a sensitivity about corruption", "a sexualisation of corporal dissolution", and "a fascination for the amorphous body, whether in the process of formation or of decomposition, for the liquid body which flows out"; he speaks of this as "a Christian affective system" and suggests that it might one of the elements of life-style that characterizes the period of late Antiquity: "Horreur du cadavre et philosophie dans le monde romain. Le cas de la patristique grecque du IVe siècle", in: F. Huiard (ed.), *La mort, les morts et l'au-delà dans le monde romain. Actes du Colloque de Caen, 20–22 novembre 1985* (Caen 1987), pp. 311–320, of which pp. 313, 315, 320. In her book *Gregory the Great. Perfection in Imperfection*, Transformation of the Classical Heritage 14 (Berkeley 1988), pp. 107–146, C. Straw emphasizes the pope's concern with self-control and "firmness" of body on the one

could this significance have been connected with his experience of the fluid contours and permeability of his own person as well as of all that he perceived?

Disintegration and wholeness

Gregory's view of the antithesis of disintegration and wholeness becomes clear in his story about the translation of the corpse of bishop Gregory of Langres, who had died a few years earlier:

> [...] While the sarcophagus was being put down with care, suddenly, I believe at the command of God, its cover shifted to one side. And behold, his blessed face became visible, so whole and undamaged (*integra et illaesa*) that one would have thought he were not dead but sleeping. Nor did there appear to be any deterioration in the clothes around his body. Thus not undeservedly did he, whose flesh was not corrupted by license (*cuius caro non fuit corrupta ludibrio*), appear glorified (*apparuit gloriosus*) after his decease. For great is the wholeness of body and heart (*corporis et cordis integritas*) that both manifests grace during the present life and, in the future one, is granted eternal life. As Paul the Apostle said: "Let us seek peace and holiness, without which no one will see the Kingdom of God".[5]

Already just after his death, Gregory had reported earlier,

> his blessed face had been so glorified (*glorificata*) [...] that it seemed (*cerneretur*) to resemble roses. While it appeared (*apparebat*) rosy, the rest of his body shone like a white-gleaming lily (*tanquam candens lilium refulgebat*), so that one would suppose him to be already at that moment prepared (*praeparatum*) for the glory of the future resurrection.[6]

---

hand, and with the transitoriness of all earthly life on the other. Professor P. Brown has been so kind as to draw my attention to these two publications. During the preparation of the present article I unfortunately did not yet have access to his last book: *The Body and Society. Men, women and sexual renunciation in early Christianity*, Lectures on the history of religions, new series, 13 (New York 1988). See on the same theme in the first four Christian centuries in the East: T.H.C. van Eyck, "Marriage and virginity, death and immortality", in: J. Fontaine and Ch. Kannengiesser (ed.), *Epektasis. Mélanges patristiques offerts au Cardinal Jean Daniélou* (Paris 1972), pp. 210–235.

[5] *Vita patrum* [*Vit. patr.*] 7.4. Hebrews 12:14.

[6] *Vit. patr.* 7.3. Similarly: *gloriosum corpus* (*Vit. patr.* 10.4).

Chastity, that is, continence, thus signified the "wholeness" of body and soul which overcomes time and death: the continent man's body remains firm and beautiful to behold. License – no doubt, especially sexual license is meant here – "corrupts" the spirit and the body, and this corruption manifests itself in physical decomposition after death. Because lust was thought to be caused by the body, the holy life was a battle of the spirit against the body: "a mortification of the flesh".[7] This derives, of course, from the tradition of the apostle Paul, according to whose writings the flesh revolts against the laws of God and leads to death, while the spirit tends toward (eternal) life and peace.[8] The chaste man is thus a harmonious being who lives the true, eternal life.

And his mortal body in this way becomes "a tabernacle" or "a temple" in which the Holy Spirit comes to dwell.[9] Already before Gregory's time, the Church had come to identify itself collectively as the community around the Old Testament Tabernacle, and this had led to purity rules for the clergy which were consciously based on those of the Old Testament priests.[10] As Gregory tells us, by himself becoming a "tabernacle", the saint was thought to live the heavenly life already during his earthly one, and to become "the new man, formed according to God in justice, holiness and truth".[11]

Leading this kind of life had consequences not only for one's own body, however. The saints, filled with the Holy Spirit, were able to restore the bodies of others: that is, to cure them from all kinds of illness. Later, it was their relics – in whatever state they might be – that constituted as it were a

---

[7] *Bellum civile [...] ut spiritus concupiscat adversus carnem* (*Hist.* 5. *prol.*); something similar also in, for example, *Glor. mart.* 105; cf. Romans 7:23. *Mortificata carne* (*Vit. patr.* 4. *prol.*); see also *Vit. patr.* 2. *prol.*. Gregory describes two saints who interpret this mortification as physical torture in *Hist.* 6.6 and *Vit. patr.* 13.1: the worms – a diabolical illusion – and the vomiting of blood (caused by wearing heavy stones around the neck) must have been understood as an imitation of martyrdom.

[8] Romans 8:6–7.

[9] Cf. 1 Corinthians 6:19f. An example in Gregory's writings: *in cordis sui tabernaculo collocavit, ut et ipse quoque templum sancti spiritus effici mereretur* (*Vit. patr.* 2. *prol.*). Similarly: *Vit. patr.* 1. *prol.*, 4. *prol.*, and 7. *prol.*. On the symbolism of the body in late Antiquity, see P. Brown, "The notion of virginity in the early Church", in: B. McGinn and J. Meyendorff (ed.), *Christian Spirituality. Origins to the Twelfth Century*, World Spirituality 16 (New York 1987), pp. 427–443, of which pp. 432–434.

[10] J.-P. Audet, *Mariage et célibat dans le service pastoral de l'Église. Histoire et orientations* (Paris 1967), pp. 110–134. See also notes 26, 27 and 28.

[11] *Novus homo, qui secundum Deum formatus est in iustitia, sanctitate et veritate* (*Vit. patr.* 3. *prol.*); cf. Ephesians 4:24. Once, Gregory tells us that resulted in their glorification already during the earthly life: *fulgebat in his et illud resurrectionis lumen insigne* (*Vit. patr.* 2. *prol.*).

direct link to God through which cures could be effected. Thus, with the help of the chaste saint – "the new man" – others too could recover their "wholeness": as Gregory sometimes says explicitly, these were *redintegrati*.[12]

Bodily discharges and the Devil

At the moment of healing, however – significantly sometimes also designated as "purgation" or "purification" – Gregory not infrequently gives unembarrassed descriptions of sudden discharges of blood, pus, mucus, faeces or a combination of these, even when it is a possessed person who is cured.[13] The suspicion that herewith the cause of the illness is also ejected is confirmed by statements such as: "by vomiting I don't know what kind of pus with blood, and therewith the demon (*daemone eiecto*), he was purged (*purgatus est*)".[14] This more or less putrid fluid is thus regarded as a product or a manifestation of demonic presence. And, although there are only scattered explicit references to this connection, one gets the impression throughout Gregory's writings that for him the Devil and his demons play a role in all cases of illness, whether of a physical or a psychic nature.[15] And there is another significant association: Gregory's view of illness as being not only a decomposition or a pollution, but also a kind of death, appears clearly when he refers to certain cures as "resurrections".[16]

Bodily discharges, the Devil and death are mutually associated in other contexts as well, even though these notions are not always made explicit. The following (likewise unembarrassed) story about bishop Nicetius of Trier is well-known:

---

[12] *Redintegratus*: *Virtutes s. Martini* [*Virt. Mart.*] 2.54, 4.23, 4.26; *reformatus*: ibid. 2.5, 2.40.

[13] "Purification": Martin *qui infirmitates nostras purgaret* (*Virt. Mart.* 3. *prol.*). Is illness a manifestation of "impurity"? Certain expressions seem to indicate this: epilepsy and leprosy (the symbol par excellence of impurity in Leviticus 13–14) will be the lot of a child unfortunate enough to be conceived on a Sunday (*ibid.* 2.24); deaf-muteness and paralysis are said to be incurred *per quoddam contagium* (*ibid.* 4.46). – Fluids appearing at the moment of healing, for example: *ibid.* 1.7, 2.8, 2.20, 2.34, 2.37, 3.16, 3.38; *Vit. patr.* 2.2.

[14] *Virt. Mart.* 2.20. Similarly: *ibid.* 2.27, and 2.37.

[15] Possession is always attributed to the Devil or his demons; but sometimes also: blindness (*Virt. Mart.* 2.15, 3.16, 3.28) and paralysis (*ibid.* 3.14 and 3.27). See also de Nie, *Views*, pp. 230–237.

[16] Death: *Quae longo tempore graviter agens, tamquam mortua putabatur superstes* (*Virt. Mart.* 2.3). Resurrection: *quasi redivivus* (*ibid.* 4.34); *ut putares eum denuo fuisse renatum* (*ibid.* 1.40); *in redivivam lucem renascens* (*ibid.* 2.8).

> Once, during a journey, when he had come down from his horse and gone into the thorny bushes to purge his bowels: behold, a most hideous shade stood before him – tall of stature, enormous in volume, black in colour. He had huge eyes spitting fire like those of a furious bull, and wide open jaws, as it were ready to gulp down the man of God. But when the bishop made the sign of the Cross against him, he vanished like rising smoke. No one will doubt that it was the Lord of evil who was shown to the bishop.[17]

It looks here as though Gregory and his contempories regarded human excrement as permeated by the spiritual quality of the Devil; just as the human debris discharged in illness, it is visible putrefaction, dissolution.

That it is the Devil who suggests and maintains the heretics' false doctrines is said more or less explicitly a number of times, and implicit everywhere.[18] And accordingly, as already indicated, Gregory's stories about heretics contain deliberate, repulsive details of bodily discharges. He repeatedly finds occasion to mention with grim satisfaction the heresiarch Arius' humiliating death: "he lost his entrails on a toilet and was given over to the flames of hell".[19] And similarly, according to Gregory's devastating wit, a heretic priest died ignominiously during a meal, as it were giving up his spirit with a loud fart, after he had gluttonously and too hastily gulped down boiling food.[20] A noble Catholic virgin, finally, who refused to be forcibly converted to Arianism "polluted (*infecit*)" the Arian baptismal water with her excrement (*fluxus ventris*).[21] For Gregory, then, bodily discharges symbolize a dissolution that is the most humiliating end that can befall a human being, and therefore a deserved punishment for those who follow the Devil in denying the divine truth.

---

[17] *Vit. patr.* 17.3.

[18] Indirectly, when a drunken "false prophet's" discharges in a church are said to smell worse than all the toilets of Paris (*Hist.* 9.6). This should be understood as in *Vit. patr.* 17.3 (Nicetius) and 11.1: *tantum fetor ut nihil aliud quam diabulus crederetur.* Explicitly, upon the occasion of an Arian antimiracle: *seductus sum ab inimico legis divinae* (*Hist.* 2.3), and of death through poison in the Arian Eucharist: *Non enim dubium est, tale maleficium esse de parte diabuli. Quid contra haec miseri heretici respondebunt, ut in sanctam* [sic] *eorum locum habeat inimicus?* (*Hist.* 3.31).

[19] *Hist.* 3. *praef.*. Further references: *ibid.* 2.23, 5.43, 9.15.

[20] *Glor. mart.* 79.

[21] *Hist.* 2.2.

Sensuality: "pollution" and "corruption"

What Gregory means by the corruption or disintegration of the flesh being caused by license becomes clear in the preface to his biography of another saint:

> Every man who knows that he possesses a body made of terrestrial matter, must be careful that earthly and carnal matters do not become dear to him. Because, as saint Paul said, "the works of the flesh are plain", full of impurity and wickedness (*immunditia et iniquitate*), rendering men who indulge in them polluted and stinking (*pollutumque et fetidum*), and condemning him in the end to eternal weeping.[22]

The carnal desires most frequently mentioned by Gregory are gluttony, alcoholism and, above all, sexual desire. That abuse of eating and of alcohol can cause illness and even death, as he shows us in his stories,[23] is less remarkable than the fact that he finds it necessary to keep pointing to this. The above quotation shows that what is at stake is not a medical notion as much as a moral and religious one. Man cannot reach God or attain eternal life except by renouncing the striving after things of the flesh in the manner of beasts (*more pecorum carnis sectatio*).[24] That the latter was thought to be regarded by God as equivalent to something like "impurity" is evident in the fact that Gallic conciliar legislation, with which Gregory must have been familiar, sometimes forbids priests to enter the church building just after they have eaten or drunk.[25] Is this attitude perhaps connected with the idea of the then ongoing process of digestion as a kind of corruption and decomposition?

Among the purity rules in Leviticus which are the foundation of Gallic conciliar legislation, seminal emission is explicitly indicated as a cause of "pollution" which makes one unfit to approach the holy.[26] Nothing is said there about sexual desire as a mental attitude. The sixth and seventh-century

---

[22] *Vit. patr.* 4.*prol.*. cf. Galatians 5:19.

[23] Through abuse of alcohol: *Vit. patr.* 8.11, *Virt. Mart.* 2.53; by gluttony: *Glor. mart.* 79.

[24] *Vit. patr.* 4.*prol.*

[25] Synodus dioecesana Autissiodorensis a. 561/605, c. 19, in: C. de Clercq (ed.), *Concilia Galliae A.511–A.695*, Corpus Christianorum Series Latina [CCSL] 148a (Turnhout 1963), p. 267.

[26] Leviticus 15:1–18. Touching a corpse also made one "impure": Lev. 21:1; 22:4. On (im)purity in the Jewish tradition see: J. Neusner, *The Idea of Purity in Ancient Judaism*, Studies in Judaism in Late Antiquity 1 (Leiden 1973).

penitential books speak of both separately, but not in a very clear manner.[27] In Gregory's writings as well as in the Gallic conciliar texts, not only coitus itself but also the desire for it are "polluting" (ejaculation is not mentioned in connection with the latter but is perhaps assumed).[28] The "pollution" concerned thus appears to be a psychic as well as physical condition which, just as in Leviticus, spreads to someone who is touched by a person in this state – a notion indicated by the use of the term "contagion (*contagium*)" in this context.[29]

The following story shows this "contagion" at work. Bishop Eparchius of Clermont, Gregory tells us, was "a very holy man, leading a pious life". However, when he entered the church one night to pray, he found it full of evil spirits and saw their ruler, the Devil, disguised as a woman laden with jewels, sitting on the episcopal throne. The bishop addressed the apparition in extreme and explicit language:

> "O cursed whore! Is it not enough for you to soil all places with your various pollutions (*variis pollutionibus infecire*)? Must you also besmirch the seat consecrated to God by the stinking contact of your rear end (*fetida sessionis tuae accessione coinquinas*)? Leave the house of God, so that it may not be further polluted (*polluatur*) by you!"

To this she replied:

---

[27] Thus P.L. Payer, *Sex and the Penitentials. The Development of a Sexual Code 550–1150* (Toronto 1984), pp. 49–52. J.A. Brundage, *Law, Sex and Christian Society in Medieval Europe* (Chicago 1987), p. 166, suggests that a seminal emission during sleep did not constitute a "sin" but rather a "ritual pollution".

[28] Gregory about bishop Brictius: *corpus meum a tactu muliebris coiti est inpollutum* (*Hist.* 2.1), and about a priest in Clermont: *pollutus erat in conscientia. Saepius enim ab eodem adulteria ferebantur admissa* (*Glor. mart.* 85). Council of Tours in 461, c. 1: *non solum cordis verum etiam corporis puritatem servantes, pro plebe supplicaturi preces suas ad divinum introire mereantur auditum*, ed. C. Munier, *Concilia Galliae A.314– A.506*, CCSL 148 (Turnhout 1963), pp. 143–144). About the conciliar legislation on this subject see Brundage, *Law*, pp. 110–113 and 150–152, and Audet, *Mariage*, pp. 128–134. S.F. Wemple, *Women in Frankish Society. Marriage and the Cloister, 500–to 900* (Philadelphia 1981), pp. 128–132, 136, and 141, gives too negative a picture of the Frankish Church's ideas about the ritual impurity of women as such. A different view of this in: G. de Nie, "Is een vrouw een mens? Voorschrift, vooroordeel en praktijk in zesde-eeuws Gallië" [Is a woman a human being? Precept, prejudice and practice in sixth-century Gaul], in: F. de Haan *et al.* (ed.), *Het raadsel vrouwengeschiedenis,* thematic issue of *Jaarboek voor Vrouwengeschiedenis* 10 (1989), pp. 51–74, especially pp. 56–64.

[29] *Ab omni voluptatis contagio impolluta* (*In gloria confessorum* [*Glor. conf.*] 32). Cf. *Vit. patr.* 16.1: *per copulam nuptialem contagio involvi mundano*; and *Vit. patr.* 16. *prol.*.

> "Because you call me a whore, I shall arrange many temptations for you through the desire for women." And after she had said this, she vanished like smoke. Then the bishop was indeed tempted through the movement of his body by desire; but, protecting himself with the sign of the Cross, the Enemy could not hurt him.[30]

In three sentences the equivalent of pollution occurs four times, and this is not even counting the qualification of "stinking" for the diabolical posterior. The association here of a state of *commotio* – an excitation that is a kind of turbulence – with the Devil and with danger is crucial here. It is the opposite of peace, which is the natural state of the spirit. Gregory's lively rendition of what must be a hundred-year-old item of oral tradition not only breathes an intense disgust and nausea felt for the genital region, but also a fear of the turbulence involved in sexuality. Man by himself is not able to resist this power: to control the turbulence in his own body he needs the strength of a superior spiritual power, invoked by a symbolic gesture. If the bishop had succumbed to the desire of his body, he would have come under the domination of the Devil and, through this, have been condemned to death. Sensuality, then, does not only imply "corruption" and "impurity", "pollution" and "contagion", but – because of all this – also a slow, insidious death. Gregory betrays this association by his metaphorical expression "the pale leprosy of sensuality (*lurida lepra luxuriae*)".[31] Just as in the story of Creation, the Devil is directly implicated in this. The human personality that, through continence, attempts to achieve a permanent wholeness is in constant conflict with the Devil, who tries to dissolve it in a psychic "corruption" that eventually leads to physical annihilation.

The fluid contours of the perceived world

We have already seen that the touch of a saint or his relics could effectuate a cure, but also that physical contact could transmit "pollution"; that the Devil or a demon could be hiding in certain, if not all, bodily discharges, but also that the latter could manifest themselves as an animal or female (!) apparition, to disappear again as smoke; and, finally, that a symbolical gesture could activate a spiritual power on the spot. Further, we have seen that the renunciation of the psychic and physical turbulence and

---

[30] *Hist.* 2.21.

[31] *Deprecans ut [...] mundet cor et mentem a lurida lepra luxuriae, purget cogitationes a concupiscentiis pravis* (*Virt. Mart.* 2.60).

"corruption" that constitutes sensuality could result in the soul and body's harmony and imperishability. In all of this, the boundaries between persons and things, between gestures, thoughts, words and realities become blurrred; all things lose their sharp contours and tend to overlap, coincide, coalesce. Many more instances could be cited in which the clear demarcation between self and world, which mainstream modern western European thought has until recently accepted as a self-evident fact, is shown not to exist for Gregory. In his view, "inside" and "outside" (a distinction which he almost never makes) merge, as it were in a dream.[32] What can this have meant for what we think of as the experience of being a human individual?

Personal identity: a skiff on turbulent water

Although indirectly, this becomes evident in still another image of fluidity that recurs in Gregory's stories: that of a boat or ship in danger on turbulent water.[33] When we look at such a story more closely, we see that here too fluidity, the Devil and death are different aspects of one and the same thing. Thus, as one story tells us, while a group of pilgrims was crossing the Loire in boats to visit and pray in the dead saint Martin's monastic cell,

> [...] there was a storm, instigated by the Tempter (*tentatoris impulsu commoto vento*), and the whole fleet sank into the deep (*in profundo demergitur*); both men and women were carried away by the river. As they were being whirled around (*rotarentur*) by the wild waves and all hope of escaping had been lost, all called out in one voice, saying: "Compassionate Martin! Save your servants from this imminent death!"
>
> Upon these words, behold, a gentle breeze lifted the submerged bodies unharmed from the waves and brought all, carried by an obedient wave, to the shore they wished to go. No one perished, and all the saved were able to celebrate the Easter feast with the greatest joy.
>
> Thus that same holy power (*virtus*) manifested itself that cleaved the waters of the Jordan and led the people on a dry path between the masses of water on each side, [...] the power that embraced the drowning Peter with a tender right hand (*pia amplectens dextera*) and saved him so that he would not perish [...].[34]

---

[32] See de Nie, *Views*, pp. 207–210, 287–290.

[33] For instance: *Glor. mart.* 68, 75, 82; *Glor. conf.* 94; *Virt. Mart.* 2.17; *Vit. patr.*17.5. Cf. Matthew 8:23–27, 14:22–33.

[34] *Virt. Mart.* 1.2.

But dissolution in a fluid chaos had once already been the punishment of sinful humanity as a whole; in his *Histories*, Gregory tells his readers:

> The Lord, however, angered by the sins of his people, who did not walk in his ways, sent the Flood that engulfed and annihilated (*diluvium inundante delivit*) all living souls from the surface of the earth. [...] But I do not doubt that the form of the Ark is the figure of our Mother Church (*quod species illa arcae matris gessisset aeclesiae*). For it is she who, passing through the waves and rocky crags of this worldly life (*inter fluctus et scupulos huius saeculi*) and cherishing us with her motherly cradling, defends us against threatening evils by her tender embrace and protection (*nos ab imminentibus malis materno gestamini fovens, pio amplexu ac protectione defendit*).[35]

We see here that turbulent water can symbolize the life in this world and that it is the motherly embrace of the Church – also through her saints – that holds a person together and protects him from dissolution in the liquid deep. Christ, Gregory writes elsewhere, does the same: "he carries the Church, redeemed by his blood, on his neck high above the turbulent water of the earthly life (*collo et super fluctus saeculi*)".[36] Fluidity and turbulence thus effect the dissolution of identity – as in the case of Chilperic's body in the boiling cauldron.

Christ, the Church, and the saint thus are symbols of "a motherly ship" that protect man from a menacing, liquefying chaos all around and under him: the turbulent water of the earthly life, the commotion caused by carnal desires, the sudden destructive blows of an illness or of robbers. For Gregory, perhaps, the individual human body too is something like a skiff: it must be whole, firm and not leak; but as such it also appears to symbolize man's personal identity.[37] Just as a small boat, the human person should be

[35] *Hist.* 1.4. Elsewhere in his writings too Gregory points to "motherly" tenderness, not only on the part of women but also of men; see de Nie, "Vrouw" (n. 28), p. 73. Brown, "Virginity" (n. 9), pp. 436–439, suggests that the Church Fathers wanted to replace the solidarity of sexual union in Christian society with that of maternal affection.

[36] Gregorius Turonensis, *In psalterii tractatum commentarius* 23, ed. B. Krusch, MGH SSrM 1.2, pp. 873–877, here p. 875. In a vision of the royal nun Radegund of Poitiers, a friend of Gregory's, Christ appears as a "ship": *vidit in visu navem in hominis specie et in totis membris eius sedentes homines* (Baudonivia, *Vita sanctae Radegundis* 3, ed. B. Krusch, MGH SSrM 2 [Hannover 1888], pp. 377–395, here p. 380).

[37] Gregory uses the term *vas* – vessel, receptacle (see A. Blaise, *Dictionnaire Latin-Français des auteurs chrétiens* [Turnhout 1954], pp. 836–837) – twice for persons: *vas*

open to "on high" – that is: ready to be filled with the Holy Spirit and guided by the stars of the sky – and closed toward "below": the carnal desires instigated by the Devil and his demons. Only the association with eternal values and persons in heaven seemed able to guarantee order, stability and self-preservation. Outside this, man is defenceless against a Devil who tries to transform all things – already blurred in their contours – into an amorphous chaos. It looks as though the smiling face of a saint – seen a number of times in the dreams and visions which Gregory reports – is the personification of a personal ideal: a higher 'self', that orients man's creative energy toward personal integration.[38]

The symbols and rituals used by the Church in Gregory's time rehearsed and thereby stabilized the attitudes necessary for the consolidation of the individual and the community.[39] I suggest that the evidence here reviewed points to the fact that those which concern "purity" are only superficially hostile to the human body as a whole. If Gregory represents the Gallic ecclesiastical view of his time, that view – although definitely one-sided – regards the body consecrated to God as beautiful and worthy of being preserved. At the same time, the body as such constitutes what is perhaps

---

electionis beatus Paulus (*Vit. patr.* 2. *prol.*); *vas electionis beatus apostolus* (*Vit. patr.* 8. *prol.*). Cf. Venantius Fortunatus, *Carmina* 8.3.397–400, ed. F. Leo, MGH Auctores Antiquissimi [AA] 4.1 (Berlin 1881), p. 191: *Opto per hos fluctus, animas tu, Christe, gubernes/ Arbore et antemna velificante crucis,/ Ut post emensos mundani gurgitis aestus,/ In portum vitae nos tua dextra locet*; and Augustine, *De beata vita* 1.1–3, Patrologia Latina [PL] 32 (Paris 1861), col. 961: *Igitur hominum quos philosophia potest accipere, tria quasi navigantium genera mihi video videre* (1.2) – On the body as an image of personal identity in the thought of Gregory the Great, see Straw, *Gregory*, pp. 114, 126, 145. The current hypotheses explaining the rise of asceticism in the fourth century emphasize social factors; see Brown, "Virginity", and n. 38, and cf. M. Douglas, *Purity and Danger. An analysis of the Concepts of Pollution and Taboo* (London (1966) 1984), p. 158: "social conditions [of a small minority group] lend themselves to beliefs which symbolize the body as an imperfect container which will only be perfect if it can be made impermeable". Gregory of Tours' experience of the body, two centuries later, in a society that, although now officially wholly Christian, had become more "primitive", deserves an empirical and unprejudiced investigation. It is possible that in this new context traditional representations have acquired an additional and new function that is more focused on the individual than on the group.

[38] *Vultu hilari* (*Virtutes sancti Juliani* 9); *hilari vultu arridens* (*Virt. Mart.* 1.24). See: de Nie, *Views*, pp. 227–251. And cf. J. Fontaine, "Thèmes et méthodes de recherche hagiographique en 1979", in: *Studi medievali*, ser. 3.20 (1979), pp. 933–945, here p. 936; and P. Brown, *The Cult of the Saints. Its Rise and Function in Latin Christianity*, Haskell Lectures in History of Religions, n.s. 2 (Chicago–London 1981), p. 57.

[39] See on this: S.K. Langer, *Philosophy in a New Key. A Study in the Symbolism of Reason, Rite and Art* (Cambridge, Mass. 1957^{3}), p. 153.

the clearest demarcation between the human person and his potentially intrusive surroundings, and thus the clearest form in which human individuality can survive death. It is a contour, a form, a whole that is recognizable, a unit upon which work can be done, whereas the “soul” and the “spirit” was more elusive. For Gregory, then, the body may have functioned as something like a point of condensation in an experience of life in which all tended to fluidity.

III

CONTAGIUM AND IMAGES OF SELF IN LATE SIXTH-CENTURY GAUL

In a contemporary history of late sixth-century Gaul, there is a story about a Frankish king that begins with one kind of contagion and ends with another. Because it exemplifies much of what can be found about *contagium* and 'self' in the sources of this period, I shall use it as a starting point and frame for discovering the interrelations between these two notions.

1. 'Contagium'

In the year 588, we are told, a merchant ship from Spain brought the 'tinder (*fomes*)' of the bubonic plague—referred to as a *contagium* or infection—to Marseilles, and the disease spread 'like wildfire' from there to the rest of Gaul.[1] The author of the story, bishop Gregory of Tours, reports that it caused 'a wound in the form of a serpent (*vulnus in modum serpentis*)' in the groin or arm-pit, whose 'poison (*venenum*)' killed its victim on the second or third day (*Historiae* (H) 4.31). This description of the wound[2] is probably meant to be more than a simile. For, as is evident throughout his writings, Gregory expected to recognize in visible phenomena shapes or images of invisible spiritual realities at work in them.[3] Here, it looks like that of

---

[1] Brought to western Europe from the eastern Mediteranean in the middle of the sixth century, the plague was to be endemic there until late in the seventh. Gregory of Tours, *Historiae* (H) 9.22; the edition plus German translation used is: B. Krusch and W. Levison (ed.), R. Buchner (tr.), *Gregorius Turonensis, Historiarum libri decem/Gregor von Tours, Zehn Bücher Geschichten*, 2 vols (Ausgewählte Quellen sur deutschen Geschichte 2 and 3), Darmstadt 1967. The most recent English translation is that by L. Thorpe, *Gregory of Tours, The History of the Franks* (Penguin Classics), Harmondsworth 1974.

[2] Today it is clinically described as a swelling of the lymph node, for which the clinical term is 'bubo'.

[3] On this see G. de Nie, *Views from a many-windowed tower. Studies of imagination in the works of Gregory of Tours*, Amsterdam 1987, 209–210, and idem, 'History and miracle: Gregory's use of metaphor', in: K. Mitchell and I.N. Wood (eds), *Gregory of Tours and His World*, Leiden 1999, (forthcoming).

the serpentine Devil himself (as in Gen 3:1, according to the Christian interpretation), exercising his poisonous power.

The Frankish King Guntram, the story continues, attempted to protect the people of his royal city Châlons against this physical infection by symbolic action:

> . . . like a good bishop, providing the remedies with which the wounds of the sinful people might be healed (*qua cicatrices peccatoris vulgi medermentur*), order[ing] all the people to come together in the church, to celebrate rogations [i.e., supplicatory litanies] with the utmost devotion, to eat nothing but barley bread and clean water, and to be continuously present at the vigils. And that was done at this time (H 9.21).

Coming immediately after the description of the serpent-like wounds, the body symbolism of spiritual 'wounds' as the result of sin here appears to imply that the spiritual ones might tend to become also physical unless precautionary measures were taken.[4] As the symbolic ritual rather than practical action also indicates, spiritual and material reality are regarded as constituting a continuum.

A comparison with another application of this same symbolism, in the context of what must also have been an epidemic—there referred to as *infirmitas*—in the acts of the second council of Tours in 567, throws some light on the matter. Its prologue tells us that certain persons had been disregarding the ancient church canons, and that this 'insane freedom generates wounds (*insana libertas generat vulnera*)' which are to be healed by 'the severity of bishops (*sacerdotalis districtio*)'.[5] Such 'wounds' can have been understood as lesions in the community or 'body' of the faithful (1 Cor 12:26), imaged in the New Testament as the body of Christ (Rom 12:5). Contemporary sources, however, show that 'wounds' of the soul was also a current metaphor for an individual state of sin.[6] And, indeed, in the concluding letter to the people the bishops mention 'the growing weight

[4] Cf. M. Douglas, *Purity and Danger. An analysis of the Concepts of Pollution and Taboo*, London (1966) 1984, 81: 'elemental forces are seen as so closely linked to individual human beings that we can hardly speak of an external, physical environment', and 92: 'the experience of organic solidarity' as the basis of such a world view; thus (128) 'rituals work uon the body politic through the symbolic medium of the body'.

[5] Council of Tours II (567), prol.; C. de Clercq (ed.), J. Gaudemet and B. Basdevant (tr.), *Les canons des conciles Mérovingiens (VIe–VIIe siècles)*, vol. 2, Paris 1989 (Sources chrétiennes 354), 348. *Infirmitas*: ibid., Epist. (Ibid., 396).

[6] The phrase occurs in the writings of Venantius Fortunatus, for instance in *Carmen* 4.14.11; M. Reydellet (ed. and tr.), *Venance Fortunat, Poèmes*, Paris 1994, 146.

of our sins (*peccata*)' drawing down 'heavenly vengeance (*caelestis ultio*)' (as in Lev 26:15–41) in the form of

> . . . the urgency of a most severe slaughter threatening to come about (*cladis gravissimae necessitas imminere*), through which no other refuge can be found than the return to the precepts of the One who wished to give us our life through His death.[7]

The rulings enacted in this council look like an attempt to restore order in a society in which laity and clerics have transgressed all kinds of divinely instituted boundaries. The general remedy (*medela*) which the bishops give is that the people should follow divine precepts: like Abraham, pay the tithe (Gen 14:20; cf. Ex 30:12), give alms to expiate their sins (as in Eccles 3:33 and Lk 11:41), and reconcile themselves to their enemies (cf. Mt 5:44). In addition, they urge those who are not yet married to postpone their wedding because it is hoped that 'the anger of the Lord (*ira Domini*) might be appeased by the chastity of the body (*castimoniam corporis*) and by the sincerity [i.e., purity] of the heart (*sinceritatem cordis*) through assiduous prayer'.[8] The latter may have taken place collectively, as in Châlons. This combination of bodily chastity with purity of heart seems to point to the apostle Paul's injunction to the whole community to reject the soul-obfuscating carnal life for the spiritual one that is wholly transparent to God (e.g., Rom 8:7–8). Contemporary literary sources speak explicitly of the 'contagion' and 'pollution' even of legitimate married life.[9]

1.1. *Sexuality and* contagium

It is only in this council's more specific rules about sexual abstinence that we find explicit mention of the notion of *contagium*. Thus incestuous unions of lay persons are said to 'soil (*macula[re]*)' those involved by 'the mixing of seed (*seminis commixtione*)'; in fact, incest is

---

[7] Tours II (567) Epist.; de Clercq-Gaudemet-Basdevant, *Canons*, 394.

[8] Tours II (567), Epist.; Ibid. 348.

[9] As in Gregory of Tours' *Vita patrum* (VP) 16.1 (as *contagium . . . mundanum*), and *In gloria confessorum* (GC) 31 (*qui coniuncti coniugio, non coitu . . . non sunt ab alterutro polluti in voluptate carnali*). The edition of his hagiographical works (also including *In gloria martyrum* (GM), *De virtutibus sancti Martini* (VtM), *De virtutibus sancti Iuliani* (VJ)) used is: B. Krusch (ed.), in: W. Arndt and B. Krusch (eds), *Gregorii Turonensis Opera* (Monumenta Germaniae Historica (MGH), Scriptores rerum Merovingicarum (SSrM)), Hannover 1885, 451–820. Cf. Lev 15:18.

somewhat cryptically said to be a 'fleshly contact/contagion (*carnale contagium*)' which 'pollutes (*pollu[ere]*)'. The specific prohibitions of Leviticus 18(:5–18 and 20) are here brought forward, reinforced by the rehearsal of a number of maledictions from Deuteronomy 27:15–20, 22–24 (canon (c.) 22 (21)). It seems likely that the notoriously polygamous and occasionally incestuous marriages of the Frankish kings were also envisioned in this canon. The wording only attempts to inspire fear, however, and does not stipulate any concrete disciplinary measures, probably because the bishops felt unable to enforce them. By contrast, those seizing the unarmed Church's property are threatened not only with a terrible curse but also with excommunication (c. 25 (24)). Gregory of Tours' stories give ample evidence that, in addition, threats with putative revenge by dead saints were the bishops' main 'weapon' to protect their properties.[10]

For the clergy—for whom, as ministers of the holy, purity, that is permanent celibacy, was prescribed[11]—everything sexual is regarded as polluting. Thus one canon says: 'on account of our jealous God (*propter zelotem Deum nostrum*)' (another Old Testament image: Ex 20:5), young boys being educated as future clergy in the bishop's household are not to be 'polluted (*polluantur*) by the proximity-contagion (*propinqua contagione*) of female servants' (c. 13 (12)), and clerics are forbidden to have unrelated women as housekeepers (c. 10).[12] Another canon even forbids monks in monasteries to take wives (*sic*!), because they would be 'soiled by such a union (*tale [sic] coniunctione fedatus*)' (c. 16 (15)).[13] In contrast to the sanctions against laymen's incest, however, there is no mention of divine punishment either of the persons themselves or of the whole community for such impurity. The sanctions are individual disciplinary measures such as excommunication, penitence and suspension from office. Over this group, I suggest, the bishops may have felt that they could exercise a feasible control.

---

[10] For instance, VJ 13–17, 20; GM 58; VtM 1.29.

[11] See on this, for instance, R. Gryson, *Les origines du célibat ecclésiastique du premier au septième siècle* (Recherches et synthèses, Section d'histoire II), Gembloux 1970, and J.P. Audet, *Mariage et célibat dans le service pastorale de l'église. Histoire et orientations*, Paris 1967.

[12] The latter are bitterly castigated as deceitful 'serpents (*serpentes*)'.

[13] If the secular judge refuses to convict them, the canon continues, and if they seek the patronage of a powerful man to support them against the episcopal authority—one sees that the secular world could aid and abet such situations—everyone involved is to be excommunicated.

The concubinage of the more difficult to supervise rural clergy, however, is dealt with separately and in a different manner. First, the practice is explicitly censured as incompatible with their consecrating the Lord's body, and designated as the Nicolaite 'heresy' which had been anathematized (*damnati*) and cursed (*subiacent maledictio*) by 'the statutes of the Fathers' (c. 20 (19)). In short, these clergy are to be removed from office. Then a highly interesting statement follows:

> [For] it is better that the diseased head (*caput morbidum*) be amputated, if it cannot be cured, than that because of (or through) it (*pro eodem*) their flock be rendered sterile (or depraved) (*infelicetur*).

It is very tempting to assume that the verb *infelicetur*, which is not found in the authoritative dictionary,[14] is a copyist's error for *inficiatur*: infected, which would fit the sense of contagion by illness here. These notions appear to be used as metaphors for the nature and influence of voluptuousness. There is no mention, however, of a divine punishment of the whole community for the resulting desecration of the altar. Instead—the bishops again evidently feeling powerless to control the situation—the people themselves are urged to reject such a pastor who, while he ought to be 'an image of the rule (*forma praecepti*)', is instead 'an image of sin (*forma peccati*)'. As in Gregory's description of the infected wound, this mode of speaking again seems to point to a contemporary habit of expecting to recognize the manifested pattern of an indwelling spiritual power in a visible appearance.

So far, all the evidence appears to point to a concept of pollution that was primarily concerned with the spiritual obfuscation caused by the yearnings of the flesh and the 'contagiousness' of this state, rather than a 'soiling' by organic fluids, as in the old Testament (Lev 15). For apart from the single reference to seminal fluid in connection with lay incest, the notion does not surface in the canons of any of the sixth-century Gallic councils. Instead, a letter of Pope Innocent I, included in the acts of the council of Agde in 506 appears to show that it is, rather, the condition of the heart that is central: that of being turned toward or away from God. The pope asks there how anyone 'who is contaminated by carnal desire (*contaminatus . . . carnali concupiscentia*)' can think that his prayers will be heard.[15]

---

[14] Cf. A. Blaise, *Dictionnaire Latin-Français des Auteurs Chrétiens*, Turnhout 1954, 440.

[15] Council of Agde (506), c. 9; C. Munier (ed.), *Concilia Galliae* (CCSL 148),

That the specific term *contagium* (derived from the verb *contingo* and *contactum*, meaning to touch) was not an idle one is shown by a canon of the council of Clermont in 535 which forbids church vessels to be used for weddings because they would be 'polluted through the ceremonies of worldly lust (*pompa saecularis luxuriae polluntur*)' and the 'touch of sinful persons (*improborum tactu*)'.[16]

1.2. Contagium *and physical pollution*

Certain canons in two sixth-century Gallic councils, however, indicate that the concept of pollution did not only pertain to a state of carnal desire and its influence upon the condition of the heart. Thus one such canon rules that the cloth that covers the Lord's body cannot be used even to cover the corpse of a bishop being carried to his tomb because, when the cloth was restored to its proper use, 'the altars would be polluted (*altaria polluantur*)'.[17] And another that the dead cannot be given the Eucharist or even be kissed.[18] These

---

Turnhout 1963, 196–9. Cf. Lev. 11:44, 1 Cor. 7:5, Rom. 8:8–9. Similarly: Orléans IV, c. 17; Mâcon I (581–3), c. 11 (de Clercq-Gaudemet-Basdevant, *Canons*, 274, 432–4). Confirming the evidence of the councils on sexual purity, Gregory of Tours uses the word *contagium* as a synonym for the pollution of sexual desire (GC 32, VP 16.1). And he tells us that the persons of the clergy can also be polluted by sexual contacts with women (H 2.21, 5.20) or by sin in general (H 5.5); not surprisingly, in Gregory's stories these tend to die violent deaths. And when rebellious nuns break their oath of fidelity to Christ, the act is said to 'pollute the temple of God (*templum Dei . . . pullui*)', the latter presumably meaning their souls and bodies as in 1 Cor. 3:16 (H 9.39); Gregory suggests that divine anger (*ira*) and punishment are likely to follow such conduct.

[16] Clermont 535, c. 8; de Clercq-Gaudemet-Basdevant, *Canons*, 214. Gregory tells us that a church is 'polluted (*polluatur*)' by physical desire, presumably on the part of its clergy (H 2.21), and adultery carried out by a layman in the building itself (H 5.49)—he is described as coming to miserable end. All this certainly points to the concept of pollution here reinforcing a difficult kind of separation between the clergy and the secular Christian world. But non-sexual sins of the heart can also contaminate the material surroundings. One story, for instance, tells us that the tomb of a saint refused to accept a piece of candle from an unwilling offerer and rolled it back towards him. Shaken by this, the man is thereupon said to 'have washed away with the flowing fount of his tears that which he had soiled with a delinquent heart (*corde delinquente foedavit*)' (Venantius Fortunatus, *Virtutes sancti Hilarii* (VtH) 33; the edition used is that of B. Krusch (ed.), *Venanti Fortunati, Opera pedestria* (MGH Auctores Antiquissimi (AA) 4.2), Berlin 1885. This edition also contains his *Vita sanctae Radegundis* (VR), *Vita sancti Albini* (VA), and *Vita sancti Germani* (VG).

[17] Clermont (535), c. 3 and 7; de Clercq-Gaudemet-Basdevant, *Canons*, 212–4.

[18] Auxerre 561/605, c. 12; Ibid. 492. But the same synod—and it is the only one in this period—ruled that a woman cannot receive the Eucharist with an uncovered hand or touch the cloth covering the Eucharist. The latter seems to be the prerogative of the male clergy; the canon may indicate that women had been assisting

prohibitions do appear to resemble the restrictions about touching the dead for the priests in Leviticus 21:1, and 11. However, as will appear below, there may be more to this than meets the eye.

1.3. *The 'contagion' of the world*

Turning now from conciliar legislation to the literary sources: the only ones to survive *in extenso* from the late sixth century are the writings of the already-mentioned Gregory of Tours and of his friend, the poet Venantius Fortunatus of Poitiers. These usually equate pollution in the Pauline manner with the worldly manner of life and purity with the saints' ascetic withdrawal from this. Thus Fortunatus speaks of 'the contagion of the world (*mundi contagium*)' (as in 2 Pet 2:20) having been 'defecated (*defecatus*)' by a nun who had been married against her will (*Vita Radegundis* 2). Likewise, Gregory quotes the apostle Paul, saying:

> Every man who knows that he possesses a body made of earthly matter, must be careful that earthly and carnal things do not become dear to him, because as St Paul said, 'the works of the flesh are plain' [Gal 5:19], full of impurity and wickedness (*inmunditia et iniquitate*), rendering men who indulge in them polluted and stinking (*pollutum et fetidum*), dooming them at last to eternal weeping (*Vita patrum* 4.prol.).

Conversely, of a saint whose corpse appeared whole and not decayed a year after his death Gregory says that this was because 'his flesh had not been corrupted by sensual pleasure (*cuius caro non fuit corrupta*

---

in church services in this region. Although the notion of pollution through the blood of menstruation is mentioned outside Gaul in this period, nothing is said about it in the Gallic councils. Whether or not silently observed, it does not seem to have been an issue. Gregory's stories seem to indicate, however, that women had just as much access to the holy as the male laity; there is no mention in any of the contemporary sources of restricted access to the holy involving menstrual blood. See on this: G. de Nie, 'Is een vrouw een mens? Voorschrift, vooroordeel en praktijk in zesde-eeuws Gallië', *Jaarboek voor Vrouwengeschiedenis* 10 (1989) 51–74. But Gregory's frequent references to innocently spilt blood—without mentioning pollution—drawing down God's vengeance (*ultio*) (*Historiae* (H) 1.41, 2.3, 2.4, 5.5, 7.3, 8.31) seem to point to the notion of an almost autonomous connection between such a crime and its divine punishment (as in Gen 4:10). When a murder is perpetrated inside St Martin's shrine in Tours, however, Gregory describes what follows as: '. . . the vengeance of God (*Dei ultio*) immediately came upon those who polluted (*polluerunt*) the holy hall with human blood' (H 7.29; cf. 9.12). What he means is that, as he tells us, the church's dependents—the poor and the possessed—attacked the murderer and his companions with fists and stones. However, Gregory's writings relate numerous forms of divine vengeance for flagrant sins, ostensibly without the notion of pollution being involved.

ludibrio)', and that he therefore possessed 'a wholeness of body and heart (*corporis et cordis integritas*)' which preserved him physically even after death (*Vita patrum* 7.4). Again, visible appearance manifested spiritual reality. However, a passage such as this also shows precisely the notion that could be associated with the handling of an ordinary corpse as the material prey of a corrupting evil power—especially that of physical desire—that might have earlier made its living soul (as we still say) dissolute.[19] One might thus surmise that this notion of decay and physical dissolution as a manifestation of the working presence of evil power will have played a role in the conciliar regulations concerning the handling of the dead.

2. *The soul-body continuum: images of self*

But this last story also substantiates the suspected connection between 'wounds' of sins in the soul and the condition of the body. That sins of the heart were indeed thought to bring down divine punishment upon the living body in the form of an analogous deformation or illness is indicated, for instance, by Fortunatus's story of an official who neglected to carry out a royal command to feed the poor; he was blinded by an eye ailment. However, Fortunatus tells us:

> Remembering his guilt (*culpa*), because of which (*unde*) so suddenly a dark error had invaded him (*illum . . . tenebrosus error invaserit*), he quickly went back and asked forgiveness so that the guilt of his heart went out [of him] (*ut culpa cordis exiit*), and the light entered his eyes (*oculis lux intravit*) (*Vita Paterni* 45).[20]

Here, personal sin—in this case doubtless understood (fleetingly imaged) as a state of spiritual blindness—appears to 'attract' (or presuppose?) a darkling, that is unclean, evil spirit that accordingly obfuscates the physical eyes; a change of heart drives it out and *ipso facto* restores sight.

---

[19] Cf. J. Neusner, *The Idea of Purity in Ancient Judaism*, Leiden 1973, 47, on Philo's view of the 'uncleanness' of a corpse: '. . . "that wretchedness is due to the different parts of the soul having been left loose and gaping and unfastened, while proper ordering of life and speech is the result of being kept close and tight" (The Worse Attacks the Better 103; Confusion of Tongues 166–167).'

[20] Likewise, Gregory uses leprosy as a metaphor for physical desire and warns those who have marital relations on Sunday that they can expect an epileptic or leprous child (VtM 2.60 and 24).

2.1. *The self as 'vessel'*

The notion of a mind-body continuum is only one of the images of self in late sixth-century sources. The many stories about possession show us another one already adumbrated in that of the serpentine wound: that of the self as a 'vessel' (as in 1 Thess 4:4, 5, 12),[21] and possibly as an 'invaded vessel (*invasum vasculum*)'.[22] The invading spirit could be described as 'evil (*malignus*)' or as 'unclean (*inmundus*)' (as also in Mt 12:43).[23] Gregory tells us a number of stories in which the exorcism of such a spirit is designated as a purification (*purgatus; Virtutes Martini* (VtM) 2.20) or cleansing (*mundatus*; VtM 2.34); the latter can be accompanied by a discharge of a putrid fluid, about which he explicitly says that the evil spirit came out with it (VtM 2.20, 34, 37). The latter is thus the visible and, especially, malodorous manifestation or result of demonic invasion. Other illness too, however, is sometimes explicitly described as caused by the machinations (*insidiae*) of an evil spirit (as in VtM 2.40).[24] Gregory nowhere spells out the specifics of the nexus of sin with illness and with personal responsibility and/or invading spirits, however, and these seem to shift about. Sometimes sin and illness are described as a personal responsibility, sometimes as brought about by evil spirits. It seems clear, however, that shielding oneself from invasion by evil spirits through avoiding contact with evil thoughts, acts and 'polluted' objects was definitely one's own personal responsibility.

2.2. *The self in the cosmos*

To return to the story about King Guntram: it also shows us an arresting image of self, continuing:

> During three days, while [the king's] alms went forth in greater quantity than usual, the whole people feared (*formidabat*) him in such a way as though he were then already not only a king but a very priest of

---

[21] Fortunatus, C 10.6.31–32; the edition used here is that of F. Leo, *Venanti Fortunati Opera poetica* (MGH AA 4.1), Berlin 1881. Alongside many shorter poems, it contains a long narrative poem to which will be referred below: the *Vita sancti Martini* (VM).

[22] Fortunatus, VR 76.

[23] Idem, VA 47.

[24] But when Gregory tells us that a man was blinded, deafened, muted and crippled 'by a certain contagion (*per quoddam contagium*)' (VtM 4.46), it is difficult to know what he means: an ostensibly physical disease or a demonic infestation? Probably both.

> the Lord: placing (*transfundens*; literally: pouring over) all his hope in the mercy of the Lord, to Whom he sent (*in ipso iactans*; literally: in Whom he threw) the thoughts that came upon him (*cogitationes quae ei superveniebant*), believing with the total wholeness of his faith that they would be transmitted to be carried out (*a quo eas effectui tradi tota fidei integritate putabat*).

Remarkably, the human inner world here appears to extend into the higher spiritual sphere from which events in the visible world were thought to be supported and directed. The notion recurs often in Fortunatus's writing. He tells us, for instance, that a male saint 'lay in prayer, pressing the ground with his body while he rose above the stars with his mind (*sidera mente transcendens*)'.[25] Such a notion is not biblical: in Isaiah 14:13, aspiring to set oneself 'above the stars' is presented as a diabolical act. The view is a commonplace, however, in the writings of the Late Antique Platonist philosophers, such as Philo, who regarded the human mind as a continuum with, and a downward extension of, the divine Mind above the stars.[26] What Gregory tells us about King Guntram's prayers appears to assume something resembling such a view of the human mind.

More usually, however, we find that God was thought of as somehow coming down to live in the human heart. Through baptism (which removed the deforming 'dirt' of original sin) and a perfect imitation of Christ, one could become—as St Martin had been—'a man full with God (*vir plenus Deo*)' (Sulpicius Severus, *Vita Martini* 3.1).[27] Thus Fortunatus writes of a holy bishop:

> Clean (*mundus*) of the enticements of the world, repelling lusts (*lasciva*), dwelling in pious temples [i.e., serving in Christian churches], you are so pure (*purus*) that your heart of hearts (*tua corda*) is a pious temple of God (*pia templa Dei*) [1 Co 3:16]; Christ chooses to hide himself in such a vessel (*vase recondi*): whoever purifies himself (*sibi purgaret*), is possessed by Him as a home (*possidet ipse domum*)' (*Carmina* 3.23a.15–8).[28]

---

[25] VG 20: *vir justus orationi incubuit, terram corpore premens et sidera mente transcendens.*

[26] As, for instance, F.E. Brenk, 'Darkly beyond the glass: middle Platonism and the vision of the soul', in: S. Gersh and C. Kannengiesser (eds), *Platonism in Late Antiquity* (Christianity and Judaism in Antiquity 8), Notre Dame, Indiana, 1992, 39–60, esp. 48.

[27] Sulpicius Severus, *Vita sancti Martini* 3.1; J. Fontaine (ed.), *Sulpice Sévère, Vie de saint Martin*, vol. 1 (SC 133), Paris 1967, 256. In fact, this epithet was also applied to our author, the later sainted Gregory of Tours, in Baudonivia's, *Vita sanctae Radegundis* (VR) 23; the edition used is that of B. Krusch (ed.), *Vitae sanctorum* (MGH SSrM 2), Hannover 1888.

[28] Gregory also speaks of 'the tabernacle of [a saint's] heart (*cordis sui tabernaculum*)' as 'a temple of the Holy Spirit' (VP 2.prol.; cf H 1.15).

How was this connection between the human heart and the furthest part of the universe more precisely envisioned? The New Testament, and later the patristic writings, had combined neo-Platonic ideas with the story of man's creation in Genesis 1:26. They regarded the human soul not as in a continuum with the uncreated divine Mind, but as created and patterned by this Mind according to its own image. Thereby—in its original state—the human soul reflected the living pattern of the divine and, through this reflection, participated in a derivative manner in this pattern (Rom 8:29; Col 1:15; 1 Cor 15:49; 1 Pet 2:21).[29]

2.3. *The interior divine image*

Fortunatus's story of the cure of two lepers—society's prime 'untouchables'—at a saint's tomb shows how this notion of the interior divine image could function as a concept of self. He tells us that the two lepers, 'deformed by blemishes (*maculis immutati*)', came to the tomb of St Hilary in Poitiers to be cured (*Virtutes Hilarii* 11–14). They stayed there and washed their heads and bodies with a potion of the dust collected from the tomb 'until the illness' variety of sores was itself captured, and left the body it had captured (*de corpore quod captiverat captiva migraret*)'. The capture of the human soul-body by a foreign spirit of uncleanness, then, is reversed or inverted by means of the equally inverted 'dirt' of the dust from the saint's tomb—as we know from Gregory's stories, it was a common remedy in this period (e.g., especially *Virtutes Martini* 3.60). The application seems to work *ex opere operato*, and indicates that physical diseases, as invasions by evil forces, may be cured by introducing holy power. Then, however, Fortunatus goes on to a different image, saying:

> After innumerable wounds, one skin was attached to all the members: the face, deleted by longstanding dirt (*diuturna deletus sordidine sua*) began to be repainted with its image and [thereby] to become recognizable [as such] (*coepit repingi imagine nec agnosci*).

How should we understand this 'image'? The notion recurs in Fortunatus' poetic version of Sulpicius' brief story of a very similar cure

---

[29] Cf. Gregory of Tours, VP 8.prol: *conformes fieri imaginis Filii sui*; and see G.B. Ladner, 'The Concept of the Image in the Greek Fathers and the Byzantine Iconoclastic Controversy', *Dumbarton Oaks Papers* 7 (1953) pp. 1–22, and J. Pépin, "Image d'image", "Miroir de miroir", in: Gersh and Kannengiesser, *Platonism*, 217–229. Cf. Y. de Andia, 'Pathos ta theia', in: Ibid., 239–258.

of a leper by St Martin, while still alive in this world, through a kiss (Fortunatus, *Vita Martini* 1.487–513). There, Fortunatus elaborates upon the idea and lets the recovery of the image of his face overlap with that of the image of God in man's interior nature—equating the saint's saliva not only with the leprosy-curing quality of the Jordan River, but also with its cleansing of original sin through baptism. The latter, of course, restores the original, inner image of God. What the author may be suggesting in both stories, then, is that the deforming and debilitating *contagium* of leprosy is a 'figure' or image of the obfuscation of God's image in man by original sin. This appears to be confirmed by the fact that, later in the poem, Fortunatus refers precisely to this incident as a metaphor of his own sinful inner condition (*Vita Martini* 2.485). The real self, then, was the interior image of God, and one way in which it could be liberated from impurities was by touching a conductor of Christ's power from on high: the physical remains of a person who, by enacting Christ's image, had been inhabited by Him.

Being cured of leprosy is thus a metaphor for the cleansing and restoration of the interior image of God which original as well as actual sin had 'deleted'. This use of the term 'deleted' is significant. For Fortunatus likewise describes Saint Hilarius's cure of a moribund child as

> suddenly he raised up by his words (*verbo operante subrexit*) the flowing fabric of the members (*membrorum fluentem fabricam*) and re-formed (*reformavit*) them in their pristine state as though there had been nothing soluble about them (*tamquam si nihil fuisset solubile*) (VtH 8).

These stories show that sin, illness, 'pollution' and death are contingently continuous states of dissolution, and that a cure is the restoration of one's identity to its pure, firm pattern: that of the image of God.

2.4. *Transparence to the divine: benign contagion*

However, King Guntram's access to divine reality also precipitated visible effects. Gregory tells us:

> For the faithful then used to relate that a certain woman, whose son was afflicted by the quartan fever [a kind of malaria] and lay in bed worrying about his illness, approached the king's back in the crowd, stealthily snatched some of the fringes of his royal cloak, put them in

water, and gave them to her son to drink. At once, the fever was extinguished and he was healed.

And I do not doubt this [to have happened], for I have often heard the evil spirits in possessed people invoking his name and—recognizing his power (*virtus*)—confess their crimes.

The resemblance to Christ's cure of the bleeding woman (Mt 9:20–22) and his exorcisms need no comment. Mary Douglas has designated such transmission of beneficent power as 'benign contagion'.[30] Gregory's stories about contemporary holy persons contain many examples of this: they are conduits for the holy power of Christ, or of the Holy Spirit, dwelling in their hearts.[31]

The most common source of benign contagion and healing in this period, however, was not the living saint but the tomb of a dead one. Thus, when Gregory tells us that St Martin, at his tomb, 'drives out (purges) our illnesses (*infirmitates nostras purgaret*) [and] washes away our wounds (*vulnera diluerat*)' (VtM 3.prol.), the phrasing already indicates that the ailments and cures must be spiritual as well as physical. Accordingly, his more elaborate description of the process of a cure begins with the enacting of a tearful contrition for one's sins, and experiences the saint's (!) 'remedy (*medela*)' of forgiveness; only thereafter does 'the touching (*tactus*) of the blessed tomb command (*imperavit*) bleedings to stop, the blind to see, paralytics to rise and even bitterness of heart to disappear entirely'.[32] Gregory's experience of all of palpable reality as a conduit for spiritual qualities and forces, then, was definitely a spiritual one that involved inner transformation, and not manipulative 'magic' as has sometimes been thought.[33]

3. *Conclusion*: contagium *and self*

What conclusions can be drawn from this evidence about *contagium* and self in late sixth-century Gallic sources?

---

[30] Douglas, *Purity*, 109.

[31] The holy hermit Hospitius, for instance, 'felt through the spirit (*sensit . . . per spiritum*) that the power of the Lord was present (*Domini adesse virtutem*)' (H 6.6).

[32] VtM 3.prol.

[33] See on this subject G. de Nie, 'Caesarius of Arles and Gregory of Tours: two Gallic bishops and "Christian magic"', in: D. Edel (ed.), *Cultural Identity and Cultural Integration. Ireland and Europe in the Early Middle Ages*, Dublin 1995, 170–96.

First, that in this period not contact with organic fluids as such, but the mental and physical preoccupation with the desires of the transitory flesh appears to be central in the concept of *contagium*. And, second, that the self was regarded as a 'vessel', originally created and patterned as 'pure heart' or true self—a common spiritual identity consisting of a resemblance to the living image-form of the Creator, Form-giver and Sustainer of the living universe, Christ, which 'attracted' His presence. Sin or impurity was a state of separation from this life-giving form and presence, and of an emptiness that attracted the invasion of 'corrupting' evil spirits, and thus in fact a condition of dissolution or non-self.

In the sixth-century West, it is not systematic theological exposition, but Gregory's gripping tales that present this world-view to a largely uneducated public. Thus he often relates that diabolically driven dark clouds caused sudden, violent storms and near-shipwrecks and drownings at sea, which were averted at the last moment by the invocation of a saint's holy power (e.g., *Gloria martyrum* 68, 75, 82; *Gloria confessorum* 94; *Virtutes Martini* 1.9, 11 and 2.17; *Vita patrum* 17.5; cf. Mt 8:23–7, 14, 22–33). These events are almost certainly parables of the soul threatened with extinction by omnipresent, invisible evil powers.[34] The indeterminate, engulfing fluidity of the sea—with the biblical story of the Flood as a paradigm (H 1.4)—was a powerful metaphor of life separated from God (cf. e.g., Ps 69.1, 14). Gregory himself elsewhere speaks of the 'waves of the worldly life (*fluctus saeculi*)',[35] and lets a would-be virgin speak of legitimate married sexual relations as immersion in 'the abyss' (*dimergo in abyssos*; H 1.47). Fortunatus likewise mentions 'the ragings of the whirlpool [or abyss] of the worldly life (*mundani gurgitis aestus*)' (C 8.3.399; cf. Gregory, H 1.47), and thus of the pull of spiritual corruption as leading to the infernal 'chaos' (cf. e.g., C 3.9.87)—an annihilating *formlessness* that also pervaded the world, and whose more recognizable name was Evil.[36]

What could happen to those who let themselves be immersed in this formlessness is made visible by the punishment which Gregory ascribes to his arch-villain, King Chilperic. This king had publicly

---

[34] Cf. Douglas, *Purity*, 161 on the symbolic equivalence of water and 'dirt', but in the positive context of creative renewal.

[35] *In psalterii tractatum commentarius* 23; B. Krusch (ed.), MGH SSrM 1.2, 873–77, here 875.

[36] As also Douglas, *Purity*, 56, 104.

vented his rage at what he regarded as the bishops' taking over royal power in Merovingian society and tried to counteract this (H 6.46). In a vision, which Gregory lets King Guntram tell as his own (!), three dead bishops throw Chilperic into a cauldron filled with boiling water—an image associated with evil in Jer 1:13, and with the sea-monster Leviathan in Job 41:13. Subsequently, the unfortunate king was 'so dissolved and liquefied (*dissolutus ac liquefactus*) . . . that no trace whatsoever remained of him' (H 8.5). In other words, his identity had been dissolved, deleted—as that of the lepers had been before their restoration at the saint's tomb. Gregory's story about King Guntram shows that the latter—in sincere faith, however—had learned how to beat the bishops at their own game: for what was the real bishop of the city doing while the king put himself in charge of the supplicatory litanies in the church?

The notion of *contagium*, then, appears to have given form to—and a handle upon—the greatest fear of a Church beset on all sides by insufficiently contained lay influence and rapacity: that of dissolution through invasion by a formlessness that was a separation from the image and presence of God. However, the notion also seems to reflect the contemporary experience of the personal self: a highly permeable vessel that needed to be protected and made firm by holy power, in a life-world in which forces of corruption and disintegration were everywhere, waiting to invade and capture the unwary.

IV

Images of invisible dynamics: self and non-self in sixth-century saints' lives

In the saints' lives of late sixth-century Gaul, notions and images reminiscent of patristic theology appear in a tissue of personal experience. For, although a number of the Germanic kings reigning there liked to imitate Roman culture at their courts, we hear no more about public higher educational institutions as a forum of intellectual exchange[1] and, probably in connection with this, what has survived from Gaul in this period is not abstract theological treatises, but stories about embodied truth.

In late Antiquity, as Peter Brown has pointed out, the Christian saint could function as an 'ideogram for one's own soul'[2]: in other words, as a model for the construction of one's interior, spiritual mode of being — the true self. Since the portrait of the saint focuses upon his assimilation to his divine model, Christ, merely natural human selfhood is a negative quality — something to be transcended. And instead of a substantive, we find only a reflexive pronoun — *se* or *se ipsum*. As such, interiority is inconsistently indicated by terms such as spirit (*spiritus*), mind (*mens*), soul (*anima* or *animus*), heart (*cor*), consciousness (*sensus*), and innards (*viscera*)[3]. We shall see, too, that instead of Augustine's — for his time unique — exceedingly subtle language of interiority[4], late sixth-century hagiographers tended to describe the abysmal

[1] Pierre Riché, 'Centers of culture in Frankish Gaul between the 6th and the 9th centuries', in: Pierre Riché, *Instruction et vie religieuse dans le haut Moyen Age*, Collected Studies Series CS 139 (London, 1981), III.

[2] Peter Brown, 'The saint as exemplar in Late Antiquity', in: J. Stratton Hawley ed., *Saints and Virtues* (Berkeley, 1987), p. 13.

[3] My focus here is not upon connecting these concepts with their origins or histories. See on this, for instance: Jean Lévêque and André Rayez, 'Interiorité', *Dictionnaire de Spiritualité* (DS) 7, col. 1877-1903; L. Reypens S.J., 'Ame', DS 1, col. 433-469; Roberto Moretti and Guy-M. Bertrand, 'Inhabitation', DS 7, col. 1735-1767. T. Sorg, 'Heart', *New International Dictionary of New Testament Theology* (NIDNTT) 2, pp. 180-184; J. Goetzmann, 'Mind', NIDNTT 2, pp. 616-620; C. Brown, 'Soul', NIDNTT 3, pp. 676-689; C. Brown, 'Spirit, Holy Spirit', NIDNTT 3, pp. 689-709.

[4] See on interiority in Augustine: Charles Taylor, *Sources of the Self. The Making of the Modern Identity* (Cambridge, 1989), pp. 127-142; on soul, body and personal identity in Augustine: John M. Rist, *Augustine* (Cambridge, 1994), pp. 92-147. Henry Chadwick, 'Philosophical Tradition and the Self', in: Glenn W. Bowersock et al. eds., *Late Antiquity. A Guide to the Postclassical World* (Cambridge, Mass.-London 1999), pp. 60-81, gives the pagan and patristic background of many of the notions and images discussed in this paper; on Augustine: *ibid*., pp. 77-80; a number of pagan philosophical motifs are referenced below.

and contradictory qualities of interior experience more traditionally as intrusions by as it were 'external' forces.

This essay invites the reader to recapture something of this early medieval self-awareness by visualizing, and thereby affectively re-enacting, the dynamic patterns in some central images of self and non-self in late sixth-century saints' lives. Such visualization may not be far from the sixth-century experience of this imagery, because there is ample evidence that in this period associative, meditational imaging was traditionally practised upon religious texts as an aid to understanding and internalizing what was regarded as the patterns of suprasensory reality manifested in their events and imagery[5].

What kind of experience is this meditative imaging? The philosopher of science and poetry Gaston Bachelard has pointed out that an image makes visible and inspectable the *psychic pattern of movement* or 'dynamism' of a specific mode of feeling. When a textual image is visualized and thereby empathetically experienced or re-enacted, as in meditative reading, it induces an affective mimesis of its energy pattern in the reader, and this, in turn, would recreate something of the psychic movement which originally brought forth the image in the mind[6]. The affectively experienced mental image is therefore in the full sense a dynamic reality[7]. Bachelard is saying, I think, that as such it is just as much a reality as the world which is grasped by the senses, but apprehensible only through imagination[8]. As we shall see, there is evidence that, in their own way, our sixth-century authors held a similar view.

In Gaul, two more or less exactly contemporary authors are responsible for almost all of the hagiography that has come down to us. They are bishop Gregory of Tours (539-594)[9] and his good friend, the originally Italian profes-

[5] E.g. Cassian, *Collationes* 14.13, CSEL 13.2, p. 414: *si eandem diligentiam... ad spiritalium scripturarum volveris lectionem meditationemque transferre*. See on this subject the seminal article of Pierre Hadot, 'Antike Methodik der geistigen Übungen im Frühchristentum', *Humanistische Bildung* 4 (1981), 31-62. On meditation and the poetical process in early Christian poetry see: Jacques Fontaine, *Naissance de la poésie dans l'occident chrétien* (Paris, 1981), especially pp. 177-194. Gregory and Fortunatus's famous contemporary Pope Gregory the Great also practised meditational imaging in the exegesis of the *lectio divina*: Claude Dagens, *Saint Grégoire le Grand. Culture et expérience chrétienne* (Paris, 1977), pp. 55-75, 233-244. On meditative reading, listening and looking in sixth-century Gaul: Giselle de Nie, 'Die Sprache im Wunder — das Wunder in der Sprache. Menschenwort und Logos bei Gregor von Tours', *Mitteilungen des Instituts für Österreichische Geschichtsforschung* 103 (1995), 1-25.

[6] Gaston Bachelard, *L'air et les songes. Essai sur l'imagination du mouvement* (Paris, 1943), pp. 10-13.

[7] *Ibid.*, p. 120: 'L'image dynamique est une realité première'.

[8] This theme and its implications for human interiority are most eloquently explored by David L. Miller in: 'Theology's Ego/Religion's Soul', *Spring* (1980), pp. 78-88; *Christs. Meditations on Archetypal Images in Christian Theology*, vol. 1 (New York 1981), pp. xv-xxiv; and 'Theologia Imaginalis', in: M. Parisen ed., *Angels and Mortals. Their Co-Creative Power* (Wheaton etc. 1990), pp. 157-176.

[9] The standard edition of his *Vita patrum* (VP) is: Gregorius Turonensis, *Opera*, ed. Wilhelm Arndt and Bruno Krusch, Monumenta Germaniae Historica, Scriptores rerum Merovingicarum

sional poet Venantius Fortunatus (c.540-c.604)[10]. Their emphases and presentations differ, but their views are essentially similar[11]. I shall first look at their images of three modes of alienation, and then at the manner in which each portrays what he regarded as the true self.

I. *Images of non-self*

A. *Corporeum vinculum*: the 'heaviness' of the body

In this period, as is well known, a great deal of alienation was experienced through the body and the latter, as Peter Brown has so eloquently shown, could be a symbol for society[12]. But the body could also function as a two-faced symbol — both positive and negative — of the self. For the worst (visionary) punishment that Gregory's villain, king Chilperic, can receive is the total dissolution and liquefaction of his body in a cauldron with boiling water; conversely, the greatest reward of a saint is that his body is found to be undecayed and even luminously beautiful years after his death. Gregory explains that this holy man's body seemed already 'glorified' for the coming resurrection because 'his flesh had not been corrupted (*non fuit corrupta*) by lust'[13]. I have explained elsewhere that this taking for granted of the congru-

(MGH SRM) 1.2 (Hannover, 1885), pp. 661-744; this edition also contains his miracle stories: pp. 451-660, 745-820. On his language and writings see: Giselle de Nie, *Views from a Many-Windowed Tower. Studies of Imagination in the Works of Gregory of Tours*. Studies in Classical Antiquity 7 (Amsterdam, 1987), pp. 1-22.

[10] Venantius Fortunatus, *Vita sancti Martini*, ed. Friedrich Leo, *Venantii Fortunati opera poetica*, MGH, Auctores antiquissimi (AA) 4.1 (Berlin, 1885), pp. 293-370; this edition includes his *Carmina*. A new edition of books 1-4 and 5-8 of the latter has appeared: *Venance Fortunat, Poèmes*, ed. and tr. Marc Reydellet (Paris, 1994, 1998). Prose lives, ed. Bruno Krusch, *Venantii Fortunati opera pedestria*, MGH AA 4.2, pp. 1-54. On his life and works see: Judith George, *Venantius Fortunatus. A Poet in Merovingian Gaul* (Oxford, 1992).

[11] For a comparison of the uses of imagery by Gregory and Fortunatus see: Giselle de Nie, 'Iconic alchemy: Imaging Miracles in Late Sixth-Century Gaul', *Studia Patristica* 30 (1997), pp. 158-166, and idem, 'Word, Image and Experience in the Early Medieval Miracle Story', in: Paul Joret and Aline Remael ed., *Language and Beyond. Actuality and Virtuality in the Relations Between Word, Image and Sound* (Amsterdam, 1998), pp. 97-122.

[12] Peter Brown, *The Body and Society. Men, Women and Sexual Renunciation in Early Christianity* (New York, 1988).

[13] *Historiae* (*Hist.*) 8.5, MGH SRM 1.1, p. 374; and VP 7.4, MGH SRM 1.2, pp. 689-690. Chadwick (*op.cit.*, p. 62) points to the treatise *Poimandres* (Corpus Hermeticum 1.18) as indicating that the sexual drive is the cause of death. Compare Augustine, *Retractationes* 1.13.8, CCSL 57, p. 40: *Si natura nostra in praeceptis et imagine dei manens in istam corruptionem non relegaretur*. Since extensive referencing to patristic sources would take too much space, random examples will be given only from Augustine's writings. See on 'self' in Gregory: Giselle de Nie, 'Le corps, la fluidité et l'identité personnelle dans la vision du monde de Grégoire de Tours', in: Marc van Uytfanghe and Roland Demeulenaere ed., *Aevum inter utrumque. Mélanges offerts à Gabriel Sanders* (Steenbrugge, 1991), pp. 75-87.

ence of spiritual and sensory reality indicates that Gregory understood the same or analogical dynamic patterns to be operative both in the mind or spirit and in the sensory world[14]. This is a fundamental assumption and represents an integrated experience of self and world, instead of the subject-object duality which we are accustomed, perhaps incorrectly, to take for granted. At the same time, however, the passages just mentioned also reveal a deep fear of physical disintegration or decay as an annihilation of self, caused by what we now regard as a physical drive which is in itself morally neutral.

The imagery used in the following passage shows which qualities of movement Gregory associated with physical existence on earth:

Everyone who knows himself (*se*) to bear a body of earthly matter should take care that he is not cast headlong (*devolvatur*) into the things that are known to be earthly and sweet to the flesh; because, according to the apostle Paul, the works of the flesh are manifest [Gal. 5, 19], full of uncleanness and iniquity, and they render the man who pursues them polluted and stinking, and relegate him in the end to eternal weeping[15].

Here the body, and matter in general, exert a downward pull[16]. The additional qualification of 'uncleanness' and iniquity, and this as leading to physical putridity or desintegration is a repulsive falling apart[17]. It adds the dimension of a contamination with destructive forces in body and mind that lead to dissolution and extreme deprivation, if not total annihilation. Instead, Gregory continues, 'captivated by the example of the saints', men should 'be lifted up to heavenly and eternal deeds'[18]. His frame of reference, then, is a vertical one[19].

Where Gregory, as pastor of souls, emphasizes the dangers of the downward pull of the flesh, Fortunatus, the elegant poet of praise, tends to focus upon his heroes' masterful control of the body as the condition for their upward movement along the vertical axis. Thus he tells us that saint Albinus, 'through his having dominated his body, triumphed over himself (*edomito corpore de se ipso potius triumpharet*)'[20]. Here, the body appears to be part of *se ipsum* or self; both it and what can only be the inner attitude of the natural, physical self (*se ipsum*) must be overcome. Fortunatus' use of the term 'the shackle of the body (*corporeum vinculum*)'[21] points by contrast to the free movement of the

[14] For instance in: de Nie, 'Word, image and experience', pp. 109-116.

[15] VP 4.*prol.*, MGH SRM 1.2, p. 673.

[16] Chadwick (*op. cit.*, pp. 72 and 77) indicates that this idea is expressed by the pagan philosopher Proclus and to a certain extent reflected by Augustine in the period just after his conversion.

[17] Similarly, Proclus, *Commentary on First Alcibiades* 104; cited in Chadwick, *op. cit.*, p. 73.

[18] VP 4.*prol.*, MGH SRM 1.2, pp. 673-674.

[19] As also was that of Plotinus and, sometimes, Augustine (Chadwick, *op. cit.*, pp. 62, 65-66 and 72, resp.).

[20] *Vita s. Albini* (VA) 14, MGH AA 4.2, p. 29.

[21] *Vita sancti Germani* (VG) 208, MGH AA 4.2, p. 27. Compare *Wisdom of Solomon* 9, 15 (cited in Chadwick, *op. cit.*, p. 63), and Augustine, *De civitate Dei* 9.10, CCSL 47, p. 258: *corporis vinculum.*

spirit. Accordingly, he reports that although saint Radegund's 'flesh was in the world, with her mind she was in heaven (*mente in caelo*)'[22].

Thus, although Church doctrine verbally defended the goodness of material creation and the body, Gregory and Fortunatus' imagery tends to point to a vertically oriented sense of cosmic dualism, and to the body as something alien, heavy and potentially decaying into nothingness. The latter's image thus evokes — and probably stands for — the fear of its dragging the heavenly, immaterial soul down with it into the annihilation of death, or non-self[23].

B. *Furor*: going around and around

A second image of alienation or non-self is that of uncontrolled mental and physical turbulence. A particularly clear example of this and its overcoming is found near the end of Fortunatus' poetic rendering of Sulpicius' *Life of saint Martin*. In his version of the monk Brictius' verbal attack on the saint, the latter first sees two demons inciting the young monk to 'puffed-up anger (*ira tumens*)'; the latter is thereby 'moved by evil (*male... motus*)', becomes 'disturbed of mind (*turbata mente*)'[24], and rushes to accuse the saint of various shortcomings. The description of Brictius' demeanor is worth quoting in full:

> Thus raving in his gestures (*gestu rabidus*), in his bitterness not knowing himself (*neque se agnoscebat*), judging and rashly inflating (*inflans*) the deeds of his own life, vaunting himself intolerably with inane (*inania*) noises, moved by the wind (*vento motus*), inert but simulating the leafy shade, stiffening (*rigens*) with a stuck-out neck, rebelling through levity, harassing his mind (*exagitans animum*), with wide-spread legs [and] protruding chest, unreasoning, swelling with inflated (*tumido*) pride, having lost his mind (*nec se mente capax*), reeling (*vacillans*) with a puffed-up mood, he fiercely (*truculenter*) heaped bitter words upon the bishop[25].

In contrast to the description of saint Albinus, the 'self' in the phrase 'not knowing himself' must here be not his natural state of fleshly living, for he was a monk but, as is indicated later, his usual self-conscious self-control as an ascetic: his true self. The absence of this is imaged as variations of essentially two dynamisms: first, a state of raving or, as it is later called, of *fury* (see below) (which includes 'moved by the wind', 'inert', 'harassing', 'having lost his mind', 'unreasoning', and 'reeling'), and, second, *emptiness*, as in 'inflating' (which includes 'vaunting', 'inane noises', 'levity', 'protruding chest', 'inert',

[22] *Vita s. Radegundis* (VR) 83, MGH AA 4.2, p. 48, possibly referring to what Plotinus spoke of as the 'undescended soul' (*Enneads* IV 8.8.1; cited in Chadwick, *op. cit*., p. 62). Augustine did not use this specific imagery; Christian poets did: e.g. the fifth-century Paulinus of Périgueux, *Vita sancti Martini* 1.297, CSEL 16.1, p. 31: during saint Martin's life on earth, his *mens plena Deo coelesti in sede manebat.*

[23] Compare Augustine, *Confessiones* 9.1 (1), CCSL 27, p. 133: *dextera tua respiciens profunditatem mortis meae, et a fundo cordis mei exhauriens abyssum corruptionis.*

[24] Respectively: *Vita sancti Martini* (VM) 4.528, 539 and 531, MGH AA 4.1, p. 365.

[25] VM 4.533-541, MGH AA 4.1, p. 365.

'swelling', and 'puffed-up'). Placed in the context of the whole poem, this composite image is a negative or shadow of what is described as the ideal: saint Martin's 'mind founded in God (*mens fundata Deo*)'[26]. After the unperturbed saint's prayer, the 'spectres (*larvae*)' that were possessing Brictius were put to flight, and 'when he returned to his [right] mind (*redit ad mentem*), the Brictius who had been furious (*furiosus*)' fell at the saint's feet to ask for forgiveness[27]. Here, then, *mens* as a state of rational self-control and self-awareness is used as an equivalent of what must in this case be the new, spiritual, 'self' (*se ipsum*) [Cf. 2 Cor. 5, 17].

Uncontrollable movement, movement that is not going anywhere, is therefore typical of the loss of self through the *furor* of possession by an external agent. In a few cases we are actually told that the possessed are going around in circles. Thus when Martin left his monastery outside the city to go to the cathedral, the crowd of the possessed there sensed his approach and 'became agitated in speech, turning around in circles (*trepidabant ore, rotatu*)'[28]. Fortunatus also repeats Sulpicius' report that some levitated and others hung upside down in the air — but without their clothes falling down[29]. These dynamics — spinning around and levitation: together a whirlwind — remind one of the Preacher's description of the emptiness of life: 'the wind goes round and round, encircling everything, and returns on its circuits (*lustrans universa circuitu pergit spiritus et in circulos suos regreditur*)' (Eccl. 1, 5). An even clearer case of rotary movement is the following:

> for when the raving (*rabiens*) enemy has invaded someone completely, and the ferocious servant of the spirit of error goes about, he — in his insane seizure — turns his prey around like a pivot (*rotat... cardine*)[30].

When interrogated by saint Martin, some demons confess to being Jupiter, or Anubis: 'vessels (*vasa*) of the abominable service of demons'[31]. The latter statement points to the fundamental, formal image of the self underlying all these stories: that of the human person as a hollow vessel [cf. Acts 9, 15; 2 Tim. 2, 21].

The image of non-self as invasion and captivity by uncontrolled turbulence, as in a whirlwind, then, points to sensations of non-direction, loss of self-awareness, powerlessness, absence of groundedness and emptiness.

C. The delusion of vanity: an *atra vorago*

This emptiness reappears intensified in the last mode of non-self that will be investigated here: the delusion of grandeur that is vanity. We find it elabo-

[26] VM 2.407, MGH AA 4.1, p. 327.

[27] VM 4.551-554, MGH AA 4.1, p. 365.

[28] VM 4.160, MGH AA 4.1, p. 353.

[29] VM 4.163-167, MGH AA 4.1, p. 353; cf. VG 187, MGH AA 4.2, pp. 25-26.

[30] VM 3.280-282, MGH AA 4.1, p. 339. Compare Augustine, *Conf.* 8.2 (3), CCSL 27, p. 114: *narravi ei circuitus erroris mei.*

[31] VM 4.170-171, MGH AA 4.1, p. 353.

rately described in Fortunatus' rendering of Sulpicius' story of saint Martin's temptation by the devil masquerading as Christ. The author begins by anaesthetizing the reader by presenting the devil as having been overcome by Christ's passion, describing him as 'perfidious and so often cast down (*perfidus et totiens elisus*), not believing in himself (*nec sibi credens*), weak and degenerated (*debilis, degener*)'[32]. He is, then, the essence of falling and its consequences. These dynamics are, course, an implicit counterimage to that of the ascensional and therefore powerful qualities of the saint. Here is Fortunatus' version of the devil's appearance:

before [the saint's] eyes stood the deformed form of the rebel, a shadow raying light, glittering with a sulphurous glow, dark with a lying brightness [that covered] an engulfing black abyss (*atra vorago*), shining because of his robes, the servant in royal dress covered with gold leaf, beautiful with an insubstantial (*vacuo*) diadem that flashed with the light of numerous rows of jewels, powerful through false attire (*falsa veste*] and gold-covered shoes, pleased and vaunting himself with the pomp of his puffed-up triumph (*tumido… triumpho*)[33].

All the alienating images of *furor* return here, magnified by latent darkness, falsity, and, most conspicuously, an engulfing utter emptiness, a 'black abyss'[34]. The latter is as it were a visualization of the invisible sickening anguish of falling into a void. Sensing the presence of the devil or evil, then, is described as sensing exactly that movement of emptiness: an endless, totally debilitating falling — as the devil himself would finally be cast into the abyss [Rev. 20, 1-3].

This feeling might resemble the acute 'sinking' feeling one has in the waking experience of sudden, intense fright or shame, or profound emotional loss. Although probably very few people have actually seen something like an abyss, most of us would feel, Bachelard writes, that we somehow know what this endless falling feels like because we have experienced it in certain dreams[35]. Thus *our imagination reveals our experienced reality to us*[36] — a reality that does not behave according to the laws of the space-time world. In their own ways, in the sixth century it is this reality's impingement upon the sensory world and the human person that Gregory and Fortunatus are above all concerned to describe.

The diabolic apparition first tried to flatter the saint into believing that it was Christ, come especially to comfort him after his heavy labours before

[32] VM 2.278-280, MGH AA 4.1, p. 323.

[33] VM 2.285-292, MGH AA 4.1, p. 323.

[34] Compare Augustine, *Sermones* 12.2, CCSL 41, p. 166: *vana pompa*; *Conf.* 1.19 (30), CCSL 27, p. 16: *vorago turpitudinis*; *Contra Faustum* 15.3, CSEL 25, p. 420: *vorago fallaciae.*

[35] Bachelard, *L'air*, p. 112; idem, *La terre et les rêveries de la volonté* (Paris, 1948), pp. 343-356.

[36] *Ibid.*, p. 353: 'c'est par le dépassement de la réalité que l'imagination nous révèle *notre* réalité'.

returning at the end of the world (thus inducing vanity), and then asked to be worshipped as such. But Martin remained silent. Not surprisingly, the description of the saint's state of mind reveals qualities and dynamics directly opposite to those of the apparition: 'His mind remained firmed (*mens solidata manens*), searching the heights and the depths; [although] blown upon by the wind, it was not turned around (*rotatur*) on a tremulous hinge'[37].

To sum up: the imagistic dynamics of non-self here examined are heaviness, falling apart, non-directional or centripetal turbulence, and an endless falling into an engulfing abyss. All these appear to point to an obsessional fear of annihilation, or death.

II. *Images of the true self*

The envisaged escape from all this is leaving heavy, potentially decaying matter behind and ascending to what was thought of as eternal youth in a spiritual reality. We have already seen that the latter was imaged as life in a future — presumably spiritualized — body in heaven beside the glorified Christ. To make this happen, the Church taught, one needed to conform to the invisible divine image in oneself as it was made visible in the life of Christ (Gen. 1, 26-27; Rom. 8, 29; Col. 1, 15).

A. Gregory: an overflowing lamp

Gregory's image of man's true self as an assimilation to Christ is nothing if not hard work. Thus he speaks of 'the cross of austere observance (*crux austerae observantiae*)' (cf. Matt. 10, 38) which is taken on by those 'who follow the Bridegroom', a significant image for male saints[38]. And he quotes the apostle John's statement that 'he who loves his soul (*anima*) shall lose it; and he who hates his soul in this world, shall keep it in eternal life' (John 12, 25). Here, 'soul' is the New Testament notion for one's natural self, and we encounter the central paradox and initiatory, transformational image of Christianity: that of achieving true life only through death. Gregory takes it to be self-evident. He goes on to another Bible quotation that shows what this taking up one's cross and this hating one's soul means in daily life: namely, 'always carrying around (*circumferentes*) the mortification of Christ (*mortificationem Christi*) in your body, so that Jesus's life (*vita*) too will be manifested in your mortal heart (*in corde vestro mortali*)' (2 Cor. 4, 10). Living according to the body, then, is the natural self; its denial, a kind of physical 'death', makes room for a totally 'other', spiritual kind of life. This is not a realization of

[37] VM 2.306-307, MGH AA 4.1, p. 324.
[38] VP 2.*prol.*, MGH SRM 1.2, p. 669.

one's own 'individuality', then, but a conscious mirroring of and thereby participation in a universal spiritual pattern[39]: that of Christ's (divine) life.

To effect this, Gregory tells us that, in addition to their abstinences, the saints meditate upon — that is affectively internalize — mental images of the suffering Christ. One inspiration for such a practice is likely to have been the apostle Paul's view of what would happen when the Christian believer 'sees' (mentally visualizes) the image of Christ prefigured in Old Testament events and images: 'seeing-mirroring (*speculantes*) the glory of the Lord, we are transformed into that same image from light to light (*in eadem imaginem transformamur a claritate in claritatem*)' (2 Cor. 3, 18). Thus Gregory writes of contemporary holy men that

through the eyes of their internal mind they keep seeing (*Aspiciebant... per illos mentis internae oculos*) how the Lord of the heavens descended to the earth, not lowly as a humiliation, but humiliated through mercy in order to redeem the world. They keep seeing Him hanging on the Cross, not as the glory of divinity, but as a pure sacrifice of the body He had taken on... And they also keep feeling in themselves (*habebant in se*) the affixing nails, when they are riveted by fear of Him and terrified of the divine Judgement, so that they bear nothing that is unworthy of his omnipotence in the dwelling of their heart/body (*cordis*, al. *corporis*)...[40].

Through this internalizing visualisation, evidently, they would not only transcend the inclinations of the natural body-centred mode of life, but indeed reflect the divine life that is imaged as light: for 'that extraordinary light of the resurrection too glows in them, the light... with which Jesus shone when he suddenly stood in the middle of the apostles' meeting within locked doors' (cf. John 20, 19)[41].

This passage shows how internalizing meditation upon the Bible was practised in this period. When Gregory adds that the blessed confessor Illidius 'placed all these [images] in the tabernacle of his heart (*cordis sui tabernaculo*), so that he too would be found worthy to be made a temple of the Holy Spirit (*templum sancti Spiritus*)', we see how this internalization of what must have been the psychic dynamics of images was used to effect processes of interior transformation[42]. And here, again, we have the basic vessel image of self, but glorified. As in the Pauline letters: when appropriately purified, body and heart can together be a dwelling for the divine (e.g. 2 Cor. 4:7; 2 Tim. 2:20-22).

Alongside that of assimilation to the suffering Christ in order to become the Tabernacle or temple of God, however, I would suggest that other, presumably more or less unselfconscious, images of the true self as assimilation to the

[39] This resembles Neoplatonic aspirations (Chadwick, *op. cit.*, pp. 65-69).

[40] VP 2.*prol.*, MGH SRM 1.2, p. 668.

[41] VP 2.*prol.*, MGH SRM 1.2, p. 668.

[42] Compare on this method in modern psychotherapy, for instance: Roberto Assagioli, *Psychosynthesis* (New York, 1962).

divine may be found in Gregory's miracle stories. My reason for including these — admittedly my own construction, because Gregory does not say there explicitly that he is talking about self — is that he indicates that he regards miracles as visible manifestations of invisible divine dynamic patterns that also work in the human mind and heart[43]. Gregory, then, in fact experiences a miracle as an event happening simultaneously in the visible world and in the interior person[44].

A particularly significant imagistic pattern in his stories is one that occurs in various transfigurations[45] — that of the miraculously created spring, with its analogues: the miraculously overflowing and/or perpetually burning oil lamp in a shrine, and divinely appearing radiating luminosities around holy persons or objects. These congruent 'imagistic structures'[46] occur a number of times and were sometimes perceived by Gregory himself. Perhaps the most arresting story is that in which he tells us about an oil lamp which, he says, he actually saw pouring forth more oil than its vessel could hold. He tells us that 'he gazed at it in awed, silent wonderment (*admiratusque silui*)'[47]. I think that we can begin to understand this kind of experience when we remember that — as modern psychology tells us — what we directly see is not the object itself but our mental representation of the incoming sensory data, and that this representation is determined by our pre-existing mental models, the patterns of our previous knowledge and expectations[48]. As the well-known art historian Ernst Gombrich wrote, we tend to see only what we already know[49]. Gregory's mental models, of course, were Sulpicius' story of oil increasing by saint Martin's power[50], and the symbols the Church had taught him: that of Christ as the 'living spring (*fons vivus*)', which he once mentions as such[51], and as the Light or lamp of the world, or the sun[52]. Gregory's gazing in awed, silent wonderment appears to have been an affective opening up to and internalizing of the dy-

[43] *In gloria martyrum* (GM).*prol.* and VP 18.*prol.*, MGH SRM 1.2, pp. 487-488, 733-734. See on this subject: de Nie, 'Die Sprache'.

[44] See on this: de Nie, 'Word, image and experience'.

[45] The concept is that of Bachelard, *L'air*, p. 13: 'On comprend les figures par leur transfiguration.'

[46] The term is Patricia Cox Miller's in her 'The blazing body: ascetic desire in Jerome's letter to Eustochium', *Journal of Early Christian Studies* 1/1 (1993), p. 43.

[47] GM 5. See on this story and its background: Giselle de Nie, 'A broken lamp or the effluence of holy power? Common sense and belief-reality in Gregory of Tours' own experience', *Mediaevistik* 3 (1990), pp. 269-279.

[48] So Rudolf Arnheim, *Visual Thinking* (Berkeley-Los Angeles, 1969), pp. 90-91.

[49] Ernst H. Gombrich, *Art and Illusion. A Study in the Psychology of Pictorial Representation*. Bollingen series 35.5 (Princeton, 1960), pp. 210-211, 223, 225-228.

[50] Sulpicius Severus, *Dialogi* 2 (3).3, CSEL 1, pp. 200-201; see: de Nie, 'Broken lamp'.

[51] *Hist.* 6.29, MGH SRM 1.1, p. 297. Compare John 4, 14: *sed aqua quam dabo ei fieret in eo fons aquae salientis in vitam aeternam.*

[52] Matt. 17, 2; Mark 9, 1; Luke 9, 28; John 8, 12 and 9, 5; Rev. 21, 23. Compare Augustine, *Enarrationes in Psalmos* 25.2.3, CCSL 38, p. 143: *sol iustitiae* (Mal. 4, 2).

namic of what, consciously or not, he perceived as a theophany. In a very real sense, he identified with it, thereby re-enacting-replicating that dynamic interiorly and becoming one with the divine[53]. I would suggest, then, that for Gregory the visual experience of the dynamic pattern of such a miracle is likely to have been a 'recognition' — the sudden awareness of a corresponding vital energy pattern in his own deepest interiority[54].

B. Fortunatus: saint Martin's *decor supernus*

Fortunatus portrays saint Martin as a 'possessor of heaven on earth (*possessor coeli in arvis*)', dwelling in Christ, adoring him night and day, 'praying inwardly the whole time (*intimus orans*), for the eyes of his heart were directed (*tendens lumina cordis*) not towards the flesh but towards heaven'[55]. Accordingly, the saint

> show[ed] forth something immortal from his mortal image: God held his face, piety his consciousness (*sensus*), and peace his heart (*cor*).... Transcending the order of his [mortal] nature, he was an angel, surpassing the heights of heaven, with his mind (*mens*) reaching beyond the clouds; free from human affairs, he entered the stars as a citizen[56].

Elsewhere, Fortunatus audaciously goes on to invent and describe the appearance of the living saint's invisible, heavenly self as 'heavenly beauty (*decor supernus*)'[57] This occurs in a much elaborated rendering of Sulpicius' brief description of the heavenly jewels once seen in a vision appearing on the saint's hand while he consecrated the Eucharist[58]. First, Fortunatus has them flashing like fireworks:

> suddenly his nourishing hand sparkled with heavenly beauty, coruscating with the varied splendour of noble stones, scattering raying light in all directions like a wheel [*undique visa rotae spargens radiatile lumen*]; his arms were vibrating lightning through beautiful [lit. purple] jewels; their brightness as well as the ruddy golden light of the metal beamed even in the sunlight, through which the miraculous character of the event was more believable. ... Thus the pious hand flashed together with the just man's faith[59].

53 As Plotinus and Augustine did by withdrawing into their deepest selves (Chadwick, *op. cit.*, pp. 66, 80).

54 Compare Augustine, *Conf.* 9.10 (23), CCSL 27, p. 147 (the mystic moment at Ostia): *sed inhiabamus ore cordis in superna fluenta fontis tui, fontis vitae, qui est apud te*; and *In Johannis Evangelium tractatus* 32.4, CCSL 36, pp. 301-302: *bibito ergo isto liquore vivescit purgata conscientia, et hauriens, fontem habebit; etiam ipsa fons erit.*

55 Respectively: VM 2.400, 410-411, 418-419, MGH AA 4.1, p. 328. Compare Augustine, Ep. 147.15, CCSL 44, p. 311: *oculi cordis.*

56 VM 2.431-432, 434-436, MGH AA 4.1, p. 328.

57 VM 4.311, MGH AA 4.1, p. 358.

58 Sulpicius Severus, *Dialogi* 2 (3).10.6, CSEL 1, p. 208.

59 VM 4.311-316, 319, MGH AA 4.1, p. 358.

Significantly, as is evident here, jewels were then thought not to reflect light but to emit it from within[60]. And, as is evident elsewhere too, the quality of faith or orientation toward heaven could actually be perceived as fiery light[61]. Here we have again the quality of sending energy outward from a centre, which we encountered in Gregory's phenomena, plus a circular motion, here represented as a 'wheel' — perhaps reminiscent of Ezekiel's visionary wheels in heaven (Ezek. 10, 13) and/or the raying disk of the sun, as we have seen a late antique symbol of Christ.

After this, however, Fortunatus suddenly leaps to envision what never appeared in Sulpicius' original story:

> O beautiful Martin, adorned by a veil of precious stones; how your new mantle [becomes you] — a coruscating texture, whose woof is ruddy-glowing topaz and whose warp jasper — and instead of woollen threads, distinguished jewels run through the robe[62]!

After raising the question of who made all this beauty, the poet ends this section by an injunction to the reader:

> These things should be brought to mind by venerating rather than by speaking. Why do you seek to understand the mysteries, when you cannot enter the hidden light? Be stunned into silence (*stupeas*) then, o man, where grace weaves its tissues[63]!

The 'hidden light' here probably points to the light of heavenly reality shining out from the jewels as traditional images of spiritual virtues: in his 'temple of the soul', Prudentius had also described such jewels[64]. Significantly, Fortunatus tells his readers to put verbal language (he means critical distancing) aside and venerate — that is affectively open up and assimilate oneself to, thus *become* — this image of heavenly harmony and beauty.

When, at the end of book four, Martin's appearance in heaven is described again, Fortunatus addresses the saint: 'you equal the sun with its rays and the moon in its courses (*cursibus*); glowing with splendour, you are beautiful as the morning star. You yourself (*ipse*), shining man, flash (*coruscas*) with the light of God'[65]. Here, the raying sun is explicitly mentioned, as is the circular course of the moon: the hidden light — God's light — is radiating outwards, then, as it was also thought to do from jewels: visible and invisible reality again coalesce.

[60] For late antique views of jewels see: Giselle de Nie, 'The poet as visionary: Venantius Fortunatus's "new mantle" for Saint Martin', *Cassiodorus* 3 (1997), pp. 65-70.

[61] A sphere of fiery light had once been seen rising from Saint Martin's head (Sulpicius Severus, *Dial.* 1 (2).2.1-2, CSEL 1, pp. 181-182; cf. Fortunatus, VM 3.53-60, MGH AA 4.1, pp. 331-332).

[62] VM 4.321-324, MGH AA 4.1, p. 358.

[63] VM 4.328-330, MGH AA 4.1, p. 358. Cf. 1 Tim. 6, 15-16.

[64] Prudentius, *Psychomachia* 851-853, CCSL 126, p. 179. Compare Augustine, *En. in Ps.* 33.2.15, CCSL 38, p. 292: *cuius cubiculum cordis plenum est tantis gemmis virtutum*; and see: de Nie, 'Poet', p. 68.

[65] VM 4.590-592, MGH AA 4.1, p. 367.

Images of the Invisible: Experiential non-spatial Dynamics of Self

In the patterns of movement which we have looked at, there are two central, opposing images of circular motion. On the one hand, the inflating, *centripetal* whirlwind of self-seeking — leading to *emptiness*, the circular engulfing abyss of annihilation or non-self. And on the other hand, the *centrifugal*, outpouring radiance of benevolence and other-centredness — leading to the *fullness* of the inhabitation of the divine as mankind's true self.

These images of non-spatial patterns of mobility reveal what Gregory and Fortunatus regarded as the dynamics of an invisible psychic-spiritual reality. The quest for an interior self that was separated from the whole of the cosmos was thought to lead to turbulent dissipation in a bottomless private void. By contrast, true selfhood could be attained by identification with Christ, not only in his suffering but also as transfigurations of a common underlying pattern — an image of the divine as the outflowing creative principle of the universe: Gregory's overflowing lamp, and Fortunatus' dazzling jewels; together, they form Boethius' *fons lucidus*[66]. Using the same images, Isaiah had already pointed to this perhaps archetypal dynamic of spiritual reality (Is. 58, 10-11):

> If you pour your soul out (*effuderis*) for the hungry and fulfill (*repleveris*) the afflicted soul, your light (*lux*) will arise (*orietur*) in the darkness, and your darkness will be as the light of midday; and the Lord will give you eternal peace,... and you will be... like a fount of waters (*fons aquarum*) that will flow for ever[67].

[66] Boethius, *Philosophiae Consolatio* 3. M xii.2, CCSL 94, p. 62.
[67] As already indicated (note 54), Augustine had said something very similar.

V

Caesarius of Arles and Gregory of Tours

Two Sixth-Century Gallic Bishops and 'Christian Magic'

In his treatise on the teaching of the faith to the uneducated, addressed to what appears to be the half-converted urban population of Romanized Africa in the late fourth and early fifth centuries (*De catech. rud.* 16.24)[1] Augustine says the following:

> ... a most joyful entrance (*laetissimum aditum*) to a beginning [of this teaching] is [to show] how great God's care (*cura*) is for us. [The listeners'] attention is thus transferred in a sensible manner from the way of miracles and dreams, to the firmer one of the Scriptures and [their] more certain oracles (*Sane ab huiusmodi miraculorum sive somniorum, ad Scripturarum solidiorem viam et oracula certiora transferenda est eius intentio*). (*De cat. rud.* 6.10)

Oracles, miracles, and dreams were prominent in late antique pagan piety.[2] The uneducated, Augustine is saying, should be persuaded to make these yield place to the solidity and certainty of the divine revelation transmitted through Scripture. Throughout the treatise, his emphasis is upon doing this through 'joy (*hilaritas*)' (e.g. 2.3; 10.14)—that is, through a love (*charitas*) that is 'pleasing (*blanda*) to some, severe to others, hostile to none, and a mother to all' (15.23). Thus, the telling of the story of God's Creation of the world and his care for the Israelites could be shown—through many events and sayings that 'prefigure' (cf. *figurare* in 19.33) the future—to lead directly to that of the contemporary Church and, beyond it, to 'the destination of love (*charitatis finis*)' (3.5) in heaven.

1 *De catechizandis rudibus liber unus*, PL 40.310–48.
2 Robert Lane Fox, *Pagans and Christians in the Mediterranean World from the Second Century AD to the Conversion of Constantine* (London 1988), p. 196 and, in general, pp. 102–261.

This essay was first published in *Cultural Identity and Cultural Integration: Ireland and Europe in the Early Middle Ages (Medieval Studies)* ed. Doris Edel, by Four Courts Press (Dublin, 1995), pp. 170–196.

Earlier in the treatise he has said, similarly, that 'the aim of [the divine] precepts and the plenitude of the Law is love (*charitas*)' (4.7; cf. 1 Tim. 1:5, Rom. 13:10). Basing his position upon Old Testament examples and the fact that Christians have incorporated the use of springs for baptism, he says elsewhere, however, that if the converted Christians wished to transfer their old buildings and morally neutral habits of worship—for instance, the giving of gifts—onto the new religion, they should be allowed to do so (*Ep.* 47.3).[3] But, he says, many nominal Christians think they can combine attending church services with striving for secular honours and watching of (often bloody) pagan spectacles which lead to the opposite of love: ambition, contentiousness, lust, cruelty (16.25). Or with pagan practices such as tying sacrilegious remedies for illness upon themselves (*remedia sacrilega sibi alligantes*). In this way, they 'have given themselves over to chanters of incantations (*praecantatores*), natural philosophers (*mathematici*), and diviners (*divinatores*) of all kinds' (25.48). Instead of trying to manipulate putative occult forces, true Christians should 'humble themselves before God and overcome the Devil through his grace (*gratia*)' (18.30). This grace can also be mediated, however. Although Augustine had earlier asserted that miracles were now no longer happening because everyone had been converted, in the last book of his *City of God*, he describes cures taking place in his church through the intercession of dead martyrs: evidently, they can transmit God's compassionate power (*Civ. Dei* 22.10).[4]

Augustine's religion is based squarely upon the Bible, especially the Psalms, the Gospels and the apostolic letters.[5] The pagans' spectacles and their gods, as well as their curative and divinatory practices based upon cosmic sympathies or powers inhering in natural objects or in demons, are to be supplanted by a radically opposed attitude toward oneself, life and the world. The turmoil and strife associated with self-aggrandizement was to make place for inner peace in the harmony of all in all through self-effacement in the love which is God. The keynote of this peace of heart is a personal relation to a God who controls the cosmos, directly or through the 'hidden seminal reasons (*occultae seminariae rationes*)' which he has put into things at their creation (*Quaest. Hept.* 2.21).[6] Thus Augustine's persuasive strategy of Christianization com-

3 *Epistolae*, PL 33.

4 *De civitate Dei*, ed. Bernardus Dombart and Alphonsus Kalb (Turnhout 1955: CCSL 47).

5 The literature on Augustine is huge. An excellent compact and comprehensive treatment is: Peter Brown, *Augustine of Hippo. A Biography* (London and Boston 1969: Faber and Faber).

6 *Quaestiones in Heptateuchum*, ed. I. Fraipont (Turnhout 1958: CCSL 33), pp. 1–377. Reference cited in Valerie Flint, *The Rise of Magic in Early Medieval Europe* (Princeton 1991: Princeton University Press), p. 167.

bined a degree of selective accommodation to pagan practices with the substitution of essentially different ones in their place.

Peter Brown has masterfully described not only Augustine's austere Psalm-based and Platonically influenced piety, but also the slow turning of all classes of the population, already during his lifetime, to dreams and to miracles through the mediation of martyrs and saints.[7] In Brown's view, the latter is intimately connected with social changes: political power no longer inhered in an élite group of equals, but in the emperor, and the way to reach him was through the mediation of powerful men. As a counterweight to the frequent abuse of such power, the Church developed the imagination of an ideal replica of the earthly situation in a more powerful heavenly court that would put things right, now or later. Thus, the personal kind of relation to a most intimate but faceless God such as Augustine had experienced, tended to be replaced by one in which an idealized human being acted as mediator to a divinity that now seemed to be primarily a majestic and distant judge.[8] The spread of Christianity in the countryside, as he says, thus involved substituting this 'vertical' pattern of personal dependence upon a saint for the centuries-old 'horizontal' pagan rites, which centered upon self-help through the propitiation of nature spirits and symbolical practices involving cosmic 'sympathies' and forces. Brown calls this process the 'hominization' of the cosmos and the natural world. What this means is that the non-human power of hidden natural forces and spirits is replaced by that operating through what he calls 'the quintessentially human relationships of friendship and intercession'.[9]

When Augustine died in 430, the Vandals were besieging his city of Hippo. During the fifth and sixth centuries Germanic peoples from outside the Roman Empire migrated into its western territories and—excepting a few enclaves, including Rome, in Italy—subjected the indigenous populations to their rule. This meant a relatively more primitive government, and because of this, insecurity and violence. It also meant the disappearance of government-run schools in the cities, with the resulting near-disappearance of classical culture.

In her erudite and penetrating book about Christian practices in this 'barbarized' society, *The Rise of Magic in Early Medieval Europe*,[10] Valerie Flint seems to overlook the affective dimensions of Brown's 'hominizing'

7 Brown, *Augustine of Hippo*; idem, *The Cult of the Saints. Its Rise and Function in Latin Christianity* (Chicago 1981: University of Chicago Press).

8 Cf. Brown, *Cult of the Saints*, pp. 51, 61, 127.

9 Ibid., pp. 125–7.

10 See above note 6.

process.[11] She recognizes its substitutive role, but as very much dominated by an accommodating, acculturative one: that between the Christian religion and the existing, especially rural, pagan practices of magic. Thus she adduces a vast array of evidence to support her view that, during the early Middle Ages, the Church developed a strategy to combat strongly entrenched pagan magic by, in effect, 'rescuing' and incorporating it as part of a neutral technology of living that was conducive to health and happiness. In such a policy of deliberate 'social and religious engineering', the Church would have incorporated the 'appearances' of practices it could not eradicate while—as she explicitly says—changing their 'essence'.[12] In the context of weather magic, for instance, she makes a statement that applies equally to other kinds of magic. She writes:

> saints' lives and miracle stories were used with a surpassing subtlety to refer to, and to retranslate, many of the magical associations which had been condemned yet required treatment of a sympathetic kind. ... The condemned influences ... do seem to have been recognized and countered with energy by supernatural interventions recounted as miracles, and very carefully devised in detail to incorporate, yet change, the old beliefs and practices.[13]

Elsewhere, she adds: 'This ... required less the replacement of past practices than the levering into mesh of parallel, and potentially or actively competing, systems of communication with the supernatural'.[14] The results she designates as 'deliberately Christianized magical compromises', 'legitimated Christianized magic' or as outright 'Christian magic'.[15]

But, are imaginative responses to social changes and the purposeful incorporation of the exterior forms of rival ideologies and practices the whole picture? Unfortunately, Flint does not make clear what—apart from the different conception of power relations in the cosmos—the changed 'essence' of these practices is. Her emphasis is upon their function in society. She regards their assimilation to biblical precedents, which we find in the sources, as a convenient mask 'disturbing our historical understanding of the situation' which, in her view, is dominated by the threat of present competition.[16] Her strongest evidence is from late tenth and early eleventh-century Anglo-Saxon

11 Although she lists three of Brown's other works, *The Cult of the Saints*, in which he develops the experiential dimension of saints' cults, does not appear in her bibliography.
12 Ibid., pp. 264, 275, 320, 396.
13 Ibid., p. 264.
14 Ibid., p. 396.
15 Respectively, ibid., pp. 320, 184, 303.
16 Ibid., p. 310.

and Latin prescriptions (full of 'mumbo-jumbo') for cures, and here her interpretation may well be right. However, she interprets Gaul's Gregory of Tours' sixth-century stories as examples of the exact same thing. In one of these, a soothsayer with his applications is sent away and a cure is effected through (in her view) Christian versions of the same: with oil and wax from the lamps and candles near or on Saint Martin's tomb.[17] In this paper I shall attempt to show that such a one-sided interpretation of Gregory's stories misses their most important point.

In Gaul, in addition to the influx of Germanic influence, there may have been a resurgence of pre-Roman, that is Gallic, culture in rural areas.[18] Both of these cultures were essentially oral in character. In the sixth century, two bishops who played an important if not crucial role in the Gallic Church have left writings from which we can distill the forms and dynamics of their piety and of their dealings with pagans and their usually only half-converted communities. Their in some important ways strikingly different pieties and strategies of Christianization may reflect something of the changing state of society in the course of the sixth century. In Arles, Caesarius was bishop from 502 to 542;[19] in Tours, Gregory officiated from 573 to 594.[20] Caesarius lived through

17 Ibid., p. 306. The story in question is *Virt. Mart.* 4.36 (see note 20).

18 William Klingshirn, *Caesarius of Arles. The Making of a Christian Community in Late Antique Gaul* (Cambridge 1994: Cambridge University Press. Cambridge Studies in Medieval Life and Thought), p. 202. See also: Régine Pernoud, *Les Gaulois* (Paris [1957]. Le temps qui court 1), p. 171.

19 On Caesarius' life and work: *Vita sancti Caesarii episcopi Arelatensis libri duo*, ed. Bruno Krusch (Hannover 1896: MGH SSrM 3), pp. 433–501; transl. William Klingshirn (Liverpool 1994: Liverpool University Press. Translated texts for historians 19 [hereafter: TTH]). The most recent modern study is that of Klingshirn, *Caesarius of Arles*; on Caesarius' strategy of Christianization and 'depaganization', see pp. 201–43. The edition of his *Sermons* used is that of Germanus Morin (Turnhout 1953: CCSL 103–104); transl. Mary M. Mueller, 2 vols (New York 1956 and Washington D.C. 1964: Catholic University of America Press. Fathers of the Church series). Unless otherwise indicated, the translations used in this paper are hers.

20 Recent accounts of Gregory's life and work are: L. Pietri, *La ville de Tours du IVe au VIe siècle: naissance d'une cité chrétienne* (Rome 1983: École francaise de Rome. Collection de l'École francaise de Rome 69), pp. 246–334, and Jean Verdon, *Grégoire de Tours* (Le Coteau 1989: Horvath). The editions of his works used are *In gloria martyrum*, *De virtutibus sancti Juliani*, *De virtutibus sancti Martini*, *In gloria confessorum*, and *Vita patrum*, [hereafter: *Glor. mart.*, *Virt. Jul.*, *Virt. Mart.*, *Glor. conf.*, *Vit. pat.*] ed. Bruno Krusch (Hannover 1885: MGH SSrM 1.2), pp. 451–820; translations of the first four works by Raymond van Dam (Liverpool 1988: Liverpool University Press. TTH 3–4); also in his *Saints and Their Miracles in Late Antiquity* (Princeton 1993: Princeton University Press), pp. 162–303; and Edward James (Liverpool 1985: Liverpool University Press. TTH 1). *Historiarum libri decem* [hereafter: *Hist.*], ed. and transl. Rudolf Buchner (Darmstadt 1967: Wissenschaftliche Buchgesellschaft. Ausgewählte Quellen zur deutschen Geschichte, Freiherr-vom-Stein-Gedächtnisausgabe 2, 3).

the changes from Visigothic to Ostrogothic and finally Frankish domination. In his sermons, reaching out to the declining literate culture of the cities and the oral one of the rural parishes in southern France, he sets forth views that are, in many ways, very close to those of his avowed model, Augustine. At the end of the century, Gregory of Tours had to contend with Frankish royalty—as well as magnates and even clergy—that did not blanch at poisoning or otherwise assassinating bishops. In contrast to Caesarius, he did not receive a classical education (but read classical authors later in life), and does not seem to be directly acquainted with Augustine's work; he may have imbibed its essentials, however, through an intermediary such as Prosper of Aquitaine. Although he also ridicules soothsayers and magicians, the attitudes and practices Gregory recommends as those of the more powerful Christian faith often appear strikingly similar to theirs. Thus he joyfully does some of the very things which Caesarius had strictly forbidden. Does this mean that his attitudes and practices are purposely 'rescued magic', as Flint would have it? What Flint does not go into, and what we need to examine in order to understand the phenomenon in question, is the nature of the Christian content of a rescued magic form (if it is that), and how it relates to this form.

In what follows I shall investigate the bishops' different kinds of piety and strategies of Christianization by comparing their views on three topics: first, their starting point: the centrality of love (*caritas*) in the Christian message; then their dominant mode of understanding divine messages, that through 'figures (*figurae*)'; and, finally, their mediating and operative symbols of divine love and holy power (*virtus*).[21] What we see happening in this comparison is not only the rise of a more practical piety concerned with naked physical survival in uncertain and violent conditions. We also see that the dreams and miracles, which Augustine, in fifth-century Africa, and Caesarius, in early sixth-century Provence, had wished to supplant—even in the unlearned—by texts ('the solid way and more certain oracles of the Scriptures'), are used by Gregory in late sixth-century Touraine as a prime vehicle for transmitting the truths of faith to these unlearned people. What does this mean? I shall conclude my article with a story about a cure that seems to exemplify something of what is happening in the meeting of Christian and pagan cultures.

21 An earlier article of mine compared magic and holy power in Gregory's writings: 'Heilige wondermacht of toverkunst? Een vroegmiddeleeuwse interpretatie [Holy power or magic? An early medieval interpretation]', in René V. Stuip and Cornelis Vellekoop (eds), *Culturen in contact. Botsing en integratie in de middeleeuwen* [Contact of cultures. Conflict and integration in the Middle Ages] (Utrecht 1988: Hes. Utrechtse Bijdragen tot de Mediëvistiek 8), pp. 129–38.

As anyone who has ever tried to investigate them knows, religion and magic are notoriously difficult—if not sometimes impossible—to distinguish from each other.[22] The characterization of religion as reverential and supplicative, and magic as manipulative and coercive, which Flint posits at the beginning of her book, and upon which she bases her whole position,[23] is not the whole picture. The sixth-century Church distinguished magic from religion through the nature of the power, diabolic or divine, that was called upon.[24] As we have already seen, these terms point to two opposing principles in human life: a self-centeredness desiring transitory things, on the one hand, and a widening of one's spirit (*animus dilatatus*, as Gregory the Great later called it in *Dial.* 2.35.6–7[25]) into the cosmic love that is God, on the other. Thus, Caesarius tells his audience that demons can only curse, not bless (*Serm.* 113.2). The Church's crucial point is that all real power that exists is, directly or indirectly, that of the God who is the Creator and sustainer of everything.

Caesarius

In one of his sermons for the rural parishes, Caesarius presents the Christian message to the uneducated in terms of their everyday experience:

> The care of our soul, dearly beloved, is very much like earthly cultivation. ... I beseech you to tell me, whoever you are who said a little while ago that you could not fulfill God's precepts because you did not know how to read—tell me, who showed you how to provide for your vineyard, at what time to plant new shoots? Who taught you this, unless you saw or heard or questioned the best cultivators as to how you should work your farm? Why, then, are you not as solicitous for your soul as you are for your estate? (6.4)
>
> Therefore, I beg and exhort you, dearly beloved, if any of you know letters, read the sacred Scriptures rather frequently; those of you who do not should listen with attentive ears when others read it. (6.2)
>
> Someone may say: I am a farmer and continually engaged in earthly matters; I can neither listen to nor read the divine lessons. How many men and women in the country remember and repeatedly sing diabolical, shameful love songs! These things which the Devil teaches they

22 Cf. David Aune, 'Magic in early Christanity', in Wolfgang Haase (ed), *Aufstieg und Niedergang der Römischen Welt* 2.23.2 (Berlin 1980), pp. 1507–57, at pp. 1510–16.

23 Flint, *Rise of Magic* (see above note 6), p. 8.

24 As in Gregory's *Hist.* 9.6. Cf. Richard Kieckhefer, *Magic in the Middle Ages* (Cambridge 1990: Cambridge University Press. Cambridge Medieval Textbooks), pp. 8–17.

25 *Dialogi*, ed. Adalbert de Vogüé, transl. Paul Antin (Paris 1979: SC 260).

> can remember and say; are they unable to keep in mind what Christ shows them? How much more quickly and to better advantage could these men and women from the farm learn the Creed, the Lord's Prayer, a few antiphons or the fiftieth and ninetieth Psalms? By getting and remembering these and saying them rather frequently they might have a means to uniting their soul to God and freeing it from the Devil. (6.3)

Caesarius' approach is a policy of substitution unmixed, as we shall see, with accommodation.[26] If people cannot read or let themselves be read to, they should memorize selected texts and keep them constantly in mind. The Creed is a profession of belief, the Lord's Prayer one of worship and submission. Which antiphons were used in sixth-century Arles I have not been able to discover. Psalm 50 (in the Vulgate) is one of compunction. It begins: 'Have mercy on me, O God, according to your compassion (*misericordia*) ...' (1) and later continues:

> Behold, you love truth; therefore show me the uncertain and hidden things of your wisdom. Purge me with hyssop, and I shall be clean. Wash me, and I shall be whiter than snow. (8–9) ... Create a new heart in me, God, and renew a stable spirit within me. (10) ... The sacrifice acceptable to God is a broken spirit; a contrite and humbled heart, O God, you will not despise. (19)

These are the themes that keep recurring in Caesarius' sermons: finding hidden wisdom, being purified, and being renewed in heart after having humbled it.

As for Augustine, so also for Caesarius: listening to God's word is the way to the life of the soul; Caesarius says that this is the way God 'talks' with men. If they don't listen to him, he won't listen to their prayers! (*Serm.* 7.3) To prevent people from gossiping in church, he instituted community singing; and to force them to listen to the sermon, he locked the doors (*Serm.* 75.3, *Vit. Caes.* 1.19; *Serm.* 73.1, *Vit. Caes.* 1.27).[27] He tells his church: '[God] deigned to send us through the patriarchs and prophets sacred writings as letters of invitation summoning us to the eternal and excellent country (...)' (7.2). 'Our country', he says there, 'is paradise, and our parents are the patriarchs and prophets, apostles and martyrs; the angels are its citizens, Christ is our King.' What he is doing here is substituting the imagination of

26 Klingshirn, *Caesarius of Arles* (see above note 18), pp. 226–43.
27 Cf. ibid., pp. 157–9.

a new, transcendent kinship, fatherland and government for what must have seemed to be the failing structures of the old.

The preacher is responsible for the souls of his flock at the Judgment (*Serm.* 4.2). Therefore, Caesarius says, quoting Isaiah: 'Cry, cease not; lift up thy voice like a trumpet, and show my people their sins' (Isa. 58:1; *Serm.* 4.2). Then he quotes an apostolic letter: 'Preach the word, be urgent in season and out of season; reprove, entreat, rebuke' (2 Tim. 4:1,2). What this means, he says, is that '[t]he word of God must be offered to those who are willing to listen; [and] it must be forced upon those who are averse to it' (4.2). In his biography, too, his clergy report that they tended to be exhausted by his energetic teaching—also during meals—never remembering, or even asking, enough to satisfy him (*Vit. Caes.* 1.52, 61, 62; 2.31–3).[28] With indefatigable and sombre energy, then, Caesarius deliberately pressed the Christian message—with its dire future penalties for those who did not listen—upon his hearers, whether they liked it or not. His most recent biographer Klingshirn suggests that the bishop's strategies were also dictated by the exigencies of exercising his authority through compelling assent to his spoken word.[29]

The whole Law and the prophets, however, depend on the two commandments to love God and one's neighbour as oneself (1.12; Mt 22:37,39), and many sermons, partly adapted from those of Augustine, have the word 'charity' in their titles.[30] For instance, when speaking of the necessity, social as well as spiritual, to give alms constantly, he tells his audience that anyone not in a situation to give material alms should forgive his enemies instead (29.4)—an idealism that his listeners found impractical, however (*Serm.* 35.2; 37.2).[31] Almost literally quoting Augustine, Caesarius says: 'Love all men with your whole heart and do whatever you wish' (35.5; cf. Augustine, *In ep. Joh. tract.* 7.8[32]). Love, finally, has the unique quality of increasing with its being spent: the more one gives it to others, the more one accumulates it in oneself (128.3–4). At the same time, Caesarius talks of Christ being the spiritual bridegroom of all chaste souls—men as well as women (155.4). Real conversion to such a religion is breaking with old habits and constantly listening, as well as talking, to the God of the Psalms in one's heart.

Although Caesarius recognized the possible intercession of the dead martyrs and wrote a few sermons in their honour (223–6), his emphasis—as that

28 See ibid., pp. 183–6.
29 Ibid., pp. 146–51.
30 Cf. ibid., p. 189.
31 Cited in ibid., p. 189.
32 *In epistolam Iohannis tractatus*, PL 35.1977–2062. Reference cited in John Burnaby, *Amor Dei. A Study of the Religion of St Augustine* (London 1938: Hodder and Stoughton), p. 142.

of Augustine—was on the individual's direct relation to God.[33] His biography—written by fellow bishops and clergy in more or less clumsy Latin in the years directly after his death—shows, however, that already during his life and more so after it, he was himself revered as a more-than-human person and expected to do miracles, also through objects that had merely touched him. When asked to cure a sick person, he almost seems to have wished to excuse himself by saying that only simple people were able to do this, and not people burdened with learning like himself (*Vit. Caes.* 2.3). His clerical disciples evidently did not attain his Augustinian kind of piety; they appear to have worshipped Caesarius' faceless God largely through what they saw as the 'angelic face' of their loving and beloved teacher (*Vit. Caes.* 1.36). Why not? Had he himself not said—perhaps inspired by Augustine (*In Ep. Joh. Tract.* 9.10)[34]—that (because God is Love) we can see God in our love of one another (*Serm.* 21.4)?

Gregory

Unfortunately, we have no contemporary Life of Gregory from which we can learn how his manner of preaching through stories was received. In his *Histories* and miracle stories he shows himself as working toward a Christian society ruled jointly by kings and bishops on the model of that described in the Old Testament.[35] Accordingly, he was also concerned above all to build up his episcopal city of Tours as the home of the patron saint of the Frankish kingdom, Saint Martin. Not, in the first place, the biblical text, then, but the deeds of the patronage of saints, are central for him.[36] In the preface to his *The glory of the martyrs*, Gregory says he intends to substitute stories about divine miracles for those about the actions and metamorphoses of immoral pagan deities; these were still part of the classical education given to young aristocrats in their homes by private tutors.[37] Instead of retelling the poets' charming fictions that induce moral turpitude, Gregory says, he will report that which, he hopes, will cause faith to be born in 'barren'—perhaps also meaning unlearned—minds. Stories about miracles—and these include dreams—then, are deliberately chosen as vehicles for conveying the essence of the Christian religion. Why? In what Venantius Fortunatus, a friend of Gre-

33 Klingshirn, *Caesarius of Arles*, pp. 166–7, says that the bishop was 'lukewarm' about the saints' cults.

34 Cited in Burnaby, *Amor Dei*, p. 161.

35 As Martin Heinzelmann, *Gregor von Tours' 'Zehn Bücher Geschichte'. Historiographie und Gesellschaftskonzept im 6. Jahrhundert* (Darmstadt 1994: Wissenschaftliche Buchgesellschaft), passim.

36 As Van Dam, *Saints and Their Miracles* (see above note 20), p. 51.

37 Pierre Riché, 'Centers of culture in Frankish Gaul between the 6th and the 9th centuries', in idem, *Instruction et vie religieuse dans le haut Moyen Âge* (London 1981: Variorum Reprints), III.

gory's and later bishop of Poitiers, says about miracles we can catch a of how they were experienced in this period: 'miracles, to be emb... delight (*delectabiliter amplectenda miracula*)' (*Virt. Hil.* 21).[38] In short, miracle stories may have been not only edifying; they may also have been aimed at taking the place of other fascinating and charming tales—not only those of Ovid and Vergil, recited in the late afternoon on the terraces of luxurious country villa's, but also the folk and heroic tales that simpler folk would tell each other around the fire in the long winter evenings. Caesarius had enjoined reading or listening to Scripture upon such occasions, but he had also included examples from daily life in his sermons and asked his listeners to transmit as much as they could remember of their content to those who had not been able to attend (*Serm.* 6.8). Gregory created lively and charming stories about saints' miracles in the context of daily life which he hoped would be carried by word of mouth into people's homes—and hearts. The Bible uses the same strategy; it cannot be called an accommodation to paganism. Rather, it is a substitution.

The most obvious difference between Gregory's and Caesarius' piety is that God is no longer approached directly, but through a dead saint who becomes not only an intercessor but also a protector or 'patron (*patronus*)' (*Virt. Mart.* 4.*prol.*), something like one's guardian spirit or angel.[39] It is now the saint who is said to exhibit love and compassion to those who show honour to him. Instead of addressing God directly through reciting or singing Psalm 50 on one's own, people are advised to go to the saint's tomb:

> For if one humbles one's soul at his tomb, and one's prayer is raised on high; if tears flow and true compunction comes; if sighs come forth from the depths of the heart and our sinful breasts are beaten—[then] the weeping finds joy, the guilt mercy, the grief of the heart attains its remedy. (*Virt. Mart.* 3.*prol.*)

Not the reading of a text, then, but the touching of a tomb now sets in motion the process of compunction and forgiveness, the creation of a new heart. Elsewhere, Gregory praises—in a language reminiscent of the Psalm passage quoted above—the saint's (God-given) curative power through the dust gathered from his tomb by saying:

> O heavenly purgative (*purgatorium*), if one may call it that ... It cleans the heart as scammony, the lungs like hyssop ... Indeed, it not only

38 *Virtutes sancti Hilarii*, 21. Ed. Bruno Krusch (Berlin 1885: MGH AA 4.2), pp. 7–11. Cf. Gregorius Magnus, *Dial.* 3.22.4: *iucunda miracula*.
39 As Brown, *Cult of the Saints* (see above note 7), pp. 55–6.

> repairs weak limbs, but, what is greater than all this, it even removes and mitigates the very stains in men's consciences. (Ibid. 3.60)

Here, man is purified interiorly as well as healed physically through the material dust from the saint's tomb that transmits his 'compassion (*misericordia*)' (ibid. 3.*prol.*), and not through God's direct action. This passage shows that Gregory's many apparently manipulative symbolic practices through objects, gestures, and words have a deeper, transformative, dimension. As already mentioned, the unfortunate flaw in Flint's otherwise very erudite and thought-provoking book is that she looks at the practices she describes from the stance of an uninvolved observer of human techniques of survival, and does not sufficiently take into account the traditional Christian affective and imaginative experience of the participants. Thus she also underestimates the affective weight of the fact that in the sources saints and their miracles tend to be equated to the apostles and Old Testament prophets rather than, as she suggests, primarily seen as an improved, Christian version of pagan *magi*.[40]

As for another kind of 'manipulative' practice: Gregory indeed lets us see that a great deal of pressure can be, and often is, put upon the saint by continued, insistent praying, and sometimes even by fasting and intimidation (e.g. *Glor. mart.* 13, *Virt. Mart.* 3.39 and 3.8). But this is not magical manipulation or coercion. Rather, it is like the personal pressure one might legitimately put upon a powerful human protector. In support of such a practice, he cites injunctions in the Gospels such as '... because of his importunity [his friend] will rise and will give to him whatever he needs' (Lk 11:8, alluded to in *Glor. mart.* 13). His stories are full of persons who, after exerting such pressure, get what they want (e.g. *Virt. Mart.* 3.8). Thus the experiential dimension of the participants' personal relation to the saint as a glorified human patron, and that of the Christian view of the transforming experience of spiritual love (*caritas*) distinguish—if, probably, not always that of many early medieval country priests and their parishioners—at least Gregory's own practices fundamentally from the manipulation of abstract forces.

Likewise, it is not the faithful themselves through their almsgiving and forgiveness of enemies, but the saint too, who, as God's agent, seems to keep society in order. In Gregory's stories, he protects and rewards those who honour him, and grimly punishes—often with death—those who insult him, for instance by seizing his church's properties. Except in one case of a feud that became a civil war in his city (*Hist.* 7.47), we do not hear Gregory exhorting us to forgive our enemies. A bishop, in the late sixth century, was

40 Flint, *Rise of Magic* (see above note 6), pp. 355ff. Examples of saints as apostles and 'prophets', in Gregory, *Virt. Mart.* 3.16 (*voce Petri*), 3.22 (*Israel nostri temporis*), *Virt. Jul.* 7 (*novus Danihel*); in *Vit. Caes.* (see note 19), 1.31 (*Danihel noster*), 2.2 (*alter Heliseus*).

unarmed in a violent society in which every self-respecting man either carried arms himself or had a body-guard. Gregory had Saint Martin. What we see here is the crucial and apparently effective role of the imagination of an idealized patronage and power system in providing protection and checking the abuse of power in an inadequately ordered society. In such a situation, forgiving incorrigible enemies was less functional than showing, often with what can only be called a grim satisfaction, that they could expect severe divine punishment, now or later.

'MORE CERTAIN ORACLES'

We come now to our second focus: 'figures' in the 'more certain oracles' of the Bible. Caesarius, as we saw, advised the substitution of Christian songs instilling divine love for 'diabolical' ones inducing the carnal variety. A contemporary of Gregory's, Bishop Martin of Braga, in his treatise *On the correction of country people*,[41] seems to see a certain, at least exterior, parallelism of pagan and Christian practices when he asserts the mutual exclusion of what he calls 'the sign of the Cross (*signum crucis*)' and 'the sign of the devil (*signum diaboli*)', meaning by the latter omens through the song of birds, or the occurring of sneezes and the like (18–21). Even more striking is his, assimilative, contrast between the 'holy incantation (*incantatio sancta*)' of the Creed and the Lord's Prayer on the one hand, and 'diabolical incantations and songs (*diabolicae incantationes et carmina*)' (23–6) on the other. In this unmistakable policy of substitution, what, then, is the difference between Christian searchings for hidden divine messages and pagan divination, and that between holy and diabolic incantations?

The shared pagan and Christian view of the cosmos, as it emerges from late antique and early Christian sources, was different from ours in two fundamental ways. First, the most 'real' reality was not that observable by the senses (the sensory world) but, as in neo-Platonist thought, considered to be that of invisible essences, as it were 'behind' sensory phenomena (the intelligible world).[42] Second, the whole cosmos of natural, human and spiritual reality was regarded as cohering, not only through mechanical and causal relations, but more essentially also as overlapping or coalescing through attractions or 'sympathies' between analogical forms.[43] As such, it was a view

41 *De correctione rusticorum*, ed. Claude W. Barlow, in idem (ed), *Martini episcopi Bracarensis opera omnia* (New Haven 1950: Yale University Press), pp. 159–203.

42 W.J.T. Mitchell, *Iconology. Image, Text, Ideology* (Chicago 1986: University of Chicago Press), p. 21.

43 Flint, *Rise of Magic*, p. 130, and Klingshirn, *Caesarius of Arles* (see above note 18), p. 221; and p. 219, n. 93, in which he takes issue with Flint's regarding pagan practices

that gave primacy to mental representations that tended to be in the form of images—images of visible objects as manifestations of higher realities. In late antique pagan circles, this manner of thinking had led to oracles, divination and dream interpretation, as well as to the curative, protective and destructive symbolical rites usually designated as magic.[44] As earlier Augustine, so Caesarius and Gregory, too, leave no doubt that many nominal Christians, some of them even clergy, engaged in such practices (e.g. resp. *Serm.* 13.4–5, 52–4, and *Hist.* 6.35, 7.44, 8.29, 9.37, etc.).[45]

A Christian example of this analogical kind of thinking is a fifth-century treatise on the spiritual meanings of all kinds of visible phenomena: Bishop Eucherius of Lyon's 'Forms of spiritual understanding' (*Formulae spiritualis intelligentiae*),[46] a work which Caesarius and Gregory must have known. It was part of a tradition, since apostolic times, to understand the Bible through images and 'figures'.[47] Both Caesarius and Gregory interpret biblical sayings and events as disguised all-time spiritual messages for the individual believer and for the Church, pointing to the present as well as the future state (e.g. *Serm.* 100.1; *In Psal. prol.*).[48] Analogy was the dominant thought mode in Late Antiquity and the early Middle Ages. Thus we can understand why Augustine, and Caesarius after him, insisted upon sacred texts instead of arbitrary personal divination, and upon 'the more certain oracles' of the Scriptures instead of ambiguous and uncontrollable dreams.

Caesarius

Caesarius speaks of the hunger and the thirst for the word of God, and about a coming 'famine' in this context (*Serm.* 4.4). He must have realized that there were not many who could preach the Word knowledgeably in his time. By legislating in a church council that there were to be seminaries for prospective clergy in the country parishes,[49] and by writing out a large number of sermons and presenting them to all clerics who came by in Arles, with the injunction to copy them for others as well as read them to their parishioners (*Serm.* 1 and 2), he hoped to do something about this situation.

as 'magic', i.e. neutral techniques of manipulation lacking 'reverence' and devoid of religious meaning.

44 See the extensive essays on these subjects in Haase, *Aufstieg* (see above note 22).

45 See Klingshirn, *Caesarius of Arles*, pp. 209–26 on what he calls 'peasant religion'. He says, however, that the 'accommodation' sometimes demonstrably comes from the people themselves, and not from the clergy (p. 225).

46 Eucherius Lugdunensis, *Formularum spiritualis intelligentiae ad Uranium liber unus*, PL 50.727–72.

47 See on this subject E. Auerbach, 'Figura', *Archivum Romanicum* 22 (1938), pp. 436–89.

48 Gregorius Turonensis, *In Psalterii tractatum commentarius*, ed. Bruno Krusch (Hannover 1885: MGH SSrM 1.2), pp. 873–7.

49 Klingshirn, *Caesarius of Arles*, p. 230.

The word of God, however, had to be 'chewed over' (the word Caesarius uses is *ruminare*; as in *Serm.* 36.8 and 69.5) before it could be understood. As we saw, under the appearance of the literal meaning, there was a spiritual meaning which was the really important one. The Old Testament is the 'type' and 'image'—or 'figure'—of the New; what is said to happen corporally there, is spiritually fulfilled in the New Testament and in us (81.1, 5). Caesarius left a large number of sermons explaining what he calls 'the obscure sacred mysteries' in the Bible text (118.1), so that his audience could arrive at 'spiritual understanding' (126.1). For instance, the prophet Elisha's throwing a vessel filled with salt into a spring and thereby making its water turn from bitter to sweet (2 Kgs. 2:19–21), is a 'figure' of Christ, filled with the salt of divine Wisdom, going into the Jordan to be baptized; by the grace of this event, the baptismal waters 'have produced a countless number of Christians like ... an exceedingly rich harvest'. Caesarius adds: 'Although we believe that this truth is fulfilled in things which are seen, still we know that it also takes place spiritually in all people' (126.1–3). Here, then, we see one of Caesarius' basic premises: visible events, in the past and in the present, represent, point to and manifest ongoing invisible processes of eternal truth. It was a habit of perception that was to gain much ground in Gregory's thinking.

How are layfolk expected to process the divine word? Caesarius says: 'I beg you and beseech you: whenever you chant the psalms, consider more carefully what should be understood and practised interiorly. Thus, while your tongue praises the Lord, the blessing of God will come to your souls' (75.3). Elsewhere, quoting the Psalms, he calls this activity 'meditation': 'let us meditate on the law of the Lord, not only during the day, but also at night' (116.2). Not only the Bible text is meditated upon in this manner, but also the Creed and the Lord's Prayer. Likewise, a miracle story as that of Christ's cure of the man born blind in John's Gospel (9:2–3). Caesarius tells his audience: 'That man, brethren, was prepared as a salve for the human race: he was bodily restored to light, in order that, by considering his miracle, we might be enlightened in heart' (172.1).

The purpose, then, of listening to, reading, chanting and meditating upon the 'figures' of God's word is not, as in the pagan divinatory practices which Caesarius repeatedly condemns, the gaining of advance knowledge of personally advantageous visible and limited future events. It is the inner transformation of oneself, according to the pattern of the living and transforming truth which is charity. This pattern is discovered as it were 'underneath' the letters of the sacred words, and constituted 'the more solid way of the Scriptures', as Augustine had said. In his list of diabolical pagan practices, Caesarius had castigated the use of 'magic letters', perhaps runes (50.2). And he expresses something essential in his position on the divine word—and also on 'Christian magic'—when he speaks of 'diabolic' priests who give men 'charms' with 'holy facts and divine lessons' as amulets to cure illness, and says: 'It would be better to keep the words of God in one's heart than to wear them in writing around one's neck' (50.2).[50] His religion is an interiorized one. He attempted to transmit the monastic meditative piety that he had learned in the seclusion of Lérins to those living and working, with little opportunity for undisturbed reflection, in an unpredictable and dangerous world.

Gregory

As is evident in his now largely lost *Commentary on the psalms*, the 'spiritual understanding' of 'figures' in the Bible is also central in Gregory of Tours' religious message (*In psal. prol.*). And, like Caesarius, he also seems to urge his readers or listeners to sing the Psalms meditatively so that the words would, at the same time, transform their hearts:

> O that each one of us would, when he begins to sing this psalm [33], at once reject the world's scandals, disregard his lusts, and leave empty ways behind to try to take the way of justice at once and without the impediment of worldly actions! (*Virt. Jul. prol.*)

On the whole, however, Gregory's emphasis is upon events, and especially miracles, rather than upon texts. And he seems to have moved closer to the sphere of divination. Gregory does not (as far as we know) listen to birds' song or pay attention to sneezes, but he does—in the manner of Roman historians and augurs—record prodigies occurring in nature, and he interprets them as messages of the Christian God.[51] For this practice, however, there is no little support in the Bible: for instance, the plagues of Egypt (Ex. 7ff.), the wonders and terrors in Joel 2:30, the Gospels' indication of the signs of the end of the world (Mt. 24:3ff., Mk 13:3ff.; Lk 21:7ff.), and the Apocalypse. And he pays attention to dreams: as literal previews of events, as visualizations or 'figures' of hidden spiritual events in past or present.[52] Although this was an eminently pagan practice, it also occurs in the Old as well as in the New Testament—together, however, with cautionary statements.[53]

Finally, Gregory does something against which fifth- and sixth-century Gallic church councils had—unsuccessfully—legislated: at moments of ex-

50 Cf. Klingshirn, ibid., pp. 223–4.

51 See on this my *Views from a Many-Windowed Tower. Studies of Imagination in the Works of Gregory of Tours* (Amsterdam 1987: Rodopi. Studies in Classical Antiquity 7), pp. 27–69.

52 See on this ibid., pp. 213–93.

53 See on this subject J.S. Hanson, 'Dreams and visions in the Graeco-Roman world and early Christianity', in Haase, *Aufstieg* (see above note 22), pp. 1395–427, and Fox, *Pagans and Christians* (see above note 2), pp. 377ff.

treme uncertainty and danger, he consults the book of the Bible, ostensibly as 'support (*consolatio*)', but in fact also as an oracle (e.g. *Hist.* 5.49).[54] On the model of the former Homeric and Vergilian oracles, this meant opening the book at random and taking the first verse that one's eyes lighted upon as a message from God—in 'figures', of course—addressed to one's specific question or situation. Gregory must have believed that God would guide his hand and eye to the right message. With what we have seen of the extensive possibilities of Bible interpretation, however, it may not have been too difficult to find some sustaining message in almost any verse.

Is Gregory's 'more certain oracle' an ingeniously constructed syncretism of 'rescued magic' and religion?[55] There is no evidence that he knew about Augustine's now well-known precedent of doing this.[56] Gregory's act is very close, I think, to simply picking up the Bible in such a moment to remind oneself of the divine sayings in general, which always insist that, if one loves and trusts in God, there is no need of fear. I do not think he was doing any conscious 'social and religious engineering' here, but—as he says—falling back on what he saw as his source of support. At other times, this was Saint Martin. As we saw, touching his tomb could cause even bitterness of heart to go away.

Alongside the oracular use of the Bible, then, not only strange natural phenomena taken to be 'signs', but also monitory and 'figured' dreams, and even miracles which function as ordeals—such as pulling a ring out of boiling water without being scalded (*Glor. mart.* 80), and being struck by lightning after perjury (*Hist.* 8.16)—are prominent in Gregory's writings. Just as Caesarius, Gregory lets invisible divine love work in the hearts of men. But he adds the presupposition—and even hopeful expectation (firmly based upon biblical precedents)—of a great deal of divine action in the sphere of visible things. As I have shown elsewhere, in his writings, earthly events and visible phenomena appear to be scrutinized with the same care and inventiveness as the text of the Bible for hidden meanings and messages.[57] Where Caesarius seems to leave more room for, as it were, independent action of nature and men, Gregory is constantly aware of the possibility of God's direct intervention in both.

If, for Gregory, the difference between God's 'figures' or 'signs' and those of the Devil—such as the divinations of witches—was that the former are

54 Cf. Klingshirn, *Caesarius of Arles*, pp. 220–1, and Flint, *Rise of Magic*, pp. 273ff.

55 Cf. Flint, op. cit, pp. 276–8.

56 In his *Confessions* 8.12.9. Ed. and transl. W. Watts (Cambridge, Mass. 1988: Harvard University Press. Loeb Library 26). Cf. Flint, op. cit., p. 274.

57 Cf. my 'Gregory of Tours' smile: spiritual reality, imagination and earthly events in the 'Histories'', in Anton Scharer and Georg Scheibelreiter (eds), *Historiographie im frühen Mittelalter* (Wien 1994: Veröffentlichungen des Instituts für Österreichische Geschichtsforschung 32), pp. 68–95.

true and the latter are always false and illusory (as in *Hist.* 5.14), does the same hold true for holy and diabolic 'incantations'? He describes a sorcerer's treatment of one of his household servants through incantation with sarcasm and scorn:

> He did not let himself be asked twice and tried to exercise his arts: he murmured incantations (*incantationes inmurmurat*), threw lots (*sortes*), hung ligatures (*ligaturae*) from the patient's neck, and promised life to the one whom he himself had just chained to death. (*Virt. Jul.* 46a)

The sick man died. In Gregory's view, sorcerers' and witches' spells are not only completely ineffective, ridiculous and pitiful (as also in *Hist.* 6.35), but they bring down upon those who use them the punishment of God. The next servant who contracted the illness was cured by drinking a potion of water with dust from Saint Julian's tomb. In another story, he reports the same dust as being carried in a capsule around a future holy man's neck (*Hist.* 8.15)—a practice that looks exactly like the pagan one of 'ligatures'.[58] The moral of the story: the Devil deceives, and the saints, as the friends of God, will give the desired cure. The technique was less important than the fact that the wrong person had been asked. As for Caesarius' rejection of biblical words functioning as amulets: it must have been not more than a few years after his death that Gregory, as a young boy, dreamed of an angel giving him instructions to cure his ill father by writing the name Joshua on a sliver of wood and putting it under his pillow; his mother carried out these instructions, and his father recovered (*Glor. conf.* 39). The story does not mention anyone engaging in supplicatory prayer; Gregory, however, may have regarded this as going without saying.

Is his use of names and letters a manipulation of spiritual powers through abstract means: in other words, as Flint calls it, 'Christian magic'? If we were able to put this question to Gregory himself, he might reply by pointing to the transforming power of the sacred words with which bread and wine become the body and blood of the Saviour. Stronger still, he adheres to the biblical view of the power of the word (taken over and developed by Augustine): everywhere in his writings we can see that, for him, words are mediating and operative symbols of compelling power.[59] Not only the written letters of holy names, but (as we see elsewhere) also those of sacred words such as

58 Flint, *Rise of Magic*, pp. 306–7.

59 Cf. my essay on this subject 'De 'kracht' van wat in het boek gezegd wordt: woord, schrift en teken in zesde-eeuws Gallië [The 'power' of what is said in the book: word, writing and sign in sixth-century Gaul]', in: *Oraliteit en schriftcultuur* [Orality and written culture] (Hilversum 1993: Verloren. Utrechtse Bijdragen tot de Mediëvistiek 12), pp. 63–88.

those telling the story of the miracles of Saint Martin, are presented as participating in, and thus making present, the 'power' to which they refer: mere contact with them effects another miracle (*Vit. patr.* 8.12). Gregory's central presupposition is that, as in the tomb, divine power is somehow present in every visible object or event that points to it, or is a 'figure' of it.[60] Carole Straw has described his contemporary Pope Gregory the Great's similarly analogical and symbolical Christian view of the cosmos as 'a sacramental vision'.[61] Gregory of Tours, similarly, tends to store, apprehend and process all knowledge in and through images of visible forms.[62]

Image-thinking, then, and its corollary analogical association, are the reason that, in Gregory's world view, everything tends to be approached and handled with appropriate symbolical actions alongside the forms belonging to personal relations. Caesarius' piety, modelled upon that of Augustine and the late antique monastery, was a deep and learned one that handled the representations of the mind as such, and with a certain psychological distance. Gregory was raised in a family and an episcopal household that cultivated the stories of saints such as the fourth-century former soldier Saint Martin, who had seen angels and demons at every turn. Gregory's later considerable learning in the Roman classics evidently did not change that perception. His view of the dynamics of divine power belonged to a less learned but no less Christian tradition. Although raised upon biblical texts, his Christianizing strategy focused less directly upon them and more on manifestations of divine power in events and objects in the visible environment. Because of this, his piety was one that could appeal to the oral folk that must have constituted the great majority of his listeners.

MIRACLES: 'CHRISTIAN MAGIC'?

This brings us to our third focus, that of holy power (*virtus*). In the early Middle Ages, we see the coalescence of two kinds of magic which would later be distinguished: the natural and the demonic. The presupposition of natural magic is that hidden cosmic powers in natural phenomena may be activated and utilized through special procedures, often also involving some kind of contact; that of demonic magic, that spirits may be called upon in a coercive

60 See my 'Die Sprache im Wunder—das Wunder in der Sprache: Menschenworte und das *Verbum Dei* bei Gregor von Tours', to appear in *Mitteilungen des Instituts für Österreichische Geschichtsforschung* in 1995.

61 *Gregory the Great. Perfection in Imperfection* (Berkeley 1988: University of California Press. Transformation of the Classical Heritage 14), pp. 47, 50.

62 See on this my *Views* (see above note 51), pp. 175–6, 109–11, 299–300.

manner, through incantations or symbolic actions, to do someone's wishes. The first category shades into natural science; the second into religion.[63]

Caesarius

Caesarius had designated as 'the pomps (displays, or appearances) of the Devil' which were formally renounced at baptism not only adultery, murder, corruption, the watching of bloody spectacles (in which people and/or animals kill each other—comparable, it seems, to modern video films such as 'Child's play III'), and divination (*Serm.* 12.4). He also mentions in this context: expecting advantages from stones, trees, or springs, and remedies from amulets and magical practices (ibid.). Such practices should be ruthlessly exterminated in oneself and others, even with violence. He tells his audience to destroy the shrines of idols, pull up trees by the roots and burn them; but also, if they have power over them—and this can only refer to estate-owners with dependent agricultural labourers, and slave proprietors—to rebuke and whip persons who engage in such diabolic practices, pull (or cut off?) their hair, and put them in chains (13.5; 14.4; 53.1–2). Caesarius's parents had been such estate-owners; Klingshirn says that in the then prevalent hierarchical view of society, uneducated labourers were not credited with as much rationality as their more fortunate brothers. And he sees the bishop's use of force as the 'depaganization' of the unconverted rather than as the 'Christianization' of the already formally converted.[64]

The latter are given substitutive practices. When ill, for instance, no sorcerers were to be consulted or herbs worn around one's neck; instead, according to the example of the apostles (Jas. 5:14–15), one should come to church to confess one's sins—for bodily sickness is related to that of the heart (19.5)—to receive the Eucharist, but also to be anointed with consecrated oil and prayed over by the priests (13.3). Caesarius seems to imply that healing, if it came, would come directly from God via the heart, and that it should take place visibly within the institutional context of the Church. Sorcerers, he says, may be able to command demons; in no way, however, can they call upon the much more powerful holy spirits, angels, or Christ or God. For, as he exclaims: 'We alone have received the power to invoke God the Father; we alone have the power to call upon his only-begotten Son!' (113.2). Through prayer, of course. Flint sees such anointing, as well as perhaps such prayer, as no more than legitimated magic and incantation.[65] This is because she overlooks the dimension of the simultaneous interior healing. Look-alike practices are only one part, and not the most important one, of the picture. As we saw,

63 Cf. Kieckhefer, *Magic* (see above note 24), pp. 8–17.
64 Klingshirn, *Caesarius of Arles*, pp. 226, 233, 239–40.
65 Flint, *Rise of Magic*, pp. 301, 311–2.

however, Caesarius' own community tended—much to his displeasure—not only to expect him to be able to cure physical illness through prayer, but also used objects he had touched to effect cures and other miracles in his absence (*Vit. Caes.* 2.42). Even among his direct pupils, the bishop's abstract religion mediated by words was giving way to one mediated by visible persons and palpable objects.

Although Caesarius' authority may have been bolstered by his cures,[66] he certainly did not, then, invent these mental attitudes as a strategy to entice pagans; they were there before him and he appears to have resisted them. By setting up a library, by instituting the singing of the monastic hours in the cathedral, and by ceaselessly urging his community to listen to and meditate on the biblical texts, he seems to have been fighting a one-man's battle to transform the forces of popular habits[67] and to create among the people something like the contemplative, textually-based piety in which he had been formed at the monastery of Lérins. It is in this context, I think, that another one of his prohibitions should be understood. He says:

> There are some people who come to the birthday festivals of the martyrs for this sole purpose, that they may destroy themselves and ruin others by intoxication, dancing, singing shameful songs, leading the choral dance, and pantomiming in a devilish fashion. While they should be doing the work of Christ, they are attempting to fulfill the service of the Devil ... If anyone wants to look for and imitate these men, they condemn themselves to eternal punishment. (*Serm.* 55.2)

Contrary to what one might expect after reading his forty-seventh letter, Augustine seems also to have censured a similar experiment in popular piety,[68] and it may have been Caesarius' model for this blanket condemnation. Klingshirn argues that both the practice and its prohibition point to gradually arising distinctions in religious culture between religious specialists, i.e. clergy, monks, and pious aristocrats, and 'everyone else'.[69] It is difficult to know whether Gregory of Tours' later speaking of dead saints 'doing a sacred dance (*tripudi[are]*' in heaven (*Virt. Jul.* 50), and referring in a sermon to such dancing on Saint Martin's feast 'throughout the world' is meant literally or metaphorically.[70] I would like to imagine him as having preserved the joy and

66 As ibid., pp. 236–8.
67 Cf. ibid., pp. 240–1.
68 E. Catherine Dunn, *The Saint's Life and the Late Roman Tradition* (Washington, D.C. 1989: Catholic University of America Press), p. 58.
69 Klingshirn, *Caesarius of Arles*, pp. 197–200. Cf. a similar situation in late fourth-century Roman Africa in Brown, *Augustine of Hippo* (see above note 5), p. 248.
70 Translated in Van Dam, *Saints and Their Miracles* (see above note 20), pp. 68, 305.

adjusted the content of such popular celebrations. In the twelfth century, a minstrel's song about the life of Saint Alexis converted the merchant Waldo of Lyon. Evidence of such oral religious culture in the intervening period is scarce.[71] Caesarius' ideal of piety and practice was an austere, monastic one. Notwithstanding his forcefulness, however, his disciples remember him also as, in his own way, an eminently caring man—in fact (as Augustine had advised), as a 'mother':

> Who will ever be able to imitate the ardour of the love (*caritatis ardor*) with which he loved (*dilexit*) all men? ... he loved them not only with a fatherly, but even with a motherly affection (*materno diligebat affectu*). ... (*Vit. Caes.* 1.53)[72]

Except perhaps through the nunnery which he had founded for his sister Caesaria, and the Rule which he wrote for it,[73] there is very little evidence of Caesarius' continuing influence in the Merovingian Church, dominated as it was by Frankish kings and politically-minded aristocratic bishops; in the eighth and ninth centuries, however, his writings and conciliar measures were used in various ways by the Carolingian religious reformers.[74]

Gregory

Gregory's writings show us that the forms of piety evident in the clerical writers of the Life of Caesarius had gained ground in the highest clerical circles of sixth-century Gaul. His piety does not revolve around texts, but around miracles. Where Caesarius had railed against worshipping trees, springs and stones, and told his hearers to whip those engaging in such practices, Gregory tells us with disarming charm about a tree growing on the place where a martyr was decapitated, the bark of which heals, and about the healing properties of water from a spring near the martyr Julian's grave (resp. *Glor. mart.* 67 and *Virt. Jul.* 3). His advice of drinking a potion of dust from Saint Martin's tomb to be cured can be seen—Flint notes[75]—as close to worshipping a stone. Is Gregory's cultivation of healing miracles through the incorporation of practices resembling pagan ones, as Flint would have it,

71 Dunn, *Saint's Life*, pp. 122–39, however, argues for a continuing tradition of song and dance in a religious context in early medieval Spain.

72 On the spiritual ideal of motherhood for men as well as women in Late Antiquity see my "Consciousness fecund through God': from male fighter to spiritual bride-mother in late antique female sanctity', to appear in: Anneke B. Mulder (ed), *Sanctity and Motherhood* (New York 1995: Garland).

73 Klingshirn, *Caesarius of Arles*, pp. 104–7, 117–24.

74 Ibid., pp. 271–2, 280–4.

75 Flint, *Rise of Magic*, p. 308.

'Christianized magic'? Or is it simply a matter of using familiar—and therefore readily acceptable—forms as bridges to an essentially different content?

Gregory throws in magic with pagan religion and defines the whole, in a general way, as the misguided worship of created things or spirits instead of their Creator (*Hist.* 2.29). A well-known case of the substitutive strategy is his story of the pagans worshipping a lake called Helarius, and propitiating it with yearly sacrifices in order to avert storms from their fields (*Glor. conf.* 2). He tells us that a priest told them that 'there is no religion in a lake'. He succeeded in convincing them to worship the true God through 'his friend' Saint Hilary of Poitiers instead, and to expect the same benefit from him when they bring their gifts to a church containing his relics. There is no way to get around the fact that this is an unmistakable case of purposeful 'social and religious engineering', recognized as such. No doubt, Gregory—as his namesake and contemporary, the pope, who (following Augustine, but not Caesarius) advised similar strategies[76]—envisioned the conversion to Christian interior values as following with time and continuous exposure to liturgy and preaching. Basic needs, then, have to be addressed first; work on interior transformation follows. Against Flint's contention, however, I would hold that the latter constitutes—in Gregory's stories too—the precise difference between the pagan and the Christian use of some very similar forms.

In his *Treatise on the Gospel of saint John*, Augustine had written that a miracle is a visible message from the invisible God; it has its own language and tells us about Christ (*Tract.* 24.1–2).[77] What I will try to show in a last story is that Gregory, too, seems to see the structure of the miraculous event or deed of holy power (*virtus*) as a pattern or 'figure': as divine truth made visible, just as the events in the Bible. As such, then, as he says explicitly (*Vit. Patr.* 19.prol.), alongside listening to and obeying the word of God, the contemplation of miracles—directly or through a story—is a means of access to Paradise.

The following story is, as it were, a 'figure' of Gregory's religious mentality too in that it is a mixture of prayer, meditation and—what Flint would regard as 'magical', but, in fact, symbolic—access to the holy through contact. In it, personal supplication and symbolic action seem to coalesce; likewise, the

76 In his well-known letter to Abbot Mellitus: *Epistola* XI.56, ed. Ludwig M. Hartmann (Berlin 1899: MGH Ep. 2), p. 331. Quoted (from Bede's History) by Flint, op. cit., pp. 76–7. As we saw, Augustine advised similar strategies in his *Ep.* 47 (see above note 3).

77 *Tractatus in Iohannis evangelium* XVII–XXXIII, ed. and transl. Marie-François Berrouard (Paris 1977: Bibliothèque Augustinienne. Oeuvres de Saint Augustine 72). Although Gregory does not mention the Church Father, he seems to be acquainted with this idea; see my forthcoming 'Die Sprache im Wunder' (see above note 60).

transformation of the heart through one's own meditation and that regarded as occurring through the power of the saint.

Here is the story. When his brother-in-law Justin once fell gravely ill, Gregory sent him one of the small candle-ends which he had taken with him from the tomb of Saint Martin, with the following message:

> 'Light it in front of him and let him pray to the Lord in the contemplation of its light and ask the omnipotence (*omnipotentia*) of the saint to save him.'
>
> The servant brought to the sick man what I had given him. When the candle had been burning a while beside his bed, they cut off the part of its wick that had already been burned and gave it to him to drink diluted in water. The moment he drank it he was immediately cured, and recovered from his illness.
>
> Later, he told us how the power of the holy bishop [Saint Martin] relieved him. As he used to tell it, at the first moment that the beam of light from the candle dispelled the darkness of night from his eyes, immediately upon the contemplation of the flame (*in contemplatione flammae*), the fever departed from his body; and his stomach, which was languishing through a long abstinence, now asked for food to restore it; the one who had been drinking only pure water to extinguish the burning fever now wanted wine. These things were brought about by the saint's power (*virtus*), which often, with an outpouring compassion (*proflua miseratione*), gives aid to the unfortunate and remedies to the sick. (*Virt. Mart.* 2.2)

In this story, the implicit metaphor—known to all—is the biblical one of Christ as the Light of the world, shining in darkness and overcoming it, illumining and saving all men. In analogical thinking, letting the light of a candle that has burned on Saint Martin's tomb shine into one's eyes is evidently a way to let—purifying and healing—light from heaven enter into one's heart and body. A metaphor is reality, because, for Gregory, every symbol not only represents, but also manifests, makes present and participates in that to which it points. If such a metaphor, then, unconceals and is reality, enacting this metaphor in a ritual precipitates a real transformation in oneself: which is exactly what Justin did. Gregory and he attribute this transformation to the saint's power, however. 'In the contemplation of the flame', and not of a Bible text, Justin—praying—experienced what he calls the saint's 'outpouring compassion'.[78]

78 On metaphor and reality in Gregory's writings see my *Views* (see above note 51), pp. 133–211. An article, 'History and miracle in Gregory of Tours: the role of metaphor', delivered as a paper at the International Medieval Congress at Leeds in July 1994,

The saint's tomb, the candles on it, the dust that collected on it, the cloth that covered it—or even a tree that grew over it or a spring near it—all these symbols, in Gregory's world view, effectively mediate divine compassion. If they were operative in even a fraction of the miraculous cures he reports, who are we to suggest that such symbols are mere means of magical manipulation, and thus not adequate to mediate the personal quality and the transformative essence of the Christian message? Calling the effecting of such transformations through these symbolic mediators 'Christian *magic*', as Flint does, is deeply misleading. In essence, it neglects to distinguish the—much wider—symbolic dimension of religion from the practice of magic. Further, directly connected with this, it overlooks the crucial fact that for many of the persons involved, a cure changed their lives entirely. They became clerics, or they devoted the rest of their lives to the service of the saint (as, for instance, in *Virt. Mart.* 2.33 and 3.22). Caesarius could not have hoped for a better result through meditation on biblical texts.

CONCLUSION

When we now look back at what we have found about Caesarius' and Gregory's text-centered and miracle-centered forms of religious experience, and their strategies of transmitting their piety to the often only half-converted pagans who filled their churches, we see two approaches. Although the core of their message—the peace of heavenly love in humbled spirit and healed heart—is the same, Caesarius' piety is a monastic, contemplative one, based on and working through texts; he expressed his love for his people by pressing this piety upon them, sometimes with force. His strategy of Christianization was that of outright substitution, and—in society at large—he was not successful. Gregory's piety is a rough and ready practical one, ultimately based on biblical and hagiographical texts, but trying to convince others primarily with lively stories about—beneficent but also punishing—manifestations of divine power through saints as recognizably human persons in the visible world. In his *Histories* he shows us that the figure of the dead Saint Martin, known through stories about his powerful acts as a protector and avenger, could be successfully used in diplomacy with rapacious and violent kings (e.g. *Hist.* 8.6). His language of personal power reflected the contemporary social and political situation, and was therefore one that his contemporaries could understand. In Gregory's writings, then, meditation upon figures and symbols in texts yielded in importance to gazing upon visible symbols

will appear in the collected papers, edited by Ian Wood, of the 1994 Gregory of Tours sessions there.

(sometimes ones that had had a pagan past) and experiencing miracles around these symbols. As we saw, 'figures' and symbols in texts were central in the Christian tradition from its inception. Gregory's emphasis upon symbols in the visible world is almost certainly connected with the well-attested general decline of literacy and the resulting increase of localism and orally based culture. Caesarius' sermons and the biblical texts he used were likely to be spread only by clergy; in a society accustomed to being entertained by stories, Gregory's tales of saints' miracles could be circulated by anyone with a gift for story-telling. He seems to have hoped that someone would versify them (*Virt. Mart.* 2.*prol.*), something that would accelerate their oral presentation; alliteration, rhythm, and rhyme, as we know, are traditional aids to memorization.

Gregory's piety is concrete and practical; it is obvious that he believes every miracle, even the most improbable one he tells, for, as he frequently repeats, nothing is impossible for God (e.g. *Hist.* 2.3). In such a view, has Christian religion sold out to a superficial fascination for the bizarre and to the covert manipulation of cosmic forces as a conscious effort to assimilate similar pagan practices and survive in a hostile environment? I hope to have shown that, at least in Gregory's thinking, the core of the transforming Christian message—self-transcendence through divine love—can be apprehended through all kinds of symbolic mediators without being essentially changed. Gregory's example shows that adopting what Flint calls 'appearances' of magic rituals did not necessarily mean that Christian religious practice degenerated into little more than manipulative strategies for physical survival masquerading as religion, as she seems to suggest. Magic and symbolic mediation more generally must be distinguished. We are all aware of the fact that we can learn and integrate nothing new into our world view except by recognizing it somehow as a variation or expansion of something we already know. As Augustine had said in the treatise quoted at the beginning of this contribution, a mother speaks to her child in the terms of his experience, so that he can understand her message (*De cat. rud.* 10.15). What he means, of course, is that adults are no different. Although, as bishop, Gregory was also a busy administrator, he was not perceived by his contemporaries as a social and religious engineer, but as a man of the stamp of his model and patron Saint Martin: a 'man filled with God (*vir plenus Deo*)'.[79]

Almost the only literature that has survived—and not much of anything has survived—from the century that followed Gregory is that of the stories of saints and their miracles. Saints, as persons with recognizable human faces,

79 Baudonivia, *Vita sanctae Radegundis* 23, ed. Bruno Krusch (Hannover 1888: MGH SSrM 2), referring to Sulpicius Severus, *Vita Martini* 3.1., ed. and transl. Jacques Fontaine (Paris 1967: SC 133).

and every palpable thing around them, were evidently experienced as the most effective symbolic mediators of the divine in a period in which civilization probably seemed to have definitively crumbled. Alongside the textually oriented tradition continuing in the relatively safe seclusion of the monasteries, in the uncertain and violent world outside it was to a large extent men and women's trust in these human and concrete symbols that made the Church's survival possible.

VI

A broken lamp or the effluence of holy power? Common sense and belief-reality in Gregory of Tours' own experience*

I myself had very often heard it said that even the lamps burning before these relics, boiling over by divine power (*ebullientes virtute divina*), brought forth (*exundarent*) so much oil that they filled a vessel placed beneath many times: and nevertheless, because of the stupidity of my hard mind (*stultitia mentis durae*) I was never moved to believe this (*ad haec credenda movebar*) until, by that which was shown (*ostensa*) in my presence, the holy power (*virtus*) reproved my brutish slothfulness (*bruta segnities*).

Therefore I will unfold (*explicabo*) what I saw with my own eyes. For pious reasons I once went to speak with this queen [Radegund] when I had visited St. Hilary's tomb. After I had entered the Convent [of the Holy Cross] and greeted the queen, I prostrated myself before the to-be-adored Cross and the relics of the saints. Then, when I had completed my prayers, I arose. [Earlier,] I had noticed a lighted lamp on my right overflowing with (*defluens*) frequent drops [of oil]; and I call God to witness that I thought the vessel was broken (*putavi quasi vas esset effractum*), because a bowl had been placed underneath, into which the spilling (*defluens*) oil fell. Turning then to the abbess, I said: "Are you so lazy-minded (*Tantane te retinet mentis ignavia*) that you are unable to take the trouble of providing an unbroken lamp, in which the oil burns, instead of a broken one from which the oil runs out (*defluat*)?"

And she replied: "That is not the case, my lord. What you see is the power (*virtus*) of the holy Cross."

Then – having come to myself (*ego ad me reversus*), recalled what I had previously heard said and turned to the lamp – I see (*video*) it overflowing in great streams (*magnis fluctibus exundare*), in that hour pouring over with swelling waves (*undis tumescentibus superfluere*), and, as I believe, increasing more and more in volume (*augeri*) in order to reprove my unbelief; so that in one hour's time the vessel brought forth (*redderet*) more than a sextarius, while it itself could not hold even a quarter of a sextarius. Having gazed at it in awed wonder, I fell silent (*Admiratusque silui*), and ever since I have preached the power (*virtus*) of the to-be-adored Cross.[1]

In this sixth-century miracle story by Bishop Gregory of Tours story we can observe what C. Geertz has called a 'leap' or a 'slip' from common sense-reality into belief-reality.[2] How can this – or any – belief-reality become so 'really real' that it can alter our perception of sensory-practical reality? Geertz's answer is well-known: the belief-world is presented as 'utter actuality' in a ritual context by an 'authority'.[3] Rituals, he states, allow the worshipper to experience the precise coincidence of the everyday world with the belief-world, and so they induce or even compel belief in the latter. One of the rituals Geertz mentions is the public recitation of a myth. Such a myth would contain and present not only *models of* the reality postulated by religion, but also – and especially – *models for* what he calls 'producing' that reality in the perception of the worshipper.[3] I suggest that Gregory's narrative, intended for reading to the church community, is just such a model of and model for religious reality.[4]

Geertz does not tell us how a remembered story can alter the perception of a sensory-practical event or object, as Gregory wants us to believe happened in his own experience. This is an exceedingly complex issue that can be approached from many different angles and that deepens at every turn. Modern psychological investigations, however, offer some interpretative models with which the historian can work, at least provisionally. In this article I present three of these, and show how they can be applied to begin providing an answer to the above question.

Mental images and perception: some models

R. Arnheim, in his *Visual thinking*,[5] says the following about recognition (in pictorial representation):

> Visual knowledge acquired in the past helps not only in detecting the nature of an object or action appearing in the visual field; it also assigns the present object a place in the system of things constituting our total view of the world. Thus almost every act of perception involves subsuming a given particular phenomenon under some visual concept. ... perception and recognition are inseparably intertwined ... [as in the] interaction between the structure suggested by the stimulus configuration and the components brought fears of the observer. ... a powerful need can impose an image of the observer's making on the scantiest objective condition. ... Often, however, there is enough ambiguity in the stimulus to let the observer find different shape patterns in it as he searches for the best fitting model among the ones emerging from memory storage.

In his *Imagery and daydream methods in psychotherapy and behavior modification*,[6] J.L. Singer states that experimental investigation has shown that ongoing image-thought processes, as in dreams, are a central part of human mentation alongside simultaneous directed, discursive thought and attention to the performance of tasks during waking hours.

He speaks of this as 'parallel processing', but says that there are also indications of 'sequential processing': shifts of attention between private imagery and the processing of external material. This latter material tends to be stored, at first, in the sensory and affective mode in which it was apprehended.[7] In addition, Singer has drawn attention to the possibility of an overlap between mental imagery and sensory input:[8]

> ... [it is a] by now reasonably well-established finding that imagery and perception seem in effect to be manifestations of a common brain process (Segal 1971) and probably use the same common pathways in the brain ... if one imagines a particular object as if appearing on a

blank screen and if a picture of the object or *if almost any visual signal* [italics supplied] is flashed faintly, but ordinarily discriminably, on the screen while the subject is imagining, the imager may not be aware of the 'real' stimulus in his visual field.

R. Assagioli, on the other hand, has drawn attention to the dynamic inherent in the images themselves. In his *Psychosynthesis*[9] he cites "the fundamental fact" that:

"Every image has in itself a motor-drive" or "images and mental pictures tend to produce the physical conditions and external acts corresponding to them."

Assagioli and his school use controlled symbolic visualization techniques to allow the patient (for instance) to "visualize living things which may change, and to experience the direction the change takes autonomously once the image begins."[10] An example is the visualization of a rosebud opening up which would initiate a process of inner blossoming in the subject.[11] Anyone acquainted with meditative techniques will at once recognize the similarity to these.[12] In my interpretation of Gregory's story I hope to show that he and his contemporaries were much more aware of the transforming qualities of images and representations than we tend to be.

To sum up the interpretative models we have looked at:

– first, Geertz's model: the recitation of a myth as 'utter actuality' and 'really real' by an 'authority' in a ritual context 'produces' a belief in the imagined reality that can alter perception of sensory-practical reality

– then, the psychological models: recognition involves choosing a visual concept stored in the memory and this choice is influenced by expectation and wishes (Arnheim)

– dreamlike mental imagery occurs alongside discursive thought and the processing of external information during waking hours; there can be shifts of attention between these thought modes and one may temporarily block out another (Singer)

– a mental image tends to be the trigger of an autonomous process of mental-emotional-physical transformation whose dynamic is analogous to its symbolic form (Assagioli).

A broken vessel or an outpouring of divine energy?

With the above interpretative models in mind, is it possible to let Gregory's story about the oil dripping from a lamp near the particle of the holy Cross yield information contributing to an answer to our query: how, more exactly, and why does the 'leap' from common sense-reality into belief-reality take place?

In his first sentence, Gregory seems to contradict Geertz's statement that hearing a religious truth in a ritual context 'produces' belief. Gregory, however, does not indicate that he had heard the story in a ritual context: he simply says that he had 'very often heard' about the oil overflowing 'by divine power'. The story appears to be part of a colloquial oral tradition. And although everywhere in his works more than willing to believe in the *possibility* of anything and everything happening through divine power,[13] Gregory, whenever possible, tries to check whether a particular event has in fact occurred. He names witnesses or quotes written sources, weighs testimonies for 'facts' whose reality might be open to doubt, and uses phrases such as 'people say (*ferunt*)' to qualify what he probably considered to be fairly reliable hearsay.[14] As appears later in the story, this particular oral tradition must have originated in the Convent of the Holy Cross itself, then still led (in fact, if not in theory) by the saintly nun-queen Radegund. That Gregory regarded her as an eminent authority is evident from the fact that he himself compares her faith to that of Empress Helena (who discovered the Cross) and lets others call her a companion of St. Martin.[15] The abbess of her convent shares in this sphere of authority. There is, then, clearly a connection with the latter, but not yet a convincing ritual context in which the story is apprehended as true. It is not enough for Gregory, this time: "and nevertheless, because of the stupidity of my hard mind, I was never moved to believe this."

This seems to be a commonsensical approach. Gregory knew as well as we do that a burning lamp consumes oil and does not 'produce' it. So, did he postpone belief in the story until he had seen the facts for himself and checked the possibility of a practical explanation? And had he, at the time, simply 'forgotten' about the alleged miracle reported of the lamps there? This is certainly what he wants us to believe when he says that, after his prostrated prayer before the Cross, "I call God to witness that I thought the vessel was broken, because a bowl had been placed underneath ..." In any case, he immediately assumes a practical cause – a very understandable reaction for us – and even speaks quite sharply about it to the abbess.

We seem to recognize the reaction; but is this the same 'common sense' that we think we have? C. Stancliffe's investigation of fourth-century belief and non-belief in St. Martin's miracles shows that there was 'hard-headed' practicality, but no such thing as what we think of as a mechanistic or 'scientific' outlook which questions the authenticity of miracles as such.[16] 'Common sense' in late Antiquity, she states, was not only down-to-earth experience of sensory-practical facts, but was also influenced by the intellectual and religious ideas held by all strata of society. These ideas held the universe to be shot through and moved by spiritual powers, good and bad. When one had offended one of these – for instance, by not pouring a libation – it would be 'common sense' to expect a bad harvest.[17] It was, then, as Gregory himself says, "the stupidity of my hard mind" – his knowledge of how sensory phenomena 'tend to behave' and not any 'scientific' attitude in our sense of the term that at first kept him being 'moved to believe' what he heard said, perhaps by visitors who had been to the convent.

Gregory's upbringing in the Christian tradition also precluded a 'scientific' doubt as to the possibility of such a miracle. Not only could he have found in the Bible that the destitute widow's oil increased when she did what she was told to do by the prophet Elisha.[18] In the Martinian tradition, too, one finds the following testimony:[19]

The priest [Arpagius] was wont to testify that he saw [medicinal] oil grow in volume through Martin's blessing (*Testabatur presbyter vidisse se oleum sub Martini benedictione crevisse*), until the overflowing abundance (*exundante copia*) spilled over the rim of the bottle. And while the vessel was being carried to the lady, too, it bubbled over by divine power (*ferbuisse virtute*), so that it billowed forth (*exundasse*) oil all the time that it was in the hands of the servant carrying it, covering his whole garment with the abundance of the liquid poured out (*copia superfusi liquoris*) ...

The pervasive image here is as it were an inexhaustible outpouring of a healing liquid generated out of nothing by divine power. It seems to function as what Geertz calls "a synoptic formulation of the character of reality".[20]

In Gregory's own writings the image recurs. Later on in *On the glory of the martyrs* he reports that at the tomb of the apostle Thomas in Edessa a lamp burns perpetually (*perpetualiter*).[21] Neither the oil nor the wick needs to be renewed because it burns "through the holy energy (*virtus*) of the apostle, [the nature of] which is unknown to men but known to the divine power (*divina potentia*)." For this fact Gregory names as his source Theodorus, who had been there to see it, and who had himself told Gregory about it.

And this is not all. In the second of the four books on St. Martin's miracles Gregory tells us that he himself saw (medicinal) rose-oil increase after it had been placed near St. Martin's tomb.[22] Interestingly, he begins this rather lengthy story by saying:

When we see such miracles (*miracula ... cernamus*) as we have described happening daily, what is to be said to those unhappy people who say that Severus lied in his Life of the holy bishop [Martin]? For I heard someone – possessed as I believe, with an evil spirit (*nequam, ut credo, repletum spiritu*) – saying that it could not have happened (*non potuisse fieri*) that oil grew in volume through Martin's blessing, nor that a flask falling on a marble floor remained unbroken.[23] Therefore I will reveal what has recently happened (*Quod ergo nuper actum est ...declarabo*), and for which I have many witnesses ...

He then proceeds to describe how after much urging on his own part, one of his deacons who was afflicted with quartan fever, finally went to pray for his health at St. Martin's tomb. He took along a half-empty flask of rose-oil with which he had been anointing himself – without much effect – and asked permission to leave it near the saint's tomb when he left. On the fourth day, when he was again attacked by fever, the deacon returned to the tomb. After he had prostrated himself and prayed for a long time, he turned to the flask to take it back with him, and found it now to be full. "Gazing in awed wonder at the holy power (*admirans virtutem*) of the bishop", he anointed himself with some of its contents and the fever soon left him. At home, however, the devil (*inimicus*) later caused the flask to be dashed to the ground and its contents were quickly absorbed by the earth. A servant, who had seen this happening, scooped up the earth into a vessel, pressed what oil he could from it, and brought the resulting mixture of oil and glass fragments to Gregory. The latter carefully transferred it to another container, wherein the oil stood about two fingerbreadths high.

Looking at it (*prospiciens*) the following morning, the height of the oil was as though (*erat ... quasi*) four fingerbreadths. I was stupefied by the power of the holy liquid (*Obstupefactus ego ob virtutem sancti liquoris*) which I had left behind covered and protected by my seal (*signaculo meo munitum*). After seven days I looked again, and found more than a sextarius [of oil] in it. Then I called the deacon and, showing it to him, gazed at it in awed wonder (*hoc ei ostendens admirabar*). He testified, with an oath, that what was now seen (*cerneretur*) in this vessel as as much as had previously been in the broken flask. And up to the present day it confers benefits upon those who ask for these in God's name ...

Even though this flask broke when it fell – a concession to those holding out in hard-headed common sense – Gregory takes back with his right hand what he has just given with his left: the oil in it was 'preserved' by St. Martin's holy power, just as it had been two centuries earlier. The fact that Gregory sealed the vessel strongly suggests that, already then remembering the earlier miracle, he was inclined to expect it to happen again, and wanted to be sure it happened under verifiably 'controlled' conditions: a thoroughly practical, experimental attitude! Can we 'explain' his – nevertheless – 'seeing' at first two fingerbreadths, then four, and then a sextarius[24] as image-model-influenced altered perception: a blocking out of sensory input by a more powerful mental image? Gregory himself seems conscious of the presence of another kind of reality – Geertz's belief-reality and psychology's altered perception – when he qualifies the phenomenon with the phrases "was as though" and "was now seen", instead of using the simple indicative "was".

Let us return to Poitiers. It is possible that Gregory's visit pre-dated the rose-oil incident, but also not unlikely that Gregory was determined to go and see for himself anyway, perhaps even with an eye to writing about it later. Not out of doubt, then, that such a thing *could* happen, but out of doubt that it *happened there*. I suggest that here, as elsewhere in his writings,[25] Gregory looked for the sensation of something happening that he did not expect: he wanted awed wonder to 'open up' his closed, 'hard' mind – an experience that he, by his strung-out description, is also trying to induce in the reader or auditor. That is why he calls God to witness that he had really 'forgotten' about the miracle he had heard about, and – in what he had earlier called his 'brutish slothfulness' – had 'thought' the lamp was broken. Gregory's repeated use of terms denoting mental laziness, earlier to refer to his own slowness (*segnities*) to believe the story, and now to what he thought was the abbess's carelessness (*mentis ignavia*), seems to me intentional. By this as it were 'backward reference' he is letting his reproach to her describe himself again: his own present inadvertence, but also (by implication) that of any similarly incredulous reader or auditor.

Then he lets the abbess's answer give him – and the reader or auditor – the jolt of *recognition*:

"That is not the case, my lord. What you see is the power of the holy Cross."

Then – having come to myself, and recalled what I had previously heard said and turned to the lamp – I see it overflowing ... in that hour pouring over with swelling waves and ... increasing even more and more in volume ... so that in one hour's time the vessel brought forth more than a sextarius, while it itself could not hold even a quarter of a sextarius ...

What has happened here? In reply to Gregory's irritated question, the abbess points to the selfsame, sensory-concrete lamp as a divine epiphany, a symbol as well as a manifestation of effluent holy power. At the same time, the convent chapel location and Gregory's just having engaged in intensive prayer there create an experiential setting removed from everyday reality and associated with ritual. Upon hearing the abbess's words in this ritual setting, Gregory recalls the story he had previously heard and suddenly he "comes to himself", to what for him is 'the really real'. He realizes that the story applies to the present situation: sensory-practical and belief-reality coincide in the visible phenomenon of the spilling lamp. In psychological terms, the model-image that is being projected onto the physical object in order to 'see' it, changes in the twinkling of an eye from the common sense-image of 'an ordinary lamp that spills because it must be broken' to the belief-image of 'the overflowing lamp as epiphany of holy power'. And Gregory now looks at it in a new way: he "gazes at it in awed wonder".

After all the verbs in the past tense, Gregory's use here of the present tense – I *see* – again suggests awareness of a 'leap' from one reality (the everyday kind) to the other (the true, spiritual reality). The present tense, in my view, points to the experienced timelessness of the image of religious truth, stored in the memory and ready to surface on the right cue, to be 'seen' again with the mind's eye whenever spoken or thought about. In this story, the sensory-concrete lamp remains just that, but it is at the same time transformed into a symbol of the *experience* of something like continuously self-generating, outpouring divine love. As such, it is stored in the memory as a dreamlike, affect-laden image that stands for something that cannot be adequately apprehended in any other way.

The verbal inexpressibility of religious truth is a commonplace in late Antiquity, and occurs also in Gregory's writings.[26] Holy truth tends to be experienced through shapes and patterns of feeling apprehended in concrete, visible objects and events: miracles, sometimes referred to as 'signs' (*signa*)[27] or 'figures' (*figurae*)[28] of this truth. It seems to me that Gregory's indications of increased volume should be understood in this way. Religious tradition had taught him to believe that God could stretch, bend and create reality on the spot. Expecting this and wishing for it to happen, he actually 'saw' it, and needed to translate this perception into objective measures to transmit his experience to others.[29]

Why was this experience of religious truth through the shapes of sensory-practical objects and visible events so attractive and – to judge from the proliferation of miracle-stories – even compelling in this period? I suggest it is because a society, such as that of late sixth-century Gaul, that depends largely upon oral communication will tend to think more in terms of visual images and vivid stories that are relatively easy to grasp and remember than in abstract concepts.[30] As a preacher, Gregory therefore presented his Christian message in this manner. A deeper reason is, however, that these shapes tended to be congruent to basic symbols expressing non-verbal, vital human experience,[31] such as those of the eternal fountain and the sun. Assagioli and others have found that such images can trigger dynamically analogous emotional processes that effectively work toward psychic health. Gregory, it is evident, felt deeply reassured and even exhilarated by what he stayed to watch in reverence as the effluence of the divine power of the Cross. He was probably assimilating the visual shape of the overflowing lamp to those of the outpouring Fount of Life and the inexhaustible Light of the world, both symbols of Christ. For, earlier in the chapter he tells us how – in the same chapel – a supernatural light once appeared during the 'dark' vigils before Easter. And immediately after the story of the lamp, he reports that a nun was once cured of blindness there. With these motifs of illumination around the image of the overflowing lamp Gregory creates a composite, dynamic image-model of the power of Christ through the holy Cross that could induce analogous affective processes of upsurging vital energy and en-light-enment in his listeners.

To return to our original question: how, more exactly, can a miracle story alter the reader's or auditor's perception of sensory-practical reality? Geertz's answer – the story's being presented as 'utter actuality' by an 'authority' in a ritual context – can be developed and refined by the psychological models indicated. If recognition involves choosing a visual concept stored in the memory and if this choice is influenced by the observer's expectation and wishes, then an emotionally rewarding 'added' reality that is matched in a persuasive manner to a sensory-concrete object or event will tend to make the former prevail when the object or event comes into view or is 'thought' about.

Gregory did not have our anthropological and psychological models, but he knew what he was doing. In his prologue to the book in which the stories here treated are found,[32] he wrote:

> ... we ought ... to write and speak of that which builds up the Church, and of that which, through holy instruction, causes knowledge of perfect faith to sprout in barren minds (*quae mentes inopes ad notitiam perfectae fidei instructione sancta fecundent*).

Gregory hopes that the awed wonder induced by his stories will produce belief in 'barren' – incredulous, i.e. 'hard', 'lazy' – minds. This is a 'leap', and Gregory was aware of it: for him it was the dynamic of the divine itself, producing new reality – here in men's hearts, through images in words.[33]

Notes

* This article is a revision of a paper given at the 25th International Congress on Medieval Studies at Kalamazoo in May 1990. I am grateful to Prof. A. Adams, to Dr. A.J. Vanderjagt and Prof. R. van Dam for suggestions regarding content and style.

1 Ego autem audiebam saepius, quod etiam lychni, qui accendebantur ante haec pignora, ebullientes virtute divina, in tantum exundarent oleum, ut vas suppositum plerumque replerent: et tamen iuxta stultitiam mentis durae nunquam ad haec credenda movebar, donec brutam segnitiem ad praesens ipsa quae ostensa est virtus argueret.

Ideoque quae oculis propriis viderim explicabo. Causa devotionis exstitit ut sepulcrum sancti Hilarii visitans, huius reginae adirem colloquia; ingressusque monasterium, consalutata regina, coram adoranda cruce ac sacris beatorum prosternor pignoribus. Denique oratione facta surrexi. Erat enim ad dexteram lychnus accensus, quem cum stillis frequentibus defluere conspexissem, testor Deum quia putavi quasi vas esset effractum, quia erat ei concha supposita, in quam oleum defluens decidebat. Tunc conversus ad abbatissam, aio: "Tantane te retinet mentis ignavia, ut integrum cicindilem laborare non possis, in quo oleum accendatur, nisi effractum quo defluat ponas?"

Et illa: "Nec est ita, domine mi, sed virtus est crucis sanctae quam cernis."

Tunc ad me reversus, et ad memoriam revocans quae prius audieram, conversus ad lychnum, video in modum ollae ferventis magnis fluctibus exundare, ac per horam ipsam undis intumescentibus superfluere, et, ut credo, ad incredulitatem meam arguendam, magis ac magis augeri; ita ut in unius horae spatio plusquam unum sextarium redderet vasculum, quod quartarium non tenebat: admiratusque silui, ac virtutem adorandae crucis deinceps praedicavi.

Gregorius Turonensis, In gloria martyrum (Glor. mart.) v. The edition used for all his hagiographical works is that of W. Arndt and B. Krusch eds., Gregorii Turonensis opera, (Monumenta Germaniae Historica, Scriptores rerum Merovingicarum i.2) Hannover 1885, 451-820.

2 C. Geertz, 'Religion as a cultural system', in: C. Geertz, The interpretation of cultures, New York 1973, 87-125, here: 122.

3 Ibid., 124, 112-3, 118.

4 Ibid., 93, 114. I am not suggesting, as Mr. J. Zwick seems to imply (in his comment on my earlier work, in 'Zur Form und Funktion übernatürlicher Kommunikationsweisen in der Frankengeschichte des Gregor von Tours', Mediaevistik 1 (1988) 193) that Gregory's imaged narratives represent a purely private imagined or dream-world. As he rightly indicates, Gregory's presentation of reality as miraculous within certain well-defined structures clearly supports the church's claim to the monopoly of spiritual power in an insufficiently ordered society (G. de Nie, Views from a many-windowed tower. Studies of imagination in the works of Gregory of Tours. (Studies in classical antiquity 7), Amsterdam 1987, 268-93 and elsewhere; eadem, 'Heilige wondermacht of toverkunst? Een vroegmiddeleeuwse interpretatie', in: R.E.V. Stuip and C. Vellekoop ed., Culturen in contact. Botsing en integratie in de Middeleeuwen (Utrechtse Bijdragen tot de Mediëvistiek 8), Utrecht 1988, 129-38). The social function is essential, but it is not my subject here.

5 Berkeley 1969, 90-1.

6 New York 1974, 173.

7 Ibid., 183, 189.

8 Ibid., 175-6.

9 New York 1965, 144, apparently citing Charles Baudoin, Suggestion and autosuggestion, London 1920 without page reference.

10 J. Singer op. cit., 111.

11 R. Assagioli, op. cit., 213-5.
12 Cf. for instance A.J. Deikman, 'Experimental meditation' and W. Kretschmer, 'Meditative techniques in psychotherapy', in: C.T. Tart ed., Altered states of consciousness, New York etc. 1969, 199-218 and 219-28 respectively.
13 As, for instance, quoting Mark ix: 23 in his Historiae (Hist) 11.3: omnia possibilia sunt credenti. Edition: R. Buchner ed., and transl. (Ausgewählte Quellen zur deutschen Geschichte des Mittelalters, Freiherr vom Stein-Gedächtnisausgabe ii, 3), Darmstadt 1967.
14 E.g.: [abbas] qui ... cum sacramento asseruit (Glor. mart. vi); Nam cum multa de eis [Francis] Sulpici Alexandri narret historia (Hist. ii.9); Nam ferunt nunc et lumen ibi divinitus apparere (Hist. vi.37); and especially: ... reprehendi ab aliquibus vereor, dicentibus mihi: "Tu cum sis junior, quomodo seniorum gesta poteris scire? qualiter ad te eorum facta venerunt? Nempe non aliud nisi conficta a te haec quae scripta sunt decernuntur." Qua de causa relatorem huius operis in medio ponere necesse est, ut hi qui veritati derogant confundantur ... quem in hoc non credo fefellisse, cum per eum Deus eo tempore, quando mihi ista retulit, et caecorum oculos illuminavit, et paralyticis gressum praestitit ... Denique si de tali relatore dubitatur, de beneficiis Dei diffiditur. (Vitae patrum xvii, prologus).
15 (Crux Dominica, quae ab Helena Augusta reperta est Hierosolymis, ...) Huius reliquias, et merito, et fide Helenae comparanda, regina Radegundis expetiit, ac devote in monasterium Pictavense, quod suo studio constituit, collocavit (Glor. mart. v); in a letter to Radegunde by a number of bishops, cited by Gregory: Sed cum paene eadem veneritis ex parte, qua beatum Martinum huc didicimus accessisse, non est mirum, si illum imitare videaris in opere, quem tibi ducem credimus iteneris extetisse: ut, cuius es secuta vestigia, filici voto conpleas et exempla, et beatissimum virum in tanto tibi facias esse socium ... (Hist. ix.39).
16 C.E. Stancliffe, St. Martin and his hagiographer. History and miracle in Sulpicius Severus, Oxford 1983, 211.
17 Ibid., 212, 215-27.
18 2 Kings: 1-7.
19 Sulpicius Severus, Dialogi (Dial.) iii.3. Edition: C. Halm ed., Sulpicii Severi libri qui supersunt (Corpus scriptorum ecclesiasticorum latinorum i) Wien 1886, 152-216.
20 C. Geertz, op. cit., 95.
21 Glor. mart. xxxi.
22 De virtutibus sancti Martini (Virt. Mart.) ii.32.
23 Dial. iii.3.
24 As a liquid measure, approximately a pint.
25 G. de Nie, Views, 81-2, 88.
26 E.R. Curtius, European literature and the Latin Middle Ages. W.R. Trask, transl., New York 1953, 159-62. Examples in Gregory's work: Quis unquam ista sic ex ordine inquirere aut referre poterit, ut ex aequo laudare sufficiat? (Virt. Mart. i.40); Insignia divinorum beneficiorum charismate, quae humano generi coelitus sunt indulta, nec sensu consipi, nec verba effari, nec scripturis poterunt comprehendi ... (Vit. part. xix. prol.). Cf. on this subject: W. Haug, Literaturtheorie im deutschen Mittelalter, Darmstadt 1985, 18-24.
27 G. de Nie, Views, 56-7, 107-8.
28 E. Auerbach, 'Figura', Archivum Romanicum xxii (1938) 436-89, and idem, Mimesis. Dargestellte Wirklichkeit in der abendländischen Literatur, Bern 1946, 74-7.
29 Cf. C. Stancliffe, op. cit., 107-8.
30 Cf. W.J. Ong, Orality and literacy. The technologizing of the word, London 1982, 49-57; similarly: 42-3, 45-6. For the other side of the picture: I Wood, 'Administration, law and culture in Merovingian Gaul', in: R. McKitterick ed., The uses of literacy in early medieval Europe, Cambridge 1990, 63-81.

31 Cf. S.K. Langer, Philosophy in a new key. A study in the symbolism of reason, rite, and art, Cambridge, Mass. 3 1979, 79-102.

32 Glor. mart. prol.

33 As I have tried to show in my Views, 112-5 and passim.

VII

Seeing and Believing in the Early Middle Ages: A Preliminary Investigation[1]

Fourteen hundred years ago, in 594 C.E., France's first historian Gregory of Tours departed from this life. He had been bishop in a sixth-century Frankish kingdom that had arisen out of the desintegrated Roman Empire, and which combined Germanic with what was left of Gallo-Roman political and social forms. His *Histories* are the only full-fledged historiographical work that has come down to us from the troubled period in the west between the fifth and the late seventh century.[2] Almost the only other literature produced seems to have been saints' lives and collections of miracles, including those which Gregory wrote. His epithet for one of his saintly subjects – *sacer heros* (*Vit. patr.* 20.4) – may indicate that the stories about saints, in general, may have functioned in some ways as the equivalent of Germanic epics about mythical heroes.[3] They also show that the saint was needed as a supernatural protector and healer who was independent of the instable and arbitrary worldly authorities. But miracles, as we see them happening in Gregory's stories, were sought not only for practical reasons such as protection or healing. As manifestations of the presence of the just and powerful invisible reality taught by the Church, they were evidently also a much-needed legitimation for hope in what seemed to be a cruel and chaotic world.

This beneficent and powerful heavenly order, however, was admitted by all to be invisible. How was it possible, nevertheless, as Gregory says, to "look towards the things that are not seen (*respic[ere] ad ea quae non videntur*)" (cf. Hebr. 11:1; *Vit. patr.* 6.*prol.*)? Is he saying that one could, in some way, "see" the invisible?

The philosopher Paul Ricoeur has designated as one of the uses of imagination the envisioning of another possible reality to contrast with the existing one in order to evaluate and work on it.[4] From the anthropological angle, Clifford Geertz has analyzed the functions of "religion as a cultural system" in a seminal article with that title. He describes the seeing of "belief reality" of religion and the acting out of its rituals as a way of constructing a coherent view of the world that, among other things, makes evil and suffering endurable. About this way of seeing the world, he says:

> The religious perspective differs from the commonsensical in that ... it *moves beyond the realities of everyday life* to wider ones which correct and complete them .... And it *differs from art* in that instead of effecting a disengagement from the whole question of factuality, deliberately manufacturing an air of semblance and illusion, it deepens the concern with fact and *seeks to create an aura of utter actuality*. It is this sense of the "really real" upon which the religious perspective rests and which *the symbolic activities* of religion as a cultural system are devoted to *producing, intensifying* and, so far as possible, *rendering inviolable* by the discordant revelations of secular experience.[5] [emphasis added]

Inspired by Eugen Drewermann's work on the interpenetration of theology and depth-psychology, I should like to reformulate this as: religion uses the symbolic activities in which imagination is implicated as a means of what I shall call "divining" what is regarded as the hidden spiritual reality – that is, perceiving the "really real" in or under the phenomena of common sense experience.[6] The prime example of this is, of course, the liturgical transformation of bread and wine in the Eucharist. And, differing with what appears to be Geertz's view of art as purposely and *only* illusionistic without any claim to truth, I hope to show that there are indications that Gregory treated religious imagination as what we would call art: the creation of something like an illusion that nevertheless stands for – and thereby participates in – the real.

An analysis of a selected few of Gregory's stories, will show something of how this early medieval bishop presented what he regarded as the connections between believing the word taught by the Church and "seeing" the reality to which it referred.

"Eyes of the heart": "eyes of faith"

In a well-known story that will serve to reveal his premises, Gregory tells us how a holy Catholic bishop cured the spiritual – and suddenly also physical – blindness of a man who had pretended, for payment, to be blind, so as to be "healed" in public by a heretic bishop who was envious of his Catholic rivals' miracles. After the unfortunate man had been told that "If you believe, all things are possible to the believer" (Mk 9:23), and had thereupon proclaimed his adherence to the Catholic view of the Trinity beginning with the phrase "I believe ...", he was cured through the laying upon of hands, the sign of the Cross and the pronouncement of the name of the Trinity. To drive his point home, our sixth-century author makes the message of this miracle-story explicit:

> Through the blindness of this man, however, it was made most clear how the bishop of the heretics was covering the eyes of [men's] hearts (*oculos cordium*)

> with the miserable veil of his doctrine, so that no one would be able to contemplate the true Light with the eyes of faith (*ne veram lucem ulli liceret fidei oculis contemplare*). O wretch, who, ... in the depravity of his own heart, tried to extinguish the torchof faith (*facem fidei*) in the hearts of the believers! (*Hist.* 2.3)

Mental and physical states are here presented as two aspects of the same phenomenon: spiritual blindness becomes physical blindness because the light of understanding is the same as that through which the bodily eyes see. Understanding, then, is thought of as, and conflated with, physical seeing, and seeing as understanding. What, however, is seen?

The "eyes of the heart" become "the eyes of faith" when they are filled with "the light of faith". This "light" consists of the decision to accept the Triune God as He is preached by the Catholic Church and – in this case, in the hope of a cure – the trust that "all things are possible" to Him. What "all things", more specifically, are, is the whole of God's dealings with men as they are recorded in the Bible. The Christian tradition of allegorical interpretation discerned, in these biblical sayings and visible events, certain underlying dynamic spiritual patterns or "figures" that represented the real – spiritual – truth. Gregory speaks of this process of discernment as "spiritual understanding" (*In psal. prol.*).[7] I suggest that in his miracle stories this same strategy of spiritual understanding is transposed from texts to sensory phenomena – here, however, the underlying truth is not only imaginatively visualized, but often reported as actually "seen".

In late antique and early medieval religious texts, however, not only extraordinary events such as miracles, but all of sensory reality tend to be regarded as symbols of invisible truth. This is evident in a compendium such as that of the fifth-century Bishop Eucherius of Lyon, with which Gregory was almost certainly acquainted.[8] According to an authority on religious symbolism in this period, Gerhart Ladner, the phenomena of the sensory world itself, as symbols, and the invisible reality to which they pointed, constituted an analogical, gradualistic, participatory – even sacramental – whole.[9] Every visible phenomenon and event could thus become an image or a "figure" of some transcendent divine truth, adumbrating religious mysteries that could not be adequately represented by (philosophical) concepts.[10] Essential in this hierarchical world view is that the spiritual form or image was the higher, "real" truth, and the sensory likeness, in which it would be recognized, a weak derivative.[11] The real truth, then, was one that was *imagined*, and never more than partly perceived by the senses.

Thus the "eyes of faith" – and this is the crux of the matter – decide to see present visible events and phenomena through the biblical patterns as dynamic models of all-time truth. This is what Geertz called the "really real" beyond common sense reality. And this is what Gregory meant by the phrase "contemplat[ing] the true Light", the latter being what the Gospel of John calls the mystery of Christ working in the present world (Jn 1:3, 9; 9:5). This Gospel calls Christ's miracles and cures "signs" of the presence of an empowering invisible reality (Jn 2:11, 4:54, etc.), and regards them at the same time as models of the continuing dynamic patterns of this new reality.[12]

Rituals, Geertz states, allow the worshipper to experience the precise coincidence of the everyday world with the the belief world, and so they induce or even compel belief in the latter. One of the rituals Geertz mentions is the recitation of a myth. Such a myth would contain and present not only models *of* the reality postulated by religion, but also – and especially – models *for* what he call "producing" that reality in the perception of the worshipper.[13] Saints' lives and miracle stories read in a liturgical context resemble such "myths", and an important means of what Geertz called "producing, intensifying and ... rendering inviolable by the discordant revelations of secular experience" the images and patterns – figures – of belief reality.[14]

It is precisely these images and figures that faith "sees", not only in dreams and apparitions, but also in or under sensory phenomena. Outside of meditative, drowsy or deep sleep conditions, the mental images and figures of belief reality seem to function as something like a waking dream. In what follows, I shall concentrate upon the combination of sensory perception with what, inspired by a central insight of modern psychotherapy, I shall show to be something like the visualization, and subsequent perception, of a dream.[15]

"Like a great star": Believing After Being Induced to See a Mental image

In the following story we see how (as Gregory tells it) the dream of the "really real" belief reality is learned: how mental images of this better reality, evoked by another's words, changed someone's perception of the sensory world and thereby transformed his life (*Hist.* 1.47).

On his wedding night, a new bridegroom found himself with a bride in tears. Only after a great deal of persuasion did she tell him what was troubling her: she had decided to be the – virginal – bride of Christ (as a nun) and had married only because her wealthy parents wished for heirs to their many properties – and now she regretted her decision, wishing she had died the day she was born:

> "For earthly beauties make me shudder, because I see (*suspicio*) the hands of the Redeemer pierced for the life of that world. Nor do I see (*Non cerno*) diadems flashing with precious jewels, when in my mind I gaze in wonder (*miror mente*)

> at the Crown of Thorns. I reject the stretches of your lands far and wide, because I long for (*concupisco*) the pleasantness of Paradise. Your terraces disgust me when I see (*suspicio*) the Lord seated [on His throne] above the stars".

Perceptions of earthly beauty and joy are consciously and purposely juxtaposed with, overlaid, and subsequently blocked out by more powerful images of a superior reality which the lady claims that she *sees* – in her imagination: the Passion, the Crown of Thorns, Paradise, Christ on the heavenly Throne.

When her new husband remonstrates with their parents' wishes for heirs, she counters that this transitory life is nothing compared to the life in heaven that is not ended by death or destruction. And then she describes this life in heaven: one remains "in eternal beatitude", "lives in never-setting sunlight", "enjoying the presence of the Lord Himself through contemplation, having been translated into the angelic state, and one rejoices with indissoluble gladness".

Placed alongside the evoked mental images of ineffable, lasting beauty and joy, earthly possibilities become wan and insubstantial. Through the experience of this mental comparison, the bridegroom decides to "refigure" his world view:[16]

> "Through your sweetest discourse," he said, "eternal life shines into me like a great star (*Dulcissimis, inquit, eloquiis tuis aeterna mihi tamquam magnum iubar inluxit*), and therefore if you wish to abstain from carnal desire, I will join you in this undertaking."

Gregory seems to want to show that it is the new composite image of the light-filled life in Paradise – "eternal life", experienced globally and affectively as "a great star" – which his new wife's words have evoked in him, that somehow transforms the feelings of the bridegroom about the world, and precipitates the decision to change his mode of life. With the "great star" of eternal life, central in the hymns of the period, constantly in his mind's eye, the sensory world, no doubt, appears "dark".[17] In his own way, Gregory here formulates the insight of modern clinical psychotherapy that images, as visualizations of emotional energies, can cross the threshold of consciousness in a way that verbal concepts cannot, and induce an involuntary affective mimesis of their dynamic patterns.[18] The latter can transform consciousness and activate the will.[19]

Gregory's story, then, shows not only how he thought this dream of the "really real" could be learned, but also how it was maintained: *believing itself is presented as seeing, and wishing to see, mental images regarded as representing the invisible truth.* The manner in which Gregory describes the incident makes it appear that he is aware of the necessary, and even crucial, role of the imagination in the act of "believing". As I hope to show in what follows, it is not too much to say that he is aware of this strategy of imagination as *an art of the real:* that of bringing out, for oneself and for others, the hidden but very much present and powerful dynamic dimensions of sensory phenomena and events.[20]

"Appear[ing] as though green": The Transformation of Perception Through Imaging an Empowering Symbol Upon Sensory Data

In the following brief story, we shall see that "believing" could bring out the patterns of invisible spiritual reality in visible phenomena:

> They even say that the thorns themselves of the Crown [of Thorns] appear as though green: if, however, their leaves would seem to have withered, they are nevertheless revived every day through divine power.
> *Ferunt etiam ipsas coronae sentes quasi virides apparere: quae tamen si videantur aruisse foliis, quotidie tamen revirescere virtute divina.* (*Glor. mart.* 6)[21]

Writing about what might be called the contact-relics of Christ in the East, Gregory is reporting hearsay. Although he has never seen the object in question, he is evidently prepared to believe the story (or he would not report it), and expects his readers to do the same. Yet the wording seems to suggest a hedge: the thorns are not said to "be" but to "appear as though" green. Surprisingly, however, the same holds for the opposite state: the possibility that the leaves "would seem to have withered" – suggesting that this appearance too is not in accordance with "reality". What, then, is this reality? Is it: that to some, the thorns "appear" fresh, and to others, "withered"? Or, more specifically: that though they have appeared as withered to unbelieving eyes, the "eyes of faith" have seen them to be fresh-and-green?

The next question goes to the heart of the matter: how can anyone see what is presumed by all to be a more than 500 years old crown of thorns as alive-and-green? and how can anyone believe that this antique object has been seen as such?

Gregory's wording suggests that the greenness is seen alongside the witheredness, or perhaps, as a transparent hue (as the images of imagination tend to be) over it, so that one could see the witheredness through it. In short, he may be saying that it was seen in another mode: that of the imagination – and that this imaginative vision of the believer represents the spiritual "really real" over against the dull opaqueness of mere sensory appearances.[22] Here again, he seems to be aware that "believing" needs a strategy of imagination – just as the strategy of "spiritual understanding": in other words, that it is an art of bringing out what is hidden in sensory appearances. But for him, and this is the crucial point, this imaginative strategy does not invalidate its truth. Quite the contrary: it is the only way to the truth.[23]

There is, however, again another way to look at this question. It has been shown that meditative vision – that is, perception uninhibited by practical concerns – can apperceive its objects and the space around them as vibrantly luminous.[24] I suggest that this sacred object, which had rested on Christ's head at the supreme moment of the Passion, is likely to be approached and perceived in such a manner: with deep, speechless awe. Elsewhere, Gregory himself insists upon reverence in everyone's dealings with objects in the religious sphere.[25] This reverence or awe, I suggest, would be for Gregory an essential element in what I have designated, less reverentially, as "a strategy of imagination".

But why should it, luminous or not, be perceived to appear as though green? What "reality" is pointed to in the "greenness" of five hundred year old thorns? As a contact-relic, the crown must have been thought of as participating in the life and power of the resurrected Saviour in heaven. And heaven was Paradise, always imaged as eternal youth in eternal spring. The latter is almost certainly the quality of life pointed to and transmitted by the sight of the greenness: what one perceived in this greenness was in effect, as Gregory says, divine renewal every day.

And this leads to the heart of the matter. Meditative seeing has been shown to decrease the self-object distinction:[26] one could thus experience the divine renewal through to some degree identifying with the holy object. This is another way of saying that, as we saw, associating such a symbol with an appropriate object and thus meditatively "seeing" it superimposed upon this object, can induce an analogous affective experience of this renewal in the perceiver. Seeing the symbol with "the eyes of the heart", then, is experiencing the empowerment it makes visible. The wish and the need for this must have been a strong influence upon perception. Gregory's wording, I suggest, seems to indicate that he sensed this, and regarded the conscious and controlled kind of imagination we have seen in this story as something like a legitimate kind of divinatory art – without, however, designating it as such.

Conclusion

What we have seen happening in Gregory's stories seems to be summed up by the words of a psychologist who has said: "The world we perceive is a dream we learn to have from a script we have not written".[27] The script of the dream is the Bible and its subsequent interpretations. The learning process is that of its visualization through mental images evoked by words. Once learned, the dream is imaged upon or recognized in sensory phenomena.

To be able to survive in early medieval society, the church had learned to play power politics along with everyone else. Certainly, miracles could be, and were, used to achieve and confirm socio-political status as well as to intimidate would-be predators with the power of the saintly patron in heaven.[28] It was clearly in the church's interest to convince all men of the dream's present and future reality. However, since it was able to tap immeasurable energies that directed lives, created institutions, alleviated misery and achieved innumerable cures, it is difficult to deny the dream's own extremely powerful reality.

Invisible and intangible, this reality seems to have been experienced as dynamic patterns of a generous cosmic energy which were representable to oneself and others only through the culturally determined imagination of the heart. One way of participating in these beneficent dynamic patterns was to let images of it, symbolized by and thereby "seen" as present in some phenomenon or event, cross the threshold of consciousness and initiate an analogous pattern of emotional energy within oneself.

The latter experience belongs to the essence of "believing" as we find it described everywhere in Gregory's writings about miracles. It was a *decision to see* intimations of a creative divine energy in all phenomena and events through the translation of spontaneous, or desired, affective experience into variations of the image-symbols taught by the church from its Scriptural tradition. In this way, religion or believing functioned, as Geertz has said, as a cultural system. But, over against Geertz, I hope to have shown that for Gregory it also functioned as a more or less conscious art of the real: a kind of "divination" that "saw" the empowering contours of spiritual reality through imaging them alongside or recognizing them in sensory phenomena.

Notes

1 This article was developed from a session of the international ERASMUS seminar "Word, image and reality in medieval texts", sponsored by the ERASMUS network "Nederlands in Europa", and held at the University of Utrecht on 27 January 1993.

2 The most comprehensive treatment of Gregory's life and works is found in Luce Pietri, *La ville de Tours du IVe au VIe siècle: naissance d'une cité chrétienne* (Roma: École francaise de Rome, 1983), 246-334. Gregorius Turonensis, *Historiarum Libri X* (*Hist.*), ed. and trans. Rudolf Buchner (Ausgewählte Quellen zur deutschen Geschichte des Mittelalters, Freiherr vom Stein-Gedächtnisausgabe 2 and 3) (Darmstadt: Wissenschaftliche Buchgesellschaft, 1967).

3 Gregorius Turonensis, *Vita Patrum* (*Vit. patr.*), ed. Bruno Krusch (Monumenta

Germaniae Historica, Scriptores Rerum Merovingicarum 1.2) (Hannover: Hahn, 1885), 661-744. See on this theme: Alison G. Elliott, *Roads to Paradise. Reading the Lives of the Early Saints* (Hanover-London: University Press of New England, 1987), 16-41 and 168-192.

4 Paul Ricoeur, "Imagination in discourse and in action", *Analecta Husserliana* 7 (1978): 3-22, here 15-22.

5 Clifford Geertz, "Religion as a cultural system", in: idem, *The Interpretation of Cultures* (New York: Basic Books, 1973), 87-125, here 103-118, 112.

6 Eugen Drewermann, *Tiefenpsychologie und Exegese* 2 (Olten-Freiburg im Breisgau: Walter-Verlag, 1985), 239, 330 and passim.

7 *In psalterii tractatum commentarius* (*In psal.*), ed. Bruno Krusch (Mon. Germ. Hist., Script. Rer. Merov. 1.2) (Hannover: Hahn, 1885) 873-877. On "figures" in this period, see: Erich Auerbach, "Figura", *Archivum Romanicum* 22 (1938), 436-489, here 450-474.

8 *Formulae spiritalis intelligentiae*, CSEL 16.1.

9 Gerhart B. Ladner, "Medieval and Modern Understanding of Symbolism: a Comparison", *Speculum* 54 (1979), 223-256, here 230, 252.

10 As Averil Cameron, *Christianity and the Rhetoric of Empire. The Development of Christian Discourse* (Berkeley etc.: University of California Press, 1992), 59: "For Christian language, like Christian art, was trying to express mysteries that were essentially inexpressible except through symbol".

11 W. J. T. Mitchell, *Iconology. Image, Text, Ideology* (Chicago: University of Chicago Press, 1986), 21.

12 Cf. Howard C. Kee, *Miracle in the Early Christian World. A Study in Sociohistorical Method* (New Haven-London: Yale University Press, 1983), 225-236.

13 Cf. Geertz, "Religion", 124, 112-113, 118.

14 See also Elliott, *Roads*, 73 and passim.

15 Silvan S. Tomkins, *Affect, Imagery and Consciousness* 1 (New York: Springer, 1962), 13. On the subject of mental imagery see now: Stephen M. Kosslyn, *Image and Brain. The Resolution of the Imagery Debate* (Cambridge, MA - London: MIT Press, 1994).

16 As Paul Ricoeur, *Time and Narrative*, vol. 3, Trans. Kathleen Blamey and David Pellauer (Chicago-London: University of Chicago Press, 1988),185.

17 Jan van Biezen and J.W. Schulte Nordholt ed., *Hymnen* (Tournai 1967), 9.

18 Compare Gerald Epstein, *Waking Dream Therapy: Dream Process as Imagination* (New York-London: Human Sciences Press, 1981), 18: "... images are the concretizations of emotions"; 149: "Imagination and will act interdependently".

19 As, for instance, Epstein, *Waking*, 18, and Roberto Assagioli, *Psychosynthesis. A Manual of Principles and Techniques* (New York: Viking Press, 1965) 177-189.

20 Compare on this view of art, Mitchell, *Iconology*, 39.

21 Gregorius Turonensis, *In gloria martyrum* (*Glor. mart.*), ed. Bruno Krusch (Mon. Germ. Hist., Script. Rer. Mer. 1.2) (Hannover: Hahn, 1885), 484-561.

22 Mitchell, *Iconology*, 17.

23 This understanding of Gregory's thinking about imagination as divination agrees with the way he very audaciously uses one of his own dreams as a diplomatic tool in *Hist.* 8.5. Cf. my *Views from a many-windowed tower. Studies of imagination in the works of Gregory of Tours* (Studies in classical antiquity 7) (Amsterdam: Rodopi, 1987) 285-287. See now also my "Gregory of Tours' smile: spiritual reality, imagination and earthly events in the 'Histories'", in: Anton Scharer and Georg Scheibelreiter eds., *Historiographie im frühen Mittelalter* (Wien-München 1994) (Veröffentlichungen des Instituts für Österreichische Geschichtsforschung 32) 68-95.

24 Arthur Deikman, "Deautomatization and the mystic experience", in: Charles T. Tart ed., *Altered States of Consciousness* (New York etc.: John Wiley and Sons, 1969), 23-44, here 32-33.

25 Compare *Glor. mart.* 5.: *admiratusque silui.* On proper reverence, for instance: *Glor. mart.* 47 and *Virt. Mart.* 1.35 (*De virtutibus Sancti Martini*, ed. B. Krusch (Mon. Germ. Hist., Script. Rer. Mer. 1.2) (Hannover: Hahn, 1885), 584-661. For a more sociological approach to *reverentia*, see P. Brown, "Relics and social status in the age of Gregory of Tours" (The Stenton Lecture) (Reading 1976). Reprinted in: Peter Brown, *Society and the Holy in Late Antiquity* (London: Faber and Faber, 1982), 222-250, especially 230-236.

26 Deikman, "Deautomatization", 33.

27 Tomkins, *Imagery*, 13.

28 As Peter Brown, *The Cult of the Saints. Its Rise and Function in Latin Christianity* (The Haskell Lectures on History of Religions, New Series 2) (Chicago-London: University of Chicago Press, 1981), 86-105.

VIII

Gregory of Tours' smile: spiritual reality, imagination and earthly events in the "Histories"

In the eighth book of his "Histories"[1], Bishop Gregory of Tours reports a conversation he had with King Guntram of Burgundy, holding court at Orléans, in the summer of 585. When the king returned from hunting,

> I spoke [to the king] on behalf of Count Garacharius of Bordeaux and Bladastis, who, as we said above, had fled to the church of St Martin because they had supported [the pretender] Gundowald. Because I had not been able to get anywhere with my previous request, this time I spoke to him as follows:
> "Let Your Majesty, O King, listen. Behold! I have been sent as ambassador to you by my lord. What shall I answer to him who sent me when you do not wish to give me an answer?"
> And he, struck by surprise (*obstupefactus*), said: "And who is this lord of yours, who sent you?"
> To which I replied, smiling (*Cui ego subridens*): "The blessed Martin sent me."
> Thereupon he ordered the men to be presented to him. But when they came into his presence, he reproached them with many treacheries and perjuries, repeatedly calling them clever foxes; nevertheless, he restored them to his good graces, giving them back the estates which had been taken away from them (8.6).

Why does Gregory smile — and, significantly: report himself as smiling — when he identifies the lord who sent him as St Martin? If the statement is part of a gentlemen's game of diplomacy, and known to all to be such, a smile is an acknowledgement of complicity. But then the king would not have been so taken aback. If, however, it is a statement about the compelling spiritual truth of St Martin's patronage, which plays a conspicuous role in Gregory's "Histo

---

[1] The editions of Gregory's works used in this paper are: Historiarum libri decem (Hist.) (ed. Rudolf Buchner, Ausgewählte Quellen zur deutschen Geschichte des Mittelalters 2, 3, 1967) 2 vols.; Gregorii Turonensis opera (ed. Wilhelm Arndt and Bruno Krusch, MGH SS rer Mer 1.2, 1885), in which (ed. B. Krusch): De cursu stellarum ratio (De cursu) 854—872, In gloria martyrum (Glor. mart.) 484—561, De virtutibus S. Juliani (Virt. Jul.) 562—584, De virtutibus S. Martini (Virt. Mart.) 584—661, De Vita Patrum (Vit. patr.) 661—744, In gloria confessorum (Glor. conf.) 744—820. The most complete account of his life is that of Luce Pietri, La ville de Tours du IVe au VIe siècle: naissance d'une cité chrétienne (Roma 1983) 246—334.

ries", not to mention his four books of the saint's miracles, humour seems out of place. Or could Gregory have been conscious of playing a serious game? In other words: was he aware of the role of imagination in his view of "reality"?

Since Gregory's historical writing usually passes for one of the most naively credulous of all sorts of more-than-natural events[2], this is a crucial question. His stories show that this courageous and in many ways very businesslike bishop grounded his position as well as his personal life squarely upon the power of Tours' dead patron saint — in short, in the sphere of an invisible spiritual reality. If it can be shown that he is aware of what we might call an imaginative strategy in apprehending and dealing with this reality, a new perspective on his complex personality seems to open.

Although Gregory's "really real" reality[3] is invisible, he implies that it is possible to "look toward" it — meaning respect, but perhaps also something more — as in the following tantalizing reference to a typical worldly noble: "nor does he look toward those things which are not seen (*nec respicit ad ea quae non videntur*)" (Vit. patr. 6. prol.). It is a different kind of looking. Of Christ's resurrection, our author says that "it inspired the minds of the faithful to the contemplation of heavenly things (*mentes fidelium ad contemplanda coelestia animavit*)" (Glor. mart. 4).

Eufrasius, a priest of senatorial family, did not look toward things unseen, however, and in what Gregory writes about him we can discern something like dual spheres of reality: "I believe that what prevented him from obtaining [the bishopric of Clermont] is that he wished to achieve these honours not through God, but through men" (4.35). Thus Eufrasius sent gifts (bought from Jews) to the king instead of trying to obtain such a position through merit; he was elegant in manners rather than chaste in living; and instead of feeding the poor, he inebriated the "barbarians" (i. e. prominent Franks). Elsewhere, making a similar point, our author paraphrases Romans 8:38: "For those who love God all things turn out well" (6.36), as, for instance, the emperor Tiberius: his enemies "were not able to do anything against the man who placed his trust in God" (5.30). In personal spiritual development: "unless [the Lord] himself shall have built the house, those who work on it labour in vain" (1.15; Ps. 127.1).

On the other hand, sinful conduct brings on divine punishment in the form of visible events: "because the people's sins were not congruous [i. e. acceptable,

---

[2] For instance, Godefroid Kurth, De l'autorité de Grégoire de Tours, in: idem, Études Franques 2 (Paris-Bruxelles 1919) 122: "il ne connaît rien de plus naturel que le surnaturel"; James W. Thompson, A history of historical writing 1 (New York 1942) 148: "the naiveté of a child"; 149—150: "credulous but otherwise honest and sincere"; Emil H. Walter, Hagiographisches in Gregor's Frankengeschichte. Archiv für Kulturgeschichte 48 (1966) 305: „. . . die gewisse Unbefangenheit und Naivität, mit der er seine Erzählungen hagiographisch stilisiert", „Indem sein frommer Sinn sich nie über ein bestimmtes Niveau unreflektierter Wundergläubigkeit erhebt. . .". Cf. however: Giselle de Nie, Views from a many-windowed tower. Studies of imagination in the works of Gregory of Tours (Studies in classical antiquity 7, Amsterdam 1987) 209.

[3] Clifford Geertz, Religion as a cultural system, in: idem, The interpretation of cultures (New York 1973) 112.

to the divine will] (*peccatis populi incongruentibus*)", the cruel and devious Leudast was sent to Tours as count (5.48). As we shall see, congruity or analogy is perhaps the central model of Gregory's thinking about spiritual reality. God is thought to "connect *(conect[ere])*" men's wills with his own (9.39; cf. 1.15), as also when King Guntram,

> pouring (*transfundens*) his whole hope in the mercy of the Lord, and throwing the thoughts coming over him [up] to [God], by whom he believed with the integrity of total faith that they would be given over to be carried out (*in ipso iactans cogitationes, quae ei superveniebant, a quo eas effectui tradi tota fidei integritate putabat*) (9.21).

With all this, Gregory is saying not only that the sphere of invisible spiritual reality has other dynamics than its sensory counterpart, but also that only these are the really effective ones in the visible world.

How, according to Gregory, can one "look toward" or "contemplate" what cannot be seen? In what follows I shall argue that what he describes as the manner of looking toward the unseen — and also as that of actually perceiving it — is analogous to what he lets us see of the late antique method of finding hidden spiritual meanings in biblical texts. But, rather than seeing "the world as a text", I suggest that he tends to see both text and world primarily in terms of images that are symbols of spiritual truths. Usually derived in one way or another from the Bible, they exhibit multidimensional religious truths that resist verbalizing, and function as mediators between the spiritual sphere and that of human understanding[4]. In other words, I shall be attempting to show that Gregory was perfectly aware of his and others' apperceiving spiritual reality through the mediation of a strategy of meditative, literary imagination that recognized analogies of spiritual symbols and dynamics in the phenomena and events in the visible world. The "real" truth, that is the spiritual rather than the sensory reality, could thus — except possibly in visions — never be directly perceived; it could only be mentally abstracted and visualized from its intimations in the visible sphere[5]. In contrast to the modern world view, this use of imagination, then, was thought to come closer to "truth" than sensory observation.

In what follows, I shall first look at what Gregory tells us about recognizing images of hidden divine messages in the sacred text, then at his reports of indirect or direct "seeing" of invisible spiritual reality in the world, and finally at two stories in which he seems to reveal his view of the role of imagination in the communication of these experiences to others.

---

[4] As also Eugen Drewermann, Tiefenpsychologie und Exegese 2 (1985) 129.

[5] Compare W. J. T. Mitchell, Iconology. Image, text, ideology (Chicago 1986) 21.

I. *Mysteria figurata*: reading with "the eyes of the heart"

When a heretic bishop, Cirola, had pretended to heal a healthy man in public from blindness in order to get even with his Catholic rivals, and the man thereupon (by divine intervention) became actually blind, Gregory makes the message of this story explicit:

> Through the blindness of this man ... it was made most clear how the bishop of the heretics was covering the eyes of [men's] hearts (*oculos cordium*) with the miserable veil of his doctrine, so that no one would be able to contemplate the true Light with the eyes of faith (*ne veram lucem ulli liceret fidei oculis contemplare*). O wretch, who, ... in the depravity of his own heart, tried to extinguish the light of faith (*facem fidei*) in the hearts of the believers! (2.3)

"The true Light" is, of course, Christ (Jn 1:9), in the Catholic view an equal part of the Trinity, and the place to "contemplate" him as such with "the eyes of the heart" (cf. Eph. 4:18)[6] is in the sacred text of the Bible. "The light of faith" in the believers' "hearts" makes these eyes "the eyes of faith", through which a hidden meaning in the text can be discerned. Gregory actually seems to be saying that they see what they wish to believe, but also: that it is really there. This is a contradiction only if one takes the understanding of a text to be derived exclusively from the latter. It is clear that Gregory's kind of understanding is meant to precede and exist independently of the text — in the reader[7].

In his brief review of Old Testament history, Gregory tells us what kind of understanding this is. Speaking of the "divisions" of the Red Sea during the Israelites' dry crossing, he says:

> These divisions should be understood spiritually and not according to the letter (*spiritaliter et non secundum littera[m] intellegere oportit*). For there also are many divisions in this life of the world, which is figurally called the sea (*in hoc saeculo, quod figuraliter mare dicitur*) (1.10).

Similarly, he says elsewhere:

> Those who narrate the deeds [of the Psalms] according to the letter in a sane manner, perceive that these have a truth of spiritual understanding (*Illi qui sane res gestas secundum litteram narrant veritatem spiritalis intelligentiae cognoscuntur habere*) (In psal...prol.).

The Psalms in their surface text, then, conceal and at the same time "show (*ostendunt*)", "show forth (*produnt*)", "teach (*docent*)", "foresee (*provid[unt]*)", "announce (*pronunci[an]t*)", "prefigured (*praefigurav[erun]t*)", and "point to

[6] Gregory nowhere mentions Augustine but the latter's central ideas must have reached him through church tradition: cf. Margaret Miles, Vision: the eye of the body and the eye of the mind in Saint Augustine's "De Trinitate" and "Confessions". Journal of Religion 63 (1983) 125—142.

[7] Karl F. Morrison, History as a visual art in the twelfth-century Renaissance (Princeton 1990) 20—47 describes "history as an art of the imagination" in Bede and in the twelfth century.

(*designa[n]t*)", the incarnation of Christ and his Redemption of the world as a deeper meaning which is the real, spiritual one. The same is true of the whole of the Old Testament. This so-called allegorical method of interpretation, evident, for instance, in 2 Cor. 3:6, was prevalent in early Christian writers. Its essence is the discernment of hidden, inhering spiritual "forms" or "figures" in the patterning of the surface text[8].

In the first part of the "Histories", Gregory writes that Adam, Noah and Joseph (and implicitly also Zorobabel) were each a *typus* — form, image, or prefiguration — of Christ, the Redeemer (1.1, 4, 9, 15; resp. Gn 2:19; 6:9; 30:24; Ezek 2:2). In addition, the Ark is the *typus* of the Church, the Red Sea crossing and the pillar of cloud the *typus* of Christian baptism, the pillar of fire the *typus* of the Holy Spirit, and the Babylonian Captivity the *typus* of the unredeemed soul's captivity in sin (1.4, 10, 15; resp. Gn 6:14; Ex 14:21—22; 13:21; 13:21; 2 Ki 25:11).

The prologue to Book 3 prepares the reader to expect to see in the following stories that those who confessed the Catholic view of the Trinity prospered and those who did not lost everything. Gregory continues:

> I will pass over, however, how Abraham venerated it near the oak, how Jacob foretold (*praedicat*) it in his blessing, how Moses recognized (*cognuscit*) it in the thorn bush, that the people followed it in the cloud and trembled before it at the mountain, and how Aaron carried it in his breastplate and David prophesied (*vaticinatur*) in the psalm. . .. (3. prol.; resp. Gn 18:1; 49:24—25; Ex 3:2; 13:21; 19:17—18; 28:25—30; Ps 28:25—30).

How much we would have liked to have had more details about his manner of finding the Trinity in these visible, verbal, and visionary forms! Some of them occur again in Gregory's angry retort to King Chilperic's attempt to dictate his (heretical) views of the Trinity to the episcopate:

> ". . . You would do better if you were to arm yourself with the faith which Abraham saw (*vidit*) at the oak, Isaac in the goat, Jacob in the stone, and Moses in the thorn bush; which Aaron carried in his breastshield, David glorified with the tympanum, and Solomon foretold (*praedicavit*) in understanding; which all the patriarchs, prophets and the law itself either prophesied in their oracles or prefigured in their sacrifices (*sacrificiis figuravit*) . . . (5.43; resp. Gn 22:13; 28:11ff).

The Trinity — impossible to clarify or defend in rational language — is apprehended, inspected and communicated as an image, even as a series of overlapping images. The same king later said to a Jewish merchant friend: "O hard mind, and ever unbelieving generation, that does not understand that the mysteries of the church were prefigured in its sacrifices (*ecclesiastica mystiria in suis sacrificiis figurata*)!" (6.5). Gregory must mean here that the inexpressible mystery of the Eucharist, representing Christ's sacrifice, is prefigured in the Old Testament sacrifices.

To a Jew, Gregory explains that Christ himself had to come in the flesh to save men because the Israelites could not be moved to understand in any other

[8] Erich Auerbach, Figura. Archivum Romanicum 22 (1938) 450—474.

way; he paraphrases Isaiah's prophecy of the suffering servant: "As (*Sicut*) a sheep that is led to slaughter; and as though a lamb (*quasi agnus*) that is silent before its shearers" (6.5; Is. 53:7). Here the qualification "as though", which will be discussed in another section, is used to point to the dominant symbol of Christ as the Lamb; it therefore indicates a spiritual truth. And when Jacob blesses Judah, Gregory describes him as speaking "as though (*quasi*) to Christ himself, the son of God" (idem; cf. Gen. 49:8 ff.).

In an attempt to convince one of his own priests of the reality of the future resurrection, Gregory again adduces many sayings from the Old Testament (*verba*) (10.13). A "proof (*indicium*)", however, is Elisha's raising of the dead boy (2 Ki 13:21). Christ's words to the rich man roasting in hell, in his parable (*in parabola*) about the same, are also brought up (Lk 16:23). Centrally, Christ's death and resurrection is the model of ours. However, "[t]here are many witnesses (*testimonia*) to these things, which prove this matter. For the elements that we see show (*demonstrant*) this resurrection . . .": the trees that lose their leaves in the autumn and, "as though rising again (*quasi resurgentes*)" clothe themselves with leaves again. Seeds sprouting in the earth "exhibit (*ostendunt*)" the same. Gregory concludes his array of proofs: "All these things are manifested to the world [to induce] belief in the resurrection (*ad fidem resurrectionis mundo manifesta sunt*)." And thus he has shown us how he continues the strategy for the discovery of hidden spiritual meaning in the sacred text in his looking at the visible world of nature.

For our author, then, the "real" truth of things could never be directly seen; it had to be mentally abstracted from analogical appearances. How, in this period, almost all visible phenomena could be perceived as symbols of spiritual reality is evident in a book such as that of the fifth-century Eucherius of Lyon — called "The forms of spiritual understanding" (*Formulae spiritualis intelligentiae*) — which Gregory must have known[9]. What we see, then, is a theology expressed in images of visible forms and events. Awareness and understanding of what are understood to be divine patterns in human experience are mediated by mental images.

II. *Fidei oculi*: seeing the invisible

When St Martin's successor to the episcopate at Tours was driven away by his people, Gregory lets him say:

> "I suffer this deservedly, because I sinned against the holy man and often called him mad and insane, and did not believe his miracles when I saw them (*cuius videns virtutes non credidi*)" (2.1).

Seeing and yet not believing is something that also occurs in the New Testament (Mk 8:18). As we have seen, in the case of the heretic bishop Cirola, Greg-

---

[9] Eucherius Lugdunensis, Formularum spiritualis intelligentiae (Migne, PL 50, Paris 1859) col. 727—772.

ory connects not seeing spiritual reality with not believing in the real (Catholic view of) God (2.3). He says something similar about the Jews in Clermont:

> When the blessed Bishop Avitus warned them repeatedly to leave behind the veil (*velamen*) of the Mosaic law so that they should understand what they read spiritually (*spiritaliter lecta intellegerent*), and contemplate with a pure heart in the sacred letters (*corde purissimo in sacris litteris contemplarent*) Christ, Son of the living God, promised by the prophetic and legal authority, there remained in their hearts not only that veil which had darkened Moses' face, but a wall (*paries*). When the bishop had been praying that they would convert to the Lord and that the veil of the letter would be torn away from them (*velamen ab eis litterae rumperetur*), one of them requested to be baptized at the holy feast of Easter... (5.11; cf. 2 Cor 3: 13—16).

When some unconverted Jews proceeded to throw rancid oil on the baptized man, however, the Christian community retaliated by destroying their synagogue completely. No doubt to avoid further violence, the bishop then invited the Jews to be baptized or leave the city, and many accepted Christianity. I think Gregory meant the visible events in this story to replicate the invisible: the destruction of the synagogue stands for the destruction of the "wall" (why use this metaphor otherwise?) in their minds. Thus we see a central strategy in Gregory's writing. He uses literary metaphor to point to an invisible truth that may also be recognized in visible events[10]. The literary image can connect the visible sensory sphere with the iconic understanding of the spiritual one.

As for the surface text — "the letter" or literal meaning — of the Holy Scripture: it is "a veil of the letter", causing a veil or even a "wall" in men's minds that prevents them from "contemplating" (the Christian view of) spiritual truth with their hearts through the letters. Thus "seeing" spiritual truth is contingent upon the prior acceptance of the model of what one is to look for: then one recognizes it in the text. Similarly, Brictius had regarded Martin's meditative attitude (the latter was always praying: *semper orabat*)[11] and his visions as absent-mindedness and phantasies or hallucinations[12]. He was not willing to see them with "the eyes of the heart" and accept them as manifestations of the sphere of the divine. Seeing spiritual reality, then, in texts and in the world, was an imagination of the heart.

In this context, we will investigate the role of imagination in the various degrees of "seeing" the invisible. Recognizing spiritual patterns in visible human events and seeing them in natural phenomena will first be considered. Then, as a preparation for what follows, Gregory's different uses of the hinge term *quasi* will be looked at. Descriptions of really "seeing the invisible" are those of miraculous appearances and of visions, which will thereupon be analyzed.

---

[10] De Nie, Views 165—176.

[11] Sulpicius Severus, Vita S. Martini 26.4 (ed. Jacques Fontaine, Sources chrétiennes 133/1, Paris 1967) 314.

[12] Cf. Clare Stancliffe, St Martin and his hagiographer. History and miracle in Sulpicius Severus (Oxford 1983) 158.

A. *Gubernatio Dei*: treasure in heaven and on earth

For Gregory, God had not only created the world, but was also still directing it in every phenomenon and event. This is clear when our author lets the holy priest Severus address God as: "Almighty God, by whose command (*nutu*) all things are directed (*gubernantur*), by whose command (*imperio*) that which is not born is created, the created live, [and] the dead are reformed . . ." (Glor. conf. 50). A detailed investigation of Gregory's views of divine dynamics in his "Histories", though no doubt rewarding, cannot be undertaken here. I shall focus upon the recognition of a few explicitly biblical patterns and several patterns that appear, at least in part, to be derived from these[13], and close with a comparison of human and divine dynamics in two rulers.

A first prominent Old Testament pattern that is mentioned in Gregory's review of the latter and which returns as an interpretation of a later event is that of subjection by alien peoples as a punishment for the people's sins, and their liberation when they repent (1.12). It reappears in the description of the Longobards' invasion of Frankish land. There the hermit Hospitius prophesies the event by saying: "The Langobards will come into the Gauls and lay waste seven cities, because their wickedness will have grown before the face of God. . ." (6.6). The underlying pattern, however, is that of enslavement through sin, also made visible in biblical history — in the Babylonian captivity: "this captivity exhibits the figure (*typum . . . gerit*) of that captivity, as I think, in which the sinful soul is abducted and lives in horrible exile, unless Zorobabel, that is Christ, should have liberated her" (1.15). In the allegorical interpretation of the Bible, visible events concerning large numbers of people can point to and stand for invisible ones in the individual.

The repeated biblical warning that he who lays a trap for another will fall into it himself (Ps. 7:16; Prov. 26:27) is one model used to explain the bad fortunes of kings warring against their own family (2.40; 4.51). Another model is that of biblical events: for instance the example of David and Absalom (2 Sam. 18). What Gregory lets King Clothar, "as a new David about to fight against his son Absalom", say in this case brings us to the view of battle as an ordeal:

> "Look down from heaven, Lord, and judge my cause [Ps. 80:15; 43:1; 1 Sam. 24:16], for I suffer unjust injuries by my son. Look down, Lord, and judge righteously [Lev. 19:15], and impose that judgment which you once imposed between Absalom and his father David" (4.20).

It is a notion that returns frequently (as for instance in 6.31; 7.14; 7.32; 7.38; 8.2). Victory in battle, then, "is in the hand of God" (7.41), and an unjust war — being sin — will bring down the wrath of God (*ira Dei*) (4.14; Jos. 9.20). The royal brothers' wars against each other are thus also the reason for their

[13] Cf. Massimo Oldoni, Gregorio di Tours e i "Libri Historiarum": letture e fonti, metodi e ragioni. Studi medievali ser. 3, 13 (1972) 672—690, and Felix Thürlemann, Der historische Diskurs bei Gregor von Tours. Topoi und Wirklichkeit (Geist und Werk der Zeiten 39, Bern 1974) 86—94.

present misfortunes: "because you do not have peace, you lack God's grace" (5. prol.). Conversely, when three warring brothers avoid war by making peace, and on the same day, far away in St Martin's church, three cripples are healed, Gregory sees a homology that reveals the action of the saint's power (4.50). Elsewhere, King Guntram is made to tell his unsuccessful army that only those who are in the right and place all their hope in God (Ps. 78:7), receive his aid in war; his army, however, has done just the opposite — killing the church's ministers, as well as destroying and ridiculing her sacred relics:

> "Where such things are done, no victory can be obtained. Therefore our hands are weak [cf. Num. 11:23], our sword becomes soft, nor does our shield defend and protect us as it used to. . ." (8.30).

This can only be "the divine vengeance (*ultio divina*), which is accustomed to deliver his servants from the mouths of rabid dogs", as Gregory writes upon another occasion (8.12). In various forms, this motif, too, recurs often (as in 4.16; 4.18; 5.18; 5.20; 7.35; 8.20; 10.22). The unarmed position of the church and the prevalence of violent revenges in the society in which Gregory found himself almost certainly have something to do with his vindictiveness here. In the same way, the frequent inadequacy of Frankish justice will have been connected with his references to God as the avenger of innocent blood, also derived from the Bible (e. g. Deut. 32:43) (2.4; 2.25; 5.5; 7.3). Gregory, then, understandably wished to see — and impress others with — as much of divine justice as he could recognize in the insufficiently ordered society in which he lived.

Not directly traceable to the Bible, as far as I know, is Gregory's predilection for analogies. For divine punishments were also recognizable, as he describes them, by their frequent similarity of form to the sin or crime committed. Noah's son Cham's case is typical: "through false power he exhibited (*ostendebat*) to men stars and fire falling from heaven"; he who taught them to worship fire, "was himself consumed divinely by fire" (1.5). Similar is the case of the warrior at Soissons who carved up the bishop of Reims' chalice with his battle axe; Clovis split the man's head with his battle axe a year later (2.27). Gregory lets Bishop Iniuriosus of Tours say to the king who attempted to levy taxes on "the poor", that is, the church: "If you wish to take away the things of God, the Lord will speedily take your kingdom away from you . . ." (4.2). The principle is made explicit in what our author lets Abbot Avitus — imitating the role of the prophet in the Old Testament — say to King Godomar:

> "If you look toward (*respiciens*) God and change your plan, so that you do not let these people [his mother's family] be killed, God will be with you, and you will go out and obtain victory; but if you kill them, you will be given into the hands of your enemies and perish through a similar lot (*simili sorte peribis*); to you and your wife and sons will be done what you shall do to Sigismund and his wife and children" (3.6).

And so both parties ended their lives at the bottom of a well. Likewise, when King Guntram's second wife poisoned his only son by an earlier marriage, she lost her own son, and later her life (4.25). And when King Guntram let Magnacharius' two sons be killed for slandering his new wife (who had been a slave in their household), he lost his own sons by a sudden death and since then remained childless (5.17). Gregory's reasoning behind all this may have been that, in the spiritual sphere, when one harms another, one in fact harms oneself. For as we shall see, when he tells King Guntram in a dream not to insult the saint by dragging the latter's protegé from his church, he says: "Don't kill yourself with your own javelin! For, if you do this, you will lose the present life as well as the eternal!" (7.22). And so, again, visible events were thought to replicate invisible ones.

In the characterization of two very different rulers we see something of Gregory's view of the way of the world as contrasted with the way of God, and the visible results of each. "The Nero and Herod of our times", the Frankish King Chilperic, oppressed his subjects in many ways, especially by cruelty and injustice, levying heavy taxes, seizing inheritances, and despoiling even the church (6.46). After a number of natural disasters had taken place, and extraordinary natural phenomena had appeared (about which more will be said below), and the kings were again preparing to go to war with each other — the disorder in nature reflects that in the kingdom — an epidemic broke out in 580. The unexpressed message of this apposition is that the latter is a divine punishment for the former[14]. And sure enough, Chilperic's sons fall ill. Gregory thereupon lets Queen Fredegunde, whom he elsewhere shows doing the most malicious things, repent of their grasping acts and deliver what can only be an invented speech to her husband, in which she expresses his own views on the matter:

> "For a long time the Divine Love has sustained us while we did evil; for he often chastised us through fevers and other ills, and there was no improvement. Behold! now we are losing our sons. Behold! now the tears of the poor, the laments of the widows, the sighs of the orphans are killing them, and no hope remains for the ones for whom we collect things. We pile up treasures, not knowing for whom we do this. Behold, our treasures, filled with the curses of robbery, will remain without a possessor! . . . Behold, we are losing the most beautiful that we have! Now, if it pleases you, come: let us burn all wicked taxation orders, and let that which was enough for our father and king Clothar be enough for our fisc!" (5.34).

Although the tax books were burned, this did not save their sons. Equally belatedly, Chilperic thereafter gave many gifts to churches and alms to the poor anyway. The dynamic pattern here is that taking from others results in losing — through divine action — what one has. In other words, the dynamic of the divine is the inverse of the earthly one: "For whoever would save his life will lose it, and whoever loses his life for my sake will find it" (Mt 16:25).

The story of Emperor Tiberius in the East exhibits this pattern from the opposite side. He is described as "capable, strong and wise, the best protector of alms and the poor" (5.19). He distributed to the poor many of the treasures that

---

[14] Cf. de Nie, Views 37.

his avaricious predecessor had collected, reminding his worried wife of the indestructible treasure that they were thus collecting in heaven (Mt 6:20): "Therefore, from what God gave, we gather [treasures] through the poor in heaven, so that the Lord might deign to give us more in this worldly life". And indeed, "the Lord gave him more and more". Two buried treasures were found and turned over to him; he gave it all to the poor — "and, because of his good will, the Lord never let him want for anything". Concrete visible events thus exhibit the dynamic that those who give, will receive spiritual treasures; and those who take from others, will lose these.

Gregory has created stories that are admixtures of fact and imagination: the speeches are clearly literary inventions and used to express his own views on the matters in question. Nevertheless, these stories are intended to exhibit the patterns or "figures" of the real, spiritual truth. Reception theory and our own experience shows us that we recreate in our imagination what we read and see, and thereby experience it[15]. Gregory intended his stories to induce in the reader the recreation of the dynamic form of the transcendent reality he portrays in action[16], so that this experience could do its work.

B. *Figura*: a sword in the sky

Not only in sacred texts and in human events does Gregory see "figures" of divine patterns, but also in the phenomena of the natural world. In this, he is combining the biblical view of God-given *signa*, *prodigia* and *portenta* that announce or accomplish his purposes with Rome's divinatory tradition as represented in its historiography[17]. His strong expectation of analogies between natural and human events, not stressed in the Bible, probably derives from Roman influence. As we have seen, however, analogies, which are also the hinge notion and central tool of the allegorical method of interpretation, structure Gregory's view of all reality. Images, patterns and forms standing for essential processes are expected and recognized in everything, and thus man's inner and outer worlds and the cosmos are experienced as constituting a continuum. Yet, as we shall see, when describing natural phenomena as signs, prodigies or portents, Gregory often uses the expressions "were shown" and "appeared". Is it because he regards their ontological status as somehow different from that of other visible reality? Does their perception have a quality different from ordinary sen-

---

[15] As, for instance, Paul Ricoeur, Time and narrative 3 (transl. Kathleen Blamey and David Pellauer, Chicago 1988) 184: "Reenactment is the telos of historical imagination . . . The historical imagination, in return, is the organon of reenactment. . . . it is still the imaginary that keeps otherness from slipping into the unsayable."

[16] Cf. Sallie McFague, Speaking in parables. A study in metaphor and theology (Philadelphia 1975) 126—127: ". . . moving from the mundane — but never leaving it behind — to the transcendent by "figuring" it in terms of the human metaphor."

[17] Cf. Raymond Bloch, Les prodiges dans l'antiquité classique (Paris 1963); and K. Berger, Hellenistisch-heidnische Prodigien und die Vorzeichen in der jüdischen und christlichen Apokalyptik, in: Aufstieg und Niedergang der römischen Welt 2.23.2 (ed. Wolfgang Haase, 1980) 1428—1469. On Gregory's treatment of prodigies in his "Histories" as a whole: de Nie, Views 27—69.

sory experience? In other words, is he aware of using a strategy of imagination — perhaps like that of the "spiritual understanding" of texts — in the recognition of these phenomena?

Closest to the Roman pattern of reacting to prodigies is the case of Vienne under its bishop Mamertus. During a whole year, it "was frightened" by repeated earthquakes and wild animals roaming about in the city; at Easter, during the mass, the royal palace was suddenly ablaze "through divine fire". When everyone had run out, thinking that the whole city would be burned or swallowed by the earth,

> the holy bishop, prostrated before the altar, implored the mercy of the Lord with sighs and tears. In short, the prayer of the eminent bishop penetrated the heights of heaven, and the river of his forthpouring tears extinguished the fire of the house (2.34).

Here again, is a metaphor that Gregory may have intended to be taken as a possible image of what is happening in the sphere of invisible spiritual reality. The bishop instituted a "rogation", to be held every year before Ascension day: a day of fasting, certain prayers and almsgiving. Thereupon the "terrors" stopped. In ancient Rome the gods had been held responsible for exactly the same phenomena, and appeasement by rituals was also customary there[18]. In a description of these events by the early sixth-century bishop of Vienne, Avitus, (which may have been Gregory's source) the prodigies are explicitly compared with God's punishment of Sodom and Nineveh[19]. Gregory may have regarded this association as self-evident.

In the first half of the "Histories", extraordinary natural phenomena tend to be interpreted as indications of divine anger and/or annunciations of imminent punishment — sometimes in the form of a royal death. Thus Gregory says in his "Treatise on the course of the stars" about comets:

> It appears (*apparet*) not always, but mostly in connection with either the death of a king or the slaughter of a region. This is the way in which it is to be understood (*intellegatur*). When a hairy head appears (*apparuerit*) flashing with a crown, it announces (*adnuntiat*) a royal death; but if, flashing, it carries (*ferens*) a sword, [and] when it scatters hairs with blackness, it shows (*monstrat*) the wiping out of the fatherland. For thus it also appeared (*apparuit*) before the pest of the region of Clermont, hanging above that region for a whole year (De cursu 34).

Gregory connects the deaths of about half of the Frankish royalty explicitly with comets or other anomalies in nature (2.20; 4.9; 4.51; 5.18; 6.33—34; 7.11). Divine anger imaged as a sword also appears in a vision of the holy Bishop Salvius, who saw it hanging over a villa of King Chilperic, twenty days before the death of his young sons. Gregory, standing beside him, and having thought his friend was joking when the latter asked him whether he saw anything besides the new roof, saw nothing (5.50). When "a great prodigy" and other strange

[18] Bloch, Prodiges 120—129; de Nie, Views 32—33.

[19] Avitus Viennensis, Homilia in rogationibus (ed. Rudolfus Peiper, MGH AA 6/2, 1883) 108—112.

sights were seen after a prince's death, however, Gregory says "[b]ut what these will have figured (*figuraverint*) I don't know" (5.23).

In two cases, he connects extraordinary natural phenomena, without designating them as signs or prodigies, however, with the death of a king. Both of these were heretics, and they had persecuted Catholic Christians. When the Vandal king Huneric died: "the sun appeared (*apparuit*) black so that scarcely a third of it shone. I believe [this happened] because of so many crimes and the spilling of innocent blood" (2.3). When, not long afterwards, the Visigothic King Euric died, "there was . . . a great earthquake" (2.20). Both a solar eclipse and an earthquake are mentioned in connection with the innocent death of Christ on the cross (e. g. Mt 27:45, 51—4); in his brief resumé of this event, Gregory himself mentions only the darkness (1.20). It seems as if every crime against the harmony of the cosmos reverberates in the whole.

In the latter part of his work, however, there are many prodigies and signs, designated as such, that Gregory does not know what to do with. He tells us that in 585, while staying with a friend in the Ardennes,

> we saw during two nights signs (*signa*) in the sky: that is, rays from the north so bright as they had not been seen to appear before (*ut prius sic apparuisse non fuerunt visi*); and from two sides, that is from east and west, bloodred clouds [were seen]. Also on the third night around (*quasi*) the second hour, these rays appeared. And behold! while we were watching them, stunned, similar rays appeared from the four corners of the earth; and we see the whole sky being covered by these. In the middle of the sky there was a glowing cloud and the rays all tended toward it in the manner of a pavilion .... Between the rays there were still other clouds flashing and gleaming brightly. This sign (*signum*) inspired us with great fear, for we suspected that some disaster would be sent upon us from heaven (8.17).

Did he indeed think of some calamity, or was he — covertly — also thinking of Luke's description of the Second Coming of Christ: "For as the lightning flashes and lights up the sky from one side to the other, so will the Son of Man be in his day (*nam sicut fulgur coruscans de sub caelo, in ea quae sub caelo sunt, fulget, ita erit Filius hominis in die sua*)" (Lk 17:24; cf. Mt 24:27)? Somewhat later, Gregory reports that two islands in the sea had burned through divine fire for two days, after which they were swallowed by the sea; and that many said that the glow he had seen in the sky — for which he then uses the expression "as though the sky were burning (*quasi ardere caelum*)" — was their reflection (8.24). Immediately after this, he reports a pond on an island near Vannes having turned into blood (8.25). Again, there maybe an unexpressed apocalyptic association here: the Book of Revelation reports that "something like a great mountain, burning with fire, was thrown into the sea", and that water turned into blood in the final cataclysm of the earth (Rev. 8:8—9; 11:6; 16:3). At the back of all this is probably Joel's rendering of the divine words: "And I will give prodigies in the sky (*dabo prodigia in caelo*) and blood upon the earth and fire and the vapour of smoke; and the sun shall turn into darkness and the moon into blood before the great and dreadful Day of the Lord comes" (Joel 2:30—1).

That this suspicion is not farfetched becomes evident in book 9. Here Gregory first reports that a new spate of prodigies appeared (*apparuerunt*) in 587: household utensils in a number of homes were inscribed with strange signs which could not be removed; in October, after the grape harvest, he saw (*vidimus*) new shoots with deformed grapes; "in other trees, new twigs and new apples were seen (*visa sunt*)"; rays appeared (*apparuerunt*) in the north; Some said they had seen serpents falling from the clouds, while others were sure that a whole villa had suddenly fallen apart and disappeared with houses and men. Gregory concludes this list with the comment: "And many other signs appeared (*signa apparuerunt*) which usually announce (*adnuntiare*) a king's death or the slaughter of a region" (9.5). Apart from enormous rainfall and consequent high water, mentioned after this, there seems to be no apposite event, however. Yet in the very next chapter, he recognizes in two wandering preachers and healers the "pseudochrists and pseudoprophets" foretold by Christ as arising in "the last times" before the end of the world (9.6; Mt 24:24).

In book 10, after having listed a number of light phenomena in the sky as well as torrential rains and thunder, high water and a subsequent epidemic of the pest (10.23), and before telling us about another impostor prophet, Gregory shares with us what he had probably been thinking already for some time:

> For these are the beginnings of the sufferings [Mt 24:8] about which the Lord spoke in the Gospel: "There will be pestilence and famine and earthquakes everywhere [Mt 24:7]; and pseudochrists and pseudoprophets will arise and give signs and prodigies in the sky (*et dabunt signa et prodigia in caelo*), so that they will lead even the elect astray" [Mk 13:22], as has been happening in the present time (10.25).

As I have explained elsewhere[20], I do not believe that Gregory attributed the celestial signs to these impostors. He must have fused Matthew's passage about the prophets giving great signs and prodigies (*dabunt signa magna et prodigia*) with Luke's similar rendering of Christ's words (without mention of the prophets) continuing with "and there will be terrors and great signs from heaven (*terrores de caelo et signa magna erunt*)" (Lk 21:11). Both are probably reminiscences of Joel 2:30 (repeated in Acts 2:19—20). Thus Gregory has changed his interpretation of extraordinary natural phenomena from one based upon Roman divinatory thinking and Old Testament examples of the chastising God, to a view based upon apocalyptic images, in the Old as well as the New Testament.

To return to our questions at the beginning of this section: why the verbs "were shown (or: exhibited)", "appeared" and "were seen" instead of simply "were", even when the things seen seem recognizable as northern lights, meteorological phenomena, and plant aberrations due to unseasonal weather? This, of course, does not hold for vanishing villas, ponds turning into blood, and unknown signs on household utensils — to name only a few. One is tempted to think, however, that a landslide, a setting sun and runes as a magical practice

---

[20] De Nie, Views 53—55.

may have been involved, and that there must be similar explanations for the many other strange happenings which Gregory reports.

But that would still not explain why Gregory at least, if not others, tended to see these happenings as created by God through direct intervention as a message to men. Gregory, in short, regards these phenomena essentially as miracles — for which he uses the same terms of showing and appearing. What in fact "appears" and "is shown" is a "figure" or image-message from God. As we saw, "ordinary" nature was already full of images supporting the truth of religion; aberrations of nature exhibited God's reply to men's disturbance of cosmic harmony by their sinful actions. Gregory senses direct divine intervention in them. God used written words and visible events to "talk" to men: it was up to men to "decipher" them. And the latter meant having the full array of Scriptural images at hand as "visual concepts"[21] to "see" them through.

C. *Quasi*: true and false imagination

In the investigation of the role of imagination[22], *quasi* is a hinge term. Broadly speaking, it is used in eight kinds of meanings in the Histories: 1) an estimate of numbers; 2) envisionings of a future reality that does not come about; 3) illusion; 4) "in the function of", "as"; 5) qualitative likeness, a simile; 6) simile as a "figure" of spiritual truth; 7) the perceptual quality of miracles; 8) the same in true spiritual visions. The last two meanings will be discussed in the sections on miracles and visions.

Estimated numbers

When Gregory writes: *Obiit autem Sicharius quasi annorum XX*, it is not difficult to see an estimate in this (9.19). The same holds for his reporting a celestial phenomenon "at about (*quasi*) the second hour" (8.17). That he sometimes, in fact, estimates is clear from what he says about a particularly destructive storm in 580: "Its space [of activity] was about (*quasi*) seven iugera in latitude, but it was not possible to estimate (*non potuit aestimare*) its longitude" (5.41). Because not all his numbers are preceded by this qualification, Gregory is probably indicating either that he is estimating or that he does know, but that the figure comes closest to this number. In both cases, the term *quasi* indicates that the number mentioned is not pure, exact fact, but a representation that stands for the facts, known or not, whatever these may be. This can also, of course, occur in a more literary context, as when, in a miracle story, he reports that monks had put "about (*quasi*) three sheaves" of grain out to dry in the sun (4.34). Here, what seems to be a literary fiction stands for the facts. We have seen Gregory doing the same with his invented speeches.

Envisionings of a future reality that does not come about

Bishop Theodore of Marseille travelled to the king *quasi aliquid contra Nicetium patricium suggesturus*: literally, this could be translated as "as though he were about to". He did so, however, but the king was not impressed, and the bishop therefore achieved

---

[21] Rudolf Arnheim, Visual thinking (Berkeley 1969) 90—91.

[22] Cf. Paul Ricoeur, "Imagination in discourse and in action", in: The Human Being in Action 2, ed. Anna-Teresa Tymieniecka (Analecta Husserliana 7, Dordrecht-London 1978) 3—22.

nothing (9.22). Elsewhere, too, the "as though" refers to intentions and plans which are viewed by the person involved as a future reality but which do not materialize. Ingitrude went to the king in a rage, *quasi filiam exhereditatura de facultate paterna*. She obtained a royal decision for an unequal division in her favor, but because her daughter refused the arrangement, nothing came of it (9.33). When King Chilperic had first tried to intimidate Gregory into agreeing to his deposing another bishop, and, when this failed, tried to trick him into it by offering him food (eating together being a gesture of mutual agreement), Gregory describes his attempt as: *At illi quasi me demulcens, quod dolose faciens potabat me non intellegere* ... (5.18). Clearly, the "as though" here does not refer to appearances, because the king was trying to conceal from the bishop — unsuccessfully, as is clear — what he was doing. It can only refer to what the king thought he was doing. And the same, in fact, applies to the other cases. *Quasi*, then, can indicate a personal intention, also when carried out in action, that does not achieve the envisioned result. I think therefore that, in these cases, the term *quasi* does not refer to the (real) intention or to its (possibly real) effectuation in action, but to the irreality of that envisioned result.

Illusion

Gregory uses the same phrasing *quasi aliquid suggesturus*, however, when he is speaking of an assassin sent under false pretences to kill King Guntram (9.3). Likewise, when King Childeric sent out a false rumour about the orphaned sons of Chlodomer *quasi parvolos illos elevaturus in regno*, intending to have them tonsured or killed instead, and achieving this (3.18). A wandering preacher and healer who may have believed himself to be sincere but is said by Gregory, from his viewpoint, to be a false prophet, is described as: "clad in skins, he prayed as though he were a religious person (*quasi religiosus*)" (9.25). In one case, Gregory is explicit about the deceit: Rauching had just made an alliance and "pretended to be about to treat of peace (*confingens se quasi tractaturus de pace*)" when he was really planning to take over the royal authority (9.9). *Quasi*, then, can refer to false pretence or false appearances.

In other cases, *quasi* is used simply to indicate that something does not correspond to reality. Just before a meal, King Guntram severely castigated a number of bishops for allying with the pretender Gundowald, but thereupon accepted their blessing, and "sat himself at the table with a cheerful and smiling face, as though (*quasi*) he had not spoken of their treason" (8.2). Similarly: "seemingly (*quasi*) apostolical canons" (5.18); "as though (*quasi*) he were already bishop" (5.49); "the king did not know that he had entered into the episcopal dwelling, but [thought that] he had taken refuge (*quasi* ... *confugisse*) in another region" (9.12). Overconfidence in one's own military strength that is to be shown up as such in the imminent battle is expressed by: "thinking that they had already killed them (*potantes eos iam quasi interfectos habere*)" (5.15). The term is also used to indicate that the heretic Oppila's thoughts about Christ are untrue: "why do you take away [Christ's] honour as though [he were] inglorious (*quasi ingloriosum*)?" (6.40). In these cases, *quasi* indicates the unreality of thoughts that do not correspond to things as they are[23].

[23] However, in 5.44: *quasi Sed[u]lium secutus*, and 6.7: *quasi Sidonium secutus*, Gregory is saying in the first case that the comparison does not hold, and in the second that the letters, of a *magnae vir sanctitatis*, presumably do resemble those of the model indicated: see below under "simile".

Function

Successful exercise of a function, as in: *Habebant autem quasi ducem tunc Godegisilum* (9.12) (he won the battle), is not irreality. The term *quasi* here seems to be used purely as a pointer to the manner in which the person in question should be regarded. Perhaps the term should be understood to indicate a temporary assignment. It is not clear whether that was the case with Ratharius, who was sent by King Childebert *quasi dux* to Marseille (8.12). A question can also be designated "as a joke (*quasi joco*)" (3.15). Less innocent seems the qualification of the former slave Andarchius, whose learning had so impressed the king that the latter entrusted him with official missions, and that "[a]s a man of honourable position (*quasi honoratus habitus*) through this" he was able to try — by dishonest means — to marry a wealthy heiress (4.46).

Simile

Sometimes the term appears to be used as an equivalent of *sicut*, *velut* or *tamquam* in the meaning of "like" or "as". In these cases, it indicates an imaginative comparison pointing to a true quality of the person, object or event in question. King Chilperic's son Clovis, for instance, was pursued by an enemy "like a fleeing stag (*quasi labentem cervum*)" (4.47). Someone is overcome by sleep "as though drunk" (3.15); another "rages as though insane" (5.43); the city of Rome restores itself after civil war "as though it rises again from the ground" (5. prol.). The meaning here is metaphorical: something is qualified by comparing it with what is perceived to be an analogy in another category of phenomena. Here, then, *quasi* indicates a resemblance that is truth.

Simile as "figure"

We have already seen a simile in Gregory's description of nature as a "figure" of the resurrection (10.13), and in the expression for something that had been, and perhaps still was, interpreted as a "figure": "as though the sky were burning" (8.24). The implication in the latter case is that the comparison, though possibly not entirely adequate, nevertheless points to a possible or real truth in the spiritual sphere. Elsewhere, Gregory reports that "a fiery column was seen (*visa est*) ... as though hanging from the sky (*quasi de caelo pendens*)" (7.11). There may have been an association here with the pillar of fire (*colomna ... ignis*) leading the Hebrews in the desert (1.10; Ex. 13:21—22). Elsewhere, the eclipsed sun "appearing hideous and pale, seemed as though in sackcloth (*teter atque decolor apparens, quasi saccus videbatur*)" (4.31). The adjectives are a reminiscence of Revelation 6:12: "When he opened the sixth seal ... the sun became black as sackcloth (*sol factus est niger tamquam saccus cilicinus*)".

We have already seen Gregory's use of *quasi* in quotes from, or to indicate figures in, the biblical text. An explicit biblical association with what is meant to be a historical story, but which sounds to us like a myth, is that of the nameless righteous man in Antioch who received three strangers in the evening with Lot: *quasi Loth ille antiqua memoratus historia*, and *velut memoratus Loth quondam in Sodomis* (10.24; Gen. 19:2). Lot is the image or "figure" of a just man — an example to be followed by all. Gregory, then, continues the strategy for the discovery of hidden spiritual meaning in the sacred text in his looking at the visible world of nature and history. Here, too, the term *quasi* can be used to to "see" the visible phenomenon as a "figure" of spiritual truth.

To sum up, for Gregory, the term *quasi* can, but need not, point to irreality: it may also reveal a deeper truth.

D. *Signa*: what Bishop Gunthar's horse saw

Close to the city of Tours, there was a chapel in which St Martin was said to have frequently prayed. When he was still abbot, Bishop Gunthar had never passed this chapel without stopping to pray there. After he had become bishop of Tours (552—555), however, he once intended to pass it without doing so. His horse thereupon stood still, with its head turned toward the chapel; neither the exercise of the whip, nor pulling at the reins, nor pricking with spurs could make it move. "The bishop then understood that he was being held by divine power (*sensit se virtute divina teneri*)", got down, and made his prayer. After this, he was able to continue his journey. Thus we are informed about the duties of greeting owed to the saint. But Gregory adds a playful epilogue:

> How I would have liked it, O courser, if the Lord had opened your mouth as he once did that of the ass [Num. 22:22 ff.], and you had said what extraordinary thing you saw (*quid vidisti spectabile*) that made you stop; whatever so lovable that you [wished to] contemplate the door of the cell (*quid amabile, ut ostium cellulae contemplareris*); whatever so awe-inspiring (*quid formidabile*), that you forced your rider to pray! Surely you would have shouted with a loud voice that, seeing the brightness of Martin (*claritatem Martini cernens*), you did not dare to move before your lord had made the visit he owed [to the saint] (Glor. conf. 8).

We can imagine him smiling as he tells this story to his audience. It is playful imagination, but at the same time it is clearly intended as a reconstruction of the situation as it must have been. Imagination "sees through" visible phenomena — the horse refusing to move — to its cause: hidden spiritual reality.

For the story of Christ and his miracles was Gregory's model of reality: "working prodigies and signs (*prodigia et signa . . . operante*)", and "doing many other miracles announced himself most clearly to the people to be God (*alia multa signa faciens manefestissime se Deum populis esse declarat*)" (1.20). Elsewhere Gregory says: "so that, . . . through his deeds of miraculous power, [Christ] might manifest himself as God (*ut . . . se virtutibus ostenderit Deum*)" (6.40). The vision of the angel at the empty tomb (as in Lk 24:4ff), and Joseph of Arimathea's liberation from prison by an angel's lifting the walls for him[24] are two events that Gregory mentions specifically (1.21); they exhibited the "working" of spiritual reality in visible events. Thus Gregory speaks of the cures and other miracles worked by Christ in largely the same terms as he does about the natural wonders. All extraordinary events are, evidently, "signs" or messages-as-events of divine activity. Later miraculous cures by saints are referred to as "signs (*signa*)" (2.3; 3.19) — but also as "powers (*virtutes*)" or "miracles (*miracula*)" (5.6) —, and, like natural wonders, they are said to be "shown" or "exhibited" (*ostenduntur*) or to "appear" (*apparent*) (2.3; 5.6). What, exactly, is thought to be "shown" or to "appear" in these events however?

---

[24] Cf. Gesta Pilati 15 (ed. Konstantin von Tischendorf, in: Evangelia apocrypha, 2nd ed. 1876, 1966) 381—382.

Gregory expects his readers to carry out most of their own imaginative associations. When he tells us that after the funeral of King Chilperic's Visigothic bride Galswintha, who (almost certainly at the instigation of the king's previous concubine and subsequent queen, Fredegunde) had been found strangled in her bed,

> God exhibited a great power (*virtutem magnam ostendit*). For the lamp — hanging on a cord — that burned near her tomb, fell onto the ground with its cord broken while no one had touched it, and the hardness of the paved floor fled before it, as though (*tamquam*) it descended into a soft element, and [although] it was half covered by it, the lamp was not at all broken. This was a great miracle for the ones who saw it (*Quod non sine magno miraculo videntibus fuit*) (4.28).

Here an element changes its nature: the pavement (marble?) behaves as though it were soft instead of hard. To us moderns, the description seems to exaggerate the events; Gregory, however — convinced, as he says, that "all is possible for those who believe" (2.3; Mk 9:23) — was prepared, and even eager, to believe everything that could point to the workings of spiritual reality. His miracle stories are visible theology. Here, the implicit message is: this person is now with God. In an elegy on Galswintha's story, Gregory's friend, the poet Venantius Fortunatus, is more explicit. He says that "[s]uddenly, a wondrous sign of things was born here (*Nascitur hic subito rerum mirabile signum*)" (Carm. 6.5.277)[25], and explains its message (perhaps to his patroness Radegund) at the end of the poem:

> The signs of [her] life remain (*Vitae signa tenet*), when, the glass container falling, neither did the water extinguish [it], nor did the stone of the floor break it. You too, Mother, receive this answer to your question by the gift of God (*habes consultum dote tonantis*) ... Believe her to be alive [in heaven], who has herself believed, [O] Christians: she who is now in Paradise should not be wept for (Carm. 6.5.365—70).

The flame of the burning lamp here is explicitly indicated as a "sign" of her continued life; its not being extinguished and the lamp not being broken by its contact with the ground are "figures" of the continued life of her soul and (new, heavenly) body notwithstanding her physical death and burial. Thus, what may have been the lucky fall of a lamp becomes a "sign" that "exhibits", in this case, the real, spiritual condition of the person concerned.

Other events and phenomena that could have natural causes are also ascribed to divine action. When the hostage Attalus and his liberator Leo escape from the barbarian's house during the night, they find the securely bolted doors of the atrium "divinely unbolted (*divinitus reseratas*)" (3.15); when an army burned down a church with relics of St Martin, the covering over the altar and the herbs on it were spared: "the power of the saint was present (*virtus beati adfuit*)" (7.12). Similarly, when a hostile army turned to flee when a relic of St Sergius is raised before them, Gregory describes their flight as "as though oppressed by the power of the martyr (*quasi martyris obpraessi virtute*)" (7.31).

[25] Edition: Venantius Fortunatus, Carmina (ed. Friedrich Leo, MGH AA 4/1, 1881).

Where spiritual causation might be seen as protecting those who trust in it, it is the preferred interpretation. But when the sarcophagi of two lovers, which had been at opposite ends of the church in the evening, were found together in the morning, Gregory says that "a new miracle, which manifested their chastity, appeared (*miraculi novitas, quae eorum castitatem manifestaret, apparuit*)" (1.47) — probably meaning that it was without precedent in the Bible. Here again, an event is given a miraculous interpretation and regarded as a "sign" of the spiritual truth about these persons.

Apart from interpretations of events that had already taken place, Gregory also tells us many stories of actual perceptions of spiritual reality. When St Martin died at midnight, "many heard psalm-singing in heaven during his passing away" (1.48). When the wealthy Ecdicius had fed all the poor he could find during a famine, "a voice came to him from out of the sky" to tell him that he and his descendants would now never lack food (2.24). In the many-windowed church in Clermont, "the awesome presence of God (*[t]error . . . Dei*) and a great brightness is seen (*claritas magna conspicitur*), and in the spring a most sweet fragrance, as if of herbs, is perceived by the devout to come there (*quasi aromatum, advenire a religiosis sentitur*)" (2.16). The term *quasi* serves here to make recognizable and communicable an experience that is felt to be of the divine. Similarly: when the holy hermit Friardus died, "his whole cell trembled" (4.37). Abbot Aredius', after a prayer, "finding" water in the ground and avoiding it from an approaching cloud exhibit the tendency to attribute all events to divine guidance (10.29).

Something else comes into play when the deacon Wulfilaicus tells Gregory about a little dust from St Martin's tomb put in a capsule and hung around his neck for the duration of a journey. It "grew so much in volume that it not only filled the whole capsule, but even spilled out from between the cracks, wherever it could find an opening. Through the light of this miracle, my soul lit up more than before to place all my confidence in his power (*Ex hoc mihi miraculi lumine animus magis accendit totam spem meam in eius virtute defigere*)" (8.15). Whereas we would tend to apply our mental model "diffusion" to this phenomenon, the deacon (and Gregory) preferred the model "divinely caused increase". It is one that recurs through Gregory's work, and is one of those that seem to visualize, and thus stand for, the affective experience of divine power as such[26].

A visible phenomenon thus tends to be interpreted through the "visual concept" that accords best not only with "the stimulus configuration", but also with the desires, hopes and expectations of the viewer[27]. Gregory presents this whole story as direct discourse by Wulfilaicus, but it has, of course, undergone literary stylization. The "light" of the miracle and the "lighting up" of the deacon's soul are complementary metaphors — or so it seems. But we have seen above that the visible flame of an oil lamp can be regarded as actually exhibiting the life of

---

[26] Giselle de Nie, A broken lamp or the effluence of holy power? Common sense and belief-reality in Gregory of Tours' own experience. Mediaevistik 3 (1990) 275.

[27] Arnheim, Thinking 90—91.

someone's soul, and also that Gregory may tend to offer possible pictures of invisible spiritual reality through a judicious use of metaphors. When spiritual truth is understood through images, metaphors — although recognized as such — can be used to suggest the forms of hidden spiritual realities.

Elsewhere, Gregory tells us that when an epidemic of the plague threatened Clermont, "the walls of houses and churches were suddenly seen to seem to be inscribed with signs (*in subita contemplatione parietes vel domorum vel ecclesiarum signari videbantur*), whence these inscriptions were called Thau by the common people" (4.5; Ezek. 9.4). Here, it is difficult to know what he means[28]. Suddenness in Gregory's writings almost always points to divine causation, and the mention of seeing as well as seeming indicates a phenomenon that is something other than straightforward sensory reality. The perception of spiritual reality, evidently, involves another kind of "seeing". As the sign Thau in the Old Testament, the sign — evidently — saved the population from the scourge, at least temporarily.

As we saw in the story of the unnamed man in Antioch who met with the three strangers, in fact angels of destruction, who later "withdrew from his eyes and did not appear (*apparuerunt*) to him again" spiritual reality can be also described without qualification; here, however, Gregory will have assumed the reader's association with the biblical text. Other perceptions can be qualified by expressions of "seeming" and "as though". When Clovis approached Poitiers to drive the heretical Visigoths from the city,

> it seemed to him as though a fiery beacon, having come out of St Hilary's church, came [to hang] above him (*visa est ei tamquam super se advenire*), in order that, aided by the light of the blessed confessor Hilary, he would more easily conquer the heretical keenness (*acies*, also meaning: army ready for battle), against which that bishop had often fought in matters of the faith (2.37).

Thus, an experience of spiritual aid is visualized as a fiery celestial phenomenon. When a known arsonist tried to swear his innocence in front of a church with St Martin's relics, however,

> it seemed to him as though he were surrounded by fire (*visum est ei quasi ab igne circumdare*). He fell to the ground at once and began crying that he was being consumed by the blessed bishop. The unhappy man shouted: "I call God to witness that I saw fire fall from heaven! It surrounds me and ignites me with its enormous heat!"
>
> And while he was saying this, he breathed out his spirit (8.16).

The qualification "it seemed to him as though" is here again used to describe an experience of spiritual reality as perceived by only one individual. Gregory treats it as an imagination which nevertheless stands for the true — ordinarily invisible — state of affairs.

When a soldier presumed to enter one of St Martin's estates to exact a penalty for not sending a contingent to the royal army, however, Gregory uses only

---

[28] Cf. de Nie, Views 288—290.

(his rendering, or invention, of) the man's own account of the event to describe what happened:

> "When I entered the hall of the house, I saw an old man holding in his hand a tree whose branches suddenly spread so as to fill the whole room. One of these branches came up against me with such a blow that I was shaken and fell" (7.42).

"A certain old man", appearing suddenly with a warning or prophecy, is a not uncommon motif in Gregory's writings (e. g. 3.5). Here, the figure is almost certainly intended to represent the saint, defending his property. When Sigiwald walked into a villa of St Julian's to take it over, he had a similar experience, without a vision being mentioned: he was "immediately struck with insanity (*statim amens effectus*)" (3.16). Such stories are powerful propaganda, probably necessary in the conditions in which Gregory found himself.

Exquisitely reassuring, by contrast, is Gregory's report about the evidently very modest Abbot Aredius' many cures (*signa*), "which, through the power (*per virtutem*) of the holy martyr Julian and the blessed confessor Martin, the Lord worked in his hands (*in eius manibus Dominus operatus est*)" (10.29). In his record of St Martin's miracles, Gregory adds: "the man of God himself asserted that he felt as it were the hand of St Martin when [during the festivities for the saint, in his church] he . . . stroked the limbs of the ill woman with a healing touch (*sensisse se quasi beati Martini manum, cum infirmae membra . . . tactu salutari palparet*)" (Virt. Mart. 4.6). The description of an otherwise incommunicable experience needs a recognizable concretization preceded by "as it were" or "as though" because the correspondence is no more than approximate or suppositional. The representation through mental images, or imagination, nevertheless is "true" in that it stands for a real experience, however indirectly expressed. Such imagination thus "sees" the hidden reality: it is divinatory.

E. *Visio*: "I speak in truth, for I saw in a dream . . ."

When the escaped Attalus and Leo reached Reims, the priest who received them said: "Indeed, my vision is true (*vera est enim visio mea*). For this night I saw (*videbam*) two doves flying toward me and sit together on my hand; one was white, the other black" (3.15). Dreams, then, can "prefigure" visible events. The wicked Bishop Priscus of Lyon, however, was not at all impressed by a deacon's story of a nocturnal vision of the late Bishop Nicetius saying he should mend his ways or else; he called it "a phantasy of dreams (*fantasia somniorum*)" (4.36). Gregory's story shows that the bishop should have recognized the dream images as corresponding to the spiritual reality of the actual situation: Priscus and his family were thereupon "struck by the power of the holy man (*a sancti viri virtute percuss[i]*)" — they became ill. Different views of dreams were thus held. In the pagan tradition, they could, in clear or "figured" manner, indicate the future, take the form of advice given by a venerable figure, or they could be empty images induced by demons, worries and/or physical conditions[29].

Although suspicious of demonic illusions, the biblical and Christian traditions valued prophetic dreams and true visions of devout persons[30]. Thus Gregory recounts Joseph's reporting himself, in his dream, as "as it were (*quasi*) binding sheaves", and "as though (*quasi*) sun and moon and eleven stars had fallen down before him" (1.9; Gn 37:5ff). Similarly, he reports that people said that in the church of St Peter in Rome, "a devout man had seen in a vision (*vidisse virum fidelem in visu*) the blessed levite Stephen as it were (*quasi*) talking to the apostles Peter and Paul" (2.6).

The following account of a dream is particularly interesting because, through the dream, it shows the same event — a city fire — happening in the visible and in the invisible spheres:

> In these days [585] there was a woman in the city of Paris who said to the inhabitants: "Flee, O [citizens], from the city, for know that it will be burned by a fire!"
> When many laughed at her, [saying that] she either reported an omen from a [pagan] oracle (*sortium praesagio*)[31] or had dreamed some empty illusions (*vana aliqua somniasset*), or indeed that she brought this forth upon the instigation of the noonday demon (*daemonii meridiani haec instinctu proferret*) (Ps 90:6; cf. Virt. Mart. 3.9), she replied: "It is not at all as you say; I speak in truth, for I saw in a dream (*nam in veritate loquor, quia vidi per somnium*) a luminous man coming out of the holy Vincent's church, holding a [lighted] candle in his hand and lighting the houses of the merchants one after another."
> Thereafter, in the third night after the woman had said this, one of the citizens went at the break of dawn into his storeroom with a lighted oil lamp; when he had taken oil and the other things he needed from there, he went out and left the lighted lamp standing near an oil barrel. The house [in question] was the first next to the city's south gate. Having caught fire from this lamp, the house burned down, and from it, other houses also began to catch fire.
> Then, when the fire came near the chained men in prison, the blessed Germanus appeared to them (*apparuit eis*); having broken the block and the chains that bound them, and opened the locked prison door, he allowed the prisoners to leave unhurt. Having gone out, they went to the church of the holy Vincent, which contains the tomb of the blessed bishop [Germanus] (8.33).

A dream, then, is not true simply because it is a dream. There can be empty and demonic ones. What makes this one true is that, like the priest's dream of the doves, it turned out to show the future in "figures" — this time, of the invisible spiritual action that would be taking place in the visible events. In such a

---

[29] Steven Kruger, Dreaming in the Middle Ages (Cambridge Studies in medieval literature 14, Cambridge 1992) 17—34.

[30] See, for instance: P.J. Budd, Dream, in: The new international dictionary of New Testament theology 1 (Grand Rapids 1975) 511—513; John S. Hanson, Dreams and visions in the Graeco-Roman world and early Christianity, in: Haase, Aufstieg 1395—1427; and Kruger, Dreaming 35—56.

[31] Cf. Dieter Harmening, Superstitio. Überlieferungs- und theoriegeschichtliche Untersuchungen zur kirchlich-theologischen Aberglaubensliteratur des Mittelalters (1979) 191—194.

case, evidently, there is no need for the two to correspond in form. Gregory does not explain why a saint should be moved to punish the merchants. Many of these appear to have been Jews in this period, however, and therefore not part of the Christian religious community; in Clermont and Orléans, Christians had destroyed a synagogue (5.11; 8.1). It is possible that similar tensions existed in Paris. Gregory has used the woman's dream here to show the spiritual dynamics of the situation.

In two highly interesting cases, Gregory describes himself as using a dream of his own as what can only be called a diplomatic tool. When King Guntram began to investigate the murder of his brother Chilperic in 584, the widowed queen Fredegund accused the chamberlain Eberulf. To escape royal vengeance, the latter fled and sought sanctuary in the church of St Martin at Tours. There he managed to offend the bishop by his unrespectful as well as immoral conduct[32]. In this predicament, Gregory tells us,

> I saw a dream (*vidi somnium*), which I related to him in the holy church, saying: "I thought myself as though celebrating (*Putabam me quasi . . . celebrare*) the sacred solemnities of the mass in this church. When the altar with the offerings had already been covered by the silken cloth, I see (*conspicio*) King Guntram suddenly entering.
>
> He shouted very loudly: 'Get this enemy of our family out here! Tear this murderer away from the sacred altar of God!'
>
> But I, when I heard this, turned to you and said: 'Take hold of the altar cloth covering the sacred offerings, you unhappy man, so that you will not be thrown out of here!' And then you took it in your hand, but loosely; you didn't really hold on to it.
>
> I, however, spread out my arms and stood chest to chest with the king, and said: 'Don't throw this man out of the holy church, lest your life be in danger, lest the holy bishop [Martin] strike you down with his power! Don't kill yourself with your own javelin! For, if you do this, you will lose the present life as well as the eternal!'
>
> But when the king resisted me, you let go of the covering and came to stand behind me. I was very angry with you indeed. And then you returned to the altar, and took hold of the covering, but let it go again. While you were loosely holding on to the covering and I was vigorously resisting the king, I woke up, terrified — not knowing what the dream might mean (*quid somnium indecaret*)."
>
> When I had narrated these things to him, he said: "The dream which you saw is true, for it accords completely with my thinking [plan] (*Verum est somnium, quod vidisti, quod valde cogitatione meae concordat*)."
>
> To which I replied: "And what does your thinking [plan] foresee (*Et quid providit cogitatio tua*)?"
>
> And he said: "I had decided that, if the king should command me to be dragged out of this place, I would hold on to the altar covering with one hand and with the other draw my sword and, after killing you first, thereafter strike down as many of the clergy as I could find. After that it would not be an injury to succumb to death, if I would have had my revenge upon the clergy of this saint."

---

[32] de Nie, Views 269—272.

Hearing this, I was stupefied, wondering what this was, since the Devil himself was speaking through his mouth (*stupens, admirabam quod erat, quia per os eius diabulus loquebatur*). For never did he have the least fear of God (7.22).

Through telling this dream, for whose content he need take no responsibility, Gregory exhibits his good intentions toward Eberulf and induces him to reveal his. And the manner in which he tells the story seems to show that he was perfectly aware of doing so, and regarded his action as a legitimate tactic in the explosive situation. His phrasing — "I saw", and "I thought myself as though" — reveal that he is conscious of the imaginative quality of the events seen. The verb "foresee" for Eberulf's plans also refer to, in this case prospective, imagination. In his dream, Gregory may have seen the chamberlain's stated intentions also carried out, but purposely have refrained from telling him about this; if so, he avoids the responsibility of an accusation and lets the man incriminate himself.

A second instance of agile diplomacy by means of a dream — which he evidently has no qualms in letting his readers know about — occurred the day before our bishop presented the two men to King Guntram in Orléans, when he sat next to the king at a meal. Talk turned to the then still unsolved mystery of the murder of Chilperic a year earlier. The king began to accuse one of Gregory's friends, Bishop Theodore of Marseille, and threatened to imprison him, saying:

"For I know that he arranged to have my brother Chilperic killed to aid the cause of [the pretender Gundowald and his supporters]. Therefore I shall not be counted as a man if I am not able to avenge him before the year is over!"
To this, I replied: "What killed Chilperic if not his own wickedness and your prayers? For he played a lot of very mean tricks on you, and it is these that are responsible for his death. This, I might as well tell you, I saw very clearly in a dream vision (*per visionem somnii inspexi*), when I saw (*cum viderem*) him, after he had first accepted tonsure, being as it were (*quasi*) ordained as a bishop; and then, preceded by burning lamps and candles, being carried around, on a bishop's chair which was bare except for a sprinkling of ashes on it" (8.5).

With these words, Gregory turns the tables on his king. He lifts the whole matter into another dimension. The spiritual dynamic of "killing oneself with one's own weapon", which we saw Gregory mention to this same king in his dream about Eberulf, is also referred to here. In the spiritual sphere, killing others is killing oneself. Very audacious indeed is Gregory's mentioning Guntram's prayers — for the welfare of the kingdom? — as also having helped to kill his brother. The spiritual dynamic is the real one in every situation; those acting in the visible events are its instruments. The dream "shows" that Chilperic was a bishop of the Devil. And so Gregory can express devastating criticism of the king's brother without incurring any responsibility for it — as well as save his friend. His belief in the truth of his dream is obviously sincere; at the same time, he is fully conscious of the imaginative component as well as of the manipulatory element in his story.

The bishop's visionary image had its effect upon the king, for the latter — much to Gregory's surprise — thereupon proceeded to relate a vision of his own:

> "I too saw another vision that announced his death (*Vidi et ego aliam visonem, quae huius interitum nuntiavit*). For three bishops led him, bound by chains, into my sight; one of these was Tetricus [of Langres], another was Agroecula [of Chalons] and the third was Nicetius of Lyon. Two of these said: 'Unfasten him, we pray, and permit him to go, after he has been chastised.'
> But Bishop Tetricus was against this and said bitterly: 'That will not happen: he is going to be consumed by fire for his crimes!'
> And while they, as it were (*quasi*) hotly debated these things amongst themselves for a long time, I saw in the distance a cauldron with boiling water above a fire. Then, while I wept, they seized Chilperic, broke his bones and threw him into the cauldron. At once, he was so completely dissolved and liquefied in the heat of the boiling water that not the least trace of him remained."
> When the king had finished saying this, we were both astonished (*admirantibus nobis*), and [then] got up, for the meal was over.

The fact that Chilperic was to be killed by a stabbing in his armpit as he alighted from his horse one evening is not felt as a contradiction: just as with the fire in Paris, and Chilperic's royal position as a veiled episcopate for the Devil, one and the same event looks different in the visible and invisible spheres of reality. In his dream, King Guntram seems to share his brother's alleged perception that it is not the kings but the bishops who are ruling the kingdom (6.46). Gregory avoids responsibility for this opinion by ascribing it to the kings themselves.

In his "Histories", dreams of devout persons which support the church's belief system are regarded as true. The invisible dynamics of events are perceived in the form of either analogous or non-analogous mental images[33].

III. *Repraesentatio*: imagination of the heart as an art of the real

There is one story, in which Gregory lets us see how he thinks mental images evoked and induced by words — in this case, with a good admixture of tears, however — can transform a life: a new bride persuading her husband to live in chastity together in order to merit Paradise. In this speech (wholly invented, of course, by our author) the bride looks through the worldly riches that her husband brings to the marriage to the — mentally visualized — reality which the Church has promised her:

> Earthly beauties horrify me because I see (*suspicio*) the hands of the Redeemer pierced for the life of the world. Nor do I see (*Non cerno*) diadems flashing with precious jewels, when in my mind I gaze in wonder (*miror mente*) at the crown of thorns (1.47).

---

[33] On dreams in Gregory: de Nie, Views 213—293. The boiling cauldron may be a reminiscence of Jer. 1:13, *ollam succensam ego video* — an image of evil.

She rejects her husband's vast lands "because I long for the pleasantness of Paradise. Your terraces disgust me when I see (*suspicio*) the Lord seated [on His throne] above the stars." As Gregory phrases it elsewhere about another, she "already possessed the kingdoms of Paradise through her mind (*iam mente possedebat regna Paradisi*)" (2.2). When her husband mentions the fact that their parents wish for heirs to their properties, she replies that this transitory life is nothing compared to the life in heaven. It is not ended by death or destruction and, there, one remains "in eternal beatitude", "lives in never-setting sunlight", "enjoying the presence of the Lord Himself through contemplation, translated into the angelic state, and rejoices with indissoluble gladness."

As Gregory presents it, the bridegroom's inner reenactment of his bride's verbalized visualization of her total experience of beauty, when contrasted with the limitations and uncertainties of the earthly life, causes him to "refigure" his world view[34]. This is evident in what he lets the bridegroom say:

> "Through your sweetest discourse," he said, "eternal life shines into me like a great star (*Dulcissimis . . . eloquiis tuis aeterna mihi vita tamquam magnum iubar inluxit*), and therefore if you wish to abstain from carnal desire, I will join you in this undertaking." (Ibid.)

This is a crucial passage. In my judgment, it unmistakably shows that Gregory knows that it was the experience of the new, composite mental image of the light-filled life in Paradise as "a great star" which the bride's words have evoked in her bridegroom, that somehow precipitated the latter's new decision. In his own way, Gregory here formulates the insight of modern clinical psychotherapy that images, as visualizations of emotional energies, can cross the threshold of consciousness in a way that verbal concepts cannot, and induce an involuntary affective mimesis of their dynamic patterns. The latter can transform consciousness and activate the will[35].

In a story of how the possessed around the tomb of St Julian complained, at his feast, about the presence of other saints upon this occasion, Gregory again reveals his view of the role of imagination. After having quoted their naming five saints with some of their identifying qualities, our author concludes:

> Saying these and similar things, they made the holy men of God so present to human minds that no one doubted them to be there (*ita sanctos Dei humanis mentibus repraesentant ut nulli sit dubium eos inibi commorari*): many of these ill people were cured, however, and departed in good health" (Virt. Jul. 30).

All he had needed to say here was that their cries proved the saints' presence, as he does elsewhere: "suddenly the possessed shouted that they were being tortured, and confessed Martin's presence to have arrived (*Martini adesse praesentiam confitentur*)" (Virt. Mart. 3.39). Instead, he stresses here the

---

[34] Ricoeur, Time 3, 170.

[35] Gerald Epstein, Waking dream therapy: dream process as imagination (New York-London 1981) 18: "images are the concretizations of emotions"; Roberto Assagioli, Psychosynthesis (New York 1965) 180, 144.

"making present to human minds" through words that results in an experience of the saints' actual presence, subsequently proved by the cures.

The bride's imaged eloquence is the model for this use of imagination. Paul Ricoeur has said:

> "Locution" — or "diction" — according to [Aristotle's] "Rhetoric", has the virtue of "placing before our eyes" and so of "making visible". An additional step is thus taken, over and beyond seeing-as, which does not prohibit the marriage of metaphor, which assimilates, and irony, which creates a distance. We have entered into the realm of illusion that confuses, in the precise sense of the term, "seeing-as" with "believing we are seeing". Here, "holding as true", which defines belief, succumbs to the hallucination of presence[36].

As I hope to have shown, Gregory, too, knew this. But the actual transformation of lives and bodies proved to him that, even as mediated through the human mind and heart, the traditional images of divine dynamics actually were "the gate[s] to the grove of Paradise" (Vit. patr. 19. prol.).

Conclusion

Why did Gregory smile — and report himself as such — when he presented himself to his king as sent by his lord Martin? If he had not used direct discourse, but described his own action, he might have used the term *quasi* for his ambassadorship — recognizing the imaginary as well as the real element in it. For the central role accorded to invisible spiritual reality in all spheres of life and government in late sixth-century Gaul required strategies, not only for "divining" it, but also for dealing with it in a social context. We have seen that Gregory applied, and was aware of applying, a strategy of imagination — analogous to that of the "spiritual understanding" of biblical texts — to "see" figures of the divine in human war and government, in strange natural phenomena, in miracles and in dream visions.

Our author may have believed all that could edify because he wished to set no limits to the power of God, but he was not naively or unreflectively credulous. For him, history was visible theology: he took the configurations of nature, history and miracle to heart as patterns of the divine manifested in the visible world. And he recognized the imagination of the heart as an art, not only of divining hidden spiritual reality in text and world, but also of making this hidden reality "present" to others through images-in-words that could lead them to "the heart of life"[37].

---

[36] Ricoeur, Time 3, 186.

[37] As Endre von Ivanka, Dunkelheit, mystische, in: Reallexikon für Antike und Christentum 4 (1959) 355, on Plotinus' light mysticism. The research for this paper has been very much stimulated by the sessions of the International *Erasmus* Seminar "Word, image and reality in medieval texts", sponsored by the Network "Nederlands in Europa".

IX

HISTORY AND MIRACLE: GREGORY'S USE OF METAPHOR

The courageous and, for his time, learned bishop whom we are honouring with these scholarly papers would have found them a strange phenomenon indeed. For him, as for Augustine, the only excuse for collecting, processing and exchanging information was not *curiositas* but the desire for a holy *sapientia*.[1] Or, as he put it in the preface to his *Glory of the martyrs*:

> it behoves us to adhere to, write and speak that which edifies the church and, through holy instruction, makes barren minds generate the knowing of perfect faith (*quae mentes inopes ad notitiam perfectae fidei instructione sancta fecundent*).[2]

What kind of "holy instruction" does Gregory have in mind? In his collection of the *Miracles of St. Martin* he tells us what he will not do:

> But why attempt in his praise (*laus*) what we are not able to fulfill? For he himself is the praise of the one [i.e. Christ] whose praise never left his lips. Would, therefore, that we should be able to unfold [no more than] the simple history (*simplicem . . . historiam explicare*).[3]

This statement should be understood against the background of the late antique stylistic ideal of high-flown, expansive and ornate language of praise, such as that which we find in the narrative panegyrical poem about St. Martin's life by Gregory's friend Venantius Fortunatus.[4] Gregory, admiring his friend's skill but conscious of his own lack of training in this manner of writing, tells us in the prologue to St. Martin's miracles that "even though my unpolished speech cannot decorate the page (*etsi non potest paginam sermo incultus*

---

[1] As H.-I. Marrou, *Augustin et le fin de la culture antique*, 4th edn. (Paris, 1958), pp. 350–1, 363.

[2] *GM*, prol., *MGH, SRM*, 1, 2, p. 487.

[3] *VM* 1, 5, *MGH, SRM* 1, 2, p. 591.

[4] Venantius Fortunatus, *Vita Martini*, ed. F. Leo, *MGH, AA* 4, 1 (Berlin, 1881), pp. 293–370. Cf. on this stylistic ideal: J. Fontaine, *Naissance de la poésie dans l'occident chrétien* (Paris, 1981), pp. 60–65.

ornare)", he hopes that his readers' prayers "will make it light up with the shining deeds of power (*praeclaris virtutibus elucere*) of the glorious bishop".[5] In the course of his writing, however, Gregory appears to have discovered that his brief stories could be at least as effective as full-blown "praise". For in the second book of St. Martin's miracles he writes:

> As we write succinctly (*succincte*) about all the individual miracles of the blessed man, we do not expand them into fuller diction (*nec ea in ampliorem sermonem expandimus*), because we greatly fear, while we apprehensively continue on the journey which we began, that perhaps wiser men should say: "An experienced [writer] could have much extended (*extendere*) these things." But it has seemed to us, being well-versed in Church doctrine, that the history (*historia*) that pertains to the edification of the Church should avoid wordiness and be woven with brief and simple speech (*brevi atque simplici sermone texatur*), so that it not only shows forth the holy power (*virtutem . . . prodat*) of the blessed bishop, but does not inflict disgust upon wiser men. Would that, through this being done, both the reader should be induced to go on and the saint be shown forth in his work (*prodatur in opere*)![6]

Now what exactly does Gregory have in mind when he says—twice—that the saint's holy power would "show forth" better in a shorter description? In a scrutiny of two of Gregory's stories I hope to answer this question, and also to show that his intentional simplicity and brevity do not mean that he intended to write completely without literary devices. Metaphor—the evocation through words of two juxtaposed and coalescing visual units or images—is one of these.

If there is one outstanding characteristic of Gregory's historical and hagiographical writings it is that he tended to describe everything in visual units—real events or images he has gleaned from reading or liturgy—rather than through abstract categories.[7] Further, his brief review of Old Testament events show him to have shared the early Christian allegorical tradition of Bible interpretation in which every person, saying and event contained a hidden, divine

[5] *VM* prol.

[6] *VM* 2, 19. Augustine had formulated this view in a number of his writings, but perhaps most trenchantly in a letter in which he says about Scripture: *invitat omnes humili sermone, quos non solum mannifesta pascat, sed etiam secreta exerceat veritate* (Ep. III 137, 18, quoted in E. Auerbach, "Sermo humilis", in idem, *Literatursprache und Publikum in der lateinischen Spätantike und im Mittelalter* (Bern, 1958), p. 41).

[7] G. de Nie, *Views from a Many-Windowed Tower. Studies of Imagination in the Works of Gregory of Tours* (Amsterdam, 1987), pp. 18, 175–6, 209.

message which was its essence. Thus Joseph (as well as Adam, Noah, and Zorobabel) "bore the image of the Redeemer (*tipum praeferens Redemptoris*)"; and the crossing through the Red Sea—"this world being called, in the mode of a figure (*figuraliter*), a sea"—is the *tipus* of baptism.[8] The history of mankind's relation with God was thus regarded as shot through with recurring divinely created images and action-patterns, the latter sometimes also called "figures", which are visual units.[9] Further, contrary to what used to be regarded as his purely "realistic"—"immediate, sensory-concrete"—presentation of contemporary events as he saw them happening,[10] Gregory's stories show that he tended to regard visible, human events in his own time, too, as manifestations of such divine images or patterns.[11]

But that is not all. He also shared the late antique world-view in which, through the eternal invisible "forms" or image-essences of things, regarded as more "real" than their manifestations or reflections in sensory phenomena, all formally analogous phenomena and acts were thought to cohere and participate in each other.[12] Thus, and this is crucial to the understanding of his world view, Gregory seems to regard and experience all objects, gestures and representations—including his own mental images—of these spiritual image-patterns, as participating in the dynamic spiritual potential of their archetypes.[13] The early Christian practice of meditation upon Scripture probably encouraged such a view. In it, mental imaging was experienced—via what we could now call the affect-laden, preverbal iconic consciousness—as the tuning into an objective, dynamic spiritual reality which could be approached only through such imaging.[14] However, Gregory's view sounds more exotic than it is. Modern psychological

---

[8] *Hist.* 1, 9 (1, 4, 15), 10.

[9] Cf. E. Auerbach, "Figura", *Archivum Romanicum* 22 (1938), 436–89.

[10] As E. Auerbach, *Mimesis. Dargestellte Wirklichkeit in der abendländischen Literatur* (Bern-Stuttgart [1946], 1988), p. 93.

[11] F. Thürlemann, *Der historischen Diskurs bei Gregor von Tours. Topoi und Wirklichkeit, Geist und Werk der Zeiten* 39 (Bern-Frankfurt am Main, 1974). See also Gregory's treatment of prodigies and history, and nature and miracles, in my *Views from a Many-Windowed Tower*, pp. 27–69, and 71–132.

[12] G.B. Ladner, *Handbuch der frühchristlichen Symbolik* (Stuttgart-Zürich, 1992), pp. 19–20; idem, "Medieval and modern understanding of symbolism: a comparison", *Speculum* 54 (1979), 227.

[13] De Nie, *Views from a Many-Windowed Tower*, p. 128.

[14] Cf. E. von Severus and A. Solignac, "Méditation: de l'Écriture aux auteurs médiévaux", *Dictionnaire de la Spiritualité* 10, pp. 906–14, and A.J. Deikman, "Deautomatization and the mystic experience", *Psychiatry* 29 (1966), 324–38.

research points to the same phenomena, albeit expressed in more self-reflexive terms: we perceive, think, live and are empowered—or crippled—by our imagination.[15] The difference between Gregory and us is not that he is "irrational" and we are "rational", but the nature of the informing model of perception. Within his model of a life-world entirely shot through with potent spiritual realities, he is eminently "rational", that is, orderly in a reasoning way—in fact, he uses the qualification "irrational" for fools who ignore what he considers to be obvious, practical truths.[16] A learned contemporary theologian who is also a psychotherapist, Eugen Drewermann, combines elements of the healing art of a nineteenth-century Amerindian shaman with the Christian concept of God: the latter would speak to us through the images in our preverbal, iconic consciousness.[17]

In Gregory's view, however, even the word actually and potently participates in the reality to which it points. Not only does the pronouncing of a saint's name immediately result in the presence of his power.[18] Gregory's reports of cures occurring during liturgy after a miracle story has been read indicate that the sounded words of a miracle story also made the saint and the miraculous "(deeds of) power (*virtus*)" referred to actively present.[19] Even a written narrative about a saint's miracles is explicitly said to contain the "power" of those miracles, and physical contact with the letters of this text effects another one.[20] As I hope to show below, this presenceing of its referent by the words and verbal images of a story about divine action is centrally involved in the "holy instruction" which Gregory hoped to write. How did he go about this?

---

[15] As S.S. Tomkins, *Affect, Imagery and Consciousness*, vol. 1 (New York, 1974), p. 13: "The world we perceive is a dream we learn to have from a script we have not written". Quoted in J.L. Singer, *Imagery and daydream methods in psychotherapy and behavior modification* (New York, 1974), p. 171.

[16] *Hist.* 4, 13: *Multae enim causae per eum inrationabiliter gerebantur, et ob hoc acceleratus est de mundo . . . Nullum autem hominem diligebat . . .*

[17] E. Drewermann, *Tiefenpsychologie und Exegese*, vol. 2 (Olten-Freiburg im Breisgau, 1985), pp. 129–41.

[18] As in *VM* 1, 23, *MGH, SRM* 1, 2, p. 600: *non solveretur a vinculo, quoadusque nomen illud sacratissimum invocasset; invocato autem, omnia solvebantur.*

[19] As in *VM* 2, 14, 29 and 49, *MGH, SRM* 1, 2, pp. 613, 619–20, 626.

[20] *VP* 8, 12: *Unum . . . admirandum de libro Vitae eius . . . memorabo miraculum: de quo virtus divina procedens . . . ad comprobandam virtutem dictorum patefecit esse plurimis gloriosum.* Gregory's view of language is discussed in G. de Nie, "Die Sprache im Wunder—das Wunder in der Sprache. Menschenwort und Logos bei Gregor von Tours", *Mitteilungen des Instituts für Österreichische Geschichtsforschung* 103 (1995), 1–25.

A. An object-miracle: "history" or metaphor?

With this question in mind, I shall first look at the role of metaphor in one of Gregory's "simple histories" of a miracle about a transformed object:

> In the same city [of Milan] there is a church of St Laurentius the deacon, whom I have already mentioned. In the church there is a crystal chalice of marvelous beauty. But once after the celebration of mass, as a deacon was carrying the chalice to the holy altar, it slipped from his hand, fell to the ground, and was smashed into small pieces. The deacon, pale and white, carefully gathered the fragments of the chalice and placed them on top of the altar; he did not doubt (*non diffisus*) that the power of the martyr would be able to make it whole (*possit solidare*). After he had spent the night in vigils, weeping and praying, he went to look at the chalice and found it made firm and whole (*solidatum*) upon the altar.
>
> The chalice was thereupon hung above the altar and, upon the request of the people, a new, annual feast in the martyr's honor was instituted.[21]

That this story is one about a miracle is evident. But is it also "history": that is, did it really happen? For many of us, historical writing is, in the terms of Paul Ricœur, a literary configuration of traces of past experience which has no reality other than that as a text.[22] Gregory, however, believed not only in the objective existence of his images of divine patterns, but also in that of history as a divine plan involving mankind.[23] Through the continuing recurrence of divine patterns in it, it is a past which lives embedded in the present. In the same chapter in which Gregory said that he would only "unfold the simple history" of the events, he shows us what it is that he means by "history". He tells us there how Bishop Ambrose, celebrating

---

[21] *Est enim apud eandem urbem basilica sancti Laurenti levitae, cui supra meminimus, ibique admirabili pulchritudine calix cristallinus habebatur. Acta vero quadam solemnituate, dum per diaconem ad sanctum altare offerretur, elapsus manu in terram ruit et in frustra comminutus est. At diaconus pallidus et exsanguis collecta diligenter fragmenta vasculi super altare posuit, non diffisus, quod eum possit virtus martyris solidare. Denique in vigiliis, lacrimis atque oratione deductam noctem, requisitum calicem repperit super altare solidatum. Quae virtus cum populis nuntiata fuisset, tanta animos devotione succendit, ut a sacerdote petrerent, nova in honorem eius Deo solemnia celebrari. Tunc pontifex loci, suspensum super altare calicem, et tunce agens, et in posterum per singulos annos devotissime instituit celebrari. GM* 45, *MGH, SRM* 1, 2, pp. 518–19.

[22] P. Ricœur, *Time and Narrative*, vol. 3., tr. K. Blamey and D. Pellauer (Chicago 1988), pp. 157, 159.

[23] Cf. M. Heinzelmann, *Gregor von Tours (538–594). Zehn Bücher Geschichte. Historiographie und Gesellschaftskonzept im 6. Jahrhundert* (Darmstadt, 1994).

liturgy in Milan, fell asleep at the altar at the moment of St. Martin's funeral in Tours, officiated there, and woke up two or three hours later to continue the ceremonies in his own church.[24] Elsewhere, Gregory will have us believe that a Gallic matron had actually come to Jerusalem "to enjoy the presence of our Lord and Saviour", and bribed the executioner of John the Baptist to let her collect the dripping blood from his severed head in order to take it home as a relic![25] A third and last example of his view of "history" is his statement that the traces of the Pharaoh's chariots in the Red Sea "remain until today" and, when occasionally disturbed by strong waves, are "divinely renewed [to be] as they were".[26] These are not events circumscribed in homogeneous space and linear time. What we see is that space and time are not stable categories; here and there, heaven and earth, past and present, tend to overlap, coalesce. Just as in his model, the Bible, there are, in Gregory's narratives of dramatic, down-to-earth events, turns, leaps, cracks and crevices through which something else becomes visible: namely, the omnipresent spiritual reality that in fact dominates everything. The stories just mentioned take place in the indeterminate, fluid time and space of the waking dreams that are "myths"—stories that are held to display fundamental truths about the world, as figured and embodied in sensory phenomena and events.[27]

Is Gregory's for us very improbable story of the broken chalice, then, presented to the uneducated as an historical event, but intended to be understood by the more sophisticated as only a "figure" or allegory: in fact, as a metaphor of spiritual reality? If the latter, then the status of all his miracle stories at once becomes questionable.

At this point, however, the nature of "metaphor" needs to be defined more precisely. Ricœur, in his study of metaphor, defines it as the effecting of a connection between previously unrelated categories of perception or thought which names and so discloses or discovers new experience, thereby creating new meaning in language.[28]

---

[24] *VM* 1, 5.

[25] *GM* 11.

[26] *Hist.* 1, 10: *Usque hodie permanere . . . divinitus renovantur, ut fuerant.*

[27] Cf. "Mythos", in: Die Religion in Geschichte und Gegenwart, vol. 4, p. 1263; "Mythos", in *Pauly's Realencyclopaedie der Classischen Altertumswissenschaft*, suppl. vol. 10, col. 1403–6; and J. Vidal, "Aspects d'une mythique", *Le Mythe, son langage et son message*, ed. H. Limet and J. Ries, *Homo Religiosus* 9 (Louvain-la-Neuve, 1983), 35–61.

[28] P. Ricœur, *The Rule of Metaphor. Multidisciplinary studies of the creation of meaning in language*, tr. R. Czerny (Toronto, 1977), pp. 239, 246.

Elsewhere, in an article on "Imagination in discourse and in action", Ricœur shows how mental imaging or imagination in fact innovates in many ways: not only by creating new meaning in language, but also by making the past and the distant experienceable (through empathy), by making the present inspectable (through a distancing which is achieved by contrasting it with imaginations of other possible presents), and by making the future moldable (through imagining plans and ideals that can materialize in and through action).[29] In his studies of historical narrative Ricœur stresses the reader's imaginative reenactment of what he calls the literary "configuration" of a story, and says that this leads to a "refiguration" of his world view.[30] In this linguistic and philosophical study of metaphor, however, he does not mention such a reenactment.

Sallie McFague has explored the reader's reception of a metaphor from a theological viewpoint. She describes a New Testament parable as "an extended metaphor" which displays otherwise not verbalizable spiritual experience in an embodied, sensory figure. And she states that the reader or listener's act of understanding—that is, inner reenactment of the dynamic pattern displayed in the story through making the "leap" from the sensory to the spiritual plane—induces an experience of this pattern. It is this actual experience that would generate belief.[31] In her view, then, the imaginative enactment of a metaphor effects an actual transformation of the heart according to its pattern. Could something like this process be what Gregory meant with his formulation of "mak[ing] barren minds conceive the knowledge of perfect faith"? And could his improbable story of the chalice be intended as a parable—or extended metaphor—to precipitate such a transformation in the listener or reader?

In his recent book, Raymond Van Dam says that the illnesses that were cured at shrines tended to be social rather than physical ailments. In the bodily miracles—cures—of late antique saints, he says, the metaphors of illness and curing that are used by Gregory are assimilated to the central religious symbols of Church doctrine, such as Christ's saving of all mankind through the Passion and the Resurrection, so that the enactment of these metaphors reinforces

[29] "Imagination in discourse and in action", *Analecta Husserliana* 7 (1978), pp. 3–22.
[30] *Time and Narrative* 3, p. 170.
[31] S. McFague, *Speaking in Parables. A Study in Metaphor and Theology* (Philadelphia 1975), pp. 138–42.

the Church's theology. At the same time, van Dam states, there are metaphors of community and of judicial power; these spell out, teach and reinforce ecclesiastical views of ideal social structures and power relations. Through a cure, a person is reintegrated into his group, the Church community, and assumes a relation of dependence with regard to the saint and his representative, the bishop. Van Dam asserts that such rituals enable people to think and talk about themselves; and, in a note, quotes an anthropologist as saying that the illness is a "text", and the cure an "interpretation".[32] In Van Dam's view, then, the Church's ideal of earthly-cum-heavenly society is something like the verbalizeable, though hidden, script of the ritual of curing.

This analysis places the cure in its social and institutional context. What Van Dam does not do, however, is to ask how such an "interpretation" of the "text" or "script" of metaphors or symbols expressing the Church's ideal—if it is indeed that—actually achieved its mental and physical effect. A contemporary cultural anthropologist who is also a psychologist—René Devisch of the University of Louvain—has recently published a study of a healing cult among the oral society of the Yaka in Zaire in which he looks specifically at the operation of metaphors in the ritual context, and formulates a new definition of this phenomenon.[33] He observes that, in this culture—uninfluenced by the "distancing self-awareness" and privileging of the mind over the senses that are connected with the use of linear writing[34]—the enactment of ritual metaphors discloses and activates the pre-verbal consciousness.[35] In ritual, he writes, metaphors do not act as linguistic phenomena in a communicative sphere: "ritual symbols are . . . corporeal devices, processes and methods or patterns that . . . arise from a potential which, akin to the dream, unconceals both images and inner energy woven into the texture of the body".[36] Thus "ritual metaphor [is] a performance that does

---

[32] R. Vam Dam, *Saints and Their Miracles in Late Antiquity* (Princeton, 1993), pp. 82–115; quotation of A. Kleinman, p. 85, n. 15.

[33] R. Devisch, *Weaving the Threads of Life. The 'Khita' Gyn-Eco-Logical Healing Cult Among the Yaka* (Chicago, 1993). This study's choices of a few of the many insights in this penetrating and innovative work are not intended to be representative of the whole of his much more intensive and extensive analysis.

[34] Devisch, *Weaving the Threads of Life*, pp. 39, 251, 255.

[35] *Weaving the Threads of Life*, p. 256.

[36] *Weaving the Threads of Life*, p 280.

actually effect the innovative interlinking that it exploratively signifies . . . [It] does not primarily aim to impose a grid of meaning or control, but rather aims to disclose and activate one".[37] Healing, then, is founded in imaginative dreamwork—including such processes as condensation, fusion, figuration—that is largely beyond dialogue and discursive reality. It can only be experienced, acted out.[38] Although the metaphorical forms of ritual and trance behavior are culturally patterned, their power of transformation is outside of what he calls the "logocentric" sphere. In sum, healing is not primarily about communication, nor is it primarily a rehearsal of right social attitudes. It is a realignment, through the dynamic of metaphorical transformation, of intrapersonal images and forces.[39]

To reassure any who may doubt whether contemporary African oral society can be used to understand a sixth-century European society using writing: first, many of the cured whom Gregory describes were almost certainly wholly or largely illiterate, and secondly, although the culturally determined images are different, there are essential similarities between the thought-worlds of the two societies. These are, notably: the use of iconic language indicating iconic thinking,[40] belief in omnipresent spiritual reality, and a blurred distinction between inner and outer events.[41] It has seemed to me, therefore, that Devisch's insight—based upon extensive, first-hand observation and upon communications by the participants—might elucidate a central element in what we see (unfortunately, relatively dimly) happening in Gregory's stories. Therefore, taking the dynamic image-pattern of the broken and restored chalice as my point of departure, I shall first point to the lateral connotations of the story—some associated images and their context which the story is likely to have called up in Gregory's listeners—and then analyze in more detail the role of the broken-restored vessel image as what Devisch calls a "threshold metaphor"[42] underlying the events in Gregory's story of a miraculous cure.

---

[37] *Weaving the Threads of Life*, p. 43.
[38] *Weaving the Threads of Life*, p. 282.
[39] *Weaving the Threads of Life*, p. 278.
[40] *Weaving the Threads of Life*, p. 132.
[41] *Weaving the Threads of Life*, pp. 50–1.
[42] *Weaving the Threads of Life*, p. 270.

B. Connotations of the broken and reintegrated vessel

One connotation may have been the image of the broken vessel that occurs in Psalm 30, 10–13.[43] Because it contains a number of elements that seem relevant for Gregory's cures, it needs to be quoted at some length:

> Have pity on me, Lord, for I am in distress. My eye is disordered (*conturbatus*) through wrath (*ira*), and so is my soul and body. . . . My strength (*virtus*) is weakened (*infirmata est*) because of my poverty, and my bones are thrown into disorder (*conturbata sunt*). I am the scorn of all my enemies, and an object of dread to my neighbors. Those who see me outside flee from me. I have been removed from the heart into oblivion as one who is dead; I have been made into something like a broken vessel (*factus sum tamquam vas perditum*).[44]

The metaphor of the individual as a vessel is a commonplace in early Christian texts. Not only is the apostle Paul called "the chosen vessel (*vas electionis*)" in Acts 9, 15 a phrase that is echoed by Gregory.[45] A key text is perhaps 2 Timothy 2, 21: "If anyone purifies himself from these [ignoble] things, he will be a vessel (*vas*) sanctified for honourable use, and useful for the Lord, ready for all good works".

The apostle Paul's metaphor of the individual heart as a temple is another version of this. In 1 Corinthians 3, 16 he writes: "Are you not aware that you are the temple of God (*templum Dei*), and that the Spirit of God dwells in you?" Gregory uses this too, and, developing this metaphor—probably with the image of the jewelled temple of the soul which he found in Prudentius' *Psychomachia*[46]—tells us early in his *Histories*:

> He [Christ] builds a temple in us in which he deigns to dwell, a temple in which faith shines as gold, and the eloquence of preaching (*eloquium praedicationis*) lights up as silver; and all the ornaments of this visible temple are bright in the beautiful virtue of our heart.[47]

---

[43] All Bible references are to the Vulgate.
[44] Jeremiah 22, 28—*vas fictile atque contritum*—appears to have a similar meaning.
[45] *VP* 2, prol. and 8, prol.
[46] Prudentius, *Psychomachia*, ll. 823–87, ed. M.P. Cunningham, *CCSL* 126 (Turnhout, 1966), 178–80.
[47] *Hist.* 1, 15.

Another relevant image, I think, is that of the glass lamp hanging near the tomb of the murdered Queen Galswinth. The incident is part of a longer section in the *Histories* about the Frankish kings, their wives and their wars. Gregory tells us that the lamp spontaneously fell onto the paved floor, sinking half into it, and yet did not break: it was, he says, "a great miracle (*magnum miraculum*)".[48] Then he goes onto other things. Everyone will have been expected to know that such a thing was possible, for something similar had happened with a glass vessel containing oil blessed by St Martin two hundred years earlier.[49] And, with his allegorical habit of mind, Gregory evidently also expects the reader to understand the message "figured" in the miracle. What message? It is Venantius Fortunatus, in his elegy on Galswinth, who actually spells out the spiritual event which this "sign (*signum*)", as he calls it, makes visible. He says:

> She [Galswinth] holds the signs of life (*signa vitae*), with the the falling glass vessel (*vas*): the water did not extinguish [its flame], nor did the stone of the floor break it. . . . One should not weep for someone who lives in Paradise.[50]

Gregory's *miraculum* and Fortunatus's *signum*, therefore, are to be understood as real events as well as metaphors, parables or figures of an invisible spiritual reality. The fact that Gregory gives only the visible event and expects the reader to do the rest instructs us how to read his "simple histories". He may well have intended the story of the chalice as a similar do-it-yourself cue.[51]

To continue with the connotations: the image of making whole is also found in the Psalms:

> The eyes of the Lord are upon the just, and his ears hear their crying. . . . and he liberates them from all their troubles. The Lord is close to the broken-hearted (*contritis corde*), and he saves the crushed in spirit (*confractos spiritu salvabit*). . . . He watches over all their bones; not one of them is broken.[52]

---

[48] *Hist.* 4, 28.

[49] Sulpicius Severus, *Dialogi* 2 (3), 3, 5–6, ed. C. Halm, *CSEL* 1 (Vienna, 1866), p. 181.

[50] *Carmina*, 6, 5, ll. 365–6, 370.

[51] Cf. for a similar expectation in twelfth-century texts, K.F. Morrison, *History as a Visual Art in the Twelfth-Century Renaissance* (Princeton 1990), pp. 20–47.

[52] Ps. 33, 16, 18–19, 21.

The New Testament uses this image to speak of the restoration of the body at the general resurrection. The first letter of Peter says, for instance: "after you have suffered a little, He Himself will make you perfect, strengthen you, and make you whole (*perficiet, confirmabit, solidabit*)".[53] Gregory, too, describes this; he tells one of his priests:

> whatever of the human body has been eaten by fish . . . or devoured by beasts, will be joined together and restored (*coniunctum . . . reparandum erit*) by the Lord in the Resurrection. For it is not difficult for Him to repair broken things (*perdita reparare*), who created the unborn from nothing. He will restore these bodies into their firm wholeness (*integritate solida . . . reparabit*) . . ..[54]

But the image also seems to be one of those underlying Gregory's thinking about miraculous cures. For in the last chapter of the third book about Martin's miracles, when he exuberantly praises the superlative healing qualities of the dust from the saint's tomb, he says: "More: not only does it make paralyzed limbs firm and whole (*debilia membra solidat*), but, what is greater than all these things, it even wipes off and polishes away the stains of those consciences".[55] Such a thought—congruent with his view of spirit and matter in general—seems to indicate that Gregory also has what we would call a holistic view of healing. The phrase "limbs made firm and whole (*solidatis membris*)" recurs elewhere for the healing of a man who had been paralyzed (*contractis nervis, debilitatur*), and made deaf and blind (he thought he was dying), through fear by a sudden storm in the fields.[56] Such a fear is understandable when we see that Gregory elsewhere describes a sudden storm as brought about by the Devil.[57] In the next—one-sentence—story, in which Gregory indeed gives just the bare essentials of a cure, he tells us: "Charimundus too, coming from Brion paralyzed (*debilis*), was put back together (*redintegratus*) by the power of the blessed bishop [Martin]".[58] But how can the cramped condition of paralysis be regarded as a having fallen apart—like a broken vessel—which needs to be put back together?

---

[53] 1 Pet 5, 10.
[54] *Hist.* 10, 13.
[55] *VM* 3, 60.
[56] *VM* 4, 22.
[57] *VM* 1, 2: *temptatoris inpulsu commoto vento.*
[58] *VM* 4, 23.

C. The miraculous cure: embodying metaphors

The terms *debilis* and *redintegratus* also occur in the following story, and it shows the scope and intensity of the imagination that could be carried out in a cure at a saint's shrine. In this case, the latter was a corner, protected by a railing, in St. Martin's monastery of Ligugé, where the saint had revived a dead catechumen 200 years earlier. Gregory tells us that once, while visiting Poitiers, he went to this monastery, and showed his respect to this corner by praying there with tears, and thereafter celebrating masses. Then he asked the abbot to tell him "whether the Lord had shown (*ostendisset*) any miracle there". In the presence of the brothers (this, of course, proves the veracity of the following statements), the abbot asserted that blind persons were frequently healed there, "and paralytics put back together (*debiles redintegrari*)". Then he proceeded to tell the following story about an event that had recently happened:

> A certain woman who is an inhabitant of this place, who had been struck with the fluid of paralysis, had completely lost the service of all her limbs. Placed on a cart drawn by oxen, she used to be carried [in this way] around the houses of the wealthy to fill the necessity of her poverty. When she had been carried to this place, she prostrated herself upon the pavement, and then she slowly approached [the corner] in a long drawn-out effort. [When she had reached it] she devoutly kissed the veil that covered the holy railing, and said:
>
> "Here, blessed confessor, I believe you to be present. Here, I tell the world (*testificor*) that you revived a dead person. I have absolute trust (*confido*), therefore, that if you wish you are able to save me, and to restore (*restituere*) health to me, just as, formerly, when you had broken open the jaws of the underworld, you brought back [from it] a dead man's soul."
>
> Having said these things [or perhaps: while she was saying these things], she flooded her cheeks with tears. Immediately after she had finished her prayer [however], whatever was withered (*aridum*), whatever was cramped (*contractum*), whatever had become disconnected (or fallen apart) (*dissolutum*), was reintegrated (*redintegratum est*) in her body for the woman by the power of the blessed bishop.[59]

---

[59] *VM* 4, 30: *Mulier quaedam vicina loci huius, paralysi humore perculsa, officio membrorum omnium usquequaque perdiderat. Quae carrucae inposita, bubus trahentibus, ferebatur, circumiens domos divitum, ut inopiae suae expleret necessitatem. Ergo dum delata ad hunc locum pavimento prosternitur, lento conamine accedens, velum quod sanctum tegebat cancellum devote osculatur, dicens: "Hic te, beate confessor, adesse credo, hic te mortuum suscitasse testificor. Confido enim, quod, si volueris, potueris me salvare ac sanitati restituere, sicut quodam, disruptis infernis faucibus, defuncti animam reduxisti."*

The woman's invocation of the saint puts into practice Christ's stress upon faith, or rather trust, in him as the operative condition of the request for a cure being granted: "Whatever you ask in prayer, believing, you will receive (*omnia quaecumque petieritis in oratione credentes accipietis*)."[60] The form of her prayer, but also that of the abbot's summing up of its effect, are not those of colloquial speech; the passages are rhythmically stylized—by Gregory, no doubt. The pounding rhythms of their repetitions hit the message home to the reader's or listener's heart.

Devisch describes the Yaka concept of illness as a disconnecting and disordering of psycho-physical energies which blocks a person's vital source.[61] The curing process undertakes to undo this through the enacting of paradoxes: "the simultaneous deployment of one connotation and its reverse", thereby perhaps "turning an opposing force against itself self-destructively".[62] The bodily enactment of such a paradox would precipitate the actual healing.[63]

In Gregory's story, what are the underlying images shaping this experience and its description? The core image is, of course, that of death. In Gregory's stories, paralysis is sometimes likened to death. Maurusa, for instance, who was also blind, "was regarded as a living dead person (*tanquam mortua putabatur superstes*)".[64] The sub-image implicit in the larger one of death is that of dissolution, disconnection, falling apart. Directly associated with death and dissolution, finally, is the image of resurrection. We saw that Gregory believed that the disconnected condition would be repaired at the Resurrection. Christ's saving death and resurrection, as Van Dam also points out, was the example for the resurrection of the faithful, but it was a model underlying the metaphors used in the descriptions of cures as well.[65] Thus Gregory not infrequently speaks of a cure as a rebirth or a resurrection, as "he made him be born anew in the world (*renasci denuo fecit in mundum*)", and "as though revived from death

---

Haec effata, genas lacrimis rigabat ubertim, ac statim impleta oratione, quicquid aridum, quicquid contractum, quicquid dissolutum fuit, redintegratum est mulieris in corpore a beati antestitis virtute.

[60] Mt 21, 22.

[61] Devisch, *Weaving the Threads of Life*, pp. 132–3.

[62] *Weaving the Threads of Life*, p. 269.

[63] *Weaving the Threads of Life*, pp. 266–7.

[64] *VM* 2, 3.

[65] Van Dam, *Saints and Their Miracles in Late Antiquity*, pp. 113–14.

(*quasi redivivus*)".[66] To draw all this together: if being paralyzed is like death, and death is a falling apart, then being cured of paralysis is being revived or reborn through being put back together again, or reintegrated. The terms *dissolutus* and *redintegratus* thus point to the broken chalice as the unexpressed root metaphor here.

Having identified what seem to be the core images and the root metaphor, how are they seen to "work"? When we compare Gregory's description of the healing process with Devisch's, we see that there are striking similarities. What we see happening in Gregory's story is the healing of the physical body by enacting metaphors of the opposing limits of human experience. Devisch says of this: "the trespassing of boundaries and exploration of liminal experiences appear to instigate a revival or reawakening in the patient".[67] Death, of course, is one of such experiences: the woman seems to have mentally imaged her paralysis as an anticipation of being held in "the jaws of the underworld"—as in Gregory's other stories, we find that past, present and future can overlap. At the same time, she expects to be, as it were, reborn.

Mentally imaging and thereby experiencing such paradoxes as actually present must have taken tremendous effort and energy. When the woman arrives at the holy place, her copious tears indicate her "broken spirit". In one of his prefaces, Gregory also speaks of *compunctio* in connection with plentiful weeping.[68] Devisch also calls the healing process one of "abreaction and catharsis": the pushing of an enactment or identification with an image to its limit, until the image transcends itself and spontaneously turns into its opposite.[69] In Gregory's story, we see this in the paralyzed woman's initial prostration, and her slow—presumably very painful—dragging herself the whole length of the room to the corner are the intensification of her pain to the limit: a kind of enactment of the death agony. This very act and quality, however, is also the supreme effort to reach the inner and outer life-giving spot to be healed there. Just as with Devisch's Yaka, for Gregory images represent realities, and (therefore) the boundaries between inner and outer events are blurred.[70] All this must have

[66] *VM* 2, 13 and 4, 34.
[67] Devisch, *Weaving the Threads of Life*, p. 268.
[68] *VM* 3, prol.
[69] Devisch, *Weaving the Threads of Life*, p. 256.
[70] *Weaving the Threads of Life*, p. 267.

brought about a liminal state in which a transformation, a reversal of the paralyzing "dissolution" and a liberating "reintegration" of emotional and physical forces, took place. As in the story of the broken chalice, the spirit and body that had both "fallen apart" were "reintegrated" by pushing the "brokenness" to—and beyond—the limit through pain, tears and prayer.

Another pair of irreconcilable yet fused opposites is that of the absence and yet presence of the saint and his holy power: the saint lives in heaven, yet he also "lives with us".[71] He is in or around his tomb or in this case in his monastery, yet he also is not. Finally, past and present are coalesced: what the saint did 200 years ago can and must happen again now. In her prayer, the woman asserts her absolute confidence that here, in the very same spot that he had revived someone else, the saint can and will repeat his action and raise her as though from the dead. The opposition between past and present is dissolved: they exist within each other, as though traces of the presence of the saint and his pattern of reviving energy or power were somehow still stored in the floor and the walls—and amenable to being called out to reenact the event.[72] And so, as in the Yaka ritual, death and rebirth or revival become different aspects of the same event. A similar Christian image is, of course, Paul's interpretation of the parable of the seeds: one has to pass through physical death to be born again spiritually.[73]

Devisch observes that the enactment of metaphors of such liminal situations in present-day oral societies induces a state of dream-awareness or trance, in which discursive reasoning is temporarily put aside for the iconic awareness, and images are preverbally experienced as affect-laden realities.[74] He writes:

> . . . the actualized trance and concomitant acts have a metamorphic effect. The cathartic trance arouses a deeply lived and bodily enacted experience of freeing and channeling life-bearing in the body, therapy group, and life-world in unison.[75]

---

[71] *VM* 2, 25: *Nobiscum inhabitat.*

[72] Cf. L. Watson, *The Nature of Things. The Secret Life of Inanimate Objects* (Rochester, Vt., 1990), pp. 31–2.

[73] 1 Cor 15:36.

[74] Devisch, *Weaving the Threads of Life*, pp. 255, 257.

[75] *Weaving the Threads of Life*, p. 211.

Gregory mentions such states in other stories about miraculous cures in the sixth century. In one, for instance, a paralyzed man attended the celebration of liturgy Palm Sunday in which everyone had chanted: "Hosanna, blessed is he who comes in the name of the Lord". After this, when he had fallen asleep alone in front of the tomb, "he suddenly went into trance (*factus est in extasi*), and, terrified by fear, lay as though dead". After a few hours, as he himself told Gregory, he woke up "as though from sleep, and suddenly came to his right mind (*ad sensum suum revertitur*): having raised himself up, he marvelled at finding himself healthy".[76] Without actually saying it, Gregory seems to suggest that the man had in some way experienced the coming of Christ or the saint "in the name of the Lord". For, as we saw, in his view, words can make their referents present. Significantly: again he does not say so explicitly. The reader or listener himself is expected to supply—thus visualizing and experiencing—the image of the saint that is missing in the picture.

Is this enactment of the metaphors for the illness—the liminal events of death, dissolution, and being caught in the jaws of the underworld, both now and in the distant past—only the replicating of a pre-existing, verbalizable script communicating about and reaffirming dependence upon community solidarity, power relations and a dominant theology? Alerted by Devisch's insights, we seem to see another dimension in Gregory's stories as well: a metaphorical "image-logic" of transformation that cannot be verbalized. Van Dam perhaps obliquely points toward the existence of something like this when he concludes that cures were more about caring than about curing.

I hope to have shown that Gregory's stories of cures seem to indicate that he was, in his own sixth-century way, aware of a transformational "logic" of enacted metaphors, which, as we saw, he perceived—perhaps for that reason—as powerful spiritual realities. As already mentioned, the same kind of logic is still operative in oral societies today. Devisch speaks of the "ritual drama" which he describes as "work[ing] on corporeal processes by using metaphorical equivalents of bodily processes" such as birth, orgasm and death.[77] This kind of healing is not confined to oral cultures, however. Some modern psychotherapy uses guided waking dream methods that effect

[76] *VM* 2, 33, p. 621.
[77] Devisch, *Weaving the Threads of Life*, p. 30.

clinically attested psychic, and even physical, healing in exactly the same way in western countries: through imaginatively enacting, and/or interacting with, either spontaneous or induced metaphors for non-verbalizable affective states and patterns. Expressed in medical terms, affect-laden mental images behave as something like bio-electrically charged patterns through which, in the hypothalamus, revitalizing—or killing—messages are given to the body's autonomous systems (such as: the central nervous system, the endocrine system and the immune system).[78]

Metaphor and miracle

The evidence here reviewed indicates that the miracle of the chalice is intended to be "history" as well as metaphor. Because for Gregory, as for Augustine, all reality is created and continuously maintained by God or Christ, it is as such inherently miraculous.[79] "All is possible for the believer",[80] and therefore a restored chalice is no more improbable than multiplied wine, bread and fish, or walking on water—events attested to in the Gospels.[81] The miracle, then, was indeed "history". But, at the same time, it was an embodied figure, metaphor or parable of a spiritual pattern operative in the world.

Gregory's appreciation of his friend Fortunatus's language, which included the use of literary devices such as metaphor, means that he must have been aware of the latter's literary use as an ornament. In the stories which he himself wrote to edify the church, however, Gregory appears to choose only metaphors that were images of invisible patterns of spiritual power, some of which could transform hearts and bodies. Apart from being figured in an event involving a physical object, the dynamic spiritual pattern of the broken and reintegrated vessel could also display itself in a "sign (*signum*)", another—telling—name for a miraculous cure.[82] Thus the miraculous cure of paralysis "reintegrated" a person who had fallen into a condition of having

---

[78] B.S. Siegel, *Love, Medicine and Miracles. Lessons Learned About Self-Healing from a Surgeon's Experience with Exceptional Patients* (New York, 1986), pp. 66–9.

[79] Marrou, *Augustin et le fin de la culture antique*, p. 156.

[80] Mk 9:23, cited in *Hist.* 2, 3.

[81] Jn 2:1, Mk 6:41–4, Mt 14:25–7.

[82] As in VM 1. prol.: *Nemo ergo de anteactis virtutibus dubitet cum praesentium signorum cernit munera dispensari, cum videat clodos erigi, caecos inluminari.*

become disordered, disconnected and thereby fractured within oneself, within the world and in one's relation to God. Gregory appears to have believed that a description of this spiritual pattern's manifestation in objects or bodies—especially if the reader or listener would also have to make an imaginative effort to supply the creative dynamic which (as we have seen) Gregory purposely leaves out of his narrative—could bring about the active presence of this creative dynamic in his heart, thus making it "conceive" the perfect faith that was the unshakeable trust and belief in her imagings as realities which precipitated the paralyzed woman's cure.

What, then, what is the role of metaphor in Gregory's "simple histories" of these miracles? It is, on the one hand, that his stories themselves tend to be embodied metaphors of spiritual patterns historically acting in and through visible and palpable human events. And on the other, he lets us see that the ritual enactment of root metaphors and core symbols of the Christian religion serves, as Devisch says, "to unconceal" non-verbal awareness: images and inner energy woven into dream consciousness and into the body that, when activated, can transform both. In other words, Gregory shows us that metaphor, as enacted imagination, can "unconceal" and create *reality*.

X

The poet as visionary
Venantius Fortunatus's «new mantle» for Saint Martin[1]

Sulpicius Severus's late fourth-century writings about Saint Martin include a one-sentence story about a vision:

> The ex-Prefect Arborius testified that he saw Martin's hand, offering the sacrifice, clothed somehow with the most noble jewels, sparkling with beautiful [lit. purple] light, and that he heard the sound of the jewels colliding among themselves upon the movement of his right hand[2].

More than 170 years later, both the length and the content of the story were expanded in a new poetic version[3]. The poet, Venantius Fortunatus (c.540-c.604), was born near Treviso and received his education in Ravenna after the restoration of imperial power there; he came to the Frankish kingdoms in 566, settled in Poitiers two years later, and died as its bishop[4]. His Life of Martin appears to have been written

[1] This essay is an expanded version of a paper given at the Gregory of Tours Centennial sessions, organized by Thomas F.X. Noble and Kathleen Mitchell, at the 29th International Congress of Medieval Studies at Kalamazoo in May 1994. I am grateful to the University of Utrecht for a research leave from September to December 1994, with a financial contribution to help cover its expenses, and to Robinson College of the University of Cambridge for the opportunity to spend that leave there, during which most of this article was written. Finally, I wish to thank Tom Noble and Martin Parmentier for their detailed comments and suggestions on the semi-final version.

[2] *Testatur Arborius ex praefecto, vidisse se Martini manum sacrifium offerentis vestitam quoddammodo nobilissimis gemmis, luce micare purpurea, et ad motum dexterae conlisarum inter se fragorem audisse gemmarum.* Sulp.Sev.,*dial.* 2(3),10,6, CSEL 1, p.208.

[3] A hundred years earlier, the first poetic version was produced: Paul.Petric.,*vita s. Mart.* [=*vit.M.*], CSEL 16, 1, pp. 17-165. The scope of this article unfortunately does not permit its inclusion in the discussion.

[4] On the poet's career, see: M. Reydellet, *Venance Fortunat, Poèmes*, vol. 1 (Collection

between 573 and 576, and it was dedicated to his patron and friend, Gregory, bishop of Tours[5]. Here is his version of the story:

> And, even more, Arborius, ex-prefect and faithful [Christian], reports a noble sign of which he was himself a witness in the city. While [the bishop] was placing the immaculate gifts to God upon the altar, while the father – in rapture – was celebrating the divine ceremonies, while the priest was blessing with his mouth the gifts of Christ – the body and blood, which had been placed on the altar – suddenly, his nourishing hand sparkled with heavenly beauty, coruscating with the varied splendour of noble stones, scattering raying light in all directions as a wheel; his arms were vibrating lightning through beautiful [lit. purple] jewels; their brightness as well as the ruddy golden light of the metal beamed even in the sunlight, through which the miraculous character of the event was more believable.
>
> At the same time, the powerful man, Arborius, said that he then heard the loud sound of jewels colliding among themselves. Thus the pious hand flashed together with the just man's faith, and transferred into the place of his cuff, an emerald shone.
>
> O beautiful Martin, adorned by a veil of precious stones; how your new mantle [becomes you] – a coruscating texture, whose woof is ruddy-glowing topaz and whose warp jasper – and instead of woollen threads, distinguished jewels run through the tunic!
>
> Which artist's hand spun the precious strands? Who was this craftsman who wove the hyacinthine wool? Who was able to twist the rigid gems into threads?
>
> These things should be brought to mind by venerating rather than by speaking. Why do you seek to understand the mysteries, when you cannot enter the hidden light? Be stunned into silence then, O man, where grace weaves its tissues!

Nobile quin etiam ex praefecto Arborius effert
signum quod vidit se teste fidelis in urbe.
Inmaculata Deo cum dona imponeret arae
et pater attonitus ceremonia diva sacraret
munera vel Christi benediceret ore sacerdos

Budé) Paris 1994, pp. vii-xxviii; J. George, *Venantius Fortunatus. A Poet in Merovingian Gaul*, Oxford 1992, pp.4-34, and B. Brennan, *The career of Venantius Fortunatus*, «Traditio» 41, 1985, pp. 49-78. Cf. also P. Godman, *Poets and Emperors*, Oxford 1987, pp. 1-37.

[5] Reydellet, *Fortunat*, cit., p. xxv. Venantius Fortunatus,*vita S. Mart.* (=*VM*) Dedicatio, F. Leo ed., MGH AA 4, 1, pp. 293-371, here p. 293. There is a French translation by E.-F. Corpet, *Oeuvres de Paulin de Périgueux suivies du poème de Ven. Hon. Clem. Fortunat*, vol. 2, Bibliothèque Latine-Française, 2nd series, Paris 1849.

inposita altari rata corporis atque cruoris
emicuit subito manus alma decore superno,
nobilium vario lapidum splendore coruscans,
undique visa rotae spargens radiatile lumen,
bracchia purpureis vibrantia fulgura gemmis,
lumen et ad solis radians lux fulva metallis,
credula quo potius fierent miracula rerum:
Vir simul ipse potens se tunc Arborius inquit
gemmarum gravium crepitantem audisse fragorem.
Sic geminante fide iusti pia dextera fulsit
inque loco manicae micuit translata zmaragdus.
O Martine decens, lapidum velamine compte,
quam nova palla tibi, cuius textura coruscans,
trama topazos erat rutilans et stamen iaspis
et tunicae insignes currunt pro vellere gemmae!
Quae manus artificis cataclyzica fila rotavit?
Quis fuit hic opifex, ubi lana hyacinthina currit?
Quis potuit rigidas torquere ad licia gemmas?
Haec venerando magis poterunt quam fando referri.
Quid secreta petis nec in abdita luminis intrans?
Est, homo, quod stupeas, ubi nectit gratia telas[6].

The poet has taken the «noble» jewels on Martin's hand which he found in his source, specified them, and imaginatively spun them into a whole «new mantle» and «tunic» for the saint. They appear to emit light[7], and the sound of their colliding proves that they are not an optical illusion[8]. Late antique saints' lives in the west tend to stress simple if not outright austere clothes on their subjects; as far as I know, such a detailed image of a jeweled saint is unique. Although he knows that his readers or listeners will realize that he has extended his source material, the poet dares to present his invention as a true vision of spiritual reality which should be venerated rather than questioned. How is all this possible, and what message is the poet trying to convey?

In late Antiquity, the accepted literary style in poetry and in prose was an elaborated, ornate and dense one: the so-called «Alexandrine»

6. *VM* 4, 305-330, MGH AA 4, 1, pp. 357-358.

7 See on this subject and on the allegorical interpretation of jewels generally: C. Meier, *Gemma Spiritalis*, vol. 1 (Münstersche Mittelalter-Schriften 34/1), München 1977, pp. 246-253 and passim.

8 As contrasted with the illusion of the Devil appearing as a bejewelled Christ in *VM* 2.278-357, MGH AA 4.1, pp. 323-325.

or «jeweled» style[9]. Instead of a continuous narrative and clear, organic composition, it preferred parallelism and «amplified» its subject matter into a loosely connected series of beautiful images, figures of speech or vignettes, like a crown of jewels or a garland of flowers – images that the poets themselves, including Fortunatus[10], use to describe their work. The connections between these units was left to the associative imagination of the reader – thus enlisting his participation in the creation of the work. Discovering the hidden meanings in another author's intentional obscurities was considered a delightful game[11]. This preference for parallel vignettes and dazzle has been connected with the contemporary taste for glittering mosaics and for the dazzling textiles decorated with interwoven with gold and jewels[12] which the poet shows us upon the saint. The stylistic ideal may help explain the long poem's unappreciated status in modern times: while its subject tended to put off classicists, its decorated poetic form discouraged hagiographers[13].

The fact that in this period everything tended to be understood in terms of images – allegorical, oneiric and visionary – appears to be another symptom of what amounts to a world view based upon analogies. It has recently been called «an insistently figural way of viewing the social, psychic, religious and philosophical dimensions of life»[14]. In Antiquity, *imago* could have many meanings: a pictorial representation, an oneiric phenomenon, a rhetorical device such as a metaphor, likeness due to resemblance, or a mental-spiritual phenomenon such as the «figure», form or archetype which, as a Platonic idea, shaped visible

[9] J. Fontaine, *Naissance de la poésie dans l'occident chrétien*, Paris 1981, pp. 60-65. M. Roberts, *The Jeweled Style. Poetry and Poetics in Late Antiquity*, Ithaca 1989; J. Fontaine, *Études sur la poésie latine tardive d'Ausone à Prudence. Recueil de travaux*, Paris 1980, pp. 164-165. See also: M. Reydellet, *Venance Fortunat et l'esthétique du style*, in M. Sot ed., *Haut Moyen-Age. Culture, éducation et société. Études offertes à Pierre Riché*, La Garenne-Colombes 1990, pp. 69-77.

[10] *VM* 3, 385-387, MGH AA 4, 2, p. 432.

[11] As Fortunatus to his friend Bishop Felix of Nantes: *Carm.* [=C] 3, 4, 3, Reydellet 1, p. 87.

[12] Roberts, *Jeweled*, cit., pp. 71, 117-118.

[13] See Fontaine, *Naissance*, cit., pp. 269-271; A. H. Chase, *The metrical lives of St. Martin of Tours by Paulinus and Fortunatus and the prose life by Sulpicius Severus*, «Harvard Studies in Classical Philology» 43, 1932, pp. 51-76; and J. Corbett, *Changing perceptions in late Antiquity: Martin of Tours*, «Toronto Journal of Theology» 1987, pp. 236-251. On Fortunatus's work in general: W. Meyer, *Der Gelegenheitsdichter Venantius Fortunatus*, «Abh. der Kön. Gesells. der Wiss. zu Gött.», Phil.-hist. Kl., N.F. 4.5, Berlin 1901. On the cult of Saint Martin in Gaul, see now R. van Dam, *Saints and Their Miracles in Late Antique Gaul*, Princeton 1993, pp. 13-28.

[14] P.C. Miller, *Dreams in Late Antiquity*, Princeton 1994, p. 104.

reality[15]. Because imagistic associations are not limited by discursive principles such as contradiction and incongruity, an image could present multileveled, dynamic truths as such in a way that abstract statements could not[16]. Letting all these associations «blossom», as Paul Ricoeur calls it[17] – we are reminded of Fortunatus's (then conventional) image of words as «flowers»: he calls his poetic predecessors «jewelled meadows» (*gemmantia prata*)[18] – is a process that Gaston Bachelard has called the «transfiguration» of a «figure»[19]. More, the brilliance of flowers and jewels itself, as Aldous Huxley has noted, can not only call up memories of past visionary experience (perhaps not yet recognized as such), but also evoke or precipitate a mode of feeling and perception that tends toward such experience[20]. Fortunatus's associative extension of the visionary image of the jewels may thus also be a journey into the visionary mode of awareness.

As I shall attempt to show in what follows, Fortunatus's elaborate visualisation of what appears to be the new heavenly robe for the elect that is only incidentally and briefly mentioned in other sources has a singularly rich associative field. Its presentation of the glorified saint for awed contemplation is, I suggest, something like an icon in the form of a mental image. At the same time, it functions as a multivalent symbol, precipitates inner illumination and visualizes a metaphor for the poem itself as scintillating language of praise. Moreover, with his description of the flashing jewels, Fortunatus purposely constructs and evokes an attitude of a dazzled awe toward the visionary image of the saint that tends to induce in the reader or listener the very visionary quality it describes. To place what Fortunatus is doing here in its sixth-century Gallo-Frankish context, a few parallels and differences with visions and luminous phenomena in the writings of his friend Gregory of Tours will be indicated. But first the poet's attitude towards an image of the saint as such will be examined in his report, at the end of the poem, of his interaction with a pictorial representation of Saint Martin in Ravenna.

15 See: TLL 7, 1, 404-414. As a visible representation (404-408); as a purely mental phenomenon (408-414); on the image as *praefiguratio, allegoria, typus* and *figura* (412); as a Platonic Idea (414).

16 As on the reading of texts in the twelfth century: K. Morrison, *History as a Visual Art in the Twelfth-Century Renaissance*, Princeton 1990, pp. 20-47.

17 P. Ricoeur, *The Rule of Metaphor*, transl. by R. Czerny et al., Toronto 1977, p. 309.

18 *VM* 1, 37, MGH AA 4, 1, p. 296.

19 «On comprend les figures par leur transfiguration», G. Bachelard, *L'Air et les songes*, Paris 1943, p. 13, quoted in Miller, *Dreams*, cit., p. 104.

20 A. Huxley, *The Doors of Perception*, Harmondsworth 1959, p. 86.

I. «Beautiful Martin»: *The form of the saint under an image*

From the end of the sixth century, there is evidence of the veneration of images in the East[21]. The evidence from Gaul in this period is spotty and ambiguous.

At least since the fifth century, St Martin's miracles, perhaps including Arborius's vision, were depicted in his church in Tours[22]. Both Gregory's and Fortunatus's writings show that pictorial representations of holy persons (in action in scenes from their lives) – sometimes designated as «icons» (*iconicae*) – were not uncommon in sixth-century Gallic churches. But also that their function was regarded, at least officially, as a commemorative, didactic and exemplary one[23]. Nevertheless, in an inscription in Saint Martin's church at Tours attributed to Paulinus of Périgueux, the addressee – who is said to be prostrating himself and praying, presumably at the saint's tomb (but this is not unambiguous) – is told to look at the mural pictures of Saint Martin's miracles. The murals not only show what the saint can do for his suppliants but also seem to function as an aid to visualizing the invisible but present saint who is being addressed[24]. The adorational gestures

[21] See E. Kitzinger, *The cult of images in the age before Iconoclasm*, «Dumbarton Oaks Papers» 8, 1954, pp. 83-150; A.Cameron, *Images of authority: elites and icons in late sixth-century Byzantium*, «Past and Present» 84, 1979, pp. 3-35; Idem, *The language of images: the rise of icons and Christian representation*, in D. Wood ed., *The Church and the Arts*, Studies in Church History 28, Oxford 1992, pp. 1-42; and R. Cormack, *Writing in gold. Byzantine society and its icons*, London 1985. Older but still valuable is:A. Grabar, *Martyrium. Recherches sur le culte des reliques et l'art chrétien antique* 2, Paris 1946, pp. 343-357, and P.J.Alexander, *Hypatius of Ephesus. A note on image worship in the sixth century*, in Idem, *Religious and Political History and Thought in the Byzantine Empire*, London 1978, VI. Cf. F. Diekamp,*Analecta Patristica*, Rome 1938, pp. 118-119.

[22] Paul.Petric.,*vers. de orant.* [=*or.*] 6-8, CSEL 16, 1, p. 165, in E. Le Blant, *Inscr. chrét. de la Gaule*, 1, n. 176, pp. 237-238.

[23] Greg.Tur.,*glor.mart.* [=*GM*] 21 (moveable *iconica* of Christ), 22, MGH SSrM 1, 2, pp. 500-501; *Vita patrum* (=*VP*) 12, 2 (mural *iconicae* of apostles and saints), MGH SSrM 1, 2, p. 713. Idem, *Hist.* [=*H*] 2, 17, MGH SSrM 1, 1, editio altera, pp. 64-65; Fortunatus, *C* 1, 5, 6, Reydellet 1, pp. 24-26, and 10, 6, MGH AA 4, 1, pp. 234-238. The latter are amply and admirably discussed in *H*. L. Kessler, *Pictorial narrative and Church mission in sixth-century Gaul*, in Idem and M.S. Simpson ed., *Pictorial narrative in Antiquity and the Middle Ages* (Studies in the History of Art 16), Washington-Hanover 1985, pp. 75-91. Cf. *Images (culte et querelle de)*, DACL 7, 1, 180-302.

[24] The following words occur in Paulinus's inscription near the pictures of Martin in his church in Tours: *Quisque solo adclinis mersisti in pulvere vultum/ humidaque inlisae pressisti lumina terrae/ attollens oculos trepido miracula visu/ concipe et eximio causam committe patrono* («whoever you are who bows to the ground, you who have rubbed your face in the dust, and pressed your wet eyes upon the uninjured earth: lifting your eyes to grasp

appear to be expressions of deep veneration toward a patron rather than worship as though of a divinity. In the sixth century, Gregory reports prostration before living persons in the past, and himself and others currently «adoring» tombs and the relic of the Cross – but not pictures – through prostration and prayer[25].

As for Fortunatus, in his Life of Martin he, too, addresses the heavenly St Martin as «delightful, to-be-adored, and venerated with the heart» (*dulcis, adorande, et mihi pectore colende*), and imagines himself prostrated, as a humble suppliant, before the saint in person as his patron: *suppliciter humilem tibi se stravisse, patrone*[26]. In his and his friend Gregory of Tours' sixth-century Gaul, communication with the divine generally tended to take place, after prayer, not through seeing but through contact with material objects that had once been 'in touch' with, and thereby made permanent conduits of, the holy. In a long diatribe on the former idolatry of the Franks as pagans, Gregory makes very clear that he does not believe that *simulacra* have any power at all[27].

Nevertheless, he repeats a story from Eusebius about a cure through a plant touching a statue of Christ in Paneas, and adds that someone who had visited it recently told him that he had seen «a wonderful brightness» in its face[28]. If he understood this to be similar to the numerous luminous apparitions which he regarded as signifying the presence of the «power» (*virtus*) of a holy person[29] – and this seems likely – then he is betraying an attitude here that he does not really want to

the miracles with a trembling seeing, commit your case to the excellent patron»), Paul.Petric.,*or.* 1-4, CSEL 16, 1, p. 165; LeBlant, *Inscriptions* 1, Paris 1856, p. 237.

25 Before a living person: *H* 1, 31, MGH SSrM 1, 1, ed. alt., p. 24; before tombs: *Virt. Jul.* [=*VJ*] 24, MGH SSrM 1, 2, p. 575: *ingredimur basilicam, adoramus sacrosancti martyris sepulturam; prosternitur et aegrotum in pavimento; GM* 5, SSrM 1, 2, p. 490: *coram adoranda cruce ac sacris beatorum prosternor pignoribus.* Cf. *Adoration*, DTC 1, 1, 437-442, and DSp 1, 210-220.

26 *VM* 2, 468, 483, MGH AA 4, 1, p. 329. Cf. *Mt* 8:2: *leprosus veniens adorabat eum.* See also M. Roberts, *St. Martin and the Leper: Narrative Variation in the Martin Poems of Venantius Fortunatus*, «Journ. of Med. Latin» 4, 1994, p. 87.

27 *H* 2,10, MGH SSrM 1, 2, pp. 58-60. Cf. *Adoration*, DS 1, 210-220; DTC 1, 437-442.

28 *Mira claritas, GM* 20, MGH SSrM 1, 2, p. 500, referring to: Eus.Caes., *HE* 7, 18, SC 41, p. 191-192. The same had occurred around the statues of pagan gods; cf. W. Elliger, *Die Stellung der Alten Christen zu den Bildern* (hereafter *Stellung*) (Studien über christliche Denkmäler, N.F. 20), Leipzig 1930, pp. 47-53.

29 For instance: *Nihil tamen praeter virtutem gloriosae Virginis aliud penitus videre potuimus, unde claritas illa fuisset exorta, GM* 8, MGH SSrM 1, 2, p. 493. See on luminous phenomena in Gregory, G. de Nie, *Views from a Many-Windowed Tower. Studies of Imagination in the Works of Gregory of Tours* (hereafter: *Views*) (Studies in classical antiquity 7) Amsterdam 1987, pp. 176-192.

know about. Or does he? For he is the first to report (non-curative) miracles around two portable pictures of Christ in Gaul. These stories suggest that, at least in Narbonne and another unidentified city, a picture of Christ could then be experienced as somehow «connected with» his person: one picture bled when pierced, and Christ appeared in a dream to protest against being shown undressed on the Cross in the other[30]. There is no indication of any «adoration» of the pictures, however. Gregory tells us only that the picture of the crucifixion in Narbonne was «continuously looked at (*assidue cerneretur*) by the people». Is this a euphemism concealing what the author regards as an embarrassing situation which he is not sure how to judge? If he had rejected the idea of any «presence» in pictures at all, he would not have told the stories, I think. As we shall see below, a story of Fortunatus will also have given him food for thought about this matter.

As is well-known from Gregory the Great's letters, around the turn of the century pictures of holy persons were being «adored» in Marseille – was it actual worship, or in fact the same gesture of deep respect for a patron? –, giving rise to the first iconoclastic action by its bishop. The pope wished to preserve the pictures of what were probably biblical and other stories so that the unlettered might learn from them what they could not read in books, and what should rightly be adored: the Trinity[31]. Gerhart Ladner has pointed to the significance for the question of images of fact that the same pope was still unquestioningly carrying out the required formal «adoration» of the statuettes of the emperor – designated as «icons» (*iconae*) –, through which he was regarded as being «present» in the West[32].

To sum up, in late sixth-century Gaul and Italy, saints were customarily «adored» in their relics; some persons, however, could evidently also experience pictures – although officially intended as commemora-

[30] R. Markus, *The cult of icons in sixth-century Gaul* (hereafter *Cult*), «Journal of Theological Studies» 29 ,1978, p. 153, says about the situation in Gaul that «the distinction between the image and the person represented was being eroded». On the subject in general see: *Images*, DACL 7.1, 210-302.

[31] Greg.Magn.,*Ep.* 9, 209 (July 599) and 11, 10 (October 600), *Reg. Ep.*, CChL 140A, pp. 768, l, 13-14, and 875, l, 60-62: *ut ex visione rei gestae ardorem compunctionis percipiant et in adoratione solius omnipotentis sanctae trinitatis humiliter prosternantur;* discussed in this context in C.M. Chazelle, *Pictures, books, and the illiterate: Pope Gregory I's letters to Serenus of Marseilles*, «Word and Image» 6 ,1990, pp. 138-153. See further: Elliger, *Stellung;* on pagan practices: E. Vacandard, *L'idolatrie en Gaule au VIe et au VIIe siècle*, «Rev. des Quest. Hist.» 33, 1899, pp. 424-454.

[32] G.B. Ladner, *The concept of the image in the Greek Fathers and the Byzantine Iconoclastic Controversy* (hereafter *Concept*), «Dumbarton Oaks Papers» 7, 1953, pp. 8, 20-22.

tive and didactic – as somehow linked with the sensibility of the heavenly person represented, and in Marseille others – perhaps influenced by practices imported there from the East – felt that pictures of holy persons deserved some kind of cultic veneration.

Hardly remarked upon, however, is the fact that, as Gregory too reports, Fortunatus is the first in the West to report a cure – his own – near a picture of Saint Martin above a window in the church of Paul and John in Ravenna[33]. As he says, «this wall holds the form of the saint under an image» (*hic paries retinet sancti sub imagine formam*). Significantly, *forma*, in that period, could mean not only appearance, but – like *imago* – also archetype of visible reality, as well as beauty[34]. As will be seen, all these meanings are relevant here as well as in the appraisal of the verbally precipitated mental image of the jewelled saint[35].

In his description of the cure, Fortunatus says that he wanted to embrace the picture because of its «sweet colour»[36] – an indication that he experienced it as lifelike, if not as actually «living». And although he does not say so, he must there have prayed to the saint for help, perhaps while looking at the picture. Did he also look «through» the visible image to the «form», beauty or appearance of the saint now living in heaven?[37] Fortunatus's phrasing suggests but does not develop this. In any case, the picture will have helped him to visualize – and thereby make quasi-present – the one to whom he was praying. But the actual cure of his eyes was brought about, as he says, by touching them from afar with the light of the lamp which was hanging near the picture and the window. Proximity to the picture is important here. Fortunatus says that the lamp's light was mediated by «blessed olive [oil]»: Gregory says explicitly that this was oil from the lamp[38]. Fortunatus suggests

[33] Greg.Tur.,*virt. s. Mart.* [=*VtM*] 1, 15, MGH SSrM 1, 2, p. 597; Fort.,*VM* 4, 672-701, MGH AA 4, 1, pp. 369-370.

[34] *VM* 4, 690, MGH AA 4, 1, p. 369. See TLL VI, 1, 1082-1087 on *forma* as *imago* or *exemplar*, including the sense of the Platonic *idea* (1086). But compare *forma venusta* as exterior appearance in C 7, 1, 31, MGH AA 4, 1, p. 154. On *forma* as divine, archetypal-pattern as well as Beauty see C. Harrison, *Beauty and Revelation in the Thought of Saint Augustine* (hereafter *Beauty*), Oxford 1992, pp. 36-52.

[35] On readerly visualization see E. Esrock, *The Reader's Eye. Visual Imaging as Reader Response*, Baltimore-London 1994.

[36] *VM* 4, 691, MGH AA 4,1, p. 370: *Amplectenda ipso dulci pictura colore.*

[37] See on *looking through* an image Harrison, *Beauty*, pp.266-269.

[38] *VM* 4, 696, MGH AA 4, 1, p. 370: *Quo procul ut tetigi benedicto lumen olivo*; Greg.Tur.,*VtM* 1.15, MGH SSrM 1, 2, p. 597: *ex oleo, quod sub imagine picturae beati Martini in cicendili ardebat, dum tetigerunt oculos, lumen rediisse confessus est*. He reports a cure through oil that had been in contact with Martin's tomb in *VtM* 2.32, MGH SSrM 1, 2, pp. 620-621.

but does not say that its proximity to the picture is what made it «blessed» – an idea that points to the picture as a source of holy power. At the same time, however, the sensory-concrete lamp was perhaps intended to be understood as a multivalent symbol: on the one hand, for the human eye, for Fortunatus (like his contemporaries) believed that the human eye emitted light; and on the other, powerfully, for Christ («the lamp» (*lucerna*) of the heavenly Jerusalem)[39]. Understood to be self-evident here is the idea that it is Christ who acts through the saints[40]. At the same time, window and eyes are probably also associatively assimilated: the eye as the «window» of the mind or soul[41].

The whole event is thus described as a purposeful kind of double vision: while Fortunatus touches his eye with the oil, he mentally images Christ (the Lamp/Light) giving light to (i.e. illumining) his soul. In addition, the image of the *forma* (inner pattern) of the saint might also, however, mediatively reveal that of Christ who – as the poet elsewhere emphasizes – was the saint's model-for-life[42]. For Fortunatus, then, powerful spiritual realities may be ritually approached through the sensory phenomena that symbolize and thereby «reveal» them. The same – sacramental – world view is found in the writings of his friend Gregory of Tours[43]. Modern clinical evidence corroborates the power of transforming symbols in showing that, in the visualisation of such symbols, mental images can be effective mediators between consciousness and the body's vital systems – sometimes triggering rapid and improbable cures[44]. But, except for the ambiguous evidence of Paulinus of Périgueux's inscription, Fortunatus appears to be the only one in the West explicitly to expand the ritual manipulation of sensory objects to include affectively contemplating a picture as an additional approach to the saint whom he is addressing: as the poet indicates with his reaction of wanting to embrace it, the picture is experienced as a quasi-presence[45].

39 Fort.,*v. Germ.* 149, MGH AA 4, 2, p. 23. Ap 21:23. All references and quotations are from the Vulgate.

40 As also Gregory, for instance in *H* 6,6, MGH SSrM 1,1, ed. alt., p. 275.

41. Cf. TLL 9, p. alt., 448.

42 As Fortunatus explicitly says in *VM* 4, 585-586.

43 In Gregory's *VtM* 2,2 (MGH SSrM 1,2, pp. 609-610) gazing at the flame of a candle that had burned upon Martin's tomb and ingesting a piece of its wick drove out fever. See: de Nie, *Views*, pp. 198-200; on his world view in general: passim.

44 B.S. Siegel, *Love, Medicine and Miracles*, New York 1986, passim.

45 See on this as an uncensored, spontaneous response D.Freedberg, *The Power of Images. Studies in the History and Theory of Response*, Chicago 1989.

If there was a relic of the saint in this church[46], in this story the picture is the focus of attention. But whereas the poet speaks of «adoring» the tombs of other saints in the city[47], he significantly does not mention such an act toward the picture. Did he assume some other gesture of veneration? The story of the cure, the first and only one of its kind in the West, shows that for Fortunatus, in any case, a pictorial representation could play a role – alongside the possible relic, the lamp and the secondary mediation of the oil – in making «the doctor present» (*praesens medicus*)[48]. (Since Fortunatus elsewhere also refers to Martin as «doctor», this must be the saint, if not also, by extension, Christ)[49].

The saint's «presence» through his relics had long been taken for granted[50]. Although the connotation of the term *forma* suggests the inherent shape-giving presence of the original in its image, the operational role of this picture itself in making the saint «present» remains – perhaps intentionally – unclear. Fortunatus's foregrounding of the picture in this story may have been influenced by eastern ideas and practices circulating in imperial Ravenna. He is careful, however, not to attribute the cure to the picture directly.

The poet gives his gratefulness for the cure as his motivation for writing the Life of Martin[51]. One modern scholar's criticism of the poem is that its presentation of the saint is not that of a human being but of «an icon»[52], that is, an idealized, non-human image to be adored. Such a mental image, I shall argue, was precisely the poet's goal. The vision of the heavenly Martin as seen by Arborius – that of the «inhabitant of heaven», as Fortunatus elsewhere calls the saint[53] – underlies the whole poem: it is the constant imaginative counterpoint for the earthly

[46] *VM* 4, 686-387 (MGH AA 4, 1, p. 370): *Martini loculum, quo iure sacelli/ ... lumen mihi reddidit auctor. Sacellus* – little bag (A. Blaise, *Dict. Lat.-Franç. des Aut. chrét.*, Turnhout 1954, p. 728) – may be associated with *sacella*, treasure (ibid.), and here may mean a relic in a reliquary. Or is *sacellum* simply 'sanctuary'?

[47] *VM* 4,682, 684, MGH AA 4, 1, p. 370: *Martyris egregii tumulum Vitalis adora/ .../ Rursus Apollinaris pretiosi limina lambe.*

[48] *VM* 4, 698, MGH AA 4, 1, p. 370.

[49] *VM* 4, 270, ibid., p. 356. Gregory also refers to Martin as a doctor in *VtM* 3, 21, MGH SSrM 1, 2, p. 637. Cf. my discussion of this theme in *Views*, pp. 243-246.

[50] As already in fifth-century inscriptions in Martin's church: *cuius anima in manu Dei est sed hic totus est praesens manifestus omni gratia virtutum* (Le Blant, *Inscriptions*, n. 178, p. 240).

[51] *VM* 4, 688, MGH AA 4, 1, p. 370: *Munera qui tribuit, saltem, rogo, verba repende.*

[52] Corbett, *Perceptions*, cit., p. 248.

[53] C 1, 5, 3, Reydellet 1, p. 24: *coeli incola*; cf. *VM* 2.465, MGH AA 4, 1, p. 329: *aeterna in saecula civis*. On this theme in the early period see: W. von den Steinen, *Homo Caelestis* 1, Bern 1965, pp. 104-114.

appearance of the saint in his customary humble attire. Double vision again. These complementary images are, as it were, the warp and woof of the poem's texture, and Martin's mantle – earthly and heavenly – is a core image throughout[54]. Fortunatus's poem may have been a factor in the subsequent tradition of the saint's soldier's mantle as a royal possession that, in the Carolingian period, was carried into battle as a protective relic[55].

Where does the image of the jeweled mantle come from? Alexandru Cizek suggests that the archetype of descriptions of ideal beauty in the early Middle Ages is the numinous light figure of the transfigured Christ on Mount Tabor: «His face shone like the sun, and his garments became white as snow»[56]. Sulpicius's description of Martin going heavenward resembles this[57]. Shining robes had also been described on heavenly beings in the Book of Revelation. The speaker to John was «one like a son of man, clothed with a long robe and with a golden girdle around his breast»[58]. The angelic riders wore «breastplates the colour of fire and of sapphire» (*igneas et hyacinthinas*)[59]. The angels emerging from the temple «were clothed with pure white stone (*vestiti lapide mundo candido*), and girded around their breasts with golden girdles»[60]. Another model may have been Ezekiel's description of the Prince of Tyre, wearing jewels that are manifestations of his original inner beauty and wisdom[61].

In late antique religious texts, a tradition had developed about a garment of glory, usually metaphorical, that would clothe the elect in heaven[62]. Especially in Gnostic circles, this could sometimes be pictured

54 I am preparing a larger treatment of Fortunatus's uses of imagination in his religious works in a study of religious imagination in the period 430-750.

55 Cf. J. van den Bosch, *Capa, basilica, monasterium et le culte de Saint Martin de Tours*, Nijmegen 1959, pp. 22-25. Fortunatus mentions the soldier's mantle in a suggestive manner in C 10,7, 57-58, MGH AA 4, 1, p. 240: *Cuius opima chlamys tremebundum texit egenum,/ Eius apostolici vos tegat ala viri.*

56 *Et resplenduit facies eius sicut sol; vestimenta eius autem facta sunt alba sicut nix*, *Mt* 17:2. Similarly, Mk 9:1 and Lk 9:28. References and further associations in A. Cizek, *Das Bild von der idealen Schönheit in der lateinischen Dichtung des Frühmittelalters*, «Mittellateinisches Jahrbuch» 26, 1991, p. 16.

57 Sulp.Sev.,*ep*. 2, 3, SC 133, p. 324.

58 Ap 1:13.

59 Ap 9:17.

60 Ap 15:6.

61 Ez 28:11-15.

62 See on this subject: A. Kehl, *Gewand (der Seele)*, in RAC 10, 945-1025; and E. Haulotte, *Symbolique du Vêtement selon la Bible* (Théologie 65), Paris 1966, pp. 324-326.

as a real garment covered with jewels[63]. Tertullian speaks in an allegorical sense of Christ taking on the sacred vestment of the Church, compared to that of the Old Testament priests of the Tabernacle which was illuminated by twelve gems: «So that gems may illuminate the sacred vestment of the church»; the latter are images for the apostles, «the [living] stones solid in faith»[64]. But the four rows of three precious stones found in this Old Testament vestment are not what we see on Martin here. In Origen's Homilies on Ezekiel, the Prince of Tyre's jeweled beauty is described as the future heavenly state of the elect[65]. Further, we find mention of jeweled persons in heaven in the fourth century in Prudentius[66], and, in the fifth, in an inscription of Paulinus of Périgueux for the church of Tours[67]. In the sixth, Gregory of Tours mentions crowns with heavenly jewels but, except for a bride of Christ, no jeweled robe or mantle[68]. It is possible, however, that he imagined the «sacrosanct mantle with which he [St Martin, at the Last Judgment] is covered through his glory» (*sacrosancto pallio, quo ille tegitur a gloria*) as such[69]. His descriptions of dead saints in contemporary visions never show them attired in jewels[70]. Fortunatus, however, mentions and describes jewels on mantles and crowns in heaven more than anyone else[71].

The rich clerical robes of later medieval times have not been found in the practice of the late antique and early medieval period[72]. As for pictorial representations: a contemporary church in Toulouse which Fortunatus may well have seen, however, pictured a «silver mantle» (*pallio ... argenteo*) and «a most precious mantle» (*palli[o] ... pretiosissimo*) on holy figures (not saints)[73]. Further, his friend Gregory tells us about the

63 As A. Hermann, *Edelsteine*, RAC 4, pp. 545-546, and E. Benz, *Die Vision*, Stuttgart 1969, pp. 341-346.

64 Ex 39. Tert.,*adv. Marc.* 4, 13, CSEL 47, p. 457-458: *ut gemmae inluminaturi sacram ecclesiae vestem*. Reference in Hermann, *Edelsteine*, RAC 4, p. 547.

65 Orig.,*hom. in Ez.* 13, 2, SC 352, p. 424.

66 Prud.,*perist.* 2, 557-560, CChL 126, p. 276 (Loeb series 398, p. 140): *videor videre inlustribus gemmis coruscantem quem Roma caelestis sibi legit perennem consulem.*

67 Paul.Petric.,*or.* 8, CSEL 16, 1, p. 165: *Terrenum non claudit opus quod regia coeli/ Suscipit, et rutilis inscribunt sidera gemmis.*

68 As in *H* 1, 28, MGH SSrM, 1, 1, ed. altera, p. 21: of martyrs, *gemmis caelestibus coronati*; 2, 3, ibid., p. 40: martyrs *gemmis immarciscibilibus coronavit*; and 6, 29, ibid., p. 297, of a nuptial robe with many jewels (see below).

69 *VtM* 2, 60, MGH SSrM 1, 2, p. 630.

70 *VtM* 1, 24 and 2, 40, *VJ* 9, MGH SSrM 1,2, pp. 601, 623, 568-569.

71 Notably in *C* 10, 7, 14; 17; 24; 27-28, and *VM* 3, 455-522, MGH AA 4, 1, pp. 239-240 and 345-347.

72 Hermann, *Edelsteine*, RAC 4, 541. Cf. *Vêtement*, DACL 15, 2, 2989-3007.

73 H. Woodruff, *The iconography and date of the mosaics of La Daurade* (hereafter:

church in Cologne in which were buried the fifty soldiers of the Theban legion who were martyred, and which «because it shone through an admirable workmanship, out of mosaics somehow made golden (*ex musivo quodam modo deaurata*), the inhabitants wished to call that church the Golden Saints» (*Sanctos Aureos*). But he reports its bishop's headache as having been cured by the dust from the well in which the martyrs had been thrown – not, then, through addressing a picture[74].

Another source of inspiration for Fortunatus's jeweled mantle, however, is likely to have been the pictorial images of jeweled persons which the poet saw in Ravenna, which we are extremely fortunate to be able to see today. In the archiepiscopal chapel in Ravenna Christ is shown as a military leader in clothing decorated with jewels[75]. The image of Saint Martin, in a white tunic with a purple mantle and carrying a crown, which we can still see in Ravenna's Sant'Apollinare Nuovo, however, does not at all look like Fortunatus's jeweled figure. In other church murals, it seems that jewels were sometimes depicted on holy persons[76], perhaps like the richly decorated mantle on Saint Demetrios in the well-known early seventh-century mosaic in Thessaloniki[77]. Thus, the possibility that the picture involved in Fortunatus's cure, which does not survive, showed Martin with a mantle woven with gold and jewels cannot be ruled out. In the church of San Vitale, however, we find not only the emperor, empress and some of their entourage wearing robes decorated with gold and possibly with jewels[78], but in the apse, Saint Vitalis' dress – as he receives a crown from a purple-robed Christ in heaven – is richly decorated. If nothing else, this could have been Fortunatus' model for Saint Martin's heavenly mantle.

In the literary context, however, Fortunatus appears to have taken the image from his model Claudian, who had described a jeweled mantle – with emerald, amethyst, sapphire, agates, pearls and coral – in his panegyric of the emperor Honorius[79]. Claudian refers to the imperial

Daurade), «The Art Bulletin» 13, 1931, p. 92. Fortunatus's poems about Toulouse's patron St Saturninus and a church dedicated to him there seem to indicate that he visited the city: *C* 2, 7, 8, Reydellet, pp. 59-63.

74 *GM* 61, MGH SSrM, p. 530.

75 On the iconography of Christ see: *Christus*, RAC 3, 1-29; as Basileus: RAC 2, 1257-1262; *Christus*, *Lex. der Christl. Ikonogr.* 1, 355-410.

76 Hermann, *Edelsteine*, RAC 4, 542.

77 Cormack, *Writing*, cit., pp. 51, 52 (plate).

78 Cf. Roberts, *Jeweled*, cit., p. 112.

79 Claud., *paneg. IV cons. Hon.* (=4 *Hon.*), 584ff., MGH AA 10, pp. 171-172 (Loeb 135,

mantle as «veils» studded with Indian stones (*asperat Indus velamenta lapis*), stressing their wide-flung origins, no doubt as an indication of the wearer's power[80]. In his poem, there does not seem to be a symbolical dimension to the jewels. The emperor Justin II's jeweled mantle as described by his contemporary Corippus in 565 may have been another model[81]. Indirectly, Fortunatus thus seems to associate the saint's status to that of the emperor, an implicit idea in Sulpicius's presentation of the saint in general, to which Raymond van Dam has pointed[82].

Should we go further and understand the poet's visionary image of Martin as a reminiscence of an imperial icon? As we saw, Gerhart Ladner has noted the similarity of the eastern worship of icons of saints with that of the – in the sixth century still continuing and unquestioned – tradition of «adoring» the emperor through his official (no doubt jewel-wearing) images in which he was thought to be «present»[83]. Had Fortunatus seen something of this sort in Ravenna? Similarly, Claudian, in the above-mentioned panegyric, explicitly assimilates the emperor being carried in state to the jewel-clad effigies (*effigies*) of gods (*numina*) being brought forth from their temples and carried around in procession to be worshipped[84]. Also through this association, Fortunatus' verbal image has the same quality: it excites a visualization, a mental image, of the saint in the reader that is to be contemplated and revered in silent awe. Was it also intended to evoke an experience of the saint's «presence»?

Martha Nussbaum has pointed to stories in general as «paradigms of emotion» that structure individual and collective feelings and attitudes[85]. I would add that an appealing or impressive image can do the same, i.e. precipitate an experience in the reader or listener that beco-

p. 328); Cizek also points to this: *Schönheit*, cit., p. 19. On Claudian in general, see A. Cameron, *Claudian. Poetry and Propaganda at the Court of Honorius*, Oxford 1970.

80 4 *Hon*. 585-586, *loc.cit*.

81 Corip.,*in laud. Iust. Aug. Min.* (=*Iust.*) 2, 86-133, A. Cameron ed. and transl., London 1976, pp. 50-51, 96-97. His word choices in 1.276-8 and 282, and 2.113-116, 129, translated on pp. 44 and 51, are very similar: resp. *intextam... vestem, auro ... gemmisque corusca ... fulvum aurum; mysterium rerum ... nobilibus gemmis ... vestis divina ... miracula vestra*.

82 R. Van Dam, *Leadership and Community in Late Antique Gaul*, Berkeley 1985, pp. 121-128.

83 Ladner, *Concept*, cit., pp. 8, 20-22. See also: *Adoration*, DACL 1, 1, 539-546.

84 4 *Hon*. 570, 572, MGH AA 10, p. 171 (Loeb 135, p. 328).

85 M. Nussbaum, *Narrative emotions: Beckett's genealogy of love* («Ethics» 98, 1988, pp. 225-54), reprinted in Idem, *Love's Knowledge*, New York-Oxford 1990, pp. 286-313, here p. 297.

mes a model shaping subsequent feelings about the subject[86]. Intended for the highly educated, and probably jewel-wearing, Gallo-Frankish aristocracy, Fortunatus's image will thus have evoked an affective pattern in connection with the saint that remained in the memory, influencing subsequent attitudes and actions.

II. «Heavenly beauty»: *a symbol*

Arborius has seen a «sign» – another word for miracle. This term is a cue for an attitude of awe and wonder, as well as an indication that the phenomenon is a symbol or «figure» of an important truth of faith[87]. Although Fortunatus elsewhere refers to the associative cluster of flowers-jewels-virtues[88], here he does not explicitly associate the vision of jewels with virtues. He also does not mention a well-known image of the saint's person and life as itself a «jewel», to which he has referred elsewhere in his poem[89]. Suggested but not said, this image underlies and intensifies the whole passage as a central subtext.

Considering the emphasis upon exterior austerity in the contemporary saints' lives, Fortunatus's focus upon beauty is not self-explanatory. Nor is the qualification «heavenly beauty», literally: «beauty from on high»[90]. A look at Fortunatus's poems to and about secular magnates in the Merovingian kingdoms shows, however, that light imagery dominates and that he used the symbolism of jewel-like beauty there too[91]. Like Prudentius[92], he tends to let visible, metaphorical and divine light coalesce, as in the following descriptions of noblemen: «Your beautiful appearance flashes with its own splendour (*forma venusta tibi proprio splendore coruscat*)», and, startlingly, «You have lights (eyes?) of the heart, the lamp of your soul raying light, and your head flashes

[86] On such models: C. Geertz, *Religion as a cultural system*, as reprinted from M. Banton ed., *Anthropological Approaches to the Study of Religion*, London 1966, pp. 1-49, in C. Geertz, *The Interpretation of Cultures*, New York 1973, pp. 87-125, here p. 93: culture patterns as both models *of* and models *for* social and psychological reality, «both by shaping themselves to it and by shaping it to themselves.»

[87] As in *vitae signa*, C 6.5.365, MGH AA 4, 1, p. 146. Cf. the seminal article of E. Auerbach, *Figura*, «Archivum Romanicum» 22, 1938, pp. 436-489.

[88] *VM* 3,385-387, MGH AA 4, 1, p. 342.

[89] *VM* 4, 24-25, MGH AA 4, 1, p. 348.

[90] As Harrison, *Beauty*, cit., shows however, heavenly beauty had been a central notion in the writings of Saint Augustine.

[91] C 6, 1.101-102, 108-111, MGH AA 4, 1, p. 127, 128.

[92] *Cathem.* (=*Ct*) 5, 29-32, 153-154, CChL 126, pp. 24, 28 (Loeb 387, pp. 40, 46).

with eternal light» (*Lumina cordis habes, animi radiante lucerna,/ Et tuus aeterna luce coruscat apex*)[93]. A halo such as that around the head of Emperor Justinian in the S. Vitale in Ravenna? Or were there other philosophical-religious ideals circulating at the Merovingian court about which we have no information?

As for the ecclesiastical tradition: there are passages in the Bible which speak of God's beauty or holy beauty made visible through jewels, and these had been commented upon by early Christian writers. We saw that the most conspicuous emphasis on human beauty through jewels is found in the description of the Prince of Tyre in the book of Ezekiel[94]. He is said to be «the signet of [divine] likeness, filled with wisdom and perfect with beauty»[95], and is also described as walking «in the midst of flaming stones»[96]. Origen's commentary, as translated by Jerome, speaks of the prince's «crown of beauty» (*decoris corona*) as that of «glory» (*corona gloriae*). The true – invisible – beauty, however, is in the Saviour[97]. The author may be indirectly referring to the passages in the Old Testament that speak of God's own beauty, such as: «let the beauty (*decor*) of our Lord God be upon us», and (more cryptically) «From Zion God appeared in perfect beauty» (*perfecta decore*)[98]. Fortunatus's *decor supernus* could derive from these passages.

Elsewhere, however, Jerome himself interprets the Prince of Tyre's jewels, in their being expressions of wisdom and beauty, as manifestations of «angels ... and heavenly Powers (*Angel[i] coelestesque Virtutes*)»[99]. And Fortunatus's wheel radiating and scattering light in all directions is almost certainly intended to evoke associations with Ezekiel's «whirling wheels» (*rotae ... volubiles*) in his vision of God surrounded by heavenly beings[100]. The saint is thereby assimilated to the heavenly hierarchies.

But the Old Testament also enjoins its readers to «adore the Lord in holy beauty» (*adorate Dominum in decore sancto*)[101]. The «holy beauty» of

93 C 7, 1.31, and 7, 5, 29-30, MGH AA 4, 1, pp. 154, 157.

94 Ez 28:11.

95 Ez. 28:12: *signaculum similitudinis plenus sapienti et perfectus decore.*

96 Ez. 28:14: *in medio lapidum ignitorum.*

97 Orig.,*hom. in Ez.* (hereafter *hom. Ez.*) 13, 2, SC 352, pp. 418-420.

98 Ps 89:17; 49:2.

99 *Comm. Is.* 15, 54.11/14, CChL 73A, p. 612.

100 Ez 10:13; or perhaps to the wheels in Ez 1:15-16. In St Mary's church in Toulouse, two archangels are described with three green globes in their right hands (Woodruff, *Daurade*, p.89).

101 1 Par [Chron] 16:29. Cf. J.A. Martin Jr., *Beauty and Holiness*, Princeton 1990, pp. 9-11.

the vestments of the priests of the Tabernacle included four rows of three precious stones[102]. Jerome interprets this arrangement as a «sign» of all the harmonies of the cosmos: the elements, the planets, and the months[103]. But he also equates them with the jewels in the diadem of the Prince of Tyre described in Ezekiel, and with the twelve jewels in the fundaments of the heavenly Jerusalem in Revelation. As such, they indicate «the order and and diversity of virtues» (*virtutum vel ordo, vel diversitas indicatur*)[104]. Further down, he interprets the four rows of stones as the four virtues of prudence, fortitude, righteousness and temperance[105]. What we see here and elsewhere is that no one was worried about multiple meanings of images. On the contrary, they appear to have been appreciated as inexhaustible sources of new meanings[106]. This is what made Fortunatus's amplification possible and acceptable.

The last biblical passage about jeweled beauty that created a tradition of interpretation is, of course, the description of the heavenly Jerusalem in the Book of Revelation:

> ... the holy city Jerusalem coming down out of heaven from God, having the glory [brightness] of God (*claritas Dei*), its radiance (*lumen*) like a most rare jewel, like a jasper, clear as crystal.... And the city does not need sun or moon to light it, for the brightness of God illuminates it, and its lamp is the Lamb (*claritas Dei inluminavit eam et lucerna eius est agnus*)[107].

In the Old Testament, the brightness or glory of God could sometimes be perceived as a visible fiery glow above or in the Tabernacle[108]. As we saw, in the New Testament, Christ too is described as shining with light.

Augustine's suspicion of sensory beauty as leading away from God is well-known[109]. Through his neo-Platonic background, however, he can distinguish this kind from an invisible beauty-to-be-embraced-for-its-own-sake (*gratis amplectenda pulchritudo*), which can only be seen

[102] Ex 27:15-28.

[103] *Epist.* 64.18, J. Labourt ed. and French transl. (Coll. Budé), *St. Jérôme, Lettres* 3, pp. 132-135.

[104] *Ep.* 64, 16, Labourt 3, p. 131.

[105] *Ep.* 64, 21, Labourt 3, p. 137.

[106] As also Morrison, *History*, cit., p. 47.

[107] Ap 21:10-11, 23. The jewels are specified in vs 19-21.

[108] As in Ex 40:32-33.

[109] Aug.,*conf.* 10, 34, 52, ChCL 27, p. 183 (Loeb 27, p. 172).

«from within» (*ex intimo*)[110]. The latter is that of God, that «beauty so old and so new»[111] whose discovery in his heart changed his life. Nevertheless, in his interpretations of the Bible Augustine spoke of «all the good qualities [virtues] that are the treasure of the interior man» – hence spiritual virtues – as «jewels»[112]. In Fortunatus's passage, then, we see the beauty of this «interior man» merging with, or mediated by, what is ostensibly exterior ornament[113].

Sulpicius appears to give the reader a pointer in this direction with the following statement in between a story of a miraculously caught fish and the story of Arborius's vision; it may apply to both:

> This true disciple of Christ – imitator of the deeds of power (*virtutum*) carried out by the Saviour, which he brought forward as an example for his saints – manifested that Christ worked in him, [Christ] who, glorifying his saint continuously, granted the gifts of various graces (*diversarum munera gratiarum*) to one man[114].

The position of the statement and its wording suggests that the term «gifts of various graces» may point to the jewels that appeared. The phrase «various graces» in the sense of spiritual capacities related to the measure of merit is found in Augustine's Commentary on the Gospel of John[115]. It also appears in the early sixth-century Homily on the Apocalypse by Caesarius of Arles. The author says there that the jewels in the foundations of the heavenly city of Jerusalem indicate «the gifts of various graces (*dona diversarum gratiarum*) which had been given to the Apostles»[116]. In the first versification of the Martin stories by Paulinus of Périgueux in the 460's, the author explicitly says that the jewels manifest the saint's merits. But his poem has a definite pastoral slant and tends to

110 *Conf.* 6, 16, 26, CChL 27, pp. 90-91 (Loeb 26, p. 326).

111 *Conf.* 10, 27, 38, CChL 27, p. 175 (Loeb 27, p. 146). Cf. P. Courcelle, *Recherches sur les Confessions de Saint-Augustin*, Paris 1968, p. 457 (n.3), and Harrison, *Beauty*, cit., passim.

112 Aug.,*serm.* 21, 8, CChL 41, p.283: *Haec omnia bona sunt, thesauri interioris hominis; gemmae, non arcae tuae, sed conscientiae tuae.*

113 As Cizek, *Schönheit*, cit., p. 33.

114 D 2(3),10, 5, CSEL 1, p. 208. Cf. 1 Cor 12:4.

115 *In Ioh. evang. tract.*, CChL 36, p. 57. A liturgical prayer for the consecration of priests speaks of *diversarum dote gratiarum* (*lib. sacr. Engol.*, CChL 159C, p. 321).

116 Ap 21:14, 19. Caes.Arel.,*expos. Apoc. Ioh.* (=*Exp. Ap.*) 19, G. Morin ed., *Sancti Caesarii Opera Omnia* vol. 2, Maredsous 1942, p. 274, l.13-15. Cf. transl. by J. Courreau, in *L'Apocalypse expliquée par Césaire d'Arles. Scholies attribuées à Origène* (collection Les Peres dans la foi), Paris 1989, p. 154. This and the following references are cited in Hermann, *Edelsteine*, RAC 4, p. 547.

emphasize the invisible «beauty of the heart» rather than the sensory kind, however symbolic[117]. Paulinus's contemporary, Eucherius of Lyon, gives a very general interpretation of jewels as «the works and miracles of apostles and saints»[118]. Another fifth-century writer, Apringius of Béja, is perhaps closer to Sulpicius in understanding the individual stones to indicate «the shining gifts and miracles of the Holy Spirit itself» (*propria ... Sancti Spiritus dona, vel miracula resplendere*)[119]. Fortunatus's friend Gregory of Tours speaks of the internal «temple (*templum*) ... in which faith lights up as gold, ... in which all the ornaments (*ornamenta*) of that visible temple shine in the honourableness of our consciousness»[120].

It is Prudentius who most clearly speaks of «gems of virtues» (*virtutum gemmae*)[121]. In a description of jewels shining as spiritual virtues in the temple of the soul, he creates an image that recalls the jewels and the light of the heavenly Jerusalem. He speaks there of [twelve] jewels «set singly in the fabric of the walls, [that] sparkle conspicuously (*distincta micant*), and the light from on high (*lux alta*) pours forth (*evomit*) from the clear deep (*liquido ... profundo*) living souls of colours (*animasque colorum viventes*)»[122]. This statement shows that an antique conception of jewels as living spiritual beings that «breathed»[123] has been carried over into Christian thinking. Now, however, they are said to transmit the breathing light of God – a highly significant statement. Elsewhere, when he describes the emerald, he says: «Emeralds shine green like meadows with the

117 Paul.Petric.,*vit. M.* 5, 695-708, CSEL 16, 1, p. 132 (the whole story). 5, 695 and 708, ibid. (jewels through merits); 709-710, ibid. (apparently referring back to the previous story about the jewels): *Nec dubium quin, praecipuae probitate fidei,/ Ultra hominem vario virtutum flore coruscet,...*; 1, 94-95, ibid., p. 22 (interior beauty and the halved soldier's mantle): *alii deformia rident/ Tegmina, nec cernunt mage verum in corde decorem.* French translation by E.-F. Corpet, Bibliothèque Latine-Francaise, 2e série, Paris 1849. See also: R. van Dam, *Paulinus of Périgueux and Perpetuus of Tours*, «Francia» 14, 1986, pp. 67-73, and Chase, *Metrical lives*, cit..

118 *Lapides pretiosi apostoli, vel sancti, sive opera ipsa virtutum.* Euch.Lugd.,*form. spir. intell.* (=*form.*) 7, CSEL 16, 1, p. 48.

119 Apring.Pac.,*tract. in Apoc.* 21, 19, ed. P.A.C. Vega, Script. Eccles. Hisp.-Lat. Vet. et Med. Aevi 10-11, Escorial 1940, p. 71. Vict.Petav.,*comm. in Apoc.* 21, 5, CSEL 49, pp. 152, 154, appears to regard the gold and precious stones as riches and powers given to the saints: *hic accipient sancti ... 'lapides pretiosos'. hoc loco 'transferet ad eos divitias maris et virtutes gentium'.*

120 *H* 1, 15, MGH SSrM 1, 1, ed. alt., p. 15. Cf. *VP* 4.prol., MGH SSrM 1, 2, p. 673: *tabernaculum ... diversisque virtutum floribus adornatur.*

121 *Psychom.* [=*Psy.*] 911, CChL 126, p. 179 (Loeb 387, p. 342).

122 *Psy.* 851-3, CChL 126, p. 179 (Loeb 387, p. 338). Cf. Ap 21, and Cizek, *Schönheit*, cit., p. 12.

123 Hermann, *Edelsteine*, cit., 506.

spring grass, and the grassy light rolls out in ever-changing waves»[124]. Such «waves» may have been another model for Fortunatus's moving light. In the latter's last lines, the *secreta abdita luminis* refers, of course, to the «unappproachable light» (*lucem ... inaccessibilem*) in which the Lord dwells, according to 1 Timothy 6:16. It could simultaneously be a reminiscence of Prudentius' *lux alta* from a *liquidum profundum*, which is probably another term for the «unapproachable light»[125]. If so, Fortunatus's jewels are indeed visualisations of spiritual virtues or graces deriving from the divine sphere. But the poet leaves this implicit because he is here more interested in putting verbal, intellectual, analytic activity aside, and gazing in silent, reverent wonder.

Is there any indication why, from the many possible ones, Fortunatus chose, besides the conventional gold, the particular jewels that he did: the emerald, topaz and jasper?[126] Are they perhaps symbolical of particular graces or qualities?[127] According to the Book of Revelation, «pure gold, clear as glass» is the building material of the heavenly city and its streets[128]. Jerome says, in his already-mentioned letter, with which Fortunatus is likely to have been acquainted, that gold stands for «the knowledge of God» (*Dei scientia*)[129]. Later, Caesarius compares the splendour of gold with that of faith (*fides ... velut aurum splendet*)[130].

The latter would accord with Fortunatus's statement that Martin's faith flashed together with his hand. In two other poems about this incident, however, he puts it alongside, and almost assimilates it to, a similar vision that occurred during another celebration of liturgy: that of a fiery globe arising from the saint's head[131]. Fortunatus's wording in the passage under discussion makes it seem likely that he is double-visioning again here, and expecting his readers to do the same. This is typo-

124 *Psy*. 862-863, CChL 126, pp. 179-180 (Loeb 387, p. 338).

125 *Psy*. 851-853, CChL 126, p. 179 (Loeb 387, p. 338).

126 Cf. Ex 28:17, 18, 20; Ez 28:13. Emerald: Ap 4:3, 21:19; topaze: Ap 21:20; jasper: Ap 4:3, 21:11, 18, 19. Cf. Epiphanius, *De XII gemmis* 2, 3, 4, C. Gesner ed., Tiguri 1565, pp. 3, 5, 8, says that the topaze is red, that the emerald is green, and that the jasper is green with mixed colours; he gives practical uses but no allegorical interpretations.

127 See on this subject Hermann, Cizek and Meier. The ancient author who is most utilized is Plinius,*nat. hist*.(=*NH*) 37, Loeb 10, pp. 164-331. Interpretations tend to be different in different texts of this period.

128 Ap 21:18, 21.

129 *Ep*. 64, 22, Labourt 3, p. 138.

130 *Exp. Ap*. 19, Morin p. 274.

131 C 1, 5.13-18, Reydellet 1, pp. 24-25, and 10, 5, 5-10, MGH AA 4, 1, p. 234.

logical, figurative and liturgical thinking: analogical spiritual realities coalesce through recalling similar time-bound discrete events.

As for the jewels: Pliny refers to jaspers as tending to be green in colour[132]. Jerome, referring to the walls of the heavenly Jerusalem, describes them as sometimes mixed with blue, white and red: «So that we might know the universal spiritual graces in the fortifications of the Church»[133]. As we saw in Revelation, however, God's glory or brightness is also said to be like that of a jasper; and the city is lighted by God's light, who is Christ[134]. Topazes could be yellowish green[135]. Pliny associated the colour of emeralds with that of young plants, and Prudentius, as we saw, with that of spring meadows, but also that of «youthful vitality»[136].

In his treatise on the saints, the fourth-century Victricius of Rouen is more specific about heavenly jewels. He speaks of the «royal garment» that is the saints' «covering of eternal light» (*aeterni luminis indumentum*) in heaven. Further, they have a crown with twelve jewels – almost certainly the ones mentioned in the vestments of the priests of the Tabernacle and the fundaments of the heavenly Jerusalem:

> «they are distinguished with diadems with the various lights of gems of wisdom, intellect, knowledge, truth, experience, fortitude, tolerance, temperance, righteousness, prudence, patience, chastity. In these individual stones the individual virtues are expressed and written (*expressae scriptaeque virtutes*). The Saviour as maker decorates the crowns of the martyrs with spiritual gems (*spiritalibus gemmis*)[137].

With the gold and what may be various shades of green jewels, then, Fortunatus here may have meant to stress the incorruptible, and eternally budding and springlike qualities of Martin's faith and spiritual qualities. These are manifested in the vision as a dazzlingly bright «heavenly beauty» that is somehow in a continuum with the divine jewel-light of the celestial Jerusalem, and perhaps even with that of heavenly hierarchies. He is showing us Martin in his present appearance of «the heavenly man».

[132] *NH* 37, 37, Loeb 419, pp. 256-261. Cf. Meier, *Gemma*, cit., pp. 152-153.

[133] *Comm. Is.* 15, 5411/14, CChL 73A, p. 613: *ut universas gratias spirituales in Ecclesiae propugnaculis cognoscamus.*

[134] Ap 21:11, 18, 23.

[135] Plin.,*NH* 37, 32, 107-109, Loeb 419, pp. 250-252.

[136] Plin.,*NH* 37, 16, 62, Loeb 419, p. 212. Prud.,*psy*. 862-863, CChL 126, pp. 179-180 (Loeb 387, p. 338).

[137] Victr. Rotom.,*de laude sanct.* 12, CChL 64, p. 89.

III. «Raying light»: *divine illumination*

We have seen that Fortunatus is the only hagiographer who emphasizes his subject's beauty. At the very end of the poem, Fortunatus speaks of the glorified saint in a more straightforward manner and emphasizes once more his total dedication to Christ: «this was your only care, to meditate upon Christ with your devout heart, to meditate upon Christ through your deeds... holding Christ simultaneously in your embrace, your heart, upon your lips»[138]. And then he makes explicit what may be the understanding of the light coming from the jewels: «You equal the sun with its rays and the moon with its courses, refulgent with splendour, you are beautiful as the morning star; you yourself, shining man, *shine with the brilliant light of God* [emphasis added], man attired in snowy white, ruddy-gleaming with a wonderful crown»[139]. As in the beginning of the Johannine Gospel and in the description of the Heavenly City in Revelation – the brightness of God illuminated it and its light was the Lamb – this light of God will almost certainly have been understood as Christ[140]. If this is indeed what he is showing us in his version of Arborius's vision, then the stunned awe he urges upon the reader is that of wordless contemplation of divine light, in other words: illumination[141]. And this illumination occurs while Martin is celebrating what Fortunatus calls «divine ceremonies»: the ritual of the Eucharist, which symbolizes, and is held to effect, the union with Christ[142].

This combination of beauty, contemplation of divine symbols in ritual, illumination, and a putting-aside of the intellect are not as clearly noticeable in other western writers in the late antique period[143]. We find

138 *Haec unica cura,/ Christum corde pio, Christum meditarier actu/ .... Iugiter amplexu Christum, corde, ore, retentans, VM* 4, 575-576, 585, MGH AA 4, 1, p. 366.

139 *Ut solem radiis et lunam cursibus aeques,/ Qui splendore nitens, pulcher quasi lucifer exis,/ Ac fulgore Dei vir fulgidus ipse coruscas,/ Tegmine vir niveus, miro diademate fulvus, VM* 4, 590-593, MGH AA 4, 1, p. 367.

140 Jn 1:9 and Ap 21:23: *claritas Dei inluminavit et lucerna eius est Agnus.*

141 Cf. *Contemplation*, DS 12, 1643-1948 and *Illumination*, DS 7.2, 1330-1338.

142 There is one description of a bishop officiating in his church that also has conspicuous light imagery: that of Avitus baptizing the Jews in Clermont at Pentecost (cf. Greg.Tur.,*H* 5, 11, MGH SSrM 1, 1, ed. alt., pp. 205-206). Here, however, the light is the «fire» of the Holy Spirit that also filled the Apostles: *Inter candelabros radiabat et ipse sacerdos,/Diffuso interius spiritus igne micans* (C 5, 5.125-126, MGH AA 4, 1, p. 111). The illumination here appears to be assimilated to the fire of the candles as sensory symbols.

143 See, however, S. MacCormack, *Art and Ceremony in Late Antiquity*, Berkeley 1981, pp. 270-271 and 275, on ceremonial images as spiritual realities in late antique panegyrics.

it, however, in an eastern source. Here, it is said that the priest, contemplating the divine symbols wordlessly in the ritual, is «filled with divine light and adorned with a loveliness suitable to his divinized state». His function is to transmit this light to the faithful. These passages occur in an early sixth-century treatise on the Ecclesiastical Hierarchy by an author who is known as Pseudo-Dionysius[144].

The history of their early reception in the West is highly obscure[145]. Gregory the Great, who had spent eight years as a papal emissary at Constantinople, refers to Pseudo-Dionysius by name and exhibits certain parallels with the latter's ideas[146]. After a reference to the presence of the treatises in Rome in the seventh century, the first time we hear of them again is when they are sent from Rome to Pepin III in the eighth century; another manuscript was sent in 827 by the eastern emperor to Louis the Pious, who requested and received a translation from Hilduin, the abbot of the monastery of St Denis in Paris[147]. As is well-known, the latter's twelfth-century abbot Suger thought he was acting according to the ideas of the one whom he regarded as his patron saint when he constructed and decorated his church according to the symbolism of the heavenly city which he hoped would lift everyone up in an anagogical manner towards the divine[148].

In the sixth century, Fortunatus wrote his complicated verse for a jewel-wearing Gallo-Frankish aristocracy that was anxious to imitate

144 His works appear in PG 3, 119-1124. There is a separate edition and translation of the *Celestial Hierarchy* [=*CH*] by R. Roques in SC 58. I have used the translation by C. Luibheid (based on the PG edition with some corrections; see p. 2) in The Classics of Western Spirituality series, New York 1987. This quotation and the reference are from the Eccles. Hier. [=*EH*] 3, 311 (PG 3, 468D, Luibheid p. 221) and *CH* 3, 3 (PG 3, 168A, Luibheid p. 155). On Pseudo-Dionysius's work and its influence in the late antique west: DS 3, 244-295, 318-320; D. Knowles, *The influence of Pseudo-Dionysius on western mysticism*, in P. Brooks ed., *Christian Spirituality. Essays in honour of Gordon Rupp*,London 1975, pp. 81-94; and P. Rorem, *Pseudo-Dionysius. A Commentary on the Texts and an Introduction to Their Influence*, New York-Oxford 1993. Further literature includes: R. Roques, *L'univers dionysien* (Théologie 29), Paris 1954; and A. Louth, *The Origins of the Christian Mystical Tradition*, Oxford 1981, pp. 159-178.

145 On this subject see: P.A. Siegmund, *Die Überlieferung der griechischen christlichen Literatur in der lateinischen Kirche bis zum zwölften Jahrhundert* (Abhandl. der Bay. Bened.-Akad. 5), München 1949, pp. 182-187; P.G. Théry, *Études Dionysiennes* 1, Paris 1932, pp. 1-9. Rorem, *Commentary*, cit., pp. 75 and 215, assumes there is no influence noticeable in the pre-Carolingian period except possibly upon Gregory the Great's angelology.

146 *Homilia in Evangelia* 2, 34, 12 (PL 76, 1254B); see DS 3,318-319.

147 DS 3, 319.

148 Sugerius, *De rebus in administratione gestis* 23, E. Panofsky ed. and transl., *Abbot Suger on the Abbey Church of St.-Denis*, second ed., Princeton (1946) 1979, pp. 62-64.

and emulate Rome's imperial and cultural tradition in every way[149]. Some of these are known to have had contacts with or to have been educated in Italy, and thus possibly exposed to influences from the East there[150]. Lacking further evidence, it cannot be proven that the poet's dazzling image of Martin was influenced – directly or indirectly – by Pseudo-Dionysian ideas of ceremonial symbolism and illumination, encountered perhaps during his student days in imperial Ravenna. In the scope of this article I can do no more than point to some conspicuous parallels, and to show that his passage is at least an indication that similar notions could crystallize in the West[151]. We shall begin by examining how Fortunatus handles the ceremonial context in this passage, and put this alongside Pseudo-Dionysius's ideas. Then Fortunatus's treatment there of beauty, illumination and wordless contemplation will be similarly compared with the eastern author's statements on these subjects.

Unlike his source and unlike other western writers (but not unlike Claudianus and Corippus)[152], Fortunatus emphasizes the ceremonial context and quality of the moment. Here, this is: purity, extasy or trance (*attonitus* literally means thunderstruck: something like stunned) during «divine ceremonies» which include the speaking of the sacred words, and the presence of Christ's body and blood under the appearance of bread and wine. Pseudo-Dionysius writes about the symbolic rite of the Eucharist that it «offers Christ to our view» also through «beautiful visions of the mind which ... sacredly and hierarchically effect our communion ... with the One»[153]. Fortunatus's phrasing appears to indicate that Martin was seeing Christ also through something like such a «vision of the mind».

149 As in C 7, 2, 3 (MGH AA, 4, 1, p. 154): *Tu refluus Cicero;* and 7, 7, 6 and 45 (ibid., pp. 159, 160): *Te duce sed nobis hic modo Roma redit ... Antiquos animos Romanae stirpis adeptus.*

150 In the sixth century, at least two men of the Arelatian family of the Parthenii were educated in Italy and maintained contacts there (K.F. Stroheker, *Der senatorische Adel im spätantiken Gallien*, Darmstadt 1970, pp. 199-200). Fortunatus's correspondent Dynamius, sometime rector of the Provence, corresponded with Pope Gregory (George, p. 142).

151 In his poem celebrating the dedication of a church to saint Dionysius the Martyr in Aquitaine, does not assimilate him to the writer: *C* 1, 11, Reydellet 1, pp. 30-31.

152 4 *Hon.* 570, 572, MGH AA 10, p. 171 (Loeb 135, p. 328); Corip., *Iust.* 2, 86-133, Cameron, pp. 50-51, 96-97.

153 *EH* 3, 3, 13 (PG 3, 469C, Luibheid p. 222), and 4, 1, 1 (PG 3, 472D, Luibheid p. 224).

Pseudo-Dionysius says of the officiating priests («hierarchs»), those who have restored God's image in themselves by being «lifted up into conformity» with him:[154]

> They must themselves virtually match the purity of the rites they perform and in this way they will be illumined by ever more divine visions, for those transcendent rays prefer to give off the fullness of their splendor more purely and more luminously in mirrors made in their image[155].

The «splendour» which he means is that mentioned in Paul's saying of the mental envisaging of Christ's life and deeds:

> And we all, with unveiled face, beholding the glory of the Lord, are being changed into his likeness from brightness to brightness as though by the Spirit of the Lord (*nos vero omnes revelata facie gloriam Domini speculantes, in eandem imaginem transformamur a claritate in claritatem tamquam a Domini Spiritu*)[156].

The ideas contained in the above passages, I suggest, are the associations implied in Fortunatus's dense formulation. If so, the poet is saying that the pure Martin, contemplating the symbols of the rite, was illuminated during his stunned beholding of the glory (brightness) of Christ, and by this transformed into the latter's likeness. It would follow that it was this likeness which Arborius then saw – through the mediation of its sensory-like appearance[157] of jewels – as «heavenly beauty».

As we saw, the word *decor* occurs in the Old Testament to refer to God, to the manner in which he should be worshipped and to the appearance of the wise man as a signet of God. In the latter two, jewels are prominent. In the New Testament, jewels are metaphors for the spiritual light and qualities of the eschatological Christian community. We saw too that Prudentius's symbolism of jewels as the virtues of the inner man makes them into an almost visionary experience of a divine reality. If we can accept Fortunatus's vision of the jeweled mantle as a metaphor that, as a visualisation of Martin's spiritual status, is itself a

[154] *EH* 3, 3, 7 (PG 3, 464A, Luibheid p. 216); cf. Rom 8:29.
[155] EH 3, 3, 10 (PG 3, 465C, Luibheid p. 219).
[156] 2 Cor 3:18. Cf. *CH* 3, 2 (PG 3, 166A-C, Luibheid p. 154).
[157] On God's self-revelation through the beauty of created sensory objects cf. Harrison, *Beauty*, cit., pp. 97-139.

spiritual reality – thereby becoming a symbol –, then the light of the jewels is likely to be that same «brilliant light of God» mentioned in the image of the saint with which we began this section, and thus a manifestation of Christ as light. We are reminded of Origen's statement that true beauty belonged only to the Saviour[158].

One of the prime characteristics of the Pseudo-Dionysian writings, however, is their frequent and central association of the One with beauty:

> ... the "beautiful" which is beyond individual being is called "beauty" because of that beauty bestowed by it on all things .... Because like a light it flashes onto everything the beauty-causing impartations of its own well-spring ray[159].

Beauty, then, is flashing, raying light – just as in Fortunatus's description of the jewels. And visible appearances of beauty are symbols that lift the mind up to this invisible, divine beauty[160].

And this brings us to the theme of illumination. In the west, it was a contemporary concern of the first order[161]. Fortunatus's friend and patron Gregory of Tours tells us many miracle stories in which the experience of supernatural light in everyday settings is central[162]. All these show experiences of illumination. Most relevant to our subject here is his story about an event in the church of the Convent in Poitiers which possessed a particle of the Holy Cross. One of the nuns wrote later how the presence of the latter was then experienced: «so that Christ would visibly live here»[163]. Gregory tells us that the relic was «adored» (*adoratur*) every Wednesday and Friday[164]. Here is his story:

> ... I shall first set forth that which the Lord deigned to reveal there in the days of his Passion. On the sixth day before Easter, when [the nuns]

[158] Orig.,*hom. Ez.* 13, 2, SC 352, pp. 18-20. Augustine developed this thought: Harrison, *Beauty*, cit., pp. 192-238.

[159] E.g. *DN* 4, 7, and *CH* 3, 1, 1 (PG 3, 761C-D and 164D, Luibheid pp. 76 and 153).

[160] *CH* 1, 3 (PG 3, 121C-D, Luibheid p. 146). Similarly, Aug.,*conf.*, 10, 34, 52, CChL 27, p. 183 (Loeb 27, p. 172).

[161] This has been shown by a monumental study of Christian funerary inscriptions from this period: G. Sanders, *Licht en duisternis in de Christelijke grafschriften*, 2 vols. (Verh. v. d. Kon. Vl. Acad. v. Wet., Lett. en Sch. K. v. Belg., Kl. d. Lett., 27.56) Brussel 1965.

[162] See on these my *Views*, pp. 176-193.

[163] Baudon.,*vita s. Radeg.* 16, MGH SSrM 2, p. 387.

[164] Cf. *Kreuz, Lex. der Christl. Ikon.*, 562-590; *Kreuz, Lex. f. Theol. u. Ki.*, 605-615.

> were staying up in vigils without light, there appeared before the altar at about the third hour of the night a small light in the manner of a spark. Then, growing larger, scattering hairs of brilliance here and there, it gradually began to rise up high. And it was made into a great beacon of the obscure night and offered light to the vigil-keeping people and suppliants. When the sky began to lighten, it gradually diminished, having been given to the earth as light, and vanished from the eyes of those gazing in wonder[165].

Gregory gives no further explanation. He appears to expect his readers to recognize the light as an epiphany of the resurrection of Christ as the Light of the world. I have chosen this story because the form of the light – scattering hairs of brilliance from on high – resembles that of Fortunatus's jewels. In the same chapter, he tells us about an oil lamp hanging near the relic of the Cross which «flowed over through divine power» (*virtute divina*). As I hope to show, all these may be perceptions or visualisations of a then well-known image or «figure» of Christ.

Fortunatus's *spargens radiatile lumen* resembles Pseudo-Dionysius's «well-spring ray» of beauty. The poet seems to have invented the word *radiatilis*[166], which indicates a specific interest in this quality. How, in fact, does Fortunatus' sudden (*subito*) burst of images of variegated flashing, raying, undulating brilliance work here? If we believe Aldous Huxley, it would evoke the very visionary trance which, as we see in the phrasing (*quod stupeas*), the poet wishes the reader to have. The saint, then, is worshipped from a distance in a trance-like state. The divine dazzles and stuns. Fortunatus's passage may have been inspired by Jerome's description of the brilliance of the Old Testament priest's mantle: «... and a mantle of scarlet beauty (*vermiculatae pulchritudinis*) is made, dazzling the eyes with its brightness» (*praestringens fulgore oculos*)[167]. Early in the fifth century, however, Augustine had described the momentary intuition of the Deity as «like, in the deepest darkness, the sparkling of brilliant light with the most rapid flashing (*velut in altissimis tenebris rapidissimo coruscamine lumen candidum intermicare*)»[168]. In these images, the dynamic pattern of overflowing, coruscating, and raying illumination is the same.

What we see in this is that the essential pattern of Fortunatus's image as a whole is something like a fountain of light. The latter phrase

[165] *GM* 5, MGH SSRM 1, 2, p. 490.
[166] D. Tardi, *Fortunat*, Paris 1927, p. 221.
[167] *Ep.* 64, 15, Labourt 3, p. 129, ll. 25-26.
[168] Aug.,*civ. Dei* 9, 16.18-19, CChL 47, p. 264.

for Christ is indeed found in one of Ambrose's hymns: *Splendor paternae gloriae, De luce lucem proferens, Lux lucis et fons luminis* ...[169]. But Pseudo-Dionysius's images are decidedly similar. He, too, speaks of God as «overflowing gift of light .. shining well-spring ... forever overflowing»[170]. The image of the Fountain of Light also resembles that of the sun, and the latter is in fact a frequent image for Christ in this period[171]. Pseudo-Dionysius explicitly says that the light of the sun is the visible image of God[172]. The image of the divine as raying light recurs in the treatises too. He refers, for instance, to the Deity's «outpouring of light»[173] and «sacred radiance»[174]. I suggest, therefore, that Fortunatus regarded his image of raying jewels as a reflection of the image of Christ, and hoped that it might somehow evoke an illumination by Christ as the Fount of Light.

Such a view is supported by Fortunatus's phrase *miracula rerum*. It recalls Prudentius's identical phrase for the miracle of the three youths in the fire, whom the author there equates with Christ[175]. The phrase may also be a reminiscence, however, of a phrase – «the miracles of pomp» (*miracula pompae*) – used by the fourth-century panegyrical poet Claudian to refer to jewels as imperial trappings[176]. If so, the heavenly and the imperial dimensions coalesce again[177].

In this visionary image of Martin, his human figure and face are not mentioned; they are obliterated by the dazzle. After his description, the poet discourages questions about its make and enjoins silent, awed contemplation. He instructs the reader or listener to remember the image directly, and thus affectively, in a venerative way without letting words get in between. And to let the stunning image do its work, without trying to analyze it or its meaning, or inquiring about its status: fiction or truth. Is Saul's blinding experience of divine light on the way to Damascus[178] a remote model here?

169 G.M. Dreves, *Analecta hymnica* (=*AH*) 50, pp. 11-12. Cf. Ps 35:9: *apud te fons vitae; in lumine tuo videbimus lumen.*

170 *CH* 9, 3 (PG 3, 260D, Luibheid p. 171).

171 For instance in the writings of Jerome: *Comm. in ep. s. Pauli ad Gal.* 2, verse 8-9, PL 26, 402C: *sol iustitiae.*

172 *DN* 4, 7 (PG 3, 701C-D, Luibheid p. 74).

173 *CH* 1, 2 (PG 3, 121B, Luibheid p. 145).

174 *CH* 3, 3 (PG 3, 168A, Luibheid p. 155).

175 *Apoth.* 138, CChL 126, p. 81 (Loeb 387, p. 130).

176 Claud., 4 *Hon.* 565, MGH AA 10., p. 171 (Loeb 135, p. 328).

177 As also Cizek, *Schönheit*, cit., p. 19.

178 Ac 9, 3, 8.

In Pseudo-Dionysius's treatises, the dazzle of the illuminating light functions to stop the ordinary functioning of the intellect so as to open the mind for pre-verbal spiritual wisdom. He says:

> the most divine knowledge of God, that which comes through unknowing, is achieved in a union far beyond the mind, ... and when it is made one with the dazzling rays, being then and there enlightened by the inscrutable depth of Wisdom[179].

About the intellectual approach he elsewhere says: «Human souls ... possess reason and with it they circle in discourse around the truth of things»[180]. In other words:

> The truth we have to understand is that we use letters, syllables, phrases, written terms and words because of the senses. But when our souls are moved by intelligent energies in the direction of the things of the intellect then our senses and all that go with them are no longer needed. And the same happens with our intelligent powers which, when the soul becomes divinized, concentrate sightlessly and through an unknowing union on the rays of «unapproachable light»[181].

As we saw, he regards such an «unknowing» union «with the dazzling rays» as an illumination by divine Wisdom[182]. He is alone in this period, however, in stressing the «darkness» at the heart of the blinding light[183]. Although it suggests blinding rather than "darkness", the attitude which Fortunatus prescribes after his description appears similar. It seems to me that, whether developed only from the ideas in the Latin tradition or (also) influenced (indirectly) by those of Pseudo-Dionysius, something like the just-quoted text may underlie Fortunatus's literally entrancing description of Martin's «heavenly beauty». The attitude he urges parallels Gregory's stunned reaction to the overflowing lamp as a theophany of Christ: «and I gazed in silent wonder» (*admiratusque silui*)[184].

As in the apostolic saying, however, such a contemplation can also induce imitation or replication of its essential pattern in the beholder,

[179] *DN* 7, 3 (PG 3, 885D, Luibheid p. 109).
[180] *DN* 7, 2 (PG 3, 880D, Luibheid p. 107).
[181] *DN* 4, 11 (PG 3, 772B, Luibheid p. 80).
[182] *DN* 7, 3 (PG 3, 872B, Luibheid p. 109).
[183] *Myst. Theol.* [=*MT*] 1, 1 (PG 3, 997B, Luibheid p. 135). Cited in Louth, *Origins*, cit., p. 175.
[184] *GM* 5, MGH SSrM 1, 2, p. 490.

who is thereby transformed into its likeness. In the fourth century, Paulinus of Nola had sent inscriptions for Sulpicius Severus's baptismal church in Aquitaine. Speaking of a «to-be-venerated image (*veneranda ... imago*)» of Martin, Paulinus states:

> It is right that in the place of human restoration Martin is painted, who bears the image of the heavenly man (*coelestis hominis imaginem ... portavit*) through his perfect imitation of Christ; so that, the to-be-imitated effigy of his heavenly soul (*imitanda coelestis animae ... effigies*) meets those leaving behind in the basin the image of their earthly oldness[185].

The contemplation of Fortunatus's image of Martin's heavenly soul mediated by the sensory-like jewels, then, might also effect an imitation, or more precisely a replication, of its image in the reader's soul. Thus he would be uplifted to participate in Christ, whose image as the Fount of Light shines through that of the glorified saint. Perhaps Fortunatus's verbal description is meant, therefore, to function as directions for constructing an elaborated mental image not only as an affective mould for thinking about, and praying to, the glorified saint, but also as a model for the reverent visualisation of what he hoped would be a transforming symbol of illumination[186].

IV. «Veil of precious stones»: *a metaphor for the poem itself*

In one of his other works, Fortunatus, after first saying that he feels struck by «thunder», says: «Perfused somehow with a starry splendour, you seem to dazzle my eyes with the brilliant light of your flashing rays» (*velut coruscantium radiorum perspicabili lumine mea visi estis lumina perstrinxisse*)[187]. Here, however, he is praising a friend's eloquence. The late antique ideal of language is thus imaged in the same manner as heavenly beauty: it stuns, dazzles and blinds[188]. As I have suggested above, it appears to be related to the contemporary proclivity for visionary perception.

[185] Paulinus Nolanus, *Epistolae* 32, 3, and 2, CSEL 29, pp. 278, 276. Cf. Von den Steinen, *Homo*, cit., pp. 106-110.

[186] The article *Contemplation* in DS 12, 1643-1948 contains a very full overview of this whole tradition in East and West until the twelfth century.

[187] C 3, 4, 2, Reydellet 1, p. 87.

[188] Cf. Roberts, *Jeweled*, cit., p. 46.

After the description, the poet asks: «Who was able to twist the rigid gems into threads?». Here again, Claudian must have been his model. Very similar questions – which go unanswered – occur after that poet's picture of Emperor Honorius' jewelled mantle[189]. With the jewelled ideal of language in mind we can recognize the dazzling «veil of precious stones» as also an image or figure of the poem itself. For at the very end of the poem we find that the image of the precious mantle – as well as that of a wreath or crown (*corona*) – as a model for what he had wanted his poem to be for the saint. Indicating that he is aware of the episodic manner of composition, he says that his book has an unraveled, knotty and «bristly texture», as of camel's hair,

> while Martin deserves to wear silk mantles (*pallia*), sparkling with a border of twisted gold thread, or a toga of interlaced blue and white wool, and [deserves] roses, lilies and jewels to paint a varied wreath [for him]. My feeble tongue is silent; request forgiveness for yourself, little book[190].

Here, the poet is referring to poetic beauties instead of spiritual virtues. The phrase as a whole would include the sense of its 'obscuring' somewhat the even greater splendour of its subject as itself a jewel. In one of Fortunatus's other poems – a ceremonial one –, he speaks of Martin's jeweled apparel as having been wrought by «angelic artistry»[191]. Here, however, he keeps us guessing. I suggest that he does so because there is a *double entendre*. After he has himself suggested the questions, he tells his readers or listeners to put them aside and just admire the tissues wrought by grace. Directly, or through the poet? He does not say.

The poem as a whole, therefore, is intended to be not only a wreath of flowers and jewels, but especially a – supposedly unsuccessful – mantle of praise (the phrasing in fact invites a counterstatement by the reader or listener). The association of «mantle» with «ornament of praise» is actually found in the fifth-century treatise of Bishop Eucherius of Lyon, the *Book of Forms of Spiritual Understanding*. There we read: *Chlamis laudis ornatus*[192].

Immediately preceding Fortunatus's last-mentioned passage, however, we find almost certainly still another layer of meaning. There, he

[189] 4 *Hon*. 593-595, MGH AA 10, p. 172 (Loeb 135, p. 330).
[190] *VM* 4, 625-629, MGH AA 4, 1, p. 368.
[191] C 10, 6, 116, MGH AA 4, 1, p. 238: *artifice angelico gemmeus iret homo.*
[192] Euch.,*form*. 7, CSEL 16, 1, p. 47.

speaks of the Last Judgment and calls upon Martin to «conceal my weak self [from condemnation to the infernal fire] with the sacred veil» (*sacro velamine*), which must also mean «mantle»[193]. The «veil of precious stones», then, which Fortunatus has just visualized for us in Arborius's vision, and which, he hopes, is at the same time his poem, is something he hopes he can hide behind at the moment of Judgment. Writing hagiography was redemptive.

Epilogue. «When grace weaves her tissues»: *the poet as visionary*

Elsewhere in the Life of Martin, too, Fortunatus supplements Sulpicius's stories by giving invented descriptions of luminous and/or jeweled heavenly appearances of the apostles and other saints which Martin said he saw. He even adds a jewel-laden Christ – with engraved pearls hanging from his ears – as the heavenly Bridegroom[194]. Here as elswhere, the poet appears to be visualizing a shared imaginary of ascetic circles in the period[195]. In Radegund's convent in Poitiers, with which Fortunatus was intimately associated, one of the nuns had a vision which Gregory of Tours reports:

> She thought, she said, that she was making some kind of journey. When she didn't know the way, a certain man came toward her and said: «If you wish to go to the living spring (*fons vivus*), I will be your guide».
> And she, thanking him, followed where he went before her. Walking, they came to a large spring, whose waters shone like gold, while the plants around it rayed in the manner of various gems in the vernal light.
> And the man said to her: «Behold the living spring (*fons vivus*), which you sought with so much effort! Quench your thirst now from its flowings, so that it may be for you a fount of living water welling up into eternal life».
> And while she was thirstily drinking from these waters, behold the abbess came from another place and, taking off the girl's clothes, covered her with royal garments, which shone with so much light, gold and jewels that one could hardly look at them. The abbess said: «Your Bridegroom sends you these gifts»[196].

[193] *VM* 4, 611, MGH AA 4, 1, p. 367.

[194] *VM* 3, 455-522, MGH AA 4, 1, pp. 345-347.

[195] Also in his C 8, 3, MGH AA 4, 1, pp. 181-191. Cf. G. de Nie, *'Consciousness fecund through God': from male fighter to spiritual bride-mother in late antique female sanctity"*, in A.B. Mulder-Bakker ed., *Sanctity and Motherhood*, New York 1995, pp. 101-190, esp. p. 138.

[196] *H* 6, 29, MGH SSrM 1,1, ed. alt., p. 297. Cf. Jn 4:14. In *H* 1.47 (ibid., p. 30) he speaks of such a robe as *puritatis stola*.

Here is again the dazzling heavenly robe, this time given to the bride of the heavenly Christ. But, as we saw in the previous section, the spring – fount – is also symbolic of Christ. The girl was so «wounded in the heart» (*compuncta est corde*) by this vision, that a few days later she asked to be walled in as a recluse so as to be able to deserve this heavenly state later. The story is another example of the tendency in this period, noted earlier, for self-awareness to be achieved through mental imaging. The nun, however, will have regarded her vision not as her own imagination but, as had happened in the Bible, a true message sent by God[197].

When Fortunatus elsewhere gives his readers or listeners images of refulgent heavenly persons he appears to be conscious of imagining these and not seeing them in a vision. In one poem he says, «There now stands, after all her tears, the excellent Radegund. *Perhaps* [emphasis added] she now holds Eugenia by the hand»[198]. He could have said something like this about his invention of Martin's new mantle. But that is not the way he speaks about it. If we accept the equivalence of the jewels in the mantle with those which (he hopes) are his poetic images, he there seems to suggest that the grace that wove the jeweled tissue was also at work in his creation of the poem[199]. He mentions Christ as the divine Word – instead of the Muses – being his inspiration at the beginning of the Life of Martin[200]. Paulinus of Périgueux had equated the poetic process with religious meditation[201]; addressing the saint, he writes:

> I pray that you will always have been manifestly present in the heart of the miserable poet, so that when the meditation of the poem shall finish, the transcribed prayer will hold your praise (*precor ut miseri manifeste in corde poetae/ Semper adesse velis, ut cum meditatio carmen/ Finierit, teneat transcripta oratio laudem*)[202].

[197] Augustine wrote about the different kinds of visions, including dreams, in his *De Gen. ad litt.* 12, CSEL 28, 1, pp. 379-435 (tr. P. Agaësse and A. Solignac, Bibl. Aug., Oeuvres de St Aug. 49, Paris 1972, pp. 328-457).

[198] C 10, 7, 25-6, MGH AA 4, 1, p. 239.

[199] As also Juvencus, according to Fontaine, *Naissance*, cit., pp. 77.

[200] *VM* Proem. 39-40, MGH AA 4, 1, p. 295: *de Verbo poscite verba;/ Si fons ille rigat, rivulus iste meat.*

[201] Fontaine, *Naissance*, cit., p. 179, designates Prudentius's lyrical poems as «une sorte de rêverie orientée, ou la méditation se mêle á l'oraison».

[202] *Vit. M.* 5, 871-873, CSEL 16,1, p. 138.

Up to now, Fortunatus's deft poetry has not been credited with a meditative dimension[203]. His «transfiguration» of Arborius's vision is poetic invention at its most audacious: the mantle as such is not reported in his source – everyone will have recognized it as the poet's invention – yet he feels free to urge its acceptance, and even veneration, as a true elaboration of the vision. He seems to be saying that his image of a jeweled Saint Martin is the real spiritual double of the visible man in his story, as well as a representation – in the imagistic mode – of what he has been saying with words throughout the poem about the saint's interior, spiritual quality as a heavenly soul. His «fictional» image provides a different, more direct, access to a real truth[204]. And the contemplation of it – as a quasi-icon in the mental sphere, as a symbol and as a point of departure for inner illumination – is an experience of «presence» that creates a new reality[205], one that structures attitudes and feelings, creating a model for subsequent thoughts about and feelings towards the saint.

Poetic creation – the spontaneous imaging through which a perception or experience becomes available for inspection – has been said to develop «an experience of reality in which invention and discovery cease being opposed and where creation and revelation coincide»[206]. In the last lines of his description of Martin's «new mantle», Fortunatus appears to be saying that the associative, transfigurative imaging process of poetry and that involved in becoming aware of the patterns of invisible divine reality, such as in visionary experience, can likewise coincide. In other words, that the poet, through inspirationally elaborating on an originally God-given image, can discover and reveal *reality*.

203 Fontaine, *Naissance*, cit., p. 270, characterizes him as a clever neo-Alexandrine poet.

204 Cf. W. Pannenberg, *Das Irreale des Glaubens* and W. Iser,*Das Fiktive im Horizont seiner Möglichkeiten. Eine Schlussbetrachtung*, in: D. Henrich and W. Iser ed., *Funktionen des Fiktiven* (Poetik und Hermeneutik 10), München 1983, resp. pp.17-34, 547-557. Although Fontaine, *Naissance*, cit., p. 189, speaks of Prudentius's «vision platonicienne d'un sensible que la contemplation résout en un réseau de signes de l'intelligible», he does not mention (pp. 269-271) this as an aspect of Fortunatus's Life of Martin.

205 Cf. Iser, ibid., p. 554: «Fiktionen ... vermögen Realitäten zu erzeugen.»

206 Ricoeur, *Metaphor*, cit., p. 246.

Iconic Alchemy: Imaging Miracles in Late Sixth-Century Gaul

After what has been called 'the linguistic turn' in modern philosophy[1], some (like W.J.T. Mitchell) would hold that we are now entering a 'pictorial turn': meaning that, through the ubiquitous dissemination of information by television and film, our modern civilization tends to think in terms of images[2]. In the reflections upon this phenomenon, a central issue is: does the logic of pictorial images resemble that of language, or does the iconic mode have its own kind of dynamic patterns?

Philip Wheelwright showed how, mostly through the evoked mental images, words can express real meanings which are other than those which logical language can formulate[3]. Earlier, Suzanne Langer pointed to the importance of symbolic forms other than words[4]. With his poetic philosophy, and his books on what he called 'rêverie' — the waking dream of the poet's creative consciousness —, Gaston Bachelard put the mental image and its dynamics at center-stage[5]. Over against those who continue to insist that they do not have them, mental images have always been a central issue in the history of human thinking about itself[6]. Plato, and later Augustine, for instance, noted a fact which modern psychology has now experimentally confirmed: that we perceive (i.e. interpret) our surroundings through an interplay between sensory data on the one hand, and stored mental images and propositions on the other[7].

[1] R. Rorty ed., *The Linguistic Turn. Recent Essays in Philosophical Method* (Chicago-London, (1967) 1988).

[2] W.J.T. Mitchell, 'The pictorial turn', *Artforum* (1992), pp. 89-94.

[3] Ph. Wheelwright, *The Burning Fountain* (Gloucester, (1968) 1982), pp. 73-101.

[4] S.K. Langer, *Philosophy in a New Key. A Study in the Symbolism of Reason, Rite, and Art*, third edition (Cambridge, Mass., (1942) 1956).

[5] G. Bachelard, *La formation de l'esprit scientifique* (Paris, 1947); *La poétique de la rêverie* (Paris, 1960) (transl. by D. Russell, *The Poetics of Reverie. Childhood, Language and the Cosmos* (hereafter *Poetics*) (Boston, 1969)); *L'air et les songes* (Paris, 1943); *L'eau et les rêves* (Paris, 1947); *La psychanalyse du feu* (Paris, 1949); *La terre et les rêveries de la volonté* (Paris, 1948).

[6] P.C. Miller, *Dreams in Late Antiquity. Studies in the Imagination of a Culture* (*Dreams*) (Princeton, 1994), pp. 14-73.

[7] R. Kearney, *The Wake of Imagination. Toward a Postmodern Culture* (Minneapolis, 1988), pp. 87-105, 117-118; S. M. Kosslyn, *Image and Brain. The Resolution of the Imagery Debate* (Cambridge, Mass., 1994).

To turn from the semiotic to the experiential aspect of mental images: today, medical and anthropological psychology has observed that mentally envisaged and/or bodily enacted images and symbols behave as psychosomatic phenomena — phenomena literally connecting mind and body. As the anthropologist René Devisch writes: 'Ritual symbols ... arise from a potential which, akin to the dream, unconceals both images and inner energy woven into the texture of the body[8].' Here, images or symbols are shown to be the actual and effective 'bridges' across which messages are carried in both directions between consciousness and the pre-verbal awareness that connects to, and activates, the body's autonomous systems. An internalized image, then, behaves as a pattern of emotional and biological energy[9]. A contemporary theologian who is also a psychotherapist, Eugen Drewermann, has made use of this evidence and put forward the idea — demonstrated through analyses of biblical prophecies as well as miracle stories — that alongside the word, certain traditional, psychically effective, religious symbols, but sometimes also spontaneous mental images and dreams, should be regarded as actual vehicles of God's communication with man. This parallel kind of communication takes place through our pre-verbal awareness: in the iconic mode[10]. In many ways, Drewermann's view is a restatement of late antique and early medieval views of symbolism[11], but now supported by empirical evidence from anthropology and psychology.

Marc van Uytfanghe has shown that miracle stories in the sixth century are often conscious continuations and adaptations of biblical ones[12]. But new motifs do appear. The images chosen reveal something about how new experiential forms of the, usually transformative, process of what was regarded as the reciprocal communication with the divine were being 'found'. 'Found' in Paul Ricoeur's sense of a discovering which cannot be distinguished from an inventing: that is, a bringing into focus, and a making inspectable, of an awareness or experience that does not yet have a shape or a name, by discovering an apt mental image or combination of images to stand for it[13]. As

[8] R.J. Devisch, *Weaving the Threads of Life. The Khita Gyn-Eco-Logical Healing Cult Among the Yaka* (Chicago, 1993), p. 280.

[9] B.S. Siegel, *Love, Medicine and Miracles. Lessons Learned About Self-healing From A Surgeon's Experience With Exceptional Patients* (New York, 1986).

[10] E. Drewermann, *Tiefenpsychologie und Exegese* (hereafter *Tiefenpsychologie*), vol. 2 (Olten-Freiburg-im-Breisgau, 1985), pp. 74-140, 239-245, 311-435.

[11] Compare G.B. Ladner, 'Medieval and modern understanding of symbolism: a comparison' (hereafter 'Symbolism'), *Speculum* 54 (1979), pp. 223-256; and Miller, *Dreams*, pp. 70-73, 92-94, 108-117, on Synesius of Cyrene, Origen and healing through dreams, respectively.

[12] M. van Uytfanghe, *Stylisation biblique et condition humaine dans l'hagiographie mérovingienne, (600-750)* (Verhandelingen van de Koninklijke Academie voor Wetenschappen en Schone Kunsten van België, Klasse der Letteren 120, Jaargang 49) (Brussel, 1987).

[13] P. Ricoeur, *La métaphore vive* (Paris, 1975), p. 310; translated by R. Czerny as *The Rule of Metaphor. Multidisciplinary studies of the creation of meaning in language* (hereafter *Rule*) (Toronto, 1977), p. 246.

Bachelard everywhere indicates, such images evoke and generate other, iconically related, images[14].

What new experiential forms? In two sixth-century miracle stories, we see, for instance, that a dead saint's compassion can be experienced through contemplating a candle flame, but also that the kiss of a living saint can be imaged as a weapon. These apparently conflicting combinations occur in stories by Gregory of Tours (539-594) and Venantius Fortunatus (c.540-c.605). In what follows, I hope to show how this dual imaging reflects what must indeed have been a two-layered experience. For, in both stories, the affective and physical assimilation to the holy by means of person-to-person relations is overlaid with assimilation through the enacting of a symbol. The latter practice is based upon the belief that it is thereby possible to bring divine power into action on the spot. For, as is well known, in the late antique analogical world view, the visible could be regarded as a figure — congruous or inverted — of the invisible, and was thereby thought to participate in the latter's qualities[15]. Depending upon their angle, some have labeled this world view as 'magical', others as 'sacramental'[16]. Is it possible to inspect the overlapping of the imaginative assimilation to a person with the enactment of an apparently unconnected symbolic pattern more closely?

In the first miracle story[17], after Gregory has just mentioned that, through candle-ends taken from St Martin's tomb, storms have been 'quieted' and

[14] As, for instance, in G. Bachelard, *La flamme d'une chandelle* (hereafter *Flamme*) (Paris, 1961), p. 12, 26, 49.

[15] Ladner, 'Symbolism', p. 225; Miller, *Dreams*, pp. 7, 31-32; but also: D.E. Aune, 'Magic in early Christianity' (hereafter 'Magic'), in: W. Haase ed., *Aufstieg und Niedergang der römischen Welt* 2.23.2 (Berlin, 1980), p. 1513.

[16] Respectively: Aune, *loc. cit.*, and C. Straw, *Gregory the Great. Perfection in Imperfection* (Berkeley 1988), p. 50.

[17] *Virtutes Martini* 2.2, MGH SSrM 1.2, pp. 609-610. The full text is as follows: Gratum arbitratus sum et illud non omittere, quod mihi in libro anteriore excidit. Nam cum retulerim de cereolis illis quos de sepulcro beati antistitis sustuli (c.34), a quibus et tempestates sedatas, et alias infirmitates prohibitas dixi, hos cum mecum detinerem, Justinus vir sororis meae in valetudinem irruit. Nam, invalescente febre, cum doloribus membrorum omnium, valde ad extremum agi coepit. Nuntius haec ad me delatus retulit, efflagitans ut si quid medicamenti reperire possem, morituro transmitterem, ne obiret. At ego in virtute beati antistitis confisus, unum ex cereolis transmitto per puerum, dicens: 'Accendite illum coram eo, et in contemplatione luminis orationem fundat ad Dominum, et deprecetur omnipotentiam antistitis, ut ei succurrat.' Missus autem puer quod dederam deportavit. Quo accenso ante lectum aegroti, favillam scirpi, quem iam ignis consumpserat, cultro eradunt, dilutumque aqua aegroto porrigunt ad bibendum. At ille ut hausit, sanitatem protinus recepit, incolumisque redditus est. Nobis postea qualiter sibi virtus beati antititis subvenit, exposuit. Nam referre erat solitus, quod ubi primum oculis eius iubar luminis progressum a cereo pepulit tenebras noctis, protinus in contemplatione flammae, febris recessit a corpore, ac stomachus qui diu languerat inedia, cibum consolationis efflagitat, et qui tantum aquam puram ad restinguendum febris ardorem haurire consueverat, nunc vinum desiderat. Facit haec virtus antistitis, quae saepe miseris opem proflua miseratione tribuit, et infirmis medicamenta largitur.

'other infirmities prohibited', he tells us how they helped his brother-in-law Justin. The latter had come down with what sounds like an extreme influenza, and it was thought that he was about to die. A messenger was sent to Gregory for some kind of remedy to prevent this. Gregory, however, as he says 'trusted in the power of the blessed bishop (Martin)' and sent him one of these candle-ends with the following instructions:

'Light it in front of his face, let him pour out a prayer to the Lord in the contemplation of its light, and let him beseech the omnipotence of the bishop to come to his aid.'

The messenger brought it, and it was lighted before the patient as Gregory had instructed. Then a piece of the wick that was already burned was cut off, probably pulverized, and stirred into a cup of water which was given to Justin to drink. Gregory tells us:

And as he was drinking it, he received his health at once and was restored safe and sound.

Later, he explained to us how the power of the blessed bishop came to his aid. For he used to say that when the first beam of light that came from the candle drove away the darknesses of night from his eyes, at once during the contemplation of the flame, the fever withdrew from his body.

Gregory concludes with the comment: 'It was the power of the bishop that did these things, the bishop who often gives aid to the wretched in outpouring compassion, and grants remedies to the sick.'

The affective pattern of compassion by a human person is expressed in terms of the human life world, through giving a 'remedy' which terminates the illness and restores health. What is at the same time 'contemplated' while being prayed in front of, however, is not the image of a human person but a candle flame. Is this really a 'new' form? Or is it the Christian version of the pagan practice — found in the magical papyri — of addressing divinities through a lighted lamp[18]? However that may be, here the moving flame appears to be experienced as somehow a visible manifestation of the Christian saint's transcendent, living and loving, 'presence'. But almost certainly also of his holy power. In his book on rêverie in front of a candle flame, Bachelard shows that it can generate iconically similar mental images[19]. Here, one of these is likely to have been that of fire as holy presence. For this is an equation that Gregory elsewhere makes explicit. In a number of other stories, he reports perceptions of mystic fire around relics — something that had also occurred around the statues of the pagan gods[20] —, and interprets these phe-

[18] E.g. *Papyri Graecae Magicae* VII.250-253, ed. K. Preisendanz, rev. ed. A. Hinrichs, vol. 2 (Stuttgart, 1974), pp. 11-12; cited in Miller, *Dreams*, pp. 119-120.

[19] Cf. Bachelard, *Flamme*, pp. 14-15, 57-59, 65.

[20] As in Aelius Aristides, *The Sacred Tales*, p. 450; translated by C.A. Behr in *P. Aelius Aristides: The Complete Works*, vol.2 (Leiden, 1981), p. 328. Cited in Miller, *Dreams*, p. 34.

nomena as indicating the presence of the saint's 'power'[21]: the power that can cure the sick. The meditative looking upon of the sensory phenomenon of the candle flame, then, is very likely to have generated not only some mental picture of the saint as a person, but also an affect-laden mental image of the powerful mystic fire, converging with it. And thus personal compassion is contemplated in the flame as the appearance of a 'present', although also transcendent, 'power': one that, it was hoped, would 'drive away' the darknesses from Justin's eyes at the same time as the (dark) heat of the fever from his body.

But the dynamic pattern of this physical illumination cannot but also have reminded of that of the central early Christian imaginative model of illumination by Christ, to which it is dynamically analogous. As the Light of the world which is also the life of men[22], Christ was thought to drive out the spirit of darkness that inhabits man when he is left to his own devices, and thereby give him the true life[23]. Gregory's instructions and their consequences may be the concretization-into-enacted-ritual of one of Jesus' metaphors: that of the eye as the lamp of the body — and we should remember that, in this period, a lamp was always something burning with a flame. In Luke's version, Jesus tells the apostles:

> Your eye is the lamp of your body; when your eye is pure (*simplex*), your whole body will be full of light; but when it is impure (*nequam*), your body is full of darkness. Therefore be careful lest the light in you be darkness. If then your whole body is full of light, having no part dark, it will be wholly bright, and illumine you as a lamp of radiance (*et sicut lucerna fulgoris inluminabit te*)[24].

What Gregory, then, called 'contemplation of the flame' may have been the metaphors of illumination by Christ and by the eye turned into a symbolic liturgy. As such, it also involved the waking but dreamlike generation of images out of one another which Bachelard called 'rêverie'. As in many miracle stories, the cluster of coalescing images is a world view in miniature.

But modern psychology, as we saw, tells us that the enactment of a metaphor — here, letting visible light drive out the darkness from one's physical eyes — initiates an imitation or replication of its pattern (illumination) in mind and body. In this way, Justin imaged and experienced an act of personal compassion as a shock of power, an *ictus*, that almost literally thrust out something that was oppressing him in a place he could not reach. In his and Gregory's view, such a purification process must have removed his internal obstructions to communication with the divine. Drewermann observes that

[21] *In gloria martyrum* (=GM) 8, and *In gloria confessorum* 20, MGH SSrM 1.2, pp. 493 and 759-760 respectively.

[22] Jn 1:3, 8:12.

[23] As in Acts 26:18 and Jn 8:12.

[24] Lk 11:34-36; cf. Mt 6:22.

such a deblocking of the preverbal sphere is the primary mode through which God revitalizes man through his love[25]. In Gregory's miracle story, the imagination of compassion affectively unites Justin to the saint as a person, while the flame, almost certainly imaged as the saint's — and Christ's — light and power, drives away the darkness which is the manifestation of a separate, debilitating force which had invaded him. And we see that it is the symbolic action that is described as having precipitated the actual cure at that specific moment. Affectively enacting a metaphor — a mental image — was thus experienced as converging with the creation of a palpable new reality: physical health.

But there is another, tactile, element. The notion of the transmission of presence or power through contact — in this story, through the candle-wick (and in the second story, through the kiss) — has been designated as 'the essence of Greco-Roman magical notions'[26]. The consensus among scholars today appears to be that magic and religion cannot be clearly distinguished[27]. The early Christian tradition in which Gregory and Fortunatus stood did distinguish between them, however, not by contrasting their strategies (say: love and power), but on the basis of which power was being called upon[28]. And this meant in practice, as we have been seeing, that this calling upon could properly take not only personal but also symbolic forms[29]. And so *proflua miseratio* could be experienced through, and as, the — beneficent — blow and shock of *virtus*.

The second story is of a different kind. Sulpicius Severus's very brief description of St Martin's kissing a leper who was thereupon instantly healed is well-known[30]. Jesus's healing of the leper, by contrast, was accomplished by touching with the hand and a command: 'Be clean[31].' His feeling compassion for the man (*misertus*) is mentioned explicitly only by Mark[32]. Thus Sulpicius's description of St Martin's kiss is a new motif, apparently developed from Mark's adjective. Fortunatus gives us a long poetic description that introduces new iconic dimensions — not images that the cured person necessarily had, but ones which the poet wishes his read-

[25] Drewermann, *Tiefenpsychologie* 2, pp. 244-246.

[26] Aune, 'Magic', p. 1536.

[27] *Ibid.*, pp. 1511-1512.

[28] E.g. Gregorius Turonensis, *Historiae* 9.6: *non sanctitate sanare sed errore nigromantici ingenii quaerebat inludere*, and *ibid.* 5.14: *A Deo haec poscenda sunt; nam credi non debent quae diabolus repromittit*, MGH SSrM 1.1, ed. alt., resp. pp. 417, 210.

[29] Cf. G. de Nie, 'Caesarius of Arles and Gregory of Tours: two sixth-century bishops and "Christian magic"', in D. Edel ed., *Cultural Identity and Cultural Integration in Early Medieval Ireland and the Continent* 3 (Dublin, 1995), pp. 191-194.

[30] Sulpicius Severus, *Vita Martini* 18.3-4, SC 133, p. 292.

[31] Mt 8:2-4; Mk 1:40-44; Lk 5:12-14.

[32] Mk 1:41.

ers to have when they think about the miracle. He as it were integrates the new kiss back into the original, probably exorcistic, model[33]. The following description may be found in his long poetic Life of Martin[34]. There, we are first given a long, horrifying description of the unfortunate leper, and then Fortunatus says:

Suddenly, however, the saint drew this man to himself and kissed him, and, by embracing the man, released him through the pouring out of a remedy. For at the moment that (the man) touched the blessed saliva with his face, and the oppression of the illness fled from the saint's ointment-like touch, his drowned figure came back, a new skin clothed his face, the original imprint returned to its mirror in the transient brow, and the long deleted image of his face was inscribed anew.

What a lofty faith of powers, when the battles of illness perish quickly through the ministry of the saint's peace, when a dire force flees through an embrace! The scourge of an evil illness fell because kisses carried out a new kind of fight[35].

Here, even the unifying and saving gesture of a living saint is overlaid with images of repelling, destroying action. Michael Roberts has pointed to the parallel here of Martin, while still in the army, winning a battle by an act of peace

[33] Aune, 'Magic', p. 1532.

[34] Venantius Fortunatus, *Vita Martini* 1.487-513, MGH AA 4.1, pp. 312-313. The full text is:

Inde Parisiacam sacer intrans concite portam,
Obviat in faciem leprosum versus euntem,
Qui sibi dispar erat, nec iam a se cognitus ibat:
Vir maculis varius, cute nudus, vulnere tectus,
Tabe fluens, gressu aeger, inops visu, asper amictu,
Mente hebes, ore putris, lacerus pede, voce refrictus,
Induerat miserum peregrino tegmine pallor.
Improvisus enim hunc sanctus ad oscula traxit,
Adstringensque virum fuso medicamine laxat.
Nam simul ut tetigit benedictas ore salivas,
Effugit unguiferum languoris sarcina tactum;
Mersa figura redit, faciem cutis advena vestit,
Ad speculum remeat peregrina fronte character,
Et deleta diu rescribitur oris imago.
Virtutum quam celsa fides, ubi concite sancti
Pacis ab officio perierunt proelia morbi.
Complexu res dira fugit; languoris iniqui
Peste cadente, novam gesserunt oscula pugnam.
Inclyta relligio Martini, cuius honore,
Foedere fida, fides formosat foeda fidelis.
O felix regio, sancti pede, lumine, tactu.
Illustris lustrante viro loca, lustra, ligustra,
Urbes, rura, domos, templa, oppida, moenia, villas,
Quaeque viri insignis tam insignia signa mereris,
Cuius ab ore sacro, magnalia cetera vincens,
Leprosi ad curam Jordanis in oscula fluxit,
Et fontem fluidae maculae lavat unda salivae.

[35] Fortunatus, VM 1.494-504, MGH AA 4.1, p. 312.

— as Fortunatus in this case also says[36]. The Pauline letters, of course, had provided the military imagery for the activity of the spiritual life which continued in the Christian tradition[37]. The war was aimed not at the person himself but at what were thought of as evil forces invading him. In sixth-century sources, too, we see that man was perceived as a vessel. If he did not take care to be filled with God or Christ, the devil or demons would take their place[38]. Unlike Justin's report of his own experience, Fortunatus's antithetical imagery is his own sixth-century addition to an existing story that did not mention it. He must have regarded the weapon image as somehow suited to his contemporaries' mental imaging of the event[39].

But, in Fortunatus's story too, a third and crucial image is generated, this time by the poet's words. As Bachelard says, not only sensory phenomena precipitate mental imaging, but words, too, 'dream'[40]. For, further on, he conflates the saint's saliva with the water of the river Jordan that had cured the leper Naaman and was believed to be still curing lepers[41]. In this image, as well as in the ones just mentioned of 'pouring' a 'remedy', the ointment, and the notion of the reinscription of the man's 'drowned' face with its original 'imprint', Roberts has, I think correctly, seen a strong reference to the act of baptism — Christ was baptized in the Jordan — and the restoration of God's image in man which this purification was held to effect[42]. Alongside the weapon image, Martin's kiss, as a kind of baptism, is thus also imaginatively assimilated to God's love for the world in Christ, which restored man to God and to himself.

Here again, then, we see three, or actually five, coalescing mental images. This time, partially analogous ones: the human kiss and the washing and anointment, or baptism; and an antithetical one: the spiritual battle. The latter inversion made visible and palpable one of the ways in which the Christian religion tended to turn all the relations of the visible world upside-down. What does such an inversion accomplish? At least, a surprise, a liberation from ingrained thinking and feeling habits, and an opening-up for a new dimension and new movement in these. Ricoeur's essay on 'Imagination in discourse and in action' shows that imagination, although it can enchant, delude and obsess,

[36] M. Roberts, 'St. Martin and the leper: narrative variation in the Martin poems of Venantius Fortunatus' (hereafter 'Leper'), *The Journal of Medieval Latin* 4 (1994), pp. 86-87.

[37] As for instance: 2 Cor 10:3-6.

[38] A. Angenendt, 'Die Liturgie und die Organisation des kirchlichen Lebens auf dem Lande', *Cristianizzazione ed organizzazione ecclesiastica delle campagne nell'alto medioevo: espansione e resistenze* (Settimane di studio del centro Italiano di studi sull'alto medioevo 28) (Spoleto, 1982), pp. 186-189.

[39] He also uses it for this miracle in C 1.6.9-10, ed. Reydellet, vol. 1 (Les Belles Lettres) (Paris, 1994), pp. 25-26; but not in 10.6.31-36 and 93-102, MGH AA 4.1, pp. 235, 237.

[40] Bachelard, *Poetics*, pp. 29-54.

[41] 2 Ki 5:14; Gregorius Turonensis, GM 16, MGH SSrM 1.2, p. 499.

[42] Roberts, 'Leper', pp. 93-95.

is at the same time the primary tool of innovation and mental liberation[43]. I would add that, as we see in these miracle stories, it is also the tool, and mode, of emotional and physical transformation.

To conclude: together with the analogical-participative world view, the notion of the openness of man's inner self and body to the invasion of what were thought to be alien deforming and debilitating forces, must be responsible for the dual imagery in these descriptions of cures. For Gregory and Fortunatus in the sixth century, symbolic action through such images of commanding 'power' was felt to be a necessary complement to the asking for and receiving of compassionate personal love in order for the latter to be effective against the faceless, powerful and omnipresent forces of destruction. The underlying model here is, of course, that of exorcism.

Our authors' descriptions of what looks like a personalized kind of liturgy may be understood also as a waking dream in which mental images are allowed to function as catalysts of miracle. For the visualization and enactment of these images appears to have helped to trigger and precipitate — I do not say effect — the cures. Embedded, then, in the distancing and discursive verbal logic of these narratives is an affective, iconic logic that is coalescent, presential and transforming. This iconic alchemy, congruent with the sixth-century participative view of the cosmos (but surreptitiously continuing in modern civilization), is in its own way no less sophisticated than the linguistic strategies with which it interacts. I suggest that it is time for those doing scholarly work on miracle stories to wake up to the crucial role of every human being's dream life in the creation of his or her *reality*.

[43] P. Ricoeur, 'Imagination in discourse and in action', *Analecta Husserliana* 7 (1978), pp. 3-22.

XII

WORD, IMAGE AND EXPERIENCE IN THE EARLY MEDIEVAL MIRACLE STORY[1]

A partir d'une analyse de deux textes de l'antiquité tardive, l'auteur s'interroge sur les conditions de compréhension d'un genre littéraire dont les deux exemples retenus mettent en cause des interrelations spécifiques entre verbe, image et réel: le récit miraculeux. L'historien moderne y est confronté à une conception de la vérité différant de la sienne: mettant en œuvre une mémoire imageante et les projections affectives de l'individu, cette "vérité" ne saurait se concevoir dans les termes, avant tout propositionnels, dont la tradition scientifique occidentale alimenta jusqu'à présent ses catégories. Certains acquis qui ouvrirent la science moderne à une conception moins restrictive de la notion d'énergie sous-jacente aux modélisations mentales – de même qu'à une participation davantage créatrice du sujet dans les processus d'élaboration de la vérité, voire de la réalité –, attesteraient cependant une attitude nouvelle, davantage susceptible de ménager au contenu le plus distinctif des textes en question une lecture que n'aurait su cautionner l'ancienne épistémé.

After a period in which many regarded verbal language as the representational paradigm of human knowledge - the so-called "linguistic turn" - (Rorty 1967), the philosopher W. J. T. Mitchell announced what he calls "the pictorial turn" (Mitchell 1992). Since television and film now reach more people than books, knowledge tends to be represented by images.

And they are being reflected upon. Researchers in art and literature have recently been devoting an increasing amount of attention to the interrelations of word and image.[2] But experimental psychologists too, leaving behind the behaviourist paradigm, have again begun to investigate the elusive phenomenon of imagination. Thus they have found ways to prove that reading, remembering, learning, and solving problems often involves visualization of the material involved: that is, calling up, constructing and manipulating various kinds of mental images (Kosslyn 1994, 1-25; Singer 1974, 171-221; Esrock 1994). Further, clinical psychologists describe an affect-laden imagistic kind of thinking as occurring in western adults alongside and in interaction with propositional, verbal thinking (Singer 1974, 183). Finally, cultural anthropologists and (medical) psychotherapists have observed the effect of bodily enacting and meditatively visualizing powerful symbols upon non-voluntary physical processes and otherwise inaccessible emotional ones.[3] Surprisingly, however, the researchers in these various disciplines have hardly ever entered into discussion with each other.

The present investigation will combine a number of insights from all these fields. My focus here will be the role of the mental image in a kind of text which still somewhat baffles medieval historians: the miracle story. For it describes, in the midst of a continuous development along an ostensibly linear course of this-worldly causation, what appear to be sudden intrusions of a completely different kind of dynamic. Until recently, present-day scholars left these inexplicable happenings aside as pious phantasies and concentrated upon extracting nuggets of "factual" information from these stories. In the past decades, however, a semiotic approach has fruitfully analyzed them as documents of social history in which the subjects act out and address contemporary ideological, social and personal concerns (e.g. van Dam 1993). But this approach does not yet explain the contemporaries' actual perception of the disruptions of ordinary causality or the reportedly real effects upon human bodies.

These two event-centred issues - the perception of an extraordinary dynamic in a sensory phenomenon and its measurable effect - are the ones I wish to address here, and I shall relate them to the manner in which the story as such is told. The so-called suprasensory, direct, perception of immaterial or spiritual phenomena is something which has not yet been inspected and described in a manner which most historical scholars are willing to accept as veridical. Without wishing to detract from this possibility, what I shall argue is that the perception involved in the early medieval miracle stories to be discussed, may also overlap with the contemporary late antique habit of discovering meaning in a religious text by mentally imaging relevant traditional "figures" of invisible reality alongside its literal meaning. And I shall compare the reported actual physical effect in a miraculous cure with the emotional and physical changes brought about through the ritual enactment of metaphors in oral cultures as well as by the meditative visualization of symbols in western psychotherapy.

Thus I hope to show that a key to the perception and experience in these miraculous events may be found in the culturally determined late antique focus upon an affective, imagistic kind of thinking rather than a discursive, propositional kind. As all artists know, alongside quasi-photographic information, images and imagistically organized configurations tend to present structures of feeling rather than discourse (Langer 1953, 59; Epstein 1981, 18). They can visualize affective patterns and modes of awareness too subtle, contradictory and complicated to be expressed by verbal propositions. This imagistic thinking then, I shall argue, is the expression of an affective rather than a propositional kind of knowledge. And it is precisely the non-discursive dynamics of this approach to life and the world which will be seen to constitute the essence of the miraculous event in its visible as well as its invisible dimensions.

In the introduction to the larger work of which the first story is a part, its author, Gregory of Tours (539-594), says something that explains his construction of the story. Namely, that he hopes his narratives will, "... through holy instruction, make inert minds fruitful in the knowledge of perfect faith (*mentes inopes ad notitiam perfectae fidei instructione sancta fecundent*)" (*Glor. mart. prol.*; cf. de Nie 1995). In my analysis of both his story and that of his friend Venantius Fortunatus (c. 540 - c. 605), I shall be concerned to show how they attempt not so much to transmit a propositional and discursive kind of knowledge as to induce an affective and transformational experience in the reader.

Word and image

Gregory was bishop of Tours in a politically unstable and physically insecure late sixth-century Gaul that was ruled by warlike and quarrelsome Frankish kings (cf. Pietri 1983, 246-334). The story I have chosen illustrates the first part of the title of this paper: word and image, and I shall focus here upon the latter's role in the perception of the miracle. The story was probably read (perhaps with improvised elaborations) by the author, during the liturgy on the feast day of the saint, in a church full of lighted oil lamps and candles.

If any present readers have not yet reflected upon their mental imagery before, I suggest that they read the story slowly and, during that process, try to notice any visual images – however fleeting and incomplete – that may present themselves to the "interior eye":

> 1 Amarandus, a martyr in the city of Albi, having completed the course of his fight for the faith,
> 2 was buried and lives in glory.
> 3 As the history of his passion declares, his tomb was hidden for a long time by a covering of briars and thorn bushes, but at the command of the Lord, it was revealed to the Christian peoples,
> 4 and the opened crypt [or hidden place] in which he was resting shone with light.
> 5 But when that area had been deserted by its inhabitants under the pressure of hostilities, residents from a distant place went there and tried to show honour to the blessed martyr as though he were their own guardian. Since Christian veneration entails offering many candles, it happened one day that someone – because of the length of his journey – did not bring the tinder for lighting the candle. And he beat with iron upon a piece of flint that he had picked up, so as to bring forth fire.
> But while he was doing this and, [although] striking the stone with numerous blows, was unable to bring forth any fire,
> 6 the candle – which had already been affixed to the blessed tomb – was lighted by [from?] the Lamp in Heaven [in this period, of course: fire];
> 7 and so it happened that that which human effort could not bring to the finish, was completed by the majesty of the Divine Name.

8 Where human effort left off, heavenly ministrations took over,
9 and the lighted candle shone with the flash of a new light.

Amarandus, autem martyr apud Albigensem urbem, exacto agonis fidelis cursu, sepultus vivit in gloria. Cuius, ut historia passionis declarat, sepulcrum diu vepribus sentibusque contectum latuit, sed, Domino iubente, christianis populis revelatum est, et cripta in qua quiescebat patefacta resplenduit.

Sed cum, hostilitate impellente, locus ille ab habitatoribus fuisset evacuatus, a longinquo venientes incolae honorem beato martyri quasi custodio proprio nitebantur inpendere. Igitur cum cereos frequenter devotio christiana deferret, quadam die contigit, ut quidam prae longinquitate itineris, incrementum ignis quo accenderetur cereus non exhiberet.

Arreptamque silicem ferro verberat, quasi ignem eliciturus. Quod dum ageret, et crebris ictibus lapidem quatiens, nihil foci posset excutere, caelesti lampadae cereus, qui iam beato sepulcro affixus erat, inluminatur; factumque est, ut quae humanae non expleverant industriae, peragerentur divini nominis maiestate. Cessante humano studio, caelestia officia ministrantur, luminisque novi fulgore cereus clarificatur accensus... (*Glor. mart.* 56).

In the first episode, we see three coalescences of similar opposites – hiddenness and glory (2), inaccessibility and revelation (3), and darkness and light (4) – which signal and exemplify the breaking into ordinary reality of a transcendent one. In the second episode (5-9), the pattern is repeated in the lighting of the candle. The story closes with another threefold repetition emphasizing that the divine comes to aid where human effort is inadequate. Contrary to Gregory – who included miracle stories in his historical writing – the modern historian usually does not accept the extraordinary happenings in these stories as "historical events". For most western scholars today tend to regard physical nature, human individuals and societies as behaving exclusively according to more or less scientifically observable this-worldly regularities.

Gregory's world, however, looked different: as he frequently indicates, he based his world view squarely upon Christ's unambiguous statements, such as: "with God all things are possible" (Mat 19: 26). This is the general biblical view of divine power as the most powerful, if invisible, reality which simultaneously transcends and is immanent in the world. It manifests itself to men through appearances, dreams and interventions in visible phenomena. Since the strange events at Amarandus' tomb conform with this world view, Gregory accepted them as fully historical: the light bursting into visibility is an epiphany of the higher spiritual reality. Our explanation could stop here.

But it is possible to refine it by considering the story in its context of early Christian literature. A recent study of late antique culture asserts that it possessed "... an insistently figurative way of viewing the social, psychic, religious and philosophical dimensions of life" (Miller 1994, 104). Early Christian tradition tended to understand, and thus "see", the phenomena and events of its world as repetitions of "figures" - biblical sayings and events manifesting the patterns that were regarded as the eternal paradigms of divine action toward men (Auerbach 1938). According to this view, what happened around the remains of the holy Amarandus could be understood as repetitions of Old Testament events: a fiery glow, for instance, had been seen in the Tabernacle (Ex 40: 38), and divine fire had descended to consume the offering there (1 Ki 18, 38). If such events could happen in the past, they could be expected to happen again.

Still, it is one thing to have this "figure" in memory storage and another to actually "see" it happen. How would such perception have come about? As already indicated, I believe that a key to this mystery lies in the contemporary habit of mental imaging as a central approach to, and mode of, knowledge. The latter is evident in a story in which Gregory shows us how meaning is arrived at in religious texts:[4] he designates the understanding that "sees" the catholic coequal Trinity figured in the Bible as that of "the eyes of faith (*fidei oculi*)" (*Hist.* 2.3). That is, heretics see the same letters and words on the page, but because of "the miserable cover" of their doctrine obstructing their "eyes of the heart (*oculi cordium*)", they do not "see" this Trinity in the messages and events to which the words refer. Underlying such phrasing is, on the one hand, the contemporary notion that understanding takes place through divine "illumination", an interior flash of light (Augustine, *Gen.* 12.9.20) - in which something must have been *seen*. On the other hand, Gregory's phrase appears to point to the practice of meditative reading and the concomitant mental envisioning as the mode of understanding and knowing.[5] The exegetical writings of Gregory's contemporary and namesake, Pope Gregory the Great, show that the images contained in religious texts were purposefully and associatively meditated upon so as to let their many levels of meaning as it were generate themselves (e.g. *Moralia in Job*, ep. ded. 2). At the end of this process, what could thus be "seen" in a text if not a composite imagistic representation combining symbolic (densely meaningful) with purely visual qualities congruent to the also visualized pattern of the literal meaning? Here, the sequential construction of referential meaning is left behind to grasp something globally. Also, the leap that the mind must make from the sound or appearance of the word to the appearance of its referent is eliminated in the direct and affective assimilation of the more mimetic visual image. Associatively moving from one image to another, however, involves another kind of leap: that moving in the qualitative dimensions of contiguity and iconic similarity.[6] It is a movement along affective, assimilative congruences rather than differentiating logical structures.[7]

In this preference for imagistic thinking we see a cultivation of the self-generating association, the budding and blossoming, of images (cf. Bachelard 1986 [1960]). Knowledge is thought to increase and cohere through a semiosis of imaginal affinities and congruences rather than through that of discursive structures. This view is part of the contemporary world picture of man and the whole cosmos as cohering through analogies or "images" and through energy patterns – "sympathies" – somehow connected with these (Miller 1994, 7). In fact, then, this world view held that the same kind of dynamics acted in the mind and in the cosmos.

In another story, Gregory shows us how the sensory world could be seen. A new bride is in tears on her wedding night: her parents forced her into the marriage because of their wish for an heir to their estates, but she would rather have remained a virgin so as to be able (as she believes) to become Christ's bride in heaven. Gregory makes her say to her astonished bridegroom:

> Earthly beauties make me shudder, because I look up to see (*suspicio*) the hands of the Redeemer pierced for the life of that world. Nor do I see (*non cerno*) diadems flashing with precious jewels, when my mind is bedazzled (*miror mente*) by the Crown of Thorns. I reject the stretches of your lands far and wide, because I long for (*concupisco*) the delight of Paradise. Your terraces disgust me when I look up to see (*suspicio*) the Lord seated [on his throne] above the stars (*Hist.* 1.47).

Her "eyes of the heart" or "eyes of faith", then, visualize affect-laden pictures of revealed belief truth alongside the incoming data of her sensory perception, and this mental imaging strongly influences the affective evaluation of what is seen. Gregory's observation of this process is confirmed by modern psychological experiments. They show that how we perceive sensory data is determined by our own pre-existing, learned as well as self-constructed, mental models of the visible world. The art psychologist Rudolf Arnheim called these "visual concepts" which are stored in memory, and chosen – according to the perceiver's expectations, hopes, wishes and fears – to identify "stimulus configurations" (Arnheim 1969, 90-91). In this theory, what we see, then, are not the objects themselves but our own mental constructions or images of them.[8] As another psychologist formulated it: "... the world we perceive is a dream which we learn to have from a script we have not written." (Tomkins 1962, 13) In general, a culture's models of reality are likely to be also the models for its perception (Geertz 1973: 87-125).

But the bride also says that she *does not see* the jeweled diadems in her visual field when her mind is bedazzled by the Crown of Thorns. In other words: these – perhaps purposefully maintained – mental images almost or wholly block out incoming sensory data. Modern psychological experiments have confirmed this too by showing that sense perception and mental imaging use some of the same pathways and processes in the brain. Visual blocking is thought to be brought about by the fact that the inspection of visual images triggered by perception (percepts) and that of purely mental images called up and constructed without an exterior stimulus, occur in the same place in the brain, a hypothetical "visual buffer" (Kosslyn 1994, 53-70). This blocking mechanism may easily be tested by the present reader: make a mental picture of the burning candle on Amarandus' grave. Are you able to discern the words on this page clearly *at precisely the same moment* that you view the mental image? But – as in the case of the lighting of the candle – if the object of perception and the mental image resemble each other, blocking means that subjects can no longer be sure whether they are seeing a sensory or a mental phenomenon – or a spiritual one. As already indicated, I emphatically do not wish to exclude the possibility of the direct actual perception – in whatever mode of consciousness – of exterior immaterial phenomena. Throughout Antiquity and the early Middle Ages, however, the spiritual tended to be approached and experienced through the often purposive foregrounding of the imaginal consciousness: in dreams and trances provoked in a cultic context (Miller 1994; Amat 1985). What I shall therefore do here is to look for relations that may have existed between the imaginal consciousness and the perception of what was thought to be spiritual reality. An explanation based upon recent psychological research could run as follows. Whatever the "stimulus configuration" was at Amarandus' tomb – and it could have been that the traveler unexpectedly managed to produce a spark near the candle long after he had given up his effort as hopeless – he imaged the Old Testament model as a visual concept to identify, and thus "see", it. Underlying this choice is, of course, the predisposition to see the event as a supernatural event rather than as the result of one's own effort – a culturally determined attitude. The subject of the story – like everyone in this period – evidently *wanted* to experience a breakthrough of the divine in everyday life, and thus to be assured in this way of divine presence enduring in the saint's protection in an environment of great physical privation and insecurity.

Thus the mental model-image that was called up by the situation is likely to have effected a selection of certain sensory data (the flame appearing) and a blocking out of others (the man's own effort at that moment), and to have caused image and perception to merged into one and the same experience. Gregory's strategy of "the eyes of faith" might thus apply not only to the recognition of divine messages in not specifically miraculous sensory phenomena and events, or to the blocking out of discordant sensory experience to focus upon belief reality. It could also pertain to the perception of a sensory event through the simultaneous mental imaging of models of belief truth in such a way that the event appeared "miraculous" (cf. de Nie 1997a). Thus the priest Brictius later confessed that he had sinned against Saint Martin because "I saw his deeds of power [i.e. miracles] and did not believe" (Hist. 2.1.). An alternative explanation was always possible.

Aside from visions - appearances or dreams (cf. de Nie 1987, 213-293), the "really real" was therefore never directly perceived, but only through its sensory dress. To "see" divine reality in daily life required not only the perception of the sensory object or event, but the recognition of the latter's underlying figure or form as congruent to one of the models of divine action stored in the memory. When closely read, Gregory's stories - as well as those of his contemporaries - reveal this kind of perception as a more or less conscious strategy (cf. de Nie 1994).

The schema below gives some of the more obvious associations which are likely to have been evoked by the sensory phenomena mentioned. They are paralleled by similar associations elsewhere in Gregory's writings (de Nie 1978, 133-211 and 1990). His phrasing here directly or indirectly evokes these imagistic models of reality in the reader's mind, so as to induce him to visualize them alongside the sensory appearances described.

Image in text	Evoked images / notions
italics sensory phenomena	CAPITALS divine reality
Amarandus, *martyr* - *fight* - *buried*	"fight the good fight of faith"(1Ti6:12) "we are buried with him by baptism"(Ro6:4)
LIVES	"because I live, you shall live also"(Jo14:19)
IN GLORY	"brightness of the glory of the Lord (Ez2:10) "shall you also appear with him in glory" (Co3:4)
his *tomb* long hidden through *briars and thorn bushes*	body as tomb of soul (Plato) "the Lord will being to light the things now hidden in darkness" (1Co4:5)
at command of THE LORD was revealed	"the glory of the Lord shall be revealed" (Is40:5)
crypt	"the vessels of mercy, which he has prepared for his glory" (Ro9:23)
opened	"to open their eyes, that they may turn from darkness to light (Ac26:18)
SHONE WITH LIGHT	"fire was in [the Tabernacle] by night" (Ex 40:38) "the true Light that enlightens every man was coming into the world" (Jo 1:9)

candle brought from afar no tinder cannot produce fire himself striking flint ineffective	(symbol for soul) [The Lord] "helped him who has no power" (Job 26:2)
candle affixed to tomb was lighted	(symbol for soul) (holy energy transmitted through contact) "thou dost light my lamp; the Lord my God lightens my darkness" (Ps18:28)
by (from) THE LAMP OF HEAVEN	"Then the fire of the Lord fell and consumed the burnt offering (1Ki 18:38) "the glory of God is its light, and its lamp is Christ" (Re 21:23)
what *human effort could not bring to the finish* was completed by MAJESTY OF THE DIVINE NAME	"our help is in the name of the Lord" (Ps 123:8)
where human effort left off HEAVENLY MINISTRATIONS took over	[The Lord] "helped him who has no power"(Job 26:2)
the lighted *candle* shone with the FLASH OF A NEW LIGHT	"as the lightning flashes and lights up the sky, ...so will the Son of Man be in his day" (Lk 17:24)

As in the biblical stories to be meditated upon, the associations make the visible a symbol or sign of the presence of invisible spiritual reality, and sensory objects and events representations of interior experience. Exterior, interior and spiritual spheres overlap and coincide. Thus tomb and crypt are analogous shapes or figures, evoking, as hollow space, the contemporary image of the soul (or interiority) as a vessel (de Nie 1991, 84-86). The candle, though not vessel-like in form, still also requires something from without to be complete; it could represent the soul. For in the late antique period light was always fire and the then still influential Stoic tradition imagined the soul as a spark of divine fire in the "tomb" of the body; but the Psalm text shows that divine illumination was an ancient theme in the biblical tradition as well (cf. de Nie 1987, 165-168). Gregory refers to it elsewhere when he speaks of someone's soul being lighted by divine fire (*Virt. Jul. prol.*). The first chapter of the Gospel of John, but also the epitaphs of the late antique period show that the divine reality was then imaged above all in terms of light and ethereal fire (Sanders 1965). The image-model of illumination, then, is the central one in the story as a whole, in the sensory as well as in the interior sphere. The multileveledness of the story imitates that of the reality it describes.

This reality is one in which the sudden leap of an interior event is perceived in an exterior one: mind or heart and world are experienced as a continuum. Modern psychology reports that this kind of perception of one's surroundings is foregrounded in the meditative mode of awareness. As it is observed today, meditation produces a kind of perception that is characterized by a tendency to see all boundaries as fluid, important objects as radiating light, the third dimension as falling away and the subject-object distinction as breaking down (Deikman 1969 [1966], 199-228). This meditative coalescing of imaginal and sensory experience is the key to the story's strange dynamics. Strange, however, only to those who have not read the Bible. Its view of a reality in which the transcendent divinity is actively immanent in the world has been masterfully described by the literary historian Eric Auerbach's book *Mimesis* (1988 [1946], 16-27 and 43-52].

Can more be said about these dynamics? As I have already indicated, recent psychological research emphasizes that an image itself – including a mental one – is a visualized pattern of feeling. Cognitive psychologists have proven, through tests with radioactive fluids, that many parts of the brain involved in feelings are directly and indirectly connected with those which contain information in a depictive rather than propositional form (Kosslyn 1994, 405). The contemporary philosopher Martha Nussbaum has powerfully demonstrated that the imaginative constructions of literature can represent affective, experiential truths which conventional philosophy cannot fit into discursive structures (Nussbaum 1990). Earlier, the literary philosopher Philip Wheelwright made a similar assertion. Such truths, he writes, are best represented by what he calls "translogical" modes of expression: indistinctness, ambiguity, multi-dimensionality, paradox, contextuality (that is, shifting about) of meaning, tentativeness, soft focus, latency, coalescence, and presentiality (Wheelwright 1982, 73-101). A close reading of the story of the miraculously lighted candle reveals some of these.

What happens is not only a discursively connected string of propositions; the real action takes place through *a multidimensional interaction of mental images*. For the story awakens associations and resonances in various directions simultaneously – thus, the candle flame is also the fire God sent in the Old Testament, Christ as Light, as well as the illumined soul, and these are the ones that act upon each other to produce the miraculous event. Such an imagined coalescence of sensory and spiritual realities induces a sense of the latter's "presence". Further, the story exhibits not the logical exclusion but *the overlapping and coalescence of opposites* that is typical of symbols of transcendence – the heavenly light in the dark earthly tomb.

But, I suggest, such a close reading also uncovers qualities and dynamics that pertain more specifically to the imagistic or iconic mode as we experience it, for instance, in meditative imaging, hypnagogic imagery, and dreams (cf. Jung 1964). The following categories are my own deductions from the material. Instead of material causality, there is *attraction through iconic congruence:* not the impact upon the flint but the attraction of divine fire toward a candle lights it. This attraction results in a sudden, category-transcending, *leap* rather than an incremental development or a causal relation. And this a leap effects a *spontaneous imitative replication:* the pattern of illumination is emphatically presented as repeating itself in various modes and dimensions. The subjacent message, however, is that this replication may also occur interiorly, in the one who is visualizing this iconic pattern while meditatively reading or listening to the story. I suggest that Gregory too, in his own intuitive way, was aware that an image is itself a visualized pattern of feeling, and that human beings tend to exhibit what has been called "affective mimesis".[9] Modern psychologists have observed that – at a level detectable by precision instruments, if not by the bare eye: that of skin tension and energy impulses in the brain – human beings spontaneously and unconsciously mimic everything they perceive (Ogden 1988; Epstein 1981, 18, 149; Assagioli 1965, 177-189). If this is true, it is of mountainous importance and deserves to be investigated and taken into account in all spheres of living.

To limit ourselves to the literary strategy in the narrative episode of the candle: combining the ordinary with the bizarre induces an experience of surprise or shock – a momentary disorientation which can be designated as "wonder". To be able to follow the narrative, the reader or listener is forced to make a mental and affective leap. In this case, he is induced to enact imaginatively the metaphor of illumination, mimicking that of the original subject. According to present-day metaphorical theology, such an experience can transform the heart according to its pattern (cf. McFague 1975, 138-142). And when it is induced by a story presented by an authority in a ritual context (as it would be if the bishop read it during liturgy), it can become the basis of a predisposition to call up and perceive through a congruent image-model of belief reality in similar situations (Geertz 1973, 112-113).

But there is more. I suggest that, in the ritual context mentioned, even a textual confrontation with such a dreamlike experience which is presented as having occurred during waking life, would create a predisposition to fall into this affective, dreamlike mode of awareness and perception when a similar ambiance recurs (Geertz 1973, 119-123). Both the model-event as a visual concept and the mode of awareness would then be stored in memory, to be called up when cued (cf. de Nie 1990). This psychical mechanism of conditioned recall has been extensively observed in transcultural psychological field-work (Sargant 1974, 18-43). In the imaginal mode of awareness thus precipitated, sensory and imaginal experience would be more likely to merge, and iconic or dream dynamics to play a larger role than in ordinary experience.

As I have already suggested, however, another way to understand the special kind of perception foregrounded in this story, is to listen to the many voices today (but also throughout human history) that claim to sense, see without using the physical eyes (so-called circumvision and tele-vision), and even register by means of mechanical instruments, more than what is regarded in our western world as the commonly visible. They would hold that the universe is entirely composed of more and less condensed energy (an insight supported by contemporary micro-physics), and that the extraordinary phenomena sometimes perceived are not projected mental images but non-material phenomena actually "out there", independent of the observer – though influenced by his energy pattern of expectation (this too has been observed in micro-physics). They would hold that all is in fact energy, and that – enveloped by a real if immaterial "dream ether" – we create our multi-leveled experiences of ourselves, our bodies and our worlds. What this adds up to is that any hard-and-fast distinction between sensory and mental experience is no longer thought to be possible. Further, some would hold that by connecting oneself with the cosmic energy that constantly creates and upholds everything, a human person would be able to participate in this continuous creation, and thus help to precipitate everything up to and including so-called miracles.[10] Seeing that medieval historians are, unfortunately, unable to interrogate their informants personally about what they actually mean with their ostensibly similar verbal statements, I feel that they should not neglect to investigate what appear to be similar contemporary world views, personally if possible, or in reports by trained observers.

With the present state of our scientific knowledge, we cannot discover whether the psychological or the spiritual model is more veridical, or to what extent there is truth in both. But there is also an intermediate position. Some, like the erudite and controversial Catholic theologian Eugen Drewermann, would hold that images and symbols can function as the effective mediators between man and a spiritual reality which he cannot approach directly. Drewermann – who is a psychotherapist as well as a priest – adapts the notion of psychological archetypes to a theological purpose. He holds that metaphors as well as visionary images, such as those found in biblical literature, are visualized energy patterns created in human mind-bodies by the invisible divine reality for the purpose of communication and interaction with mankind. That is, we do not invent these provenly potent symbols ourselves, but "find" them in us (Drewermann 1985, 74-140). The philosopher Paul Ricœur speaks of the poet's spontaneous creative imaging as something similar: at the frontier between what he calls *bios* and *logos* (pre-verbal and verbal awareness) images are "discovered" at the same time that they are "invented" – a word whose original Latin meaning is, of course, "finding" (Ricœur 1975, 310). In such an intermediate view, then, it matters less whether we think of such, usually imagistically represented, energy patterns as "out there" or "in the mind" – a relatively recent either-or distinction which (also in the physical sciences, as we have seen) is becoming less and less tenable anyway.

Gregory's miracle story, then, is inexplicable only as long as one attempts to understand it as a discursive statement about sensory-concrete events. If we can accept the possibility of ourselves and our world being as multidimensional and multidynamic as we in fact experience them, and the story as an imagistic literary construct standing for this and attempting to evoke an experience of it, it becomes an invitation to wake up and discover past – and possibly present – contours of human experience. A more direct initiation into the "other world" of the imaginal consciousness, however, might be the reading of Virginia Woolf's novel *The Waves*, which tells a story exclusively through "poetic" mental-experiential images of her characters.

Image and experience

The second story, by Gregory's friend, the originally Italian poet Venantius Fortunatus (cf. George 1992), may be said to illustrate the second part of my title: image and experience. It also revolves around illumination, but centres upon a picture of a saint – not a tomb. In it, the poet evokes mental images in the reader to reconstruct and reenact an awareness of a spiritual reality so experientially "present" that it precipitated the cure of his eye ailment. In contrast to Gregory's story, this one was meant to be read to a small group of highly educated persons capable of understanding the poetic language and the intricate allusive structure.

At the end of his long poem about the *Life of saint Martin*, the poet is addressing his own "little book", as he calls it, and imaginatively sending it from Poitiers, where he wrote it, back to Ravenna where he had studied:

> A From there, go with pleasure to the agreeable city of Ravenna; visit the sacred shrines of the saints, adore the tomb of the excellent martyr Vitalis, and [that of] the gentle and blessed Ursicinus, equal in destination: lying as a suppliant on the ground, kiss the threshold of the [church of the] precious Apollinaris, and make haste to visit all the churches.

> B Look for the little place [chapel?] of Martin, where through the law of the shrine, the artist gave me back the light [of my eyes] of which I had already despaired: for the gifts he gave, I pray, repay him at least with words.

C There is the peak of a church dedicated to Paul and John. Here, a wall holds the form of the saint under an image – a picture to-be-embraced because of the very sweetness of its colour.

D Under the feet of the just man the wall has, through art, a window; there is a lamp, whose fire swims in a glass bowl. While I hastened to this place tortured by a severe pain, lamenting that the light was disappearing from the windows of my eyes – as soon as I touched the light through the blessed olive [oil], the fiery vapour withdrew from my wilting brow, and the doctor – present – put the illnesses to flight with his soothing ointment.

E My lights [eyes] have not forgotten the gift of the saint to me, for the cure of my eyes comes back before the eyes of the believer, and I shall remember it while I remain in light and body.

Inde Ravennatum placitam pete dulcius urbem;
Pulpita sanctorum per religiosa recurrens,
Martyris egregii tumulum Vitalis adora,
Mitis et Ursicini parili sub sorte beati:
Rursus Apollinaris pretiosi limina lambe,
Fusus humi supplex, et templa omnia curre;
Expete Martini loculum, quo iure sacelli
Iam desperatum lumen mihi reddidit auctor:
Munera qui tribuit, saltem, rogo, verba repende.
Est ibi basilicae culmen Pauli atque Johannis.
Hic paries retinet sancti sub imagine formam,
Amplectenda ipso dulci pictura colore:
Sub pedibus iusti paries habet arte fenestram,
Lychnus adest, cuius vitrea natat ignis in urna.
Huc ego dum propero valido torquente dolore,
Diffugiente gemens oculorum luce fenestrae,
Quo procul ut tetigi benedicto lumen olivo,
Igneus ille vapor marcenti fronte recessit,
Et praesens medicus blando fugat unguine morbos.
Non oblita mihi mea lumina munere sancti,
Nam redit ante oculos oculorum cura fidelis,
Et memor illud ero dum luce et corpore consto.
(*Vita Mart.* 4.680-701)

Fortunatus' story is the first in the West, and as far as I know the only one in this period, explicitly to mention an experience of the healing "presence" of a saint through his picture, rather than a relic or a tomb. For official Christian opinion in the West – basing itself upon the many biblical strictures against idol-worship – refused to allow pictorial images a cultic role.[11] The schema on this page shows what may have been the central associations in the story:

Image in text	Associated images/notions
italics (metaphors of) self	CAPITALS (symbols of) divine
A adore *tomb*	"presence" of saint in relics, tomb
prostrate on ground	gesture of client towards patron prostration in East before statues
B law of the shrine	relics or chapel as such habitation of holy power?
Light	inner light shining out through eyes
AUTHOR	God the Creator; Christ: Light of World (true Light enlightening all men)
C wall holds FORM of saint under an IMAGE	forma: appearance, beauty, inner pattern imago: likeness, symbol, essence "presence" of original through resemblance
a PICTURE to be embraced BECAUSE OF ITS SWEET COLOURS	gest. of patronage; illusion of presence colours as spiritual qualities
D *through art the wall has a window**	analogous to human body
LAMP FIRE *glass vessel**	Christ: lamp of heavenly Jerusalem. (Ap 21:23) mystical "fire" of holy power analogous to human eye as window of soul
light disappearing from *windows of my eyes**	analogous to daylight, inner illumination "the lamp of the body is the eye"(Mt6:22)
touched ... LIGHT	assimilation through (mediated) contact
blessed ... oil**	mediation / assimilation through analogy and possibly contact
DOCTOR PRESENT	Martin (+ Christ) is (are) present through relic (adored?), picture ("embraced"), lamp / fire / light ("touched")
SOOTHING OINTMENT**	analogous to olive oil
E *my lights*	the eye is the light of the body (Mt 6:22)
gift of the saint	saint is effective mediator
returns to *believer's eyes*	memory image for eye of mind / heart

cure of my eyes	illumination of eyes of mind, soul, heart
while I remain *in light and body*	coalescence present / future life

As Gregory's story tells of a man travelling to come to Amarandus' tomb, *Paragraph A* leads us to Ravenna: there is a significant displacement in time and space. First, the saints there are greeted by the ritual of "adoration" – that is: prostration – at their tombs (DTC 1.1 437-442; DS 1 210-220). Although their souls were thought to live in heaven, and their bodies to remain on earth until the resurrection, they were – as we saw in Gregory's story – nevertheless regarded as also being very much "present" in their tombs and contact-relics (cf. Brown 1981). A fifth-century writer explains this presence by pointing to their essential unity with Christ who is also immanent everywhere (Victricius Rot., *Laud.* 7).

In *paragraph B* the phrase "the law of the shrine" – an abstract, unemotional formulation – may suggest that the cure to be described took place according to the then generally accepted principle of holy power exuding from the saint's relics kept there. For the contemporary practice in Gaul is that a chapel cannot be consecrated without the presence of relics (e.g. *Vit. pat.* 8.8). In Gregory's renderings of other Italian miracles which Fortunatus told him about, however, the event is always brought about through (indirect) contact with or proximity to a chapel or church of saint Martin: relics are not mentioned (*Virt. Mart.* 1.13-16). Thus, there may not have been any relics of saint Martin in the church of Paul and John, but only a place to pray near his picture. With this formulation, an absence of relics would make the chapel – and not, as the subsequent story would lead one to suppose, the picture – the habitation of holy power. Is Fortunatus defending himself from a possible charge of idolatry?

"The artist" must be the saint, for he is to be repaid by the poem about Martin. Some lines earlier, too, Fortunatus says explicitly that Martin gave him back his "light" (*lumen*) (4.667) – the same word that is to be used of the oil lamp near the picture. But the word *auctor* also evokes the Creator of light: God, and Christ as "the Light of the world" (Jn 8: 12) and "the true Light enlightening all men" (Jn 1: 9). In Gregory's other stories of miraculous cures, too, it is Christ who is said to do all the healing through the saints (e.g. *Hist.* 6.6). So there is an imaginative coalescence or unity of Martin and Christ – one which, as Fortunatus explicitly tells us, the saint had continuously attempted to achieve during his life (4. 585-586). But another coalescence is also suggested: that of visible light, the light shining from human eyes (Miles 1983, 124-129), and Christ as the inner Light, enlightening all men (Jn 1: 9). Through the mental images entertained then, external and internal phenomena, visible and invisible, human and divine realities, overlap and coalesce. Even more densely than in Gregory's story, sensory objects become symbols and epiphanies of invisible but very much present spiritual realities.

Paragraph C introduces the picture of the saint. Although the church of John and Paul which Fortunatus mentions survives (much changed) (Deichmann 1976, 333), the picture unfortunately does not. There is one portrait of Martin that we can still see, however, and Fortunatus himself certainly saw it: that in the church now called Sant' Apollinare Nuovo, in the author's time dedicated to Martin. There, high up above the columns but below the windows, he deferentially leads the row of martyrs to the throne of Christ.[12]

The fourth-century pagan philosopher Plotinus had expressed the imagistic-analogical world view so prominent in late Antiquity when he said that the statue as a mimetic object provides a sympathetic space for the presencing of the gods because they are mutually attracted by the similarity of their forms (Miller 1994, 31-32). In this context, Fortunatus' phrase "the form of the saint under an image" is highly suggestive. In his poems, Fortunatus uses the word *forma* for exterior appearance, often in the sense of beauty (e.g. *Carm.* 7.1.31). Another current use of *forma*, however, is the Platonic one of invisible, eternal essence or archetype, or inner pattern underlying the sensory appearance (TLL 6.1: 1082-1087; cf. Harrison 1992, 36-52). The same is true of the word *imago*, which can mean both likeness and inner pattern (TLL 7.1: 414). The central and similar Christian use of this term is, of course, God's creating man "according to his image (*ad imaginem suam*)" (Gen 1: 27). Thus, although Fortunatus appears to be saying only that the saint's visible appearance is represented as a picture (*pictura* is the term used in the next line), the other possible meanings of *forma* and *imago* as essence hover around. The picture can thus also be understood as a representation manifesting, through the mediation of visual material, the pattern of Martin's invisible inner soul-form, presumably manifesting the image of God.

Just as with Gregory's "eyes of faith", the discernment of this pattern would require some extra mental activity, however. How can one perceive such a "form"? Augustine had answered a similar question when he wrote that one sees God - who is Love - when one sees (in a manner which cannot be verbalized) divine love in someone's face (*Ev. Joh. Tract.* 9.10). It would have been easier to project a self-contructed mental image of Christ as the incarnate God upon the picture of Martin: for, as already indicated, He had been the saint's explicit soul-model. Like Gregory with visible events and objects, Fortunatus appears to be trying to let the reader look through sensory appearance of the picture to the iconically congruous invisible heavenly reality. But, for his own reasons, he does not develop this.

Paragraph D continues the strategy of overlaying and coalescing sensory objects with mental images whereby the former come to be perceived and experienced as symbols and epiphanies of dynamic immaterial realities. The wall having, through art, a window, is an analogon to the body, made by the Creator, having eyes. We see the image of windows being explicitly used for his eyes further down. The image also points forward to the saint's art (he was earlier called *auctor*, artist: 687) by which he will pierce the "wall" of the illness obstructing Fortunatus's eyes or windows. Window of the soul was a well-known metaphor for eyes (TLL 9.2: 448]). Just as in Gregory's story, the cure is doubtless intended to be understood as not only physical but also spiritual: as interior illumination.

Likewise, the description of the lamp – fire swimming upon oil (on water, so as to prevent overheating) in a glass container – points not only toward the sensory object. It also functions as a figure (or visualization) and theophany of Christ as "the lamp (*lucerna*)" of the heavenly Jerusalem (Ap 21: 23), who is the same as "the brightness of God (*claritas Dei*)". In one of Fortunatus's poems, he describes the interior of a church as a "figure" of, and as assimilated to, heaven with its stars, moon and eternal light (*Carm.* 3.7.41-50). At the same time, the image of the lamp functions as an image of that which he hopes his own "lights" or eyes – *mea lumina* – will become. I suggest that he may be imaging the light of his eyes – as we saw, in this period thought of as shining *out* of them – as becoming that of the saint's holy power which often manifested itself as light in the lamp. For in one story, his friend Gregory actually describes the eyes of a cured blind man in Tours as "adorned with the light of [the saint's] holy power" (*Virt. Mart.* 3.16). There, the saint has, as it were, lighted an interior fire in the heart of man – like the candle on Amarandus' tomb.

The light disappearing from the windows of the poet's eyes, then, is daylight but also the inner light which is Christ. And Christ, acting through the saint, returns both. Fortunatus says that this took place when he "touched the light (*lumen*)" near the picture through the oil. Through this gesture, he imaginatively assimilated his body, especially his eyes of course, with the light as a manifestation of Christ and the holy power of the saint. The oil was almost certainly taken from the lamp, as Gregory tells us explicitly in the short prose version of Fortunatus's story in *The Miracles of St Martin* (*Virt. Mart.* 1.15). Assimilating light by touching oil is again coalescing sensory with spiritual realities by means of superimposed mental images. What Fortunatus calls his "wilting brow" may at the same time be an evocation of the disturbed image of God in man. Thus, as the poet tells it, he mentally collapsed the images of light-Christ-lamp-saint with those of his eye and his interior self, imaged the oil as a medicinal ointment as well as an extension and mediation of the lamp's light, and perceived the visible picture as a manifestation of the saint's heavenly self. Coalescing sensory perception and mental images, he thus experienced as he says "the doctor present" – a spiritual reality – and this experienced "presence" of a known healer in which he had absolute confidence evidently brought on the cure.

How are we to understand this imaginative strategy as precipitating what was reportedly a real cure? One way is to compare it to similar experiences happening outside as well as inside organized western religion today. Certain anthropologists and psychologists have observed that metaphors can behave as bridges between the human consciousness and the so-called preverbal awareness, including that of the body. The Belgian anthropologist René Devisch writes:

> ... ritual symbols are ... corporeal devices, processes and methods or patterns that ... arise from a potential which, *akin to the dream*, unconceals both images and inner energy woven into the texture of the body (Devisch 1993, 280; my italics).

Physical healing, then, is founded in imaginative dreamwork – including such processes as condensation, fusion, figuration – that is largely beyond dialogue and discursive reality: it can only be experienced, acted out (Devisch 1993, 282). This enactment in fact induces a state of dream-awareness, in which discursive reasoning is temporarily put aside for the iconic awareness or trance, and images are experienced as affect-laden realities (Devisch 1993, 255, 257):

> ... the actualized trance and concomitant acts have a metamorphic effect. The cathartic trance arouses a deeply lived and bodily enacted experience of freeing and channeling life-bearing in the body, therapy group, and life-world in unison (Devisch 1993, 211).

Likewise, an American surgeon and psychotherapist observes that in the meditative visualization of symbols, affect-laden mental images act as bioelectrically charged patterns through which, in the hypothalamus, revitalizing messages are given to the body's autonomous systems (Siegel 1986, 66-69). Bodily-affectively enacting or imaginatively / affectively contemplating a mental image thus mediates and transmits its inherent structure of (emotional) energy to the preverbal consciousness and the body, thereby transforming it according to its pattern.

Fortunatus's miracle story, focusing upon a picture, shows that someone's carrying out symbolic actions while mentally imaging them as giving access to a living and "present" healer could bring about a similar result.

Paragraph E is a small epilogue, serving as a kind of framing device, which again suggests the continuum between interior and exterior eyes and light – confirming once more the open frontier between seeing, imaging and spiritual reality.

Mental image and miracle

In these miracle stories, then, vision – that is, sensory perception, mental imaging and "seeing" spiritual reality – is the means to knowledge. The latter increased and cohered through the explosively expanding semiosis of imagistic congruences and affinities rather than through the interrelations of discursive structures.

The episodes examined appear to describe quasi-liturgical acts in which a sensory event in a ritual context is consciously or unconsciously overlaid and collapsed with mental images – visualized patterns of feeling – of a spiritual reality. In this meditative or daydreaming state, the miraculous event is perceived as an ostensibly sensory phenomenon that exhibits the same pre-verbal dynamics as the mental images involved, namely: multidimensionality, coalescence of opposites, presentiality, assimilation with or coalescence through iconic resemblance, transformational leaps, and imitative replication in the affective as well as the bodily sphere.

As literary constructs, the miracle stories use imagistic dynamics in material objects to stand for and evoke a real – if imaginal – experience in the reader or listener of a leap mimicking that of the creative-supportive "divine" dynamic. In the ritual situation, this enactive experience of the leap would be the basis of a belief that would store this image as a model for subsequent perception in the religious sphere. In addition, it could establish the predisposition to foreground the meditative-affective – that is, imagistic or "dream" – mode of awareness, in which such dynamics operate, in situations within the religious context.

And that is a central point I wish to make in this paper: in late Antiquity the imaginal sphere was not, as today, trivialized. On the contrary, it was regarded as perhaps the most important mode through which to approach and experience spiritual reality. Gregory and Fortunatus's imagistically structured stories of the merging of the sensory, the imaginal and the spiritual, present and mediate non-discursive patterns of an affective and transforming kind of knowledge that is at least as sophisticated as the intellectual, propositional kind.

NOTES

1 I wish to express my gratitude to Professor Karl F. Morrison for his helpful critique of an earlier version of this explorative essay.

2 The scholarly journal *Word and Image* presents this line of research. The literature is vast. Studies in the general field that I have found useful are: Suzanne Langer *Philosophy in a New Key* (1957 [1942]) and *Feeling and Form* (1953); Gaston Bachelard *La poétique de la rêverie* (1986 [1960]); Rudolf Arnheim *Visual Thinking*

(1969); Dan Sperber *Rethinking Symbolism* (1974); Paul Ricœur "Imagination, in discourse and in action"(1978); Brunner H et al. Ed. *Wort und Bilt* (1979); Gerhart Ladner "Medieval and modern understanding of symbolism: a comparison" (1979); W. J. T. Mitchell *Iconology. Image, Text, Ideology* (1986) and *The Language of Images* (1987); Richard Kearney *The Wake of Imagination* (1988) and *Poetics of Imagining* (1991); David Freedberg *The Power of Images* (1989).

3 Studies that I have found useful are: Carl G. Jung, *Man and his Symbols* (1964); Roberto Assagioli, *Psychosynthesis* (1962); Wolfgang Kretschmer, "Meditative techniques in psychotherapy" (1969); Singer, *Imagery and Daydream Methods in Psychotherapy and Behavior Modification* (1974); and Peter E. Morris & Peter J. Hampson, *Imagery and Consciousness* (1983).

4 Gregory's writings show, however, that he is fully capable or reading non-religious texts in a quite different, critical and analytical manner. See on the ideological embedding of his reading processes: de Nie (1993).

5 The Church Father Augustine had used the expression eye of the mind or heart as a synonym for the imagination as an intermediate stage between sensory perception and intellectual understanding; the latter leaves images behind and is like a flash of divine light (*De Genesi ad litt.* 12; Miles 1983). David Chidester *Word and Light. Seeing, Hearing and Religious Discourse* (1992, 14-24), speaks of the Christian equation of word and light as a synaesthesia indicating the transcendence involved in this process.

6 Morrison (1990, 43) speaks of likeness, contiguity and contrast.

7 I am not suggesting that the mental images generated in this manner are necessarily fully developed or that imaging is a simple matter. Quite the contrary. Obviously, the degree and the contours of visualization differ not only between individuals but also in the same person according to the situation, the purpose of the reading, and the state of mind. In the mind's speed and economy, the image can also consist of only a visual trace suggesting the rest: "visual hints and flashes" (Arnheim 1969, 107-109). Moreover, distinctions should be made between: voluntary and involuntary imaging, that during waking and sleeping, incidental / brief and consciously recalled or constructed, maintained and developed imagery, and the purely inspectional visualization of referents as opposed to the immersive, affective imaging of symbols such as in meditation. Research on mental images has only just begun.

8 This is dramatically confirmed by the experience, after successful eye-surgery, of a fifty-two-year-old man born blind: all he saw at first was a big blur; it took him days to put together a few faces (Henn 1983).

9 Morrison (1990, 47) uses this term for the twelfth-century reader's reception of religious texts.

10 Arthur Koestler, *Roots of Coincidence* (1972) dicusses overlaps between science and parapsychology. In her *Dreams, Illusion and Other Realities* (1984, 189-197 and elsewhere), Wendy Doniger O'Flaherty compares reality testing by modern western scientists with the Indian mentalistic view of the universe. James Gleick, *Chaos. Making a New Science* (1987) explains new scientific paradigms to the general reader. Lyall Watson *The Nature of Things: The Secret Life of Inanimate Things* (1990) offers

case studies in parapsychology. James Redfield's *The Celestine Prophecy* (1993) is a well-known personal view.

[11] On the pictures of the holy in the west see: Ernst Kitzinger "The cult of images in the age before iconocmasm" (1954); Robert Markus "The cult of icons in sixth-century Gaul" (1978); Herbert L. Kessler "Pictorial narrative and Church mission in sixth-century Gaul" (1985); Celia Chazelle "Pictures, books and the illiterate: Pope Gregory's letters to Serenus of Marseilles" (1990). I have placed Fortunatus' story in its larger context in my "The poet as visionary: Venantius Fortunatus's 'new mantle' for Saint Martin" (de Nie 1997).

[12] Paulinus of Nola mentions a fourth-century picture of Martinus in his friend Sulpicius Severus' baptistery in Gaul (Paulinus Nol., *Ep.* 32.2-3; cf. de Nie 1997b).

WORKS CITED

Primary Sources

Augustinus, Aurelius. 1954. *In Johannis Evangelium Tractatus*. Ed. Willems, R. [Corpus Christianorum Series Latina (CCSL) 36]. Turnhout: Brépols.

---. 1970 [1894]. *De Genesi ad litteram*. Ed. Zycha, Josephus. [Corpus Scriptorum Ecclesiasticorum Latinorum (CSEL) 28]. New York: Johnson.

Fortunatus, Venantius. 1881. *Vita sancti Martini*. Ed. Leo, Friedrich. [Monumenta Germaniae Historica (MGH), Auctores Antiquissimi (AA) 4.1]. Berlin: Weidmann, 293-370.

---. 1881. *Carmina*. Ed.Leo, Friedrich, [MGH AA4]. Berlin: Weidmann, 293-292.

Gregorius, Georgius Florentius. 1885. *In gloria martyrum*. Ed. Krusch, Bruno. [Monumenta Germaniae Historica, Scriptores rerum Merovingicarum (MGH SSRM) 1.2]. Hannover: Hahn, 484-561.

---. 1885. *De virtutibus sancti Juliani martyris*. Ed. Krusch, Bruno. [MGH SSRM 1.2]. Hanover: Hahn, 562-584.

---. 1885. *De virtutibus sancti Martini*. Ed. Krusch, Bruno. [MGH SSRM 1.2]. Hanover: Hahn, 584-661.

---. 1885. *Vita patrum*. Ed. Krusch, Bruno. [MGH SSRM 1.2]. Hanover: Hahn, 661-744.

---. 1951. *Historiae libri X*. [ed.alt.] Eds. Krusch, Bruno & Wilhelm Levison. [MGH SSRM 1.1] Hanover: Hahn.

Gregorius Magnus. 1979. *Moralia in Job*. Ed. Adriaen, Marc. [CCSL 143-143b]. Turnhout: Brépols.

Paulinus Nolanus. 1894. *Epistolae*. Ed. Hartel, Wilhelm von. [CSEL 29]. Wien: Tempsky.

Victricius Rotomagensis. 1985. *De laude sanctorum*. Eds. Mulders, I & Roland Demeulenaere. [CCSL 64] Turnhout: Brépols, 69-93.

Modern Works

"Adoration", *Dictionnaire de Théologie Catholique* [DTC] 1.1 437-442.

"Adoration", *Dictionnaire de Spiritualité* [DS] 1.210-220.

Amat, Jacqueline. 1985. *Songes et visions. L'au-delà dans la littérature latine tardive*. Paris: Études Augustiniennes.

Arnheim, Rudolf. 1969. *Visual Thinking*. Berkeley: University of California Press.

Assagioli, Roberto. 1962. *Psychosynthesis*. New York: Esalen.

Auerbach, Erich. 1938. "Figura." *Archivum Romanicum* 22: 436-489.

---. 1988 [1946]. "Mimesis." *Dargestellte Wirklichkeit in der abendländischen Literatur*. [8e Aufl.]. Bern-Stuttgart: A. Francke.

Bachelard, Gaston. 1986 [1960]. *La poétique de la rêverie*. Paris: Quadrige / Presses Universitaires.

Brown, Peter L. 1981. *The Cult of the Saints*. Chicago: University of Chicago Press.

Brunner, H. et al., eds. 1979. *Wort und Bild*. München: Wilhelm Fink.

Chazelle, Celia. 1990. "Pictures, books and the illiterate: Pope Gregory's letters to Serenus of Marseilles." *Word and Image* 6: 138-153.

Chidester, David. 1992. *Word and Light. Seeing, Hearing and Religious Discourse*. Urbana: University of Illinois Press.

Dam, Raymond van. 1993. *Saints and Their Miracles in Late Antiquity*. Princeton: Princeton University Press

Deichmann, Friedrich W. 1976. *Ravenna. Hauptstadt des Abendlandes*. [vol. II, Commentary part 2]. Wiesbaden: Franz Steiner.

Deikman, A.J. 1966. "Deautomatization and the mystic experience." *Psychiatry* 29: 324-338. [Reprinted in: Ed. Tart, Charles T. 1969. *Altered States of Consciousness*. New York: John Wiley and Sons, 23-44.]

Devisch, René. 1993. *Weaving the Threads of Life*. Chicago: University of Chicago Press.

Drewermann, Eugen. 1985. *Tiefenpsychologie und Exegese*. [vol. 2]. Olten / Freiburg-im-Breisgau: Walter.

Epstein, Gerald. 1981. *Waking dream therapy*. New York: Human Sciences Press.

Erenstein, Robert L. 1988. *Theatre and Television*. Amsterdam: International Theatre Bookshop.

Esrock, Ellen. 1994. *The Reader's Eye*. Baltimore: Johns Hopkins University Press.

"Forma." *Thesaurus Linguae Latinae* [TLL] 6.1: 1082-1087.

Freedberg, David. 1989. *The Power of Images*. Chicago: University of Chicago Press.

Geertz, Clifford. 1973. "Religion as a cultural system." Geertz, C. *The Interpretation of Cultures*. New York: Basic Books, 87-125.

George, Judith. 1992. *Venantius Fortunatus. A Poet in Merovingian Gaul*. Oxford: Clarendon.

Gleick, James. 1987. *Chaos. Making a New Science*. New York: Viking.

Harrison, Carol. 1992. *Beauty and Revelation in the Thought of Saint Augustine*. Oxford: Clarendon.

Henn, Volker. 1983. "Der Sehvorgang – Wie Auge und Gehirn ihre Umwelt analysieren." Ed. Svilar, Maja, 201-218.

"Imaginalis ... imago." *Thesaurus Linguae Latinae* [TLL] 7.1: 401-414.

Jung, Carl G. 1964. *Man and His Symbols*. London: Aldus Books.

Kearney, Richard. 1988. *The Wake of Imagination*. Minneapolis: University of Minnesota Press.

---. 1991. *Poetics of Imagining*. London: Harper Collins Academic.

Kessler, Herbert L. 1985. "Pictorial Narrative and Church mission in sixth-century Gaul." Eds. Kessler, Herbert L. & Marianna Shreve Simpson, 75-91.

Kessler, Herbert L. & Marianna Shreve Simpson, eds. 1985. *Pictorial Narrative in Antiquity*
and the Middle Ages. [Studies in the History of Art 16]. Washington.

Kitzinger, Ernst. 1954. "The cult of images in the age before iconoclasm." *Dumbarton Oaks Papers* 8: 83-150.

Koestler, Arthur. 1972. *The Roots of Coincidence*. London: Hutchinson.

Kosslyn, Stephen M. 1994. *Image and Brain*. Cambridge, Mass.: MIT Press.

Kretschmer, Wolfgang. 1969. "Meditative techniques in psychotherapy." Ed. Tart, Charles T., 219-228.

Ladner, Gerhart B. 1979. "Medieval and modern understanding of symbolism: a comparison." *Speculum* 54: 223-256.

Langer, Suzanne. 1957 [1942]. *Philosophy in a New Key*. [Third edition]. Cambridge, Mass.: Harvard University Press.

---. 1953. *Feeling and Form*. New York: Charles Scribner's Sons.

McFague, Sallie T. 1975. *Speaking in Parables*. Philadelphia: Fortress.

Markus, Robert. 1978. "The cult of icons in sixth-century Gaul." *Journal of Theological Studies* 29: 151-157.

Miles, Margaret. 1983. "Vision: the eye of the body and the eye of the mind in Saint Augustine's *De trinitate* and *Confessions*." *The Journal of Religion* 63: 125-142.

Miller, Patricia Cox. 1994. *Dreams in Late Antiquity*. Princeton: Princeton University Press.

Mitchell, W. J. T. 1986. *Iconology. Image, Text, Ideology*. Chicago: University of Chicago Press.

---. 1987. *The Languages of Images*. Chicago: U. of Chicago Press.

---. 1992. "The pictorial turn." *Artforum*: 89-94.

Morris, Peter E. & Peter J. Hampson. 1983. *Imagery and Consciousness*. London: Academic Press.

Morrison, Karl F. 1990. *History as a Visual Art in the Twelfth-Century Renaissance*. Princeton: Princeton University Press.

Nie, Giselle de. 1987. *Views From a Many-Windowed Tower. Studies of Imagination in the Works of Gregory of Tours*. [Studies in Classical Antiquity 7]. Amsterdam: Rodopi.

---. 1990. "A broken lamp or the effluence of holy power? Common sense and belief reality in Gregory of Tours' own experience." *Mediaevistik* 3: 269-279.

---. 1991. "Le corps, la fluidité et l'identité personelle dans la vision du monde de Grégoire de Tours." Eds. Uytfanghe, Marc van & Roland Demeulenaere, 75-87.

---. 1993. "De 'kracht' van wat in het boek gezegd wordt: woord, schrift en teken in zesde-eeuws Gallië." ["The power of what is said in the book: word, script and sign in sixth-century Gaul."] Eds. Stuip, René E. V. & Cees Vellekoop.

---. 1994. "Gregory of Tours' smile: spiritual reality, imagination and earthly events in the 'Histories'." Eds. Scharer, Anton & Georg Scheibelreiter, 68-95.

---. 1995. "Die Sprache im Wunder — das Wunder in der Sprache. Menschenwort und Logos bei Gregor von Tours." *Mitteilungen des Instituts für Österreichische Geschichtsforschung* 103: 1-25.

---. 1997a [1993]. "Seeing and believing in the early Middle Ages: a preliminary investigation." [*Selected Essays from the Third Conference of the International Association of Word and Image Studies* (1993)]. Amsterdam: Rodopi.

---. 1997b. "The poet as visionary: Venantius Fortunatus's 'new mantle' for Saint Martin." *Cassiodorus* 2.

---. 1997c. "History and miracle: Gregory's use of metaphor." Ed. Wood, Ian N. [forthcoming].

Nussbaum, Martha. 1990. *Love's Knowledge. Essays on Philosophy and Literature.* Oxford: Oxford University Press.

"Oculus." *Thesaurus Linguae Latinae* [TLL] 9.2: 441-452.

O'Flaherty, Wendy Doniger. 1984. *Dreams, Illusion and Other Realities.* Chicago: University of Chicago Press.

Ogden, Dunbar. 1988. "The mimetic impulse or the Doppelgänger effect." Ed. Erenstein, Robert L., 21-49.

Pietri, Luce. 1983. *La ville de Tours du IVe au VIe siècle.* Roma: École française de Rome.

Redfield, James. 1993. *The Celestine Prophecy.* New York: Warner Books.

Ricœur, Paul. 1975. *La métaphore vive.* Paris: Seuil.

---. 1978. "Imagination, in discourse and in action." *Analecta Husserliana* 7: 3-22.

Rorty, Richard. 1988 [1967]. *The Linguistic Turn. Recent Essays in Philosophical Method.* Chicago: University of Chicago Press.

Sanders, Gabriel. 1965. *Licht en duisternis in de christelijke grafschriften.* [Verhandelingen van de Koninklijke Vlaamse Academie voor Wetenschappen, Letteren en Schone Kunsten van België, Klasse der Letteren 27.56. 2 vols.] Brussels: Paleis der Academiën.

Sargant, William. 1974. *The Mind Possessed.* Philadelphia: J.B.Lippincott.

Scharer, Anton & Georg Scheibelreiter, eds. 1994. *Historiographie im frühen Mittelalter.* Wien: R. Oldenbourg Verlag

Siegel, Bernie S. 1986. *Love, Medicine and Miracles.* New York: Harper.

Singer, Jerome L. 1974. *Imagery and Daydream Methods in Psychotherapy and Behavior Modification.* New York: Academic Press.

Sperber, Dan. 1974. *Rethinking Symbolism.* [transl. A. Morton]. Cambridge: Cambridge University Press.

Stuip, René E. V. & Cees Vellekoop, eds. 1993. *Oraliteit en schriftcultuur* [*Orality and the culture of the written word.* Utrechtse Bijdragen tot de Mediëvistiek 12]. Hilversum: Verloren.

Svilar, Maja, ed. 1983. *'Und es ward Licht' Zur Kulturgeschichte des Lichts*. [Universität Bern Kulturhistorische Vorlesungen 1981 / 82]. Bern-Frankfurt am Main: Peter Lang.

Tart, Charles T., ed. 1969. *Altered States of Consciousness*. New York: John Wiley.

Tomkins, Sylvan S. 1962 / 3. *Affect, Imagery and Consciousness*. [2 vols.] New York: Springer.

Uytfanghe, Marc van & Roland Demeulenaere, eds. 1991. *Aevum inter utrumque. Mélanges offerts à Gabriel Sanders*. [Instrumenta Patristica 23]. Steenbrugge: Abbatia s. Petri.

Watson, Lyall. 1990. *The Nature of Things: The secret Life of Inanimate Things*. London: Hodder and Stoughton.

Wheelwright, Philip. 1982. *The Burning Fountain. A Study in the Language of Symbolism*. [New rev. ed.]. Gloucester, Mass.: Peter Smith.

Wood, Ian N., ed. 1997. *The World of Gregory of Tours*. Ithaca: Cornell University Press. [forthcoming].

XIII

FATHERLY AND MOTHERLY CURING IN SIXTH-CENTURY GAUL: SAINT RADEGUND'S *MYSTERIUM*

Introduction

In Poitiers, probably around the year 590, the Italian-born poet and priest Venantius Fortunatus (c. 540–c. 605) wrote one of the first biographies of a holy woman in the West: that of his intimate friend, the then just-deceased nun Saint Radegund (c. 520–87).[1] She was a Thuringian princess, captured on the battlefield, who had become a Frankish queen, but had later managed to leave her royal husband to embrace the religious life and found a convent in the above-mentioned city. Although she had been revered by most people as a saint already during her lifetime, her powerful personality and independent interpretation of the monastic life-style prescribed by the Rule of her convent—Fortunatus' poems show that, instead of strict withdrawal from the world, she cultivated religious friendships and literary tastes—had alienated the city's bishop; he resented being unable to assert his rightful authority as the convent's ecclesiastical supervisor. When the nuns' revolt after Radegund's death called the headstrong queen's reputation into question,[2] it was probably to restore the latter that Fortunatus undertook to write his encomiastic biography, in which we see only ascetic piety, humility and loving care.

---

[1] Venantius Fortunatus, *Vita sanctae Radegundis*, ed. B. Krusch, Monumenta Germaniae Historica (= MGH), Auctores Antiquissimi (= AA) 4.2 (Berlin, 1885), pp. 38–49. Tr. J.A. McNamara and J.E. Halborg, *Sainted Women of the Dark Ages* (Durham-London, 1992), pp. 70–86. On Fortunatus' life and career see: B. Brennan, "The career of Venantius Fortunatus", *Traditio* 41 (1985), pp. 49–78, and J. George, *Venantius Fortunatus: A Poet in Merovingian Gaul* (Oxford, 1992), pp. 4–34.

[2] Gregorius Turonensis, *Historiae* (ed. B. Krusch and W. Levison, MGH Scriptores rerum Merovingicarum (= SSrM) 1.1, editio altera (Berlin, 1951)) 10.16.

At approximately the same time that Fortunatus was writing, his friend and patron, the historian and hagiographer Bishop Gregory of Tours (539–94) included some holy women in his numerous brief notices on Gallic saints and their miracles, and wrote a biography of one: Monegunde. But he also wrote brief, admiring, passages about Radegund, stressing her queenly as well as her saintly qualities.[3] About fifteen years later, Baudonivia, a nun in Radegund's convent, wrote another biography of the saint to supplement that by Fortunatus, who is mentioned in her preface as then being bishop of Poitiers. Baudonivia presents Radegund as a queenly personality and a teacher, aspects which Fortunatus had, it seems intentionally, omitted.[4]

Although Greek women saints' miracles were being reported at least since the fourth century, in the West sainthood and miraculous curing had up to then been attributed only to men,[5] and the latter's cures tended to resemble those of their model, the fourth-

---

[3] Gregorius Turonensis, *In Gloria Confessorum* (ed. B. Krusch, MGH SSrM 1.2 (Hannover, 1885), pp. 484–561) 5, 16, 18, 24, 33, 42, 89, 102, 104, 107; Saint Monegunde: idem, *Vita Patrum* (MGH SSrM 1.2, pp. 661–744) 19. About Radegund: *Historiae* 3.4, 7; 6.29, 34; 7.36; 9.2, 42; and *In Gloria Confessorum* 104.

[4] Baudonivia, *Vita sanctae Radegundis*, ed. B. Krusch, MGH SSrM 2 (Hannover, 1888), pp. 377–95. Tr. McNamara and Halborg, *Sainted Women of the Dark Ages*, pp. 86–105. This biography reports only one other direct cure—in a manner which is not indicated, of a woman's eye-ailment—during her lifetime (c. 11), and an unspecified number through her tomb, especially of possessed and fevers but including that of an abbot's toothache (c. 25–8). On Radegund's life and career, see: B. Brennan, "St Radegund and the early development of her cult at Poitiers", *Journal of Religious History* 13 (1985), pp. 340–354. Recent studies of Radegund include: (Comité du XIVe Centenaire), *La riche personalité de Sainte Radegonde: Conférence et homilies* (Poitiers, 1988); Jean Leclercq, "La sainte Radegonde de Venance Fortunat et celle de Baudonivie", *Fructus Centesimus: Mélanges offerts à Gerard J.M. Bartelink*, eds. A.A.R. Bastiaensen et al., Instrumenta Patristica 19 (Steenbrugge, 1989), pp. 207–216; S. Gäbe, "Radegundis: sancta, regina, ancilla. Zum Heiligkeitsideal der Radegundisviten von Fortunat und Baudonivia", *Francia* 16 (1989), pp. 1–30; C. Papa, "Radegonda e Batilde: modelli di santita regia femminile nel regno Merovingio", *Benedictina* 36 (1989), pp. 13–33; R. Folz, *Les saintes reines du Moyen Age en Occident (VI–XIIIe siècles)*, Subsidia hagiographica 76 (Brussels, 1992), pp. 13–24. On the position of women in Frankish Gaul, see also: H.-W. Goetz, *Weibliche Lebensgestaltung im frühen Mittelalter* (Cologne, 1991), pp. 7–44.

[5] Cf. A. Rousselle, "La sage-femme et le thaumaturge dans la Gaule tardive. Les femmes ne font pas de miracles", *La médecine en Gaule. Villes d'eaux, sanctuaires des eaux*, ed. A. Pelletier (Paris, 1985), p. 248. On Greek women saints performing miracles, see: E. Giannarelli, "Women and miracles in Christian biography", *Studia Patristica* 25 (1991), pp. 376–380. See also: H.-W. Goetz, "Heiligenkult und Geschlecht: Geschlechts-spezifisches Wunderwirken in frühmittelalterlichen Mirakelberichten?", *Das Mittelalter* 1 (1996) 2, pp. 89–111.

century Saint Martin of Tours. Fortunatus and Gregory are thus the first to tell us about women's cures in Gaul, both during their lives and through their tombs after death. As far as we can tell from the reports, most of these cures do not differ significantly from those by men. Since the two women saints that we know most about, Monegund and Radegund, lived in a cloistered sphere, this must be one reason why they are reported as healing more women than men: very few men had access to them. Another reason is likely to be that women patients tended to feel more comfortable with a woman healer.[6] Not surprisingly, both saints also associated themselves closely with the memory of Saint Martin. Monegund established her monastic community in the *atrium* of his very church in Tours, and Radegund visited his various shrines before establishing herself in Poitiers, close to a Martinian monastery. One of her last reported acts was to request an official in a dream to rebuild a chapel for the saint.[7]

All three authors describe Radegund as an independent and unconventional, as well as a forceful, personality. As I hope to show in what follows, Fortunatus' biography contains indications that she may have innovated in her exercise of the existing male curing tradition as well. Focusing upon a notion that keeps recurring in crucial places—that of *mysterium*—, I shall place his stories of Radegund's cures alongside his descriptions of those by a contemporary living male saint (whom he also knew personally), Bishop Germanus of Paris (555–76). In this way, what may be her unique contribution will become visible.

The Term Mysterium

What, however, is a *mysterium*? The term occurs in the following story about a cure by Radegund which is significantly qualified as 'a new kind of miracle'. Fortunatus tells us that

> the nun Animia was so completely swollen with dropsy that she had reached her end. The appointed sister nuns were around her, expecting her to expire at any moment, when she saw in her sleep that the

[6] As also Goetz, "Heiligenkult und Geschlecht: Geschlechtsspezifisches Wunderwirken in frühmittelalterlichen Mirakelberichten?", p. 104.

[7] Gregorius, *Vita Patrum* 19.2; Fortunatus, *Vita sanctae Radegundis* 33–34, 87–89.

> blessed Radegund, with the venerable abbess, ordered her to descend nude into a bath (*in balneo*) without water. Then, with her own hand, the saint was seen to pour oil over the head of the sick woman, and to cover her with a new robe. After this mystery had been enacted (*peracto mysterio*), she awoke from sleep and nothing of the illness was left; she had not lost the water through perspiration but it had been consumed within. By this new kind of miracle (*novo sub miraculo*) the illness left no trace in her womb (*uterus*). For she who had been believed to be ready to be carried to the grave (*tumulum*), lifted herself at once from her bed, with the scent of the oil remaining upon her head and the fact that there was nothing harmful in her belly (*venter*) as a testimony (*testimonium*) [to the truth of the event].[8]

What we see here is that the *mysterium* is the hinge event in this story: the transformational moment. In the Gospels, the term is used by Christ to refer to manifestations of the invisible presence and working of the Kingdom of God in the human life-world.[9] According to the authoritative dictionary of early Christian Latin, the term later came to denote: a symbol of a divine truth or its content; a revealed divine doctrine; the effectuation of Christ's redemption of man; a (pagan or) Christian rite or mystical celebration, especially that of the transformation of bread and wine into the body and blood of Christ: i.e. the Eucharist; and the (ritual) Eucharistic prayer.[10]

The term 'mystery', then, was used to indicate a pattern of transformational divine action in the human life-world, an event which cannot be rationally analyzed or understood; it can only be pointed to in a specific event or metaphor functioning as a symbol, and entered into through ritual symbolic action. According to the then already established church tradition, certain Old and New Testament events could be identified as such 'mysteries'. For they could have more than only an empirical meaning in that their contours were perceived to manifest the archetypal patterns or 'figures'[11] of transtemporal modes of divine interaction with humankind. With this in mind, Bible exegesis flourished, and particularized meanings of the term *mysterium* emerge. Thus, two hundred years before Radegund, bishop

---

[8] Fortunatus, *Vita sanctae Radegundis*, 80–81.

[9] As in Matthew 13:11, Luke 8:10, and John 1:3, 9; 9:5.

[10] A. Blaise, *Dictionnaire Latin-Français des Auteurs Chrétiens* (Turnhout, 1954), pp. 547–548. Gregory of Tours refers to the Eucharist as a *mysterium* in his *Virtutes sancti Martini* (ed. B. Krusch, MGH SSrM 1.2, pp. 584–661) 2.1.

[11] As E. Auerbach, "Figura", *Archivum Romanicum* 22 (1938), pp. 436–489.

Hilary of Poitiers had written the *Tractatus mysteriorum*, which lists and explains a number of visible biblical events as revealing specific divine prophecies about the future of the Church and its members.[12] As we shall see, this tradition is reflected in Fortunatus' writing, and Radegund must also have been aware of it.

Another fourth-century treatise, Bishop Ambrose of Milan's *Liber de mysteriis*, describes the symbolic actions involved in the ritual of baptism and explains how they effect the catechumen's rebirth into a new life.[13] Here, then, *mysterium* is a symbol as enacted and effectuated in and through human ritual. Although Radegund may have read Ambrose's treatises on virginity,[14] she would not have been likely to have known this one; as a priest, however, Fortunatus would. These two treatises show that in this period *the term 'mysterium' could be understood as pointing to the effective operation of (biblical) symbols or 'figures' of divine activity in present sensory reality through their ritual enactment.* In what follows, I hope to show that Fortunatus may have used the notion of 'mystery' in a striking new way: to indicate both the symbolic ritual through which Radegund precipitated a miracle as well as the event itself as a visual manifestation of an invisible divine transformational dynamic or pattern of action. It seems to me that Fortunatus would have had no reason to invent her new curing rituals, and thus that it was very likely Radegund herself who was, more or less consciously, innovating here.

In the story above, her 'new kind of miracle' took place during another's dream, and a dream—in late Antiquity—was regarded as the privileged manner in which an objectively existing spiritual reality could be perceived.[15] As we saw, the successive acts of descending into a bath, and being anointed and clothed with a new robe that, together, appear to have precipitated the cure are referred to as an '*enacted* mystery'. This phrase appears to refer to the performance of a ritual that actualizes and activates the religious symbol. The symbol here could be that of baptism, because all the acts

[12] Hilaire de Poitiers, *Traité des mystères*, ed. and tr. J.P. Brisson, Sources chrétiennes (= SC) 19bis (Paris, 1967).

[13] Ambroise de Milan, *Des mystères*, ed. and tr. B. Botte, SC 25 (Paris, [1950]), pp. 107–128.

[14] Ambrosius Mediolanensis, *De virginibus Libri Tres*, ed. E. Cazaniga, Corpus Scriptorum Latinorum Paravianum (Torino, n.d.).

[15] As also P.C. Miller, *Dreams in Late Antiquity: Studies in the Imagination of a Culture* (Princeton, 1994), p. 40.

described in this story also appear in the late antique north Italian and Gallican rites of baptism which, as we saw, was designated as a *mysterium*.[16] But, as we all know, dreams can condense various symbols into one. Thus, the presence of the abbess alongside Radegund may indicate that the dream acts were at the same time the equivalents of the ritual profession of a nun as the bride of Christ.[17] (Since the fourth century, the veiling of a religious woman was celebrated as her affiancing to Christ.)[18] Gregory of Tours reports a dream of another of Radegund's nuns in which the abbess brings her a bridal robe, sent by 'the Bridegroom' (i.e. Christ), in a setting that can only be Paradise.[19] This dream event made such an impression upon her that she asked to be walled in as a recluse, which was ceremonially carried out, Radegund presiding. Significantly, both of these events, then, have a ritual dimension, both take place in the imaginative or spiritual world, and both effect a transformation. In the curing dream, however, there is almost certainly another dimension that is specifically connected to its status as a cure: that of an associative overlap with the apostolic (and contemporary) ecclesiastical ritual of anointing the sick,[20] another ritual of transformation.

It remains to explain why the whole event is designated as 'a new kind of miracle'. As we see elsewhere in Fortunatus' biography, Radegund—as the first sainted queen and a pioneer in miracle-doing holy womanhood in the West—is *explicitly* compared only to male models of saintliness and exercise of holy power.[21] However, her non-miraculous actions resemble those of some earlier ascetic women, with whom Fortunatus compares her explicitly in one of his poems.[22]

---

[16] See: "Baptême", *Dictionnaire d'Archéologie chrétienne et de Liturgie* (= DACL) 2.1b, col. 318–320, 325–326; "Bains", Ibid., col. 98, and "Huile", DACL 6.2, col. 2779–2783.

[17] In the rite of the late antique consecration of virgins, as Duchesne describes it, there is only a veiling and no anointing: L. Duchesne, *Christian Worship: Its Origin and Evolution*, Tr. M.L. McClure, 4th ed. (London/New York, 1912), pp. 422–427.

[18] J. Bugge, *Virginitas. An Essay in the History of a Medieval Ideal.* International Archives of the History of Ideas, series minor 17 (The Hague, 1975), pp. 59–67, esp. p. 66.

[19] *Historiae* 6.29.

[20] Mark 6:13; James 5:14–17.

[21] Fortunatus, *Vita sanctae Radegundis* 4 (Israel), 7 (Samuel), 13 (three youths in Babylon), 37 (Germanus), 84 (Martin). In chapters 11 and 44 her actions imitate those of Saint Martin without his name being mentioned.

[22] Venantius Fortunatus, *Carmina* (ed. F. Leo, MGH AA 4.1 (Berlin, 1881)) 8.1.41–46. See on this topic: G. de Nie, "'Consciousness fecund through God': from

The only explicit female model—consonant with the self-effacing image of the saint that Fortunatus, to restore the saint's reputation, is here concerned to present—is the very humble one of Martha, who served Jesus and his disciples while her sister Mary sat and listened to their conversation.[23] We shall see, however, that Fortunatus may be slipping in one part of his subject's innovations in a less conspicuous manner, and that this could be what he meant with the qualification 'new kind of miracle'.

In what follows, I shall first examine the male curing tradition as Fortunatus describes it in the acts of Saint Germanus of Paris. Then I shall attempt to show that the contours of the events in the dream cure cited above may imply and involve, alongside the traditional Christian symbolism already mentioned, a new image that highlights woman's role in a cure. For in this and in one other 'new kind of cure'—which Fortunatus also explicitly designates as such—, a symbolic dimension appears to become visible which displays a new powerful role model for Christian women. And I shall argue that, in these, the term *mysterium* points precisely to *the transformation of the human body through the ritual enactment of a powerful image, archetypal pattern of transformational divine action, or symbol.* But we must begin by a brief look at some more general preconceptions underlying the view of cures in this period.

Late Antique Views of Healing

A late twentieth-century layman's view of healing tends to be couched in terms of a purely empirical conception of the material world inherited from the nineteenth century. In this world view, a 'miracle' is theoretically impossible: it is assumed that each phenomenon or event must have a 'natural' explanation, even though it has not yet been found. The late antique person, however, whether pagan or Christian, looked at the human life-world from a different perspective. First, although the material and the spiritual dimensions were conceptually distinguished, they were not perceived as being in fact separated

male fighter to spiritual bride-mother of Christ in late antique female sanctity", *Sanctity and Motherhood: Essays on Holy Mothers in the Middle Ages*, ed. A.B. Mulder-Bakker (New York/London, 1995), pp. 139–151.

[23] Luke 10:38–42. Fortunatus, *Vita sanctae Radegundis* 42.

from each other. Quite the contrary. Throughout material objects, animals and human persons good and evil *spiritual forces and powers* were thought to be present and active; there was no neutral territory or vacuum.[24] Illness too, therefore, was not only a physical thing; we see in Gregory of Tours' stories that it is frequently described as the effect of a malign power which had invaded the person from without, and which needed to be driven out again.[25]

A second crucial difference from modern views is that for sixth-century Christians contemporary events, and especially miracles, could also be interpreted—like those in the Bible—as signs revealing divine action patterns. Their internal contours or 'figures', too, were thought to reveal archetypes of spiritual truth which were being divinely replicated since biblical times. In fact, the whole palpable and visible world was thought to be a veil that covered the *archetypal forms or figural patterns of the 'really real' spiritual world*, which could sometimes be perceived in dreams or visions. The central example of such an archetypal form or pattern of spiritual truth was, of course, the visible event of Christ's death and resurrection as imaging or 'figuring' the victory over all evil and the entrance into eternal life; this was the central Christian *mysterium.*

A last, essential, difference with modern thinking is that—in pagan as well as in Christian circles—*all phenomena in the cosmos were thought to participate in each other through resemblance in form.*[26] This meant that the ritual enactment of a particular symbolic form would effect the celebrant's participation in (the power pattern of) the archetype at the place of action. Thus, even Augustine regards the human sounding of the word of God as effecting its actual presence: Christ as the divine Logos or Word is actively present in and working through the human words of the preacher.[27] Two centuries later, Gregory of

---

[24] As A. Angenendt, "Die Liturgie und die Organisation des kirchlichen Lebens auf dem Lande", *Cristianizzazione ed organizazzione ecclesiastica delle campagne nell'alto medioevo: espansione e resistenze*, Settimane di Studio del Centro Italiano di Studi sull'alto medioevo 1 (Spoleto, 1982), p. 186. On the intellectual background, see: L. Thorndike, *A History of Magic and Experimental Science*, vol. 1 (New York, 1923), pp. 540–547.

[25] As in his *Virtutes sancti Martini* 4.37. Cf. G. de Nie, *Views from a Many-Windowed Towe: Studies of Imagination in the Works of Gregory of Tours.* Studies in Classical Antiquity 7 (Amsterdam, 1987), pp. 230–237.

[26] G.B. Ladner, *Handbuch der frühchristlichen Symbolik* (Stuttgart/Zürich, 1992), pp. 19–20.

[27] Based upon 1 Thessalonians 2:13 and John 1.1–4, 9; Augustine, *De magistro*

Tours reports that the pronouncing of a saint's name precipitates the presence of his holy power, and that even reverent contact with the written letters of the miracle stories of a saint (who happened to be his uncle) healed someone's blindness.[28] To sum up, the coalescence of the material and the spiritual and the participation of phenomena in each other through the resemblance of 'figured' patterns and/or analogy were the underlying reasons that late antique medical practice, pagan and Christian, tended to combine physical remedies with symbolical acts. The latter were intended to invoke and bring to the spot beneficent spiritual powers or power-patterns to drive out the disease-causing spirit as well as its bodily effects.[29]

In the Christian tradition which we see in late sixth-century saints' lives and miracle stories, the saint's healing action tends to follow a similar pattern. For here too, the use of spiritual 'power' is often, but not always, simultaneous with practical therapy. Generally speaking, an act of prayer to ask for power from Christ usually came first. Then, touching or anointing to transmit this healing 'power', and/or symbolical gestures such as the sign of the Cross, the invocation of the divine name, or the speaking of ritual words followed. All this is not infrequently combined with cleansing, and herbal or other physical treatment of the patient.[30] Something like the Old Testament view that "unless the Lord builds a house those who work on it labor in vain" may be said to underlie these therapies.[31]

(ed. K.D. Daur, CCSL 29 (Turnhout, 1970), pp. 156–203) 11.30 and 12.40. Cf. G. de Nie, "Die Sprache im Wunder—das Wunder in der Sprache. Menschenwort und Logos bei Gregor von Tours", *Mitteilungen des Instituts für Österreicheische Geschichtsforschung* 103 (1995), pp. 1–25.

[28] Gregorius, *Virtutes sancti Martini* 23 and *Vita Patrum* 8.12. The latter resembles the use of amulets—along with herbs and potions—in Marcellus's pagan magical medicine; see: A. Rousselle, "Du sanctuaire au thaumaturge: la guérison en Gaule au IVe siècle", *Annales* 31 (1976), p. 1093.

[29] See: "Médecins", DACL 11.1, col. 109–180. On pagan women doctors: col. 119–20; the Merovingian period and healing saints: col. 149–154, and Rousselle, "Du sanctuaire au thaumaturge: la guérison en Gaule au IVe siècle."

[30] A. Rousselle, *Croire et guérir: La foi en Gaule dans l'Antiquité tardive* (Paris, 1990), pp. 83–96, 114–128. Cf. idem, "Du sanctuaire au thaumaturge: la guérison en Gaule au IVe siècle."

[31] Psalm 126 (127).1.

Male Cures: 'The Miracle-Doing Doctor'

The male curing tradition in sixth-century Gaul becomes most visible in Saint Germanus of Paris, because of all the male saints whose deeds Fortunatus records, he effected by far the most cures: including indirect ones, forty-eight, against seven by his nearest male rival.[32] Accordingly, the saint is repeatedly referred to as a "doctor",[33] and praised as a "miracle-doing doctor (*mirificus medicus*)", a "healing leader (*medicabilis praesul*)", and one who "outdoes all the art of doctors (*omnem artem medicorum . . . superasse*)".[34] As may be expected, ordinary physicians are therefore disparaged.[35] Although Radegund's cures number fourteen, she is only once referred to as a 'doctor', perhaps as a reminiscence of the Roman tradition of women doctors.[36]

In what follows, I shall focus upon the curing methods that appear to be similar to Radegund's, but also indicate accents that differ. The cures through anointing and washing will be looked at first, and the stroking and holding which this involved have been included also when these occur by themselves. I shall begin by putting alongside Radegund's above-quoted cure of Animia's dropsy (which will be further analyzed in the section on Radegund's cures) the single similar one by Germanus, and then survey his rituals of anointing, stroking and washing. This section will be concluded by looking at the use of the term *mysterium* for one of Germanus' miracles, and its meanings elsewhere in Fortunatus' prose saints' lives.

Dropsy

The one cure of dropsy recorded of Germanus tells us that Daningus,

> given up by the doctors, and at the end of his strength, turned to the holy man for a remedy (*remedium*). When the patient had taken off his clothes and the saint had anointed him with his sacred hands (*sacris manibus peruncto*), the fluid of the dropsy inside his body was at once consumed by the fluid on the outside, and the infusion of water was

[32] Saint Albinus (in: Fortunatus, *Vita sancti Albini* (ed. B. Krusch, MGH AA 4.2, pp. 27–33)).

[33] Fortunatus, *Vita sancti Germani* (ed. B. Krusch, MGH AA 4.2, pp. 11–27) 72, 109, 137, 146, 149, 157, 185.

[34] Ibid. 137, 141, 109.

[35] Ibid. 146, 159.

[36] Fortunatus, *Vita sanctae Radegundis* 29; Roman female physicians: DACL 11.1, col. 119–120.

> dried up by the oil. In this astonishing manner (*modo admirabili*) neither did the humor come out nor was it held inside, and a humor was dried up by a humor in a praiseworthy manner.[37]

The here evident trope of the inversion of everyday reality or paradox is not infrequently stressed by Fortunatus; it points to Christianity's more general inversion of everyday values.[38] But, as I hope to show later, paradox is likely to have played a central role in the healing processes themselves too. In the above story, the oil and the touching by the saint's 'sacred hands' are highlighted. As I have already indicated, it is of course the treatment which the apostolic letter of James had prescribed:

> If anyone among you is ill, let him call for the priests of the church, and let them pray over him (*super eum*), anointing him with oil in the name of the Lord. And the prayer of faith shall save the ill man, and the Lord will raise him up. And if he has committed sins, they will be forgiven. . . . The assiduous prayer of a just man is very powerful, for Elijah was a man of like nature with ourselves. . . .[39]

This prophet not only averted as well as brought on rain, as James writes, but had also healed and revived the dead.[40] We may assume that, in Fortunatus' story, the prayer is taken for granted. Early in the sixth century, Bishop Caesarius of Arles had repeated these instructions for healing in one of his sermons, and added the ingestion of the Eucharist.[41] Concerned with the healing of the soul as well as

---

[37] *Vita sancti Germani* 146–147. On the importance of humors in the ancient and medieval view of illness, see: R. Fahraeus, "Grundlegende Fakten über die Pathologie der Körpersäfte und ihre Relikte in Sprache und Volksmedizin", *Volksmedizin. Probleme und Forschungsgeschichte*, ed. E. Grabner, Wege der Forschung 63 (Darmstadt, 1967), p. 448.

[38] Centrally, of course, through that of life through death and power through humility. Inversion in general is stressed, for instance, in *Vita sancti Germani* 67: "in inverted order (*versa vice*)". And see on its corollary, the inversion of emotions: Fortunatus, *Vita sanctae Radegundis* 11: "believing she would lose whatever she did not give to the poor (*hoc se reputans perdere quod pauperibus non dedisset*)", and 17: "she was fulfilled by a long fast with tears as though she were satiated with delicious food (*quasi repleta deliciis sic longo ieiunio satiaretur in lacrimis*)." And G. de Nie, "Visies op St. Radegunde's 'vlammende geest'. Zesde- en twintigste-eeuwse gevoelspatronen in ideaal, verhaal en beeldspraak" [Views of Saint Radegund's 'flaming spirit'. Sixth and twentieth-century patterns of feeling in ideals, narratives and imageries], *Emoties in de Middeleeuwen* [Emotions in the Middle Ages], ed. R.E.V. Stuip and C. Vellekoop, Utrechtse Bijdragen tot de Mediëvistiek 15 (Hilversum, 1998), pp. 49–78.

[39] James 5:14–17.

[40] 1 Kings 17:1, 18:1, 41–35; 17:17 ff.; 2 Kings 4:32–34.

[41] Caesarius, *Sermones* (ed. G. Morin, Corpus Christianorum Series Latina (= CCSL) 104 (Turnhout, 1953)) 184.5.

of the body, he says that the priest's prayer will effect divine forgiveness of the patient's sins—also a central issue in some of Christ's cures.[42]

Anointing

Anointing is involved in twenty-one of Germanus' cures. Preceded by prayer, he treats in this way: paralysis, cramped open mouths, lacerations by a wolf and temporary insanity, blindness, gout, muteness, gangrene, and, as we saw, dropsy.[43] Sometimes the touching and stroking is highlighted. In the case of a woman whose mouth stood open, the saint is said to "have touched her head all around (*palpato undique capite*)".[44] Another time, however, the same malady was cured in this manner while calling upon Christ's name.[45] But the power of the oil itself, too, may be the center of attention. When someone's contracted hand "had touched the oil, the latter's power poured the remedy into it (*Qua contacta oleo virtus infudit remedium*)"; the right hand is said to have been "purged" of its disability (*purgata vitio*).[46] Something, then, was driven out, and the cure is therefore also a kind of exorcism. In another case, a paralytic is healed by having

> sanctified oil poured over him: when it had touched his whole skin, strength entered his inner parts (*sanctificati olei liquore perfuso, cum cutem summam tetigisset, vigor medullas introiit*).[47]

The adjective "revived (*redivivus*)" is here used of his hands, and it is said that "the whole fabric of his limbs was restored (*tota membrorum fabrica reparatur*)". In this case, then, the model of death and resurrection is made explicit. When a withered hand "revived (*revirescit*)" and "bloomed again (*reflorescit*)", through contact with "sacred oil" and Germanus' hands,[48] the same association appears to be evoked, but here the saint's hands are evidently a parallel conduit of holy power.

---

[42] Loc. cit.; Matthew 9:2, Luke 7:48.
[43] *Vita sancti Germani* 47, 49, 50, 55, 56, 72, 74, 75, 82, 103, 106, 109, 121, 131, 133, 137, 138, 141, 145, 147, 157.
[44] Ibid. 49.
[45] Ibid. 56.
[46] Ibid. 50–51.
[47] Ibid. 106–107.
[48] Ibid. 157.

The common sense remedy of hot water and cabbage leaves, in combination with the anointing with 'blessed oil', cured gangrene. Significantly, this cure is said to have taken place through the "poultice (*malagmate*)".[49] The saint, then, combines practical remedies of independent efficacy with the holy power of the oil. It is not impossible that he used oil or an ointment with special ingredients prepared by himself, like the ointments of pagan doctors.[50] Neither here nor anywhere else is there any suggestion of an incompatibility between 'natural' and 'holy' medicine: it is in fact here that the saint is designated as a 'miracle-doing doctor'.

Washing

Germanus is nowhere described as washing anyone's whole body, but he does clean and wash parts of it as needed. In one case, the bishop makes the sign of the Cross over an old woman's blind eyes and, the next day, when they are seen to be bleeding, washes them with warm water.[51] Elsewhere, a blind slave girl's eyes were anointed and prayed over; then she was given bread and salt over which the sign of the Cross had been made, and told to go home; the next day, Germanus cleaned and washed her then bleeding eyes with warm water (*fovens et abluens*). One was thereupon healed; the other, anointed once more, bled again at night, and was healed the next day, probably by another washing.[52] Here, it looks as though symbolic gestures—the sign of the Cross, the anointing with the blessed oil, the consumption of blessed bread (the Eucharist?)[53] and salt—triggered a somewhat slower healing process which was aided by nutrition and washing. For, like so many others in Gaul in this period, the woman was probably undernourished and ill cared for.[54]

Touching

There are a few cases of anointing in which not the oil or the dressing is highlighted, but the quality of Germanus' touch itself. When

---

[49] Ibid. 137.
[50] Rousselle, "Du sanctuaire au thaumaturge: la guérison en Gaule au IVe siècle", p. 1099.
[51] *Vita sancti Germani* 112.
[52] Ibid. 73–75.
[53] Cf. Caesarius, *Sermo* 184.5.
[54] Cf. "Médecins", DACL 11.1, col. 149–150.

a man was brought to the saint who had been lacerated by a wolf, contracted gangrene and slipped into insanity through the shock and pain, Germanus

> turned to the support of his [healing] art (*suae artis*); when he had anointed the arm all around with the blessed liquid of the oil, and had stroked the man in a healing manner with his holy fingers, that illness which had invaded his heart with violent pain fled from the obsessed places (*sacris eo digitis medicabiliter adtrectato, pestis illa quae viscera dolore grassante pervaserat loca fugit obsessa*). The flesh which had already been dissolved in rotting was restored to its pristine vigor, [and] without delay—as though he were awakening from sleep—the pain receded and his [right] mind returned.[55]

Here, not only is the gangrenous arm anointed but the whole, crazed, man is stroked (rubbed or massaged?) 'in a healing manner', and thereby cured and brought back to his right mind. The story may present a longer healing process in a condensed manner. As we see in the wording, the stroking was thought to have driven out a possessing, disease-causing agent who had taken over the patient's mind as well. Germanus elsewhere cures a possessed person also by the imposition of hands.[56] In another case, when he has first applied saliva,[57] and then oil, his touching as such is praised:

> For the holy man, in the matter of illnesses, curing is the same as touching (*Nam causas infirmitatis hoc erat sancto viro curare quod tangere*).[58]

Elsewhere, when he has only made the sign of the Cross—but evidently thereby touching the skin of the mute, paralytic girl—it is said that "for the saint touching was reviving (*hoc fuit apud sanctum vivificare quod tangere*)".[59] Finally, in one case, someone's withered hand is said to have been healed "between the hands of the doctor (*inter manus medici*)".[60]

Christ, of course, had touched to heal.[61] And Saint Martin had healed a mute and completely paralyzed girl through prayer, pouring oil into her mouth, and stroking her limbs.[62] A holy man is per-

---

[55] *Vita sancti Germani* 72.
[56] Ibid. 78.
[57] As Christ had done to heal blindness in John 9:6 ff.
[58] *Vita sancti Germani* 82.
[59] Ibid. 127.
[60] Ibid. 157.
[61] For instance, in Matthew 8:3.
[62] Sulpicius Severus, *Vita sancti Martini* (ed. J. Fontaine, SC 133 (Paris, 1967)) 16.

ceived as powerful because, through continuous prayer, he is 'filled with God (*plenus Deo*)' or Christ—a description of Saint Martin, the apostle of Gaul, which can also be used for holy men in the sixth century.[63] At the same time, however powerful Germanus' touch is perceived to be, it is evidently also—as all the examples show—warmly caring. For he once healed a mute paralytic servant boy by "anoint[ing] him continually for three days with sacred oil (*quem continuatim per triduum sacro liniens oleo*)".[64]

Mysterium

In two cases, however, Fortunatus qualifies a cure through anointing as a 'mystery'. In one story, the anointing of a contracted hand with blessed oil is described as:

> When the liquid of the blessed oil had been poured out, or rather the ointment of the mystery had been spread about (*mysterii potius unguento resperso*), [the saint] restored him to health by another prayer.[65]

The term here appears to point, in one way or another, to the transforming power of the anointing ritual as precipitating the cure. In the second story, taking place in the city of Nantes, the lady Tecla asked the bishop for help for her husband, the merchant Damianus. First, a deacon was sent who 'touched' the patient; evidently to no effect. For

> the next day, the bishop himself, having been asked to do so, went to the ill man, who was to be pitied, for he was shamelessly oppressed by the double torture of great pain from gout [in both hands and legs]. At the same moment that the priest of the Highest [Deity] anointed the sick man with blessed oil, he at once snapped (*prosilivit*) completely out of the illness by the straightening of his hands and the strengthening of his legs.
>
> But, so that the mystery (*mysterium*) should be duplicated in one house . . ., Maria, his daughter, who was blind, deaf and dumb, was presented to him. They placed the living corpse (*vivum cadaverem*) before the feet of the saint, saying: 'Good shepherd (*bone pastor*), apply to this

---

[63] Sulpicius, *Vita sancti Martini* 3.1; about Gregory of Tours: Baudonivia, *Vita sanctae Radegundis* 23. Saint Martin as the apostle of Gaul: Gregorius, *Historiae* 1.39: "then our sun too arose . . . for it was in this time that the most blessed Martin began to preach in Gaul (*tunc iam et lumen nostrum oritur . . . hoc est eo tempore beatissimus Martinus in Gallias praedicare exorsus est*)."

[64] *Vita sancti Germani* 109; the case in chapter 58 is perhaps similar.

[65] Ibid. 138.

ill girl whatever remains of your medicine (*medicina*) [i.e. the oil]. For we believe her to have been reserved for you, so that you would receive the praise, and so that, given back to her family, she would acquire from the priest what she lacks from her parents.'

When their outstanding piety was supported by tears, the warrior at once turned to the arms of his warfare, and the powerful orator offered prayers to obtain the victory (*ad militiae suae belliger arma convertitur et ad obtinendam victoriam preces offert fortis orator*). Thereupon the holy man rose from his prayer, anointed all places of the girl's head with blessed oil, and drove out the illness three times in the name of the Trinity. At once, the paths of the ears and the eyes were opened, and while, everyone applauded, the mute girl was given the faculty of speech. When this had been done, each merchant of the city of Nantes gave or sent as much as he could for this healing to the holy man to be devoutly dispensed to the poor.[66]

The terms in which the above cure is described may be said to make it into an embodied miniature of the central Christian belief of life as death except when revived to eternal life through the power of One who had himself entered the true life through death. We saw that this redemption itself could be termed a *mysterium*: a hidden but actively powerful dynamic pattern or archetype of spiritual truth. In this story, the term *mysterium* appears to point to that redemption itself as well as to the manner in which its pattern was replicated in the curing ritual of anointing. Here, then, the *mysterium* is the empowering truth of a transforming archetype or symbol as activated by its re-enactment in a ritual.

A few other uses of the term *mysterium* in Fortunatus' saints' lives are possibly relevant to our argument.[67] In the story of a beacon of light rising from the church of Saint Hilary to hang over the Frankish king Clovis (486–511) as he was about to give battle (c. 507) to the Arian king Alaric and his Visigoths,[68] Fortunatus speaks of it as a "sign of light (*signum luminis*)" and a "royal mystery (*regalis mysterium*)"; but he also writes: "I should like to know why there was a hidden mystery of such fire (*tanti ardoris secretum mysterium*) and so clearly revealed (*manifestum prolatum*)". And then he explains that it is a replication and re-enactment—in visual form—of Saint Hilary's verbal

---

[66] Ibid. 130–133.

[67] The meaning of the term in Fortunatus' *Vita sancti Hilarii* (MGH AA 4.2, pp. 1–7) 12 is unclear to me, and that in ibid. 34 appears to indicate something like a vision or revelation.

[68] Fortunatus, *Virtutes sancti Hilarii* (ed. B. Krusch, MGH AA 4.2, pp. 7–11) 20–23.

battle against the Arian emperor Constantius, approximately a hundred and fifty years earlier. Here again we see the early medieval tendency to transpose the contours of events and notions into images. The terms "prodigy (*prodigium*)" and "miracle (*miraculum*)" also designate the phenomenon, however, and it is compared to the pillar of fire preceding the Hebrews in the desert.[69] Gregory of Tours refers to this pillar (again an image) as "the archetype (*tipus*) of the Holy Spirit"[70]—a very clear example of the contemporary habit of thinking in terms of images rather than of concepts. Fortunatus, however, says that by this beacon Saint Hilary "showed (*ostenderet*)" what he also expressed in words[71]—presumably through an apparition or in a dream. Here, then, 'mystery' appears to mean a visual manifestation of an actively present, but ordinarily hidden, dynamic pattern of spiritual reality.

But Fortunatus also uses the term for the strange behavior of a candle given to Saint Hilary's tomb by two merchants, one of whom did not really want to give it; it split in two, and one half rolled away: the saint had rejected it as an unwilling gift.[72] The incident is thereupon designated as a "judgment (*iudicium*)", probably meaning that the event functioned as an ordeal. For, if we are to believe Gregory's stories, false oaths on saints' tombs in this period tended to be followed by an instant, visible punishment.[73] Here again an event in the invisible dimension is revealed by a visible one; or, to approach it from the other side: the contours of a visible event are perceived and understood as revealing an already known, invisible and significant pattern.

Finally, in his Life of Saint Marcellus of Paris, Fortunatus uses the term 'mystery' twice. One of these cases, the saint's victory over a dragon, will be discussed in another context. The other is when the young Marcellus' sinful bishop is punished by the loss of his voice, and the future saint cures him through asking him to say, 'in the name of the Lord' (a ritual formula, invoking the Lord's power),

---

[69] Exodus 13:21.

[70] *Historiae* 1.10.

[71] *Virtutes sancti Hilarii* 21: "It would not have been enough for [the saint] to show this sign to support the king if he had not added [in a dream or apparition] a clear warning with his voice (*Parum illi fuit pro solatio regis signum ostendere luminis, nisi aperte monitus addidisset et vocis*)."

[72] Ibid. 30–33.

[73] E.g. Gregorius, *In gloria martyrum* 19.

what he wishes him to do. Fortunatus comments—showing the crucial importance of the spoken word as a means of pastoral care and ecclesiastical government—:

> Truly worthy is the blessed Marcellus' speaking (*sermo*), so that the one who gave his shepherd health should rule the flock of the Lord.[74]

The *mysterium* here is the indirect manifestation of the then still hidden, but in the spiritual sphere evidently already present, reality of Marcellus' future as bishop. In sum, then, also in his other saints' Lives, Fortunatus uses the term to mean both a transforming symbolic ritual and the visible manifestation and operation of a transcendent divine reality pattern.

Male Curing: The ideal Father

The manner in which Fortunatus describes his subject tells us a great deal about the author's perceptions of the role of the Christian bishop in mediating holy power. As we have seen, in the patriarchal society of sixth-century Gaul, Germanus is continuing an established tradition of the holy bishop as a father, a shepherd, an orator, and a 'warrior' against the evils threatening his flock.[75] In addition, he is elsewhere compared to Moses.[76] Over against such an impressive figure, complete subjection and dependence is the only adequate attitude, and we see this reflected in the stories. Fortunatus is certainly writing propaganda for an unarmed church depending upon the general belief in its monopoly of spiritual power to survive as an institution in a violent, inadequately ordered society, one in which every self-respecting man could and did defend his interests with physical weapons. Conversely, however, the insecurity which such a situation engendered among the weak and helpless cannot but have created a pressing need for protection by someone of power. The ideal figure of the saint as we find it in the biographies being written in this period is tailored to satisfy this need.[77] Accordingly, at the end of the biography, Fortunatus refers to the bishop as "the father and the shepherd of the people (*pater et pastor populi*)".[78] I have shown

---

[74] Fortunatus, *Vita sancti Marcelli* (MGH AA 4.2, pp. 49–54) 27–35.

[75] See on the perceptions and duties of bishops in this period: G. Scheibelreiter, *Der Bischof in merowingischer Zeit* (Vienna, 1983).

[76] *Vita sancti Germani* 22–25.

[77] Cf. De Nie, *Views from a many-windowed tower*, pp. 251–287.

[78] *Vita sancti Germani* 205.

elsewhere that others in this period sometimes ascribed explicitly 'motherly' qualities to contemporary holy men as well.[79] Fortunatus, however, chooses to describe Germanus' loving care of his patients as that of a father figure.

Tomb-Bath-Womb: The 'Doctor' as Mother?

As already mentioned, Radegund had no tradition of holy women performing miracles behind her (Monegund was a contemporary, and probably only known in and around Tours), and was therefore perceived as following male clerical role models—especially that of Saint Martin. We see this perception most clearly in a letter addressed to her by a council of bishops during her lifetime, in which she is spoken of as his 'companion'—the greatest compliment that could be given.[80] Although, Fortunatus' biography stresses her deference to males, including saints,[81] the number of her miracles (fourteen) shows that her power to do these was evidently not perceived as inferior to theirs. But how could a woman be described as 'powerful'? In his preface to the Life, Fortunatus refers to the "strong victories (*fortes victoriae*)" won by holy women of 'fragile bodies' through the "power of a distinguished mind (*virtute mentis inclitae*)".[82] These words recall the male model of the 'warrior', evidently the most conspicuous one indicating strength and power in holiness.[83] But, further on, Fortunatus appears to present his subject also in terms of another, only indirectly expressed, model.

In his friendship poems to her, Radegund appears as a strong-spirited and warm-hearted spiritual mother to her nuns and to the poet himself.[84] Spiritual motherhood was a late antique Christian

---

79 As in *Vita sancti Caesarii* (MGH SSrM 3, pp. 457–501) 1.53: "for he loved them not only with a fatherly but also with a motherly affection (*ille tamen eos non solum paterno, sed etiam materno diligebat affectu*). Cf. also: G. de Nie, "Is een vrouw een mens? Voorschrift, vooroordeel en praktijk in zesde-eeuws Gallië" [Is a woman a human being? Precept, prejudice and practice in sixth-century Gaul], *Jaarboek voor Vrouwengeschiedenis* 10 (1989), pp. 72–73, and idem, "'Consciousness fecund through God'. From male fighter to spiritual bride-mother in late antique female sanctity", pp. 101–102.

80 Gregorius, *Historiae* 9.39.

81 As in Fortunatus, *Vita sanctae Radegundis* 19–20, 30–32.

82 Ibid. 1.

83 Cf. De Nie, "'Consciousness fecund through God': From male fighter to spiritual bride-mother in late antique female sanctity", pp. 116–123, 139–151.

84 As Fortunatus, *Carmina* 8.8.1: *O regina potens*; 11.1: *Mater opima*. Gregory, *Historiae*

ideal for monastic men as well as women who had renounced physical procreation. For, replicating the 'figure' or archetype of the Virgin Conception, spiritual 'children' were thought to be conceived and born through the pouring of the word of God into others' hearts.[85] Although, as far as we know, Radegund never had children of her own, her actions may indicate that this ideal was a central one for her.[86]

For in his biography, Fortunatus appears to show that, from the beginning, she embodied this ideal in acts of practical, loving care: washing, stroking and anointing were prominent in Radegund's relations to others; this is evident, too, in the cure we have already looked at. When she was being educated at the estate of Athies before her marriage, she founded a hospital for poor, sick women, in which she "washed them in baths".[87] Later at Saix, when she had left her husband, she again cared for the poor and the sick: she bathed them on Thursdays and Saturdays, cleansed their sores, deloused hair, treated infected wounds, extracted worms, and (in a reference to James) "in the evangelical manner, overcame illness through the pouring out of oil". Here, the oil itself appears to be doing the curing. But elsewhere, "lying", says Fortunatus, "that it would be of use to her", she uses a vine leaf over which she has made the sign of the Cross to cure an ulcer.[88] He means that she is trying to hide her miraculous healing under the guise of a herbal remedy. And she uses an apple to heal unspecified illnesses, equally miraculously.[89] For the rest, the practices here mentioned appear to be a medical kind of care rather than miraculous healing. Women were bathed with soap from head to foot; when necessary they were given new clothes and, in any case, meals. In implicit imitation of Saint Martin, Radegunde embraced and kissed leprous women with

---

9.39, quotes a letter of a council of bishops to Radegund telling her that her nuns "leave their parents and choose you whom grace, not nature, makes their mother (*relictis parentibus, te sibi magis elegant, quam matrem facit gratia, non natura*)."

[85] Cf. De Nie, "'Consciousness fecund through God': from male fighter to spiritual bride-mother in late antique female sanctity", pp. 101–102.

[86] Ibid., pp. 139–151.

[87] Fortunatus, *Vita sanctae Radegundis* 12. She may have been imitating the fourth-century Fabiola's hospital, known through a letter of Hieronymus (Jerome): *Epistolae* (ed. J. Labourt, vol. 4 (Paris, 1954)), 77.6. But Bishop Caesarius had also founded a hospital in Arles: *Vita sancti Caesarii* 1.20.

[88] Fortunatus, *Vita sanctae Radegundis* 47.

[89] Ibid. 49. Cf. 78, in which an absinth leaf she had carried against her chest cures an ulcer.

joy.[90] As we saw, all this earns her the somewhat dubious praise of the epithet "new Martha".[91] There simply was no traditional role model for a holy healer who happened to be a woman!

When she was settled in Poitiers, however, something happened which Fortunatus describes as follows:

> A certain nun shivered with cold by day and burned with fire by night through an entire year. And when she had lain lifeless (*exanimis*) for six months, unable to move a step, one of her sisters told the saint about her infirmity. Finding her almost lifeless (*perinanis*), she bade them prepare warm water and had the sick woman brought to her cell and laid in the warm water. Then she ordered everyone to leave, only the sick woman and the doctor (*medica*) themselves remaining for almost two hours. She held the whole form of the body in her arms and [stroked] the weak limbs from head to foot (*Quantum est corporis forma a capite usque ad plantam infirma membra conbaiulat*). Through which, wherever her hand touched, the pain fled from the patient. And she who had been placed in the bath by two persons, came out of it in full health. The woman who had previously been disgusted by even the smell of wine now accepted it, drank it and was refreshed. What more shall I say? The next day, when she had been expected to migrate from this world, she came forth (*processit*) cured into the community.[92]

Ostensibly, a persistent fever has been stopped by the application of heat and stroking. As we have seen, the latter also occurs—without a bath—in Saint Martin's cure of the paralyzed girl, and in cures by her older contemporary Saint Germanus.[93] Radegund's holding and stroking for two hours of 'the whole form of the body" and "the weak limbs from head to foot" are reminiscent of Saint Martin's "gradually, at his touch, her individual limbs began to revive (*paulatim singula contactu eius coeperunt membra vivescere*)".[94] To raise an actually dead person, Martin had—in imitation of Elijah—placed his body upon that of the deceased, perhaps to transmit vitality and warmth (or did he already practice artificial respiration?), and prayed.[95] Radegund's treatment of a warm bath and holding is perhaps another way to do this. Although prayer is part of the proceedings in

---

[90] Ibid. 39–42.

[91] Ibid. 42.

[92] Ibid. 68–70.

[93] *Vita sancti Germani* 109.

[94] Sulpicius, *Vita sancti Martini* 16.8.

[95] *Vita sancti Martini* 7; 1 Kings 17:21. Cf. L. Bieler, "Totenerweckung durch synanáchrosis", and O. Weinreich, "Zum Wundertypus der synanáchrosis", *Archiv für Religionswissenschaft* 32 (1935), pp. 228–245, 246–264.

Radegund's other cures, it is not mentioned here. Probably, it is assumed. After having thus been 'recreated', as it were, in the warm bath by Radegund's hands, the nun 'came forth' again into the community.

The saint's treatment resembles the therapeutical bathing and massage which were part of the pagan water sanctuaries' care for women, the care which was taken over after their demise by 'wise women' or birth-helpers, about whom we unfortunately know very little.[96] Radegund appears to be acting in this tradition. At the same time, however, there are symbolical and spiritual dimensions to her act. One is that the pain is said to have 'fled' upon her touch. Such a notion must be based upon the holy person as 'filled with God', an epithet that, as we saw, had been used of Saint Martin, Radegund's model.

Martin's earthly remains, and therefore the center of his cult, were at Tours. What Fortunatus prudently omitted, and Baudonivia, when the danger has passed, reveals is that from 568 on—much to the annoyance of the city's later bishop Maroveus—Radegund created her own center of spiritual power in Poitiers. For, like certain other late antique women,[97] she managed to associate herself with another even more prestigious and hence presumably more powerful relic: that of the Holy Cross, a particle of which was sent to her at her request from Constantinople by the reigning Emperor and Empress;[98] after its installation there, Radegund renamed her convent after the Holy Cross. Radegund herself is supposed to have said that, with the relic, "Christ will visibly live here".[99] And with that fact, Radegund's convent must have become something close to the spiritual center of the Frankish kingdoms. Her second biographer accordingly speaks of her ruling "a heavenly rather than earthly kingdom".[100] But Radegund's appropriation of the Holy Cross relic also associated her with Christ's presence in a special way. This special way may give an added dimension to Fortunatus' introduction of Radegund's cure

---

[96] Rousselle, "La sage-femme et le thaumaturge dans la Gaule tardive: Les femmes ne font pas de miracles", pp. 249–250.

[97] Ibid., p. 246.

[98] Baudonivia, *Vita sanctae Radegundis* 16; Gregorius, *Historiae* 9.40.

[99] Baudonivia, *Vita sanctae Radegundis* 16.

[100] Ibid. 10: "where she seemed to reign, she prepared for herself a kingdom that was more heavenly than of this earth (*ubi dum regnare videretur, sibi magis caeleste quam terrenum praeparavit regnum*)."

of Animia's dropsy as one of the "wondrous events which the compassionate mercy of Christ effects (*mirabilia quae Christi misericors operatur clementia*)".[101]

The therapeutic immersion we saw in the cure just quoted resembles that in our very first story: Animia's being anointed and thereupon newly clothed in an empty bath. To recapitulate the latter story: the phrase *peracto mysterio* there seems to assimilate these acts to a religious ritual, possibly the purificational liturgy of baptism, in which anointing took place before and after the immersion. In the sources of the time we find that the unbaptized were thought to be *ipso facto* possessed by the Devil.[102] As already mentioned, however, invasion by the Devil or one of his demons was also held to be responsible for illness. And the anointing and clothing by the abbess as well as Radegund, finally, may point to the ritual of a nun's ceremonial entrance into the religious life. In contemporary symbolism, however, a new robe can also be a symbol of a new body.[103] This symbolism, in turn, appears to point to still another dimension: that of the whole event as, at the same time, an enacted ritual of a (Christlike) death and burial in a tomb—Animia is said to have been on the point of death and sleeping—, and a resurrection. Such a comparison is far from unusual; Gregory, too, not infrequently couches his descriptions of cures in terms of death and resurrection, pointing towards the last heavenly one to come.[104] In Radegund's cure, it is the combination of a densely symbolic ritual with the sensory replication of central Christian events and symbols, then, which appears to be indicated by the term *mysterium*.

One word, however, appears to point to the possibility that Animia's illness was not so much in her belly as in her womb: the word *uterus* can mean both.[105] It is tempting to suspect a hysterical pseudo-pregnancy here in connection with what appears from other sources about the convent to have been very lively—even physical—imaginations there of being the beloved bride of Christ.[106]

---

[101] Fortunatus, *Vita sanctae Radegundis* 80.

[102] Angenendt, "Die Liturgie und die kirchlichen Organisation auf dem Lande", p. 185.

[103] See on this subject: A. Kehl, "Gewand (der Seele)", *Reallexikon für Antike und Christentum* 10, pp. 945–1025.

[104] As in *Vita sancti Martini* 2.3 and 4.34.

[105] Blaise, *Dictionnaire latin-français des auteurs chrétiens*, p. 862.

[106] Fortunatus, *Carm.* 8.3.125–128, and Appendix 23.19, 23–4 (to the abbess): "If

This brings us to the possibility that there could be yet another symbolic dimension. For the uterus and the bath are analogical or congruent images. Thus the whole ritual may also point symbolically to something like the patient's new conception (through the oil), gestation (her presence in the bath, being anointed there, and clothed, while asleep, in a new robe—as we saw, a late antique symbol for a new body), and birth (she arose from her bed, and came forth from seclusion in the cell). If so, the structure of Animia's cure—that of rebirth—is remarkably similar to the one in which the feverish nun was restored through holding and stroking in a real warm bath.

A third story is similar. It shows us how Radegund revived a dead girl, probably an oblate in her convent. The whole event is explicitly introduced as a repetition of a model miracle of Saint Martin, but Christ too is mentioned:

> Let the model of an ancient miracle in the manner of Saint Martin in the present time (*more beati Martini tempore praesenti antiqui norma miraculi*) be proclaimed in praise of Christ.[107]

This is again an indication of the importance then accorded to doing things in a (male-dominated) recognizable tradition. The somewhat obscure wording in this story appears to indicate that the bath in which the girl's dead body was about to be washed was already warm (*Quae mortuam sororem nuntiavit infantulam et, frigida qua lavaretur, paratam esse iam calidam*). Upon her hearing of the death, Radegund commanded the corpse to be brought into her cell and secluded herself with it, sending everyone away. Did she also ask for the bath, as she did in the earlier story? While everyone outside was preparing for the girl's funeral, she stroked (*tractat*) the body in her cell for almost seven hours—in the warm bath, as in the first story? We are not told. Its use as an indication of the time elapsed since the girl's death does not exclude its also being used by Radegund, as in the other cures. It is tempting to suspect that the author took its use to be self-evident. It is not clear, however, what is so Martinian about this cure; perhaps the revival as such, or the prolonged stroking, as

---

sleep overtakes you, keep Christ in your heart . . . let yourself go legitimately in his embrace: for whoever holds him need fear no sin (*Si sopor obripiat, retinendo in pectore Christum/ . . . /huius in amplexu te totam effunde licenter:/ Illum quisquis habet crimina nulla timet*)." Cf. Hieronymus, *Epistolae* (ed. Labourt, vol. 1 (Paris, 1949)) 22.26.

[107] Fortunatus, *Vita sanctae Radegundis* 84.

in the previous story. However that may be, Fortunatus concludes by saying that Christ, seeing the saint's faith, gave the girl her health again: "as the saint arose from her prayer, the girl arose from death". The saint, therefore, from time to time also prostrated herself in prayer. Again, the paradox of the Christian religion of new life—or rebirth—through death is made visible here.

In the three stories we have just looked at, the core elements are a warm bath, or the strong suggestion of one, and the stroking or anointing's effecting of a new body. Is it only the dressing-up of the effect of ordinary bathing and massage as a miracle? Or should these experiences be understood as being formally analogous to being conceived and formed in the womb, and emerging through birth? This view accords with their all being said to have passed from (near-) death to a new life. Although the latter is a frequent motif in sixth-century cures, the combination of bathing and stroking with this motif which we see in Radegund's miracles is unique. It looks as though she is continuing the tradition of gynecological therapy and the birth-helper's craft, but in the spiritual dimension.

If the above sounds far-fetched, it should be noted that this symbolism can also be recognized in the curing rituals of certain present-day oral societies. Thus Felicitas Goodman identified in the different acts of touching in South American Indian healing rituals—previously analyzed only by men:

> the ritual transmutation of the mother's labor pain, the newborn's issuing from her womb, its being welcomed, attended and finally placed at the mother's breast to draw nourishment.[108]

But a male anthropologist who is also a psychologist reports similar structures in an African curing ritual. René Devisch describes the Yaka concept of illness as a disconnecting and disordering of psycho-physical energies which blocks a person's vital source.[109] The ritual curing process undertakes to undo this through the enacting of paradoxes: 'the simultaneous deployment of one connotation and its reverse', for instance, death and birth.[110] The bodily enactment of such a paradox would precipitate the actual healing.[111] And so, in

[108] F. Goodman, *Ecstasy, Ritual and Alternate Reality: Religion in a Pluralistic World* (Bloomington/Indianapolis, 1988), p. 32.

[109] R. Devisch, *Weaving the Threads of Life: The 'Khita' Gyn-Eco-Logical Healing Cult Among the Yaka* (Chicago, 1993), pp. 132–133.

[110] Ibid., p. 269.

[111] Ibid., pp. 266–267.

Yaka ritual, death and rebirth or revival become different aspects of the same event. We have seen the same thing happening in sixth-century cures.

And, just as in the late antique period, here too dream consciousness is observed to play a central role. For the ritual enactment of metaphors of liminal situations in present-day oral societies, Devisch says, induces a state of dream-awareness in which discursive reasoning is temporarily put aside for iconic 'thinking', and images are preverbally experienced as affect-laden realities[112]—just as in Animia's dream. He writes:

> . . . the actualized trance and concomitant acts have a metamorphic effect. The cathartic trance arouses a deeply lived and bodily enacted experience of freeing and channeling life-bearing in the body, therapy group, and life-world in unison.[113]

In this context, then, ritual symbols are not just mental images; they are

> corporeal devices, processes and methods or patterns that . . . arise from a potential which, akin to the dream, unconceals both images and inner energy woven into the texture of the body.[114]

And "ritual metaphor [is] a performance that does actually effect the innovative interlinking that it exploratively signifies. . . .".[115] This kind of healing is founded in imaginative dreamwork—including such processes as condensation, fusion, figuration—that is largely beyond dialogue and discursive reality. It can not be verbalized but only experienced, acted out.[116] This, too, we have seen happening in Radegund's cures.

Is all this peculiar only to oral societies? Apparently not, for in western countries certain schools of modern psychotherapy use guided waking dream methods that effect clinically attested psychic, and even physical, healing in exactly the same way: through imaginatively enacting, and/or interacting with, either spontaneous or induced *images as metaphors for non-verbalizable affective states and patterns.* For the *human mind-body continuum is observed to imitate, affectively, internally, what*

---

[112] Ibid., pp. 255, 257.
[113] Ibid., p. 211.
[114] Ibid., p. 280.
[115] Ibid., p. 43.
[116] Ibid., p. 282.

it sees. Expressed in medical terms: affect-laden mental images are observed to behave as though they were bio-electrically charged patterns through which, in the hypothalamus, revitalizing—or killing—messages are given to the body's autonomous systems.[117]

These modern views show the central function of the mind's symbolizing for bodily well-being and, I suggest, make Radegund's apparently exotic symbolic ritual something we might begin to understand. Apart from the medical terminology, however: how can the seeing of an image be understood to transform the beholder? From personal experience most people will know that one can 'fall in love' at first sight with a face, a house, a landscape, a vase—perhaps unconsciously, affectively recognizing the contours of a dream image of happiness. Marcel Proust's Swann fell *back* into love through the hearing of Vintueil's musical phrase, which had previously seemed to coincide with—and thus affectively represent or 'figure'—the contours of his then blossoming love for Odette.[118] Experiencing a visual image in such a manner, then, as an affective, dynamic pattern, might precipitate a transformation in mind and body.

To return to Radegund: the effect of ritually enacting death and birth metaphors in the sixth century then, I suggest, is likely to have resembled that in today's oral societies. As Fortunatus describes it, Radegund appears to have acted just as intuitively with her womb-like baths and creative stroking—as it were metaphorizing an imminent tomb into a bath which becomes a recreating womb. As far as I know, it is a ritual that occurs nowhere else in late antique saints' lives. The fact that Fortunatus uses the term 'new kind of miracle' for the dream bathing ritual seems to indicate that he was aware of this. In his intricate and many-layered poems he shows himself to be a master of imagistic allusion. The hagiographical genre in this period, however, required unadorned, colloquial speech. Nevertheless, alongside the largely implicit symbolism of the rituals of a nun's profession, baptism and anointing of the sick, as well as that of Christ's death and resurrection, he appears to be subtly pointing to a womb

[117] B.S. Siegel, *Love, Medicine and Miracles: Lessons Learned About Self-Healing from a Surgeon's Experience with Exceptional Patients* (New York, 1986), pp. 66–69.

[118] M. Proust, *À la recherche du temps perdu*, vol. 1: *Du coté de chez Swann* (Paris, 1954), p. 283: "the little phrase of Vintueil's sonata . . . continued to remind Swann of the love he had for Odette (*la petite phrase de la sonate de Vinteuil . . . continuait à s'associer pour Swann à l'amour qu'il avait pour Odette*)."

symbolism that reveals Radegund's acting out and realizing her ideal of spiritual motherhood.

Trampling the Serpent Underfoot: Christian Woman as the New Eve?

Radegund's second kind of innovative cure involves a different ritual: that of an exorcism in which the possessing agent appears as a serpent. Only one of Germanus' cures resembles it. Here, the saint heals a possessed person who was a member of the clergy in a manner about which we are not told—perhaps by prayer and/or the imposition of hands[119]—and "the bystanders saw the spirit (*umbra*) that was driven out emerge from the possessed man's head like a small bird".[120] When it was caught,

> the holy man himself crushed it with his feet (*contrivit vestigiis*). When he stepped upon it (*cum pede comprimeretur*), the False One was at once turned into blood in a double praise, so that it would not be trampled underfoot (*nec calcaretur*), and so that, by the testimony of his fall (*sui casus indicium*), the omnipresent Artificer would be shown up as the bloodstained perpetrator of murders.[121]

That the bird, as the visible manifestation of the possessing agent should be killed is obvious. Showing the 'figurative' habit of mind in this period, Fortunatus assimilates the saint's catching and crushing the bird to the 'fall' of the evil angel Satan from heaven,[122] and its turning to blood as a manifestation of its murderous nature. He does not highlight the gesture of grinding underfoot. In Psalm 90 (91):13, however, we read: "You will tread upon (*calcabis*) the adder and the basilisk; you will trample the lion and the dragon underfoot (*conculcabis*)". These animals are, of course, figures of spiritual evil.[123] Jesus' perhaps derivative statement that the apostles have been given the power to tread upon serpents[124] may resonate as well. The

---

[119] As in *Vita sancti Germani* 53 (prayer: *exorante*), and 78 (hands on head).

[120] Ibid. 142. Cf. P. Dinzelbacher, "Der Kampf der Heiligen mit den Dämonen", *Santi e demoni nell'alto Medioevo occidentale (secoli V–XI)* Settimane di Studio del Centro Italiano di Studi sull'alto Medioevo 36 (Spoleto, 1989), pp. 675–682.

[121] Ibid. 143.

[122] Revelation 12:9.

[123] Cf. "Serpent", DACL 5.1, col. 1353–1356; and "Dragon", DACL 4.2, col. 1537–1539.

[124] Luke 10:19.

figure of Christ trampling upon Satan as a serpent and/or dragon has been found in early Christian iconography.[125] But these associations are evidently not the author's focus of attention in the context of a cure.

Outside that context, however, the overcoming of serpents is a well-known motif in male saints' lives. Saint Martin had commanded water snakes to retreat.[126] And Fortunatus himself reports in his Life of Saint Hilary of Poitiers that the man of God had chased snakes off a certain part of an island. He did this with the sign of the Cross and the invocation of the name of the Lord. These acts must have accompanied a command however because, in the same passage, Fortunatus praises Hilary for "commanding serpents" and confining them through his "speech" to a certain region, making the rest of the island safe for human habitation. The author's subsequent stress on Hilary's "charm (*dulcedo*)" in all this, however, appears to point to the event as a metaphor for containing evil in the bishop's human community.[127] The story shows again that speaking was a typically male power role. But Fortunatus here also explicitly and significantly contrasts the first Adam's being overcome by a serpent with Hilary, as a servant of Christ—the new, second Adam—overcoming them. Elsewhere, he recounts a similar event in Saint Marcellus' "triumphal mystery (*triumphale mysterium*)", in which the saint tamed and drove away the dragon who had been infesting the suburbs of Paris "in the spiritual theatre (*in spiritale theatro*)" in front of all the people.[128] The male saint, then, is presented as overcoming the serpent through the power of the word, and not through physically treading upon him. Gregory and Fortunatus' writings abundantly show that rhetoric—as an instrument of power—was highly prized in men in this period, but never attributed to women.[129]

Two of Radegund's cures, however, show a trampling of the disease-causing agent underfoot, and in one case the latter looks like a serpent. In both cases, the illness is possession without other physical symptoms. Here is the first story:

---

[125] See: "Serpent", DACL 5.1, col. 1353; and "Dragon", DACL 4.2, col. 1537.
[126] Sulpicius Severus, *Dialogi* (ed. C. Halm, Corpus Scriptorum Ecclesiasticorum Latinorum (= CSEL) 1 (Vienna, 1866), pp. 152–216) 2 (3).9.4.
[127] *Vita sancti Hilarii* 35–39.
[128] *Vita sancti Marcelli* 40.
[129] For instance: Gregorius, *Historiae* 2.22 and Fortunatus, *Carmina* 3.4.

> A certain woman labored so heavily under an invasion by the Enemy that the rebellious Foe could scarcely be brought to the saint. She commanded the Adversary that he should prostrate himself with his fear on the pavement. At the very moment that the blessed lady spoke he threw himself upon the ground, and the one who had been feared was now himself afraid of her. When the saint, full of faith, stamped upon his neck, he came out in a flux from her belly (*cum calcasset in cervice, fluxu ventris egressus est*).[130]

In late antique possession stories, the actions and speech of the person concerned are not their own but those of the possessor.[131] The curing of possession by purgation in one way or another was a late antique medical prescription, and is also reported in one of Saint Martin's cures.[132] But this ritual of a, presumably rather uncomfortable, stamping on the possessed's neck is not found elsewhere. The specific mention of the neck seems to me to point to the passage in Genesis in which it is said that the seed of the woman—and, in this context, Eve's descendants must be meant—will crush the head of the serpent who is the image of Satan: "she shall bruise your head (*ipsa conteret caput tuum*)".[133] As we saw, Radegund was a dominating figure, through her prayers and miracles said to 'rule' Gaul as 'a spiritual kingdom' alongside the secular government of her stepsons. It is tempting to believe that she is here, against the patriarchal ordering of society, pointing to a woman's version of world history: to the descendants of a new, independent and powerful Eve alongside the new Adam who was Christ—now 'living' in her chapel at Poitiers—, and who had also acted through male saints such as Saint Hilary, whose tomb was not far from the convent. Was she, as spiritual queen, spiritual mother, teacher and custodian of the relic of the Holy Cross, in fact providing an intrinsically female role of power over against that of the male father, shepherd, doctor, warrior and orator?

The second story, just as the one about Animia, announces innovation, but Fortunatus cautiously calls it "a new healing of Christ (*nova Christi curatio*)". He tells us that when Radegund was still at her

[130] Fortunatus, *Vita sanctae Radegundis* 71–72.

[131] As P. Brown, *The Cult of the Saints: Its Rise and Function in Latin Christianity* (Chicago, 1981), p. 111.

[132] *Vita sancti Martini* 17.5–7. Cf. Rousselle, *Croire et guérir*, p. 116.

[133] Genesis 3:15. Cf. DACL 5.1, col. 1353.

country estate, a woman called Leubila, in the countryside, was also greatly "troubled (*vexaretur*)" by the Adversary; but

> the following day, while the saint prayed, she was publicly healed through a new cure of Christ. For the skin of her shoulder opened with a rustling sound and a worm came out. She reported that when she trampled that same worm underfoot, she was liberated.[134]

The worm is, of course, a kind of serpent. Gregory's story of another woman's cure shows that violent intestinal illness incurred through sorcery (*maleficium*) could be, probably correctly, diagnosed as 'serpents'—meaning worms—in the belly, which eventually became visible after purgation.[135] In the Third World today, there are diseases in which worm-like larvae of certain kinds of flies can penetrate the skin, incubate in the underlying tissue for days or weeks, and emerge again and drop on the ground. These diseases are not described as happening in Europe today.[136] The possibility that they occurred in the extremely unhygienic conditions of the sixth-century Gallic countryside cannot, however, be excluded.[137] Such a worm-like larva could easily be perceived, and treated as, the serpent who is Satan. Crucial, however, is that Leubila overcame the 'serpent' not by words, but by means of a visible symbolic ritual that seems to enact the biblical promise.[138]

If—as seems to be the case—the saint indeed only prayed and the girl enacted her own ritual, this is an uncommonly active role for a patient in this period. For in all other reported contemporary miracles, the living saint—man or woman—always does, or is always regarded as doing, everything for a passive, powerless sufferer. Radegund's life story shows, however, that she was capable of almost anything: like—against all custom—leaving her royal husband, getting

---

[134] Fortunatus, *Vita sanctae Radegundis* 67.

[135] Gregorius, *Vita patrum* 19.3.

[136] Subcutaneous myiasis, Dermatobia hominis, and Dermal myiasis: P.E.C. Manson-Bahr and D.R. Bell, *Manson's Tropical Diseases*, 19th ed. (London etc., 1987), pp. 911–917.

[137] Quartan fever, which is also frequently mentioned by Gregory, is designated as a kind of *paludisme* or malaria by M. Rouche, "Miracles, maladies et psychologie de la foi à l'époque carolingienne en Francie", *Hagiographies, cultures et sociétés IV–XIIe siècles* (Paris, 1981), p. 322.

[138] Cf. G. de Nie, "Text, symbol and 'oral culture' in the sixth-century Church: The miracle story", *Mediaevistik* 9 (1996), pp. 115–133.

herself consecrated as a deaconess when not only she was still legally married to the king, but the female diaconate was already abolished, and persuading her rejected husband to support and finance her founding of the convent.[139] In this last cure, too, she was acting independently and innovating.

The 'Mysterium' of the New Eve

At the end of Fortunatus' story of Radegund's life, he tells us that a tribune severely suffering from a constriction of his throat had a dream in which Radegund comes to visit him. As will be seen, the discomfort may have been connected with his resisting popular pressure to perform certain actions. Radegund does three things. First, she takes him by the hand and shows him a place in which there were 'relics' of Saint Martin, and in which, according to the wish of the people of the region, a church should be built in his honor. Fortunatus goes on: "What a mystery (*Quale mysterium*)! The fundament and pavement [of an older church?] were found, where the church was built."[140] Here, the dream image appears to be the 'mystery'—showing something that is hidden but real, and which, when found, will transform people's lives. The next thing Radegund did was to stroke the tribune's jaws and throat for a long time, finally saying: "I came so that God might confer better health upon you". Finally, she requested him to release, for her sake, those whom he held in his prison—which he carried out after his awakening. A messenger later confirmed that she had died at the very hour of the tribune's dream, and, as Fortunatus writes,

> through the triple mystery (*triplici mysterio*) of the opened prison, the tribune cured and the temple built, the oracle of the saint was confirmed (*sanctae probavit oraculum*).[141]

The dream about the saint, then, was an 'oracle' whose truth was proven by the occurrence of the events it had announced. Why are these events themselves designated as 'a triple mystery'? Because, I

---

[139] Fortunatus, *Vita sanctae Radegundis* 26–28; Baudonivia, *Vita sanctae Radegundis* 5. On the abolition of the female diaconate in Gaul, see: S.F. Wemple, *Women in Frankish Society: Marriage and the Cloister 500–900* (Philadelphia, 1981), pp. 138–141.

[140] Fortunatus, *Vita sanctae Radegundis* 87–89.

[141] Ibid. 90.

would suggest, they are all manifestations and effects in sensory reality of 'figural' patterns or symbols of the Kingdom of God: those of Christ's salvation of man from sin and from illness (the latter is likely to be perceived as a punishment as well as a manifestation of the former), and of the building up of the Church. As so often, here again the contours of the visible events are perceived as those of biblical images and 'figures'.

To summarize and conclude: focusing upon the concept of *mysterium*—meaning the human enactment of a divine symbol as well as its manifestation in the sensory sphere—, a comparison between Fortunatus' descriptions of Saint Germanus' and Saint Radegund's cures reveals many similarities between them. But it also brings out the uniqueness of two of the latter's healing rituals for women. For whereas Germanus is presented as behaving in a quintessentially male and patriarchal manner, Radegund is seen to exploit her ideal of spiritual motherhood and experiment with the specific potential of Christian womanhood. She transforms the image and symbol of Christ's death and resurrection—through whose contours miraculous cures were then not infrequently perceived—, and makes the Old Testament prophecy of woman's treading upon the serpent a present reality. In the first ritual—which is designated as 'an enacted mystery'—, the bath in which the patient is laid symbolically turns from a tomb (into which everyone else was about to lay her) into a womb from which the patient emerges, as it were, reborn: the event mimics and replicates woman's natural reproductive capacity. The second ritual appropriates the biblical 'figure' highlighting woman (one which is, as far as I know, not mentioned anywhere else in this period) and expels the disease-causing agent—imaged as a serpent—by enacting and thereby fulfilling the prophecy. What we see happening here also occurs in oral societies today: a patient's affective enacting of a significant metaphor or symbol can precipitate a real physical transformation through what one might call 'iconic alchemy'.[142]

That Radegund was indeed especially remembered as a spiritual mother seems also to be evident in Baudonivia's report that, just after her decease, Gregory of Tours was startled to see in her face

[142] Cf. G. de Nie, "Iconic alchemy: imaging miracles in late sixth-century Gaul", *Studia Patristica* 30 (1997), pp. 158–66.

a reflection of that of "the Mother of the Lord".[143] Fortunatus' other, overlapping, image of Radegund as the new Eve is also—if dimly—visible, however, in what a mid-sixth-century religious poet in Rome, notwithstanding the grinding inequality of women in everyday life, presented as the official church view:

> Mary . . . the gateway of God, the virgin mother of her own Creator. . . . The second virgin put to flight the woes of Eve's crime; . . . she restored what the first took away. . . . [Eve] begetting mortal things and [Mary] bearing divine, she through whom the Mediator came forth into the world (*mortalia gignens/Et divina ferens, per quam Mediator in orbem/Prodiit*). . . .[144]

[143] Baudonivia, *Vita sanctae Radegundis* 23.

[144] Arator Subdiaconus, *De actibus apostolorum* (ed. A.P. McKinlay, CSEL 72 (Vienna, 1951)) 1.57–60, 66–68. Tr. R.J. Schrader et al., *Arator's On the Acts of the Apostles (De actibus apostolorum)*, Classics in Religious Studies 6 (Atlanta, 1987), pp. 26–27.

XIV

Poetics of Wonder: Dream-Consciousness and Transformational Dynamics in Sixth-Century Miracle Stories[1]

Almost a hundred years ago, in his famous book *The Varieties of Religious Experience*, the philosopher and experimental psychologist William James wrote:

> [t]he further limits of our being plunge, it seems to me, into an altogether other dimension of existence from the sensible and merely 'understandable' world [....] we belong to it in a more intimate sense than that in which we belong to the visible world.[2]

Thus he asserts that in a state of what he calls "prayerful communion",[3] this other dimension is accessed in modes of consciousness different from that of everyday common sense:

> [...] whatever it may be on its farther side, the 'more' with which in religious experience we feel ourselves connected is on its hither side the subconscious continuation of our conscious life.[4]

For:

> [...] our normal waking consciousness, rational consciousness as we call it, is but one special type of consciousness, whilst all about it, parted from it by the filmiest of screens, there lie potential forms of consciousness entirely different [...].[5]

---

[1] Original English version of "Eine Poetik des Wunders: bildhaftes Bewusstsein und Verwandlungsdynamik in den Wundererzählungen des späten sechsten Jahrhunderts", in: M. Heinzelmann *et al.* (ed.), *Mirakel im Mittelalter: Konzeptionen Erscheinunsformen, Deutungen* (Stuttgart 2002), pp. 135–150.

[2] W. James, *The Varieties of Religious Experience* (New York 1902; 1958), pp. 388f.

[3] *Ibid.*, p. 394.

[4] *Ibid.*, p. 386.

[5] *Ibid.*, p. 298.

Probably, we all experience at least hints and flashes of such kinds of awareness every day without paying attention to them. The well-known anthropologist Clifford Geertz observes that there is a ritualized slipping back and forth between what he calls the "common sense" and the "belief" mode of consciousness in religious contexts.[6] Probably few people reflect upon what they are asked to do when, in the Eucharistic ritual, the priest says or chants "lift up your hearts (*sursum corda*)". All over the world, in fact, religions encourage their adherents, at the appropriate moments, to experience the truth of their myths or theology and their ritual in altered states of consciousness, including more and less deep trances.[7] In such states, images – mentally visualized and/or emotionally and physically enacted – tend to be the vectors of reality. In late Antiquity, the frequency of reports of dreams, visions and apparitions point to a world view and experience of reality that combined practical common sense with acute attention to this imagistic mode of thought and perception.[8]

In what follows, I shall investigate evidence in late sixth-century miracle stories of the experiential role of what must be many different kinds of non-common-sense states of consciousness. As already indicated, this is a state in which the functioning of the common-sense frame of reference is temporarily diminished or even eliminated, and the otherwise more or less submerged affective sensing and pre-verbal, imagistic thought processes tend to predominate.[9] For convenience, therefore, I shall lump them together and designate them with the greatly oversimplified term "dreamlike state of consciousness". First, its influence upon perception will be looked at, and

---

[6] C. Geertz, "Religion as a Cultural System", in: C. Geertz ed.., *The Interpretation of Cultures* (New York 1973), p. 119.

[7] E. Bourguignon, *Religion, altered States of Consciousness and Social Change* (Columbus, Ohio 1973), pp. 9–11. Cf. F.D. Goodman, *Ecstasy, Ritual and Alternate Reality. Religion in a Pluralistic World* (Bloomington–Indianapolis 1988), p. 36; E. Bourguignon, "Foreword", in: F.D. Goodman, J.H. Henney and E. Pressel, *Trance, Healing and Hallucination. Three Field Studies in Religious Experience* (New York 1974), p. xv: "90% [of stable traditional societies] have one or more forms of institutionalized, ritualized altered states of consciousness". An overview and analysis of the subject and the relevant literature may be found in: M. Winkelman, "Trance States: A Theoretical Model and Cross-Cultural Analysis", *Ethos* 14 (1986), pp. 174–203.

[8] See on this: P. Cox Miller, *Dreams in Late Antiquity. Studies in the Imagination of a Culture* (Princeton 1994).

[9] So R.E. Shor, "Hypnosis and the concept of the Generalized Reality-Orientation", in: C.T. Tart (ed.), *Altered States of Consciousness* (New York etc. 1969), pp. 246f. On imagistic thought processes see for instance W. Kretschmer, "Meditative Techniques in Psychotherapy", in: Tart, pp. 219–228.

then its role in the transformational process of what are presented as miraculous cures. To put this sixth-century phenomenon into perspective, I shall briefly point to its role in similar phenomena in present-day societies, including our own.

I. "Awed admiration": a different mode of perception

Modern psychologists approach the great variety of these modes of consciousness from an experimental angle.[10] They have observed that such states can occur through great concentration upon one limited sector of experience to the exclusion of the rest, either intentionally or through extreme stress or fear, or through sensory deprivation.[11] Healthy adults, the same psychologists tell us, also have momentary altered states of consciousness when, without realizing it, they profess opinions, have feelings and carry out acts which have been learned or accepted in earlier moments of altered consciousness and which are contrary to their everyday reality picture;[12] in fact, without being aware of it, many of us would more or less constantly be slipping back and forth between these two states.[13]

The sixth-century bishop and hagiographer Gregory of Tours tells us an extraordinary story in which he lets us see how this can happen in the religious context. Once when he prayed before the relics of the holy Cross in the chapel of saint Radegund's convent in Poitiers, he noticed a dripping oil lamp hanging beside it. After finishing his prayers, he turned to the abbess and said with unconcealed irritation,

> "Are you so lazy that you are unable to take the trouble of providing an unbroken lamp, in which the oil burns, instead of a cracked one from which the oil runs out?"

---

[9] On these, see for instance: A.M. Ludwig, "Altered States of Consciousness", in: Tart, pp. 9–22.

[11] As, for instance, W. Sargant, *The Mind Possessed. A Physiology of Possession, Mysticism and Faith Healing* (Philadelphia–New York 1974), p. 30: "All sorts of prolonged excitements and stresses can [...] exhaust the nervous system. Music, singing, dancing, [...]. Trance can even be caused in sensitized persons by [...] the reciting of prayers". Also: Shor, pp. 240f., and J.H. Henney, "Spirit-Possession Belief and Trance Behavior in Two Fundamentalist Groups in St. Vincent", in: Goodman, Henney and Pressel, p. 70.

[12] As Sargant, p. 31.

[13] R.E. Shor, "Three Dimensions of Hypnotic Depth", in: Tart, p. 253.

> She replied, "That is not the case, my lord. What you see is the power of the holy Cross".[14]

These words changed his perception of the phenomenon. Suddenly, he writes, they caused him to remember a story he says he had "often heard" about the lamp and now look at it in wonder: in his own words, "having gazed [at it] in awed admiration, I fell silent (*admiratus silui*)". For he now saw, not a broken lamp leaking oil but a whole one that, instead of burning oil, produced it. He tells us that he saw it overflowing "with swelling waves (*undis tumescentibus*)", and in one hour's time bring forth more than a sextarius (about half a litre), while it itself could not hold more than a quarter of that.

If we adhere to our ordinary western common sense view of reality, we must assume Gregory's perception and measuring to have been inaccurate. But what in fact happened is less important for this investigation than the fact that the bishop, quite intentionally it seems, lets us see how his memory of a miracle story functions: as a cue that triggers a temporary suspension of the practical common-sense view of the physical world. Suddenly, the mental image which was originally evoked by the story emerges from memory storage and slides over that which the common-sense frame of mind had formed of the incoming sensory data. Modern psychological experiments indicate how this occurs. In normal perception, what we actually see is not the sensory object itself but our own constructed mental image of it.[15] As in a Rorschach test, we ourselves generate this image by selecting from the incoming sensory data that which fits a learned model image or pattern stored in the mind. All our perception, then, is determined by the contours of these models or paradigms. Desires, fears and expectations, however, as well as conditions of mind and body, influence which of

---

[14] *Tantane te retinet mentis ignavia, ut integrum cicindilem laborare non possis, in quo oleum accendatur, nisi effractum quo defluat ponas? Et illa: Nec est ita, domine mi, sed virtus est crucis sanctae quam cernis*. Gregorius Turonensis, *In gloria martyrum* 5, ed. B. Krusch, Monumenta Germaniae Historica [MGH] Scriptores rerum Merovingicarum [SSrM] 1.2, (Hannover 1885). For a more detailed discussion of this story, see G. de Nie, "A broken lamp or the effluence of holy power? Common sense and belief-reality in Gregory of Tours' own experience", in: *Mediaevistik* 3 (1990), pp. 269–279.

[15] S.S. Tomkins, *Affect, Imagery, Consciousness*, vol. 1 (New York 1962), p. 13: "the world we perceive is a dream which we learn to have from a script we have not written". See V. Henn, "Der Sehvorgang – Wie Auge und Gehirn ihre Umwelt analysieren", in: M. Svilar (ed.), *'Und es war Licht'. Zur Kulturgeschichte des Lichts*, Universität Bern Kulturhistorische Vorlesungen 1981–1982 (Bern–Frankfurt am Main 1983), pp. 201–218.

the available models is chosen for recognition, and hence the selection of the available sensory data perceived and their interpretation.[16]

The memory image of the miracle story here instantly focuses Gregory's attention on discerning, and affectively experiencing, a non-spatio-temporal dynamic of the "really real" reality taught by the Church. He refers to what he came to recognize as the endlessly creating, overflowing movement as the "power of the to-be-adored Cross (*virtus adorandae crucis*)". Perhaps not quite consciously, it would have reminded him of and, I suggest, made him experience interiorly, the boundlessly creative divine generosity he knew about in the early Christian symbols of Christ: the living spring (which he once mentions as such), and as the Light or lamp of the world, the sun, and the "fountain of light".[17] In short, Gregory may have experienced something like an illumination; the previous miracle of the Holy Cross in the same chapel which he describes in the same chapter is in fact that of a luminous apparition. Elsewhere in his writings, many more luminous phenomena are described: some as seen by all present, others as seen only by a select few;[18] all of these are extraordinary perceptions.

Judging by his *Histories*, this bishop was capable of acute critical judgement, adult psychological finesse and great practical common sense in the administration of his diocese in very turbulent period.[19] What his story of the lamp appears to show is that he, as well as others, had learned to go back and forth consciously between the common-sense mode and the affective mode of "awed admiration" required in the confrontation with phenomena in the religious sphere. His narrative is an artistically crafted invitation for the reader to do the same. Today, anthropological research has likewise observed that trained individuals – especially shamans, but also ordinary people with multiple trance experiences – can regulate and control their dreamlike states or trances and even combine them usefully with the more complicated resources of everyday consciousness.[20] In this story and

---

[16] R. Arnheim, *Visual Thinking* (Berkeley 1969), pp. 90–91.

[17] Respectively: John 4:14 and Gregorius Turonensis, *Historiae 6.29*, ed. B. Krusch and W. Levison, MGH SSrM 1.1, ed. altera (Hannover 1951). Bible references: John 8:12 and 9:5; Matthew 17:2. Cf. Boethius, *Philosophiae consolatio* III.12m.2: *fons lucidus*, ed. L. Bieler, Corpus Christianorum, Series Latina [CCSL] 94 (Turnhout 1957).

[18] See on this: G. de Nie, *Views from a Many-Windowed Tower. Studies of Imagination in the Works of Gregory of Tours*, Studies in Classical Antiquity 7 (Amsterdam 1987), pp. 176–192.

[19] The most detailed recent biography of Gregory is that of L. Pietri, *La ville de Tours du IVe au VIe siècle: naissance d'une cité chrétienne* (Rome 1983), pp. 246–334.

[20] Sargant, p. 173; Shor, pp. 253, 257.

elsewhere, Gregory would then be turning to an altered state of consciousness to become aware of non-material phenomena too subtle for ordinary perception.

Is this kind of perception possible only for religious visionaries such as Gregory? Perhaps not. For a well-respected voice from the abstruse world of theoretical physics – Professor David Bohm, lately of Birkbeck College in London – asserts that modern experimental science indicate that the spatio-temporal field of everyday experience must be only a small part of what actually is. What he makes clear to non-scientific readers such as myself is that there is indirect evidence of a seemingly measureless, higher, non-material and multi-dimensional ground of both mind and matter which is not only mankind's primary experience as children, but also the essence of human intelligence and our deepest inwardness[21] – a view, incidentally, which resembles that of Augustine.[22] This not directly accessible dynamic process or "implicate order", Bohm writes, is most veridically experienced in the process of poetic intuition and in the perception and experience of movement, as for instance in music.[23] If he is right, Gregory's "awed admiration" of what he perceived as the generous *creatio ex nihilo* dynamism of the overflowing oil begins to look like poetry or post-scientific perception....

As is well-known, however, not only Gregory's story but almost every sentence of early Christian writings points to the pre-eminence of a dynamic alternate reality behind everyday sensory appearances. From the fourth century onward, Christian monks developed an art of approaching this reality through a process of moral purification accompanied by a meditative discipline; the latter silenced sensory experience and transformed its memories to focus exclusively upon discerning and associatively developing ideas and images in Scripture that would lead the mind and heart to the invisible God.[24] Thus the fifth-century monastic authority John Cassian describes the monk's ideal state as that of ceaseless prayer or union with God; he writes that this state makes the soul so light that it rises naturally to

---

[21] D. Bohm, *Wholeness and the Implicate Order* (London–New York 1980), pp. 52–53, 59, 206, 209.

[22] See on this: C. Taylor, *Sources of the Self. The Making of the Modern Identity* (Cambridge 1989), pp. 127–142.

[23] Bohm, pp. 55–56, 63, 199, 206.

[24] M. Carruthers, *The Craft of Thought. Meditation, Rhetoric and the Making of Images, 400–1200*, Cambridge Studies in Medieval Literature 34 (Cambridge 1998), p. 155 and passim.

God,[25] an image that, as we shall see, is also found in the writings of Gregory of Tours' Italian-born friend, the poet and hagiographer Venantius Fortunatus (c.540–c.604). Another image which Cassian uses for this state is that of a tower reaching into heaven;[26] Gregory of Tours describes something like this in a sixth-century saint's dream.[27] This state, Cassian writes, could culminate in moments of sensory oblivion and wordless rapture, in which one is suffused by a fiery kind of energy: the "prayer of fire (*oratio ignita*)". It could be suddenly triggered by small as well as by great things: for instance, by the singing of a psalm, by someone's beautiful voice or spiritual advice, by someone's death, or by the memory of one's own moral laxity.[28] It is clearly an altered state of consciousness focused upon interior experience. Gregory of Tours describes one of these states as having been perceived as a fiery glow by one observer – himself probably using extraordinary perception.[29]

The ordinary, in this period often non-literate, believer was told during church services to approach God by "lifting up his heart" – that is, by intentionally leaving behind his common-sense material reality picture. In such a state of mind he would have listened to (and mentally imaged) stories about biblical or saintly persons, sung psalms (and imaged these) and, especially, participated in the Eucharist (enacting a mentally imaged symbol). All these are imagistic modes of access to the unseen, non-common-sense religious reality that was accepted on faith. As we have seen in Gregory's story of the lamp, a non-common-sense or faith attitude was also required to recognize a miraculous phenomenon as such; and he indicates that such an attitude also played a decisive role in the physical cures that occurred at saints' shrines.[30] Since his friend Fortunatus' saints' lives have been less extensively utilized, I shall concentrate in this paper on the evidence in these.[31] Let me emphasize at the outset, however, that I take Fortunatus' all too brief descriptions not as necessarily accurate reports of

---

[25] Johannes Cassianus, *Collationes* IX.4, ed. M. Petschenig, Corpus Scriptorum Ecclesiasticorum Latinorum [CSEL] 13.2 (Vienna 1886), IX.4, p. 253.

[26] *Ibid.*, IX.2.

[27] *Vita patrum* 17.5, ed. B. Krusch, MGH SSrM 1.2.

[28] *Collationes* IX.25–26.

[29] *In gloria confessorum* 37, ed. B. Krusch, MGH SSrM 1.2.

[30] As, for instance, in *Virtutes sancti Juliani* 4, ed. B. Krusch, MGH SSrM 1.2 (Hannover 1885): *fide plena et de martyris pietate secura.*

[31] *Vita sancti Hilarii, Liber de virtutibus sancti Hilarii, Vita sancti Germani, Vita sancti Albini, Vita sancti Paterni, Vita sanctae Radegundis, Vita sancti Marcelli*, ed. B. Krusch, MGH Auctores Antiquissimi [AA] 4.2 (Berlin 1885), pp. 1–54. *Vita sancti Martini*, ed. F. Leo, MGH AA 4.1, pp. 293–370.

what actually happened in these particular cases, but as purposely stylized pointers to what the whole, mixed church community should be encouraged to believe and imitate.[32]

II. "With her mind in heaven": altered states of consciousness in the saints

To begin by looking at altered states of consciousness as Fortunatus describes them in the saints themselves: what we see is that their intentional reduction or blocking out of ordinary consciousness and sensory reality to focus exclusively upon an affective sensing of the heavenly one is praised as a great virtue and accomplishment – thus motivating the reader to attempt the same. For instance, while saint Radegund (c. 520–587) was praying, she did not hear secular songs being sung outside the walls of her convent because, as Fortunatus writes, "she was with her mind in heaven (*mente ... esset in caelo*)".[33] And about the holy bishop Albinus of Angers (538–550) we are told that

> he regarded himself as so much in the monastic enclosure that when he went outside it he always remained enclosed in the prison of his heart, and preferred not to see anything outside himself except Christ, whom he carried in his heart as a faithful porter.[34]

This behaviour too is held up for imitation: the physical world being one of transient and delusive appearances that could lead to temptation, one should attend only to affectively discerning the immanent Christ working in and shining through everyone and everything – as Gregory appears to have done in the spilling lamp.

Here and there, Fortunatus reports how the saints went about achieving this state of mind. His clerical listeners are likely to have been acquainted with Cassian's subtle and detailed instructions for fine-tuning the mind and heart into a receiving mode for God. But Fortunatus, mindful of his in-

[32] See on this also: R. Collins, "Observations on the form, language and public of the prose biographies of Venantius Fortunatus in the hagiography of Merovingian Gaul, in: H.B. Clarke and M. Brennan (ed.), *Columbanus and Merovingian Monasticism*, BAR series 114 (Oxford 1981), pp. 111–118.

[33] *Vita s. Radegundis* 83.

[34] [...] *talem se intra monasterii saepta tractavit, ut vel si quando processit ad publicum esset infra carcerem sui cordis semper inclusus, nec aliud extra se respiciendum praetulit quam Christum quem in pectore fidelis portitor baiulavit. Vita s. Albini* 17.

tended, mixed audience, keeps it simple. Thus we are told about bishop Germanus of Paris (555–576):

> How great was his constancy in singing psalms, when his flesh held out as though clothed with the rigor of iron, while the frost made the stones fall apart and congealed water into ice! [...] he went into the church at the third hour of night and thereafter did not stop solemnly singing the whole series of the psalms according to the canons until day had begun to dawn and the series was completed.[35]

Psychological research shows that practices such as the sleep deprivation and the prolonged fasting, prayer and chanting described in Fortunatus' Lives themselves alter the body's chemistry to produce altered, dreamlike states of consciousness.[36] The latter, then, have a physiological component, and this can be intentionally brought about. As with the Old Testament prophets, but also as with shamanistic healers in present-day traditional societies, a saint's deprivational practices could lead to clairvoyance:[37] he prophesies about others and has prophetic dreams about his own future.[38]

III. "Stupefaction": others' slips into non-common-sense awareness

Not only professionals like Gregory, however, but also ordinary believers are sometimes reported to have been stunned into speechlessness and thereby experienced temporary slips out of the discursive thought mode and everyday reality frame. As we have seen, one such slip occurs when a miracle is recognized as such. Probably because all miracle stories take the generation of astonishment for granted, however, they rarely advert to it. Nevertheless, in one case Fortunatus tells us that people were "terrified (*terrerentur*)",[39] and that after another cure, "a stupor took hold of all (*cunctos stupor amplectitur*), [and] a great cry was lifted up to the sky

---

[35] *Quanta vero ad psallendum fuit constantia, dum velut ferri rigore induta caro subsisteret, dum saxa frigus decrustaret et aquas in crustam verteret? [...] tertia noctis hora ingreditur in ecclesiam, non est egressus ulterius psallentium ab ordine, donec clariscente die decantatus sollemniter cursus universus consummaretur ex canone. Vita s. Germani* 202–203.

[36] Sargant, pp. 193–195; W.N. Pahnke and W.A. Richards, "Implications of LSD and Experimental Mysticism", in: Tart, p. 417.

[37] M. Eliade, *Le chamanisme et les techniques archaïques de l'extase* (Paris 1983), pp. 83–85.

[38] Respectively: *Vita s. Germani* 27, 39, and *Vita s. Paterni* 46.

[39] *Vita s. Germani* 11.

(*clamor in caelo educitur*) [...]."[40] The phrasing resembles some of the New Testament descriptions of bystanders' reactions to Christ's miracles.[41] Such conventions point to the community's shared perceptual paradigms and expectations, however, and as such to what is therefore, sooner or later, likely to have been the manner in which people actually experienced the event.

A story of a miracle which Fortunatus himself saw yields first-hand information, and therefore perhaps a more trustworthy report. The author tells us that bishop Germanus of Paris once could not enter a church because the doors were locked. When the keys had been asked for but did not open the lock, the saint

> opened the [lock on the] bolt by making the sign of the Cross. Stupefaction took hold of the people at the beholding of the miracle of the opening by holy power what a key could not. These venerable things [...] took place in my presence.[42]

One wonders here whether making the sign of the Cross was the only thing the saint did. Important for our investigation, however, is that in this situation apparently everyone concerned was culturally conditioned to attribute miraculous power to the sign of the Cross and thus – whatever else the saint also did – to perceive the event as a miracle. Not only because the figure of the idealized, miracle-doing saint had become a perceptual paradigm[43] that generated an urgently needed feeling of empowerment and protection in these times of great want and insecurity – perhaps comparable to the deplorable situation in some of the Third World states today. But also, as Fortunatus' description here and elsewhere appears to show, because the church taught men to look for and expect in the visible world the same patterns of divine action that were manifested in its history of the salvation

---

[40] *Ibid.* c. 109; cf. 119.

[41] As for instance: *videntes autem turbae timuerunt et glorificaverunt Deum* (Matthew 9:8), and *et videntes discipuli mirati sunt* (*ibid.* 21:20). On biblical stylization in the texts of this period see Marc van Uytfanghe, *Stylisation biblique et condition humaine dans l'hagiographie mérovingienne (600–750)*, Verhandelingen van de Koninklijke Academie voor Wetenschappen, Letteren en Schone Kunstern van België, Klasse der Letteren, Jrg. 49, Nr. 120 (Brussels 1987).

[42] [...] *sic reseravit pessolum facto crucis signaculo. Stupor anim[o]s invasit praesenti miraculo aperire de virtute quod clave duce non potuit. Haec [...] veneranda praesente me gesta sunt. Vita s. Germani* 176–177.

[43] See on this: P. Brown, *The Cult of the Saints. Its Rise and Function in Latin Christianity* (Chicago 1981).

of mankind.[44] The symbolism implicit in the opening of the church door through the ritual gesture that presenced the power of the Cross is likely to have been that of Christ's passion opening the door of Paradise for the saved. Fortunatus' poems indicate that church buildings – with their trance-inducing combination of fragrances and flickering lights, reflected in colourful mosaics – were meant to evoke associations with Paradise.[45]

A striking example of such a looking through sensory phenomena to discern belief images and patterns is one woman's perception of bishop Germanus as he entered her house. She is quoted as saying:

> "Behold, it seemed to me that the blessed Germanus came in with horns on his head, so that I could hardly look at the holy man shining in a new way with horns, or speak with him."
>
> The woman was in consternation at being able to see a man of our time in the figure of Moses;[46] and it is to be believed that [the saint] too, after his talking with the Lord, could be perceived by the woman as exalted by horns. Because he was affrighted by this event, [the master of the house] Aebro did not dare to sit near the saint that day for two reasons: his affliction and his fear.[47]

The phrase "it is to be believed" is a give-away: it points to the story's exemplary function as a model of belief reality. The woman had evidently heard story of Moses in church, and it had left an image in her mind that emerged into awareness when she was later confronted with what must have been saint Germanus' charismatic presence. And just as Gregory did with the lamp, she must have suddenly perceived the saint through the filter of this mental image: psychological experiments have shown that vision and imagination use some of the same pathways in the brain.[48] This is a sign that

---

[44] As also: Collins, pp. 112f.

[45] As, for instance, in *Carmina* 1.1.11–14, ed. Friedrich Leo, MGH AA 4.1: *Emicat aula potens, solido perfecta metallo, / Quo sine nocte manet continuata dies. / Invitat locus ipse deum sub luce perenni, / Gressibus ut placidis intret amando lares.*

[46] Exodus 34:29.

[47] *Ecce beatus Germanus cornuta facie mihi videtur incedere, quod paene vix valeo aut intuere lumine aut sermone conferre sanctum virum novo more cornibus radiantem. Consternataque mulier hominem nostro tempore in figura Moysi potuisse conspicere, credendum, quod et iste post conloquium domine potuit a muliere cornu exaltatus agnosci. Cuius causae pavore Aebro eadem die iuxta sanctum sedere nullatenus praesumpsit duplice pro merito, maerore pariter et terrore. Vita s. Germani* 23–25.

[48] J.L. Singer, *Imagery and Daydream Methods in Psychotherapy and Behavior Modification* (New York 1974), pp. 175f.

her common sense awareness must have been significantly diminished, and that she had slipped into a mode of consciousness in which mental images predominate. As is well known, in this period the dreams and visions of the devout were valued as veridical perceptions of an otherwise hidden reality.[49] Since it validates his presentation of the saint, Fortunatus presents this dreamlike mode of perception as eminently truthful and thereby encourages his listeners to have similar experiences. It must be added, however, that in this period any extraordinary perceptions whose content did not accord with church views – such as that of folk healers claiming divine aid but resisting episcopal authority – were demonized and vigorously repressed.[50]

IV. "Enacting the mystery": symbolic action and transformation

To turn now to the state of mind during the physical transformation that takes place in cures: Fortunatus explicitly describes one cure as having taken place in a dream.[51] He writes:

> The nun Animia was so completely swollen with dropsy that she had reached her end. While the appointed sister nuns were around her, expecting her to expire at any moment, she saw in her sleep that the blessed Radegund, with the venerable abbess, ordered her to descend nude into a bath without water. Then, with her hand, the saint was seen to pour oil over the head of the sick woman, and to cover her with a new robe. After this mystery had been enacted (*peracto mysterio*), she awoke from sleep and nothing of the illness was left; she had not lost the water through perspiration but it had been consumed within. In this new kind of miracle the illness left no trace in her womb. For she who had been believed to be ready to be carried to the tomb, lifted herself from her bed to walk: the scent of her head was a testimony of the oil and nothing harmful [remained] in her belly.[52]

[49] See on this: J. Amat, *Songes et visions. L'au-delà dans la littérature latine tardive* (Paris 1985).

[50] As Gregory of Tours tells us in his *Historiae*, 9. 6.

[51] See on the curing ritual in this and similar stories: G. de Nie, "Fatherly and motherly curing in sixth-century Gaul: Saint Radegund's *mysterium*", in: A.-M. Korte (ed.), *Women and Miracle Stories: A Multidisciplinary Exploration* (Leiden 2001), pp. 53–86.

[52] *Animia monacha dum tantò hydropis morbo tumefacta tenderetur, ut salus esset in ultimo, et deputatae sorores spectarent, quo momento exhalaret spiritum, visa est illi per soporem cum veneranda abbatissa beata Radegundis in balneo sine liquore nudam iubere descendere. Deinde manu beatae visa est oleum aegrotae super caput effundere et nova veste contegere. Quo peracto mysterio, evigilanti de sopore de morbo nihil apparuit, ita ut nec subsudasset et intus aqua consumpta sit. Quo novo sub miraculo non reliquit in utero nec*

Whether the illness was indeed dropsy (a disease in which watery fluid collects in cavities or tissue of the body) or not, is not important for our investigation. Central for us here is that this story presents the enactment of symbolic ritual in the dream as having had a transformational effect upon the nun's body. For the term *mysterium* was also used for church sacraments, and the bath as well as the anointing appear in the rite of baptism as it was then carried out.[53] Descending into the pool – similar in form to the tomb mentioned later – thus may have symbolized not only purification but, as the apostle Paul had said, the death of the old unspiritual nature; and rising up out of it the resurrection or the creation of the new spiritual nature, created after the likeness of God.[54] In addition, I suggest, there may be – as in certain present-day oral cultures – implicit feminine imagery. Since the healer is in this case a woman, the bath may also have had the affective connotation of a womb, in which a new creature would be formed.[55] The nun had therefore "enacted the mystery" of death and resurrection or rebirth into a new, heavenly life. The image of the new robe possibly reinforces this: in late Antiquity, it could symbolize not only a nun's marriage to Christ,[56] but also a new body or vehicle for the soul.[57]

The symbolic action in this early medieval story also bears a generic resemblance to a curing ritual in one present-day African oral culture as it is described and analyzed by Professor René Devisch of the University of Louvain. In this society, illness is regarded as a disconnecting and disordering of psycho-physical energies which blocks a person's vital source.[58] The ritual curing process undertakes to undo this through the enacting of liminal situations such as death, gestation (in a symbolic version of the primal Womb, the Life Source), and rebirth.[59] This enactment, Devisch writes, takes place in a state of dreamlike awareness or trance, in which discursive reasoning is temporarily put aside for imagistic 'thinking', and

---

morbus vestigium. Nam quae credebatur deferri praeceps ad tumulum, levat ad cursum de lectulo, ut olei testimonium odor inesset capitis et ventris nulla pernicies. Vita s. Radegundis 80–81.

[53] As in Ambrosius of Milan, *Des mystères,* ed. and tr. B. Botte, Sources Chrétiennes [SC] 25 (Paris 1950), pp. 107f.

[54] Ephesians 4:22–24.

[55] Cf. Goodman, p. 32.

[56] As in Gregorius, *Historiae* 6.29.

[57] See on this: A. Kehl, "Gewand (der Seele)", in: *Reallexikon für Antike und Christentum* 10, pp. 945–1025.

[58] R. Devisch, *Weaving the Threads of Life. The Khita Gyn-Eco-Logical Healing Cult Among the Yaka* (Chicago–London 1993), pp. 132f.

[59] *Ibid.*, p. 269.

images are preverbally experienced as affect-laden realities.[60] He asserts that "[s]uch healing is founded in imaginative dreamwork [...] that is largely beyond dialogue and discursive reality. It can not be verbalized but only experienced, acted out".[61]

By comparison: in the Christian tradition, the gifted, twentieth-century American healer and author Agnes Sanford describes successful healing as an imaginative and affective connecting to the omnipresent higher spiritual energy of God. She insists, however, that the healing message must be relayed to the body's unconscious "control center" by repeatedly making a mental picture of the afflicted part as completely healthy while, at the same time, believing firmly that it is being healed at that very moment.[62] This accords with what psychologists tell us: namely, that the imaginative experience of an image produces an involuntary affective mimesis of its dynamic pattern in the beholder.[63] Thus an apparently agnostic American surgeon at Yale, Bernie Siegel, found that meditative, affective visualizations of dynamic, health-inducing imagery helped bring about improvement or even cures of cancer patients. Offering an explanation of the mimetic process from a medical point of view, he asserts that the lower part of the brain or hypothalamus relays such affectively experienced mental images as commands for the body's autonomous systems, such as the central nervous system and the endocrine and immune systems.[64]

This evidence from different cultural contexts appears to indicate that affect-laden images, especially when experienced in an imaginal or dream-like mode of consciousness, can in fact give transforming messages to the body. Is there any trace of this happening in the other cures which Fortunatus describes? In one of the two other dream cures reported, a blind woman prayed with tears for three nights to saint Germanus; during the third night, she was cured by the saint's appearing and making the sign of the Cross over her eyes. Fortunatus writes, significantly: "so that the image of the holy man thus seen in a dream was the remedy (*ita ut sancti viri sic visa per somnium esset imago remedium*)".[65] Here, the image of the saint as the embodiment of all her hopes, strengths and ideals – indirectly perhaps as an idealized image of self – must have focused her imagination upon her

[60] *Ibid.*, pp. 255, 257.

[61] *Ibid.*, p. 282.

[62] A. Sanford, *The Healing Light*, revised ed. (New York 1972), pp. 22f.

[63] So R. Assagioli, *Psychosynthesis* (New York 1965), p. 144.

[64] B.S. Siegel, *Love, Medicine and Miracles. Lessons Learned About Self-Healing from a Surgeon's Experience with Exceptional Patients* (New York 1986), pp. 66–69.

[65] *Vita s. Germani* 98; cf. *ibid.* 179.

certainly becoming whole again, and his empowering gesture was perceived as triggering the final breakthrough. Several other cures are preceded by advice in dreams to go to the saint that as it were guarantee future wholeness.[66] Such stories clearly point to the transforming and enabling power of the image of a culture hero when perceived affectively in a dream or a dreamlike state.

As for the transformational effect of other religious symbols: as we have seen, Fortunatus' reports of cures can suggest the involvement of imagistic patterns that point to central church symbols and doctrines of salvation. The implication is, of course, that sin and illness are two aspects of the same phenomenon. Thus we hear about a royal official who incurred an eye ailment by not carrying out the king's order to distribute alms; when he became conscious of the fact that his "darkening error (*tenebrosus error*)" was the cause of his physical condition, he asked forgiveness "so that with the departure of the guilt of his heart, light would enter into his eyes (*ut culpa cordis exiit oculis lux intravit*)".[67] Here, it is explicitly the purification of the heart, perhaps also through some formal penitential act, that results in the healing of the body. Whether or not the cured themselves always had these images in mind at the time of their healing is unclear; what is clear is that Fortunatus intends his hearers to have them in mind to guide their imagination while praying for a future cure. For he presents his stories, as he says in one of his prefaces:

> so that whoever shall have apprehended this as he should, through a trustful listening, may rejoice in knowing about earlier events, and have confidence that similar things will be done by the confessor's holy power in the future.[68]

In other words, his stories are intended to be models, not only for the future perception of miracles, but also for the future enactment of cures.

It is in his poetic rendering of Sulpicius Severus' stories about Saint Martin, however, that Fortunatus tells us in the greatest detail how he himself was once healed by enacting symbols. In a story that is unique in early western hagiography he describes how, during the prayerful contemplation of a picture of the saint, the experience and manipulation of

---

[66] *Ibid.* 73 and 102.

[67] *Vita s. Paterni* . 45.

[68] [...] *ut quisquis haec fideli sicut condecet auditu perceperit, et praeterita recognoscere gaudeat et similia fieri virtute confessoris in futuro confidat. Virtutes s. Hilarii* 5.

sensory objects as symbols of analogous spiritual realities helped bring about the cure of his eye-ailment:

> Under the feet of the just man the wall has, through art, a window; [close by] there is a lamp, whose fire swims in a glass bowl. I hastened to this place tortured by a severe pain, lamenting that the light was disappearing from the windows of my eyes.
>
> [But] as soon as I touched the light from afar through the blessed olive [oil], the fiery vapour withdrew from my wilting brow: the doctor – who was present – put the illnesses to flight with his soothing ointment.[69]

In the state of prayerful communion with Christ that is here assumed, there are two levels of symbolism. First, the application of oil from the lamp near the saint's picture to the eye is imagined as "touching light" – a symbolic gesture that was almost certainly intended to enact Christ's beneficent illumination of the spirit as well as the body. Through the mediation of the saint, seen and sensed to be actively present through his picture, Christ's light would have been imagined as chasing the painful, darkening and obstructing fire away. At a second, indirect symbolic level, the juxtaposition of sensory objects, such as the fire in the glass bowl and the window in the wall, with what the author calls "the light [...] [in] the windows of my eyes", implicitly suggests that their presence prefigures, and somehow perhaps even helps to bring about, the healing of the author's eyes. Fortunatus' description is a poetical rendering of what looks like a sacramental perception of sensory phenomena in a faith state of imaginal consciousness. Presumably alongside prayer and complete confidence in the power of Christ through the saint, what is here presented as a dreamlike act of intense affective assimilation to a cluster of empowering symbols is perceived as having helped to precipitate a physical transformation.[70]

---

[69] *Sub pedibus iusti paries habet arte fenestram: / Lychnus adest, cuius vitrea natat ignis in urna. / Huc ego dum propero, valido torquente dolore, / Diffugiente gemens oculorum luce fenestris, / Quo procul ut tetigi benedicto lumen olivo, / Igneus ille vapor marcenti fronte recessit / Et praesens medicus blando fugat unguine morbos. Vita s. Martini*, 4.692–698.

[70] For a more detailed analysis of this story see G. de Nie, "Word, image and experience in the early medieval miracle story", in: P. Joret and A. Remael (ed.), *Language and Beyond. Actuality and Virtuality in the Relations between Word, Image and Sound*, Studies in Comparative Literature 17 (Amsterdam 1998), pp. 109–116.

V. Conclusion

To conclude: our texts show that the sixth-century church had institutionalized the inducement of altered states of consciousness as modes of access to the hidden spiritual reality, and that it tended to present its symbols of Christ's salvation of the soul as the divine dynamisms made manifest in miracles and physical cures. As we have seen, different kinds of modern evidence also appear to indicate that controlled imagistic or dreamlike perception may be an affective mode of accessing and inspecting otherwise only dimly apprehended experience of very subtle but real, if non-material, phenomena. Artists, visionaries and charismatic healers have always known this. But I think most of us would recognize that we have also experienced such moments at one time or another. Further, we have seen indications that – in present-day as well as in early medieval societies – the affective experience or enactment of the dynamisms of power-laden symbols in meditational or dreamlike states of mind can help direct the transformation of the body. Perhaps, then, our own ancestors' 1400-year-old stories can help us to recover a mode of perceiving ourselves and our environment that might be something like a poetics of wonder.

XV

The 'Power' of What is Said in the Book: Word, Script and Sign in Gregory of Tours*

Because this book needs to be brought to an end, however, I will relate one more miracle that deserves admiration – this one concerning the book about [Bishop Nicetius'] life which I mentioned above as having been written by an unknown author. The divine power coming forth from it (*de quo virtus divina procedens*) did not leave [the saint] inglorious, but in order to confirm the power of what is said [in it] (*ad comprobandam virtutem dictorum*), manifested to many people that he is glorified.

For [when] a deacon of the city of Autun, who was labouring under a painful blindness of his eyes, heard about that which God, the Glorifier of his saints, was carrying out at the tomb of this saint, he said to his companions:

"If I go to his tomb or take [from there] something of the holy relics, or certainly if I touch the cloth with which the limbs of the holy man are covered, I shall be made healthy."

And while he was saying this and words of this kind to his companions, suddenly a certain clerical person stood before him, and said:

"You believe in the right manner; but if you wish to be even more sure of these powers (*virtutes*), here is a book of parchment which has been written about these things, so that you may more easily believe that which you have heard."

But before [the deacon] felt the desire to read, he said – inspired by respect toward the divine Beneficence – :

"I believe that God has the power to work excellent things through his servants". And at once he placed the book upon his eyes.

Immediately, the pain was put to flight and the obscuring veil [over his eyes] broken through: he was found worthy to receive the use of his eyes from the power of the book (*voluminis a virtute*). And he was given so much clarity of vision that

---

* Author's translation of "De 'kracht' van wat in het boek gezegd wordt: woord, schrift en teken in zesde-eeuws Gallië", in: R.E.V. Stuip and C. Vellekoop (ed.), *Oraliteit en schriftcultuur*, UBM 12 (Utrecht 1993), pp. 63–88.

he learned about the [saint's] deeds of power (*virtutum gesta*) through reading about them with his own eyes.

For it is one and same Lord who does these things: He who is glorified in his saints, and who makes these chosen ones glorious through shining miracles.[1]

This story, written by Gregory, bishop of Tours (573–594), one of the only two authors in troubled late antique Gaul of whom a substantial corpus of writings survives, shows us some of the attitudes of the contemporary clerical milieu[2] towards the spoken and the written word. Is the initial choice to touch the written words before reading them a symptom of a relapse into orality, as that which would occur in the seventh century, the so-called "dark age"? Or are other factors, too, involved?

A hundred years earlier, the Roman Empire in the West had fallen apart into Germanic kingdoms. Franco-Gallic society[3] in which our author found himself resembled that of some of those in the Third World today: a well-educated, privileged élite, a pragmatically literate commercial class, and below that the mass of the rural population, still living in primary orality. Gregory is aware of a difference between the society of his time and that of the Roman period. For in the well-known prologue to his *Histories* he writes:

> Many people, very often, keep sighing and saying: "Woe to our days! For the study of letters has disappeared from among us, and there is no one among the people who is able to make the present events known in writing (*promulgare possit in paginis*)".[4]

As a result of the long period of Roman domination, however, written documents were still being used in administrative affairs.[5] The Church,

---

[1] Gregorius Turonensis, *De vita patrum* [*Vit. patr.*] 8.12, ed. B. Krusch in: W. Arndt and B. Krusch (ed.), *Gregorii Turonensis opera*, pars II: *Miracula et opera minora*, Monumenta Germaniae Historica, Scriptores rerum Merovingicarum [MGH SSrM] 1.2 (Hannover 1885). Gregory's other hagiographical writings, mentioned below, are also contained in this edition.

[2] See on this: R. van Dam, *Leadership and Community in Late Antique Gaul*, The Transformation of the Classical Heritage 8 (Berkeley 1985), pp. 177–302.

[3] The most recent and fullest treatment of this is: E. James, *The Franks* (Oxford–New York 1988).

[4] Gregorius Turonensis, *Historiarum libri decem* [*Hist.*] *praef. prima*, ed. B. Krusch and W. Levison, MGH SSrM 1.1, editio altera (Hannover 1951).

[5] I.N. Wood, "Administration, law and culture in Merovingian Gaul", in: R. McKitterick (ed.), *The Uses of Literacy in Early Medieval Europe* (Cambridge 1990), pp. 63–81.

especially, promoted the continuation of the Roman administrative methods within her organization, also in her own interest. And the Church too was now the only institution that had schools in cities and rural parishes, in part to educate and train its own future personnel.[6] For, except for one not very clear reference,[7] there is no indication that the former state-run city schools and universities were still functioning after the Franks came into power;[8] the families that could afford it employed private tutors.[9]

Apart from using writing for practical matters, the Church based its teachings upon a centuries' old written tradition. The central text was, of course, the Bible as the written record of God's dealings with the human race. But His deeds continued in the present time. And Gregory says more than once that he records such deeds in writing to prevent their being forgotten. In his view, then, a local oral tradition, such as that around Martin's tomb in Tours, is evidently not sufficient to preserve the memory of the saint's miracles. His four books on *The miracles of St Martin*, probably intended not only for the generations to come but also for a broad contemporary public,[10] record these deeds of power in written form. The importance to Gregory of the certainty of the written word is evident in what he says at the end of one of his miracle stories:

> As we have said, there have been [other] men of illustrious merit [in Clermont] whose names, although are not known to the inhabitants, are preserved – as we believe – in written form in heaven (*scripta tamen, ut credimus, retinentur in coelis*).[11]

The central assertion in Walter Ong's *Orality and Literacy* is that dealing with the word as a written mark or sign creates distance from the original auditive experience of the spoken word as a live event in which one participates affectively. Because of this, in his view, working with written texts instead of oral communication would itself transform thinking and the

---

[6] As is evident, for instance, in *Hist.* 6.36 and *In gloria confessorum* (*Glor. conf.*) 77.

[7] *Hist.* 5.44.

[8] Cf. P. Riché, "La survivance des écoles publiques en Gaule au Ve siècle", in: *Le Moyen Age* 63 (1957), pp. 421–436.

[9] P. Riché, "Centres of culture in Frankish Gaul between the 6th and the 9th centuries", in: P. Riché, *Instruction et vie religieuse dans le haut Moyen Age* (London 1981), III.

[10] Gregorius Turonensis, *De virtutibus sancti Martini* (*Virt. Mart.*) 1. *prol.*.

[11] *Glor. conf.* 36; cf. Philippians 4:3.

attitude toward language: "writing restructures consciousness".[12] Can this alienating effect of the written word be recognized in what Gregory tells us about himself and his contemporaries?

The story with which we began occurs in a series of biographies which he wrote about the holy life of a number of exceptional persons in his century, some of whom he had known personally. As already indicated, it also tells us something about his views of the spoken and the written word and how they relate to an invisible but all-determining reality. Gregory's conviction of the existence of this reality is evident from the number of times (eight) that the concepts for holy power or miracle – often with overlapping meanings – occur in this story (and this is without counting the seven indirect references). In addition, the biblical theme of not seeing and yet believing,[13] and of seeing (also in the metaphorical sense) through believing,[14] are demonstrated here. The longer we look at the story, the more layers of meaning emerge and the more complicated it becomes.

Our focus here, however, is how spoken and written words function in relation to holy power. Does this (sometimes healing) power reach human beings only in non-verbal ways through the touching of holy objects "filled" with this power, as Gregory first lets the deacon say? Or, in one way or another, (also) through the word? And if the latter is the case, what is more effective: the spoken or the written word? Was it the spoken words about the miracles that brought the deacon to his original faith in a cure, and/or the spoken words of the suddenly appearing cleric (perhaps an apparition[15]), who – in an ostensible paradox – privileges the book, and/or the spoken words of the deacon himself, through which he verbalized his faith and thereby enacted it? Or was it after all "the power of the book (*voluminis ... virtus*)"; and if so, does this phrase point to the power of the written words as such or to something else? Or was it "the divine power coming forth [from the book] (*virtus divina procedens*)", which revealed Nicetius' glorification "in order to demonstrate the power of what is said (*virtus dictorum*)"? But precisely what does Gregory mean with the phrase "the power of what is said": power to convince, or perhaps something more? In the end, however, it was nevertheless the physical contact with the book that precipitated the cure.

[12] W. Ong, *Orality and Literacy* (London–New York 1988), pp. 78–81.

[13] John 20:29.

[14] John 9:38–39.

[15] In Gregory's writings, as in *Glor. conf.* 109, the words "suddenly" and "a certain" may be read as pointing to an apparition.

It looks as though it is not possible to isolate any one of these elements as the sole determinant: they are all necessary and inextricably intertwined. One fact is significant: that the miracle had already happened, and needed to happen, before the deacon could learn about the saint's previous miracles through reading the written letters with his own eyes. And that brings us to the question whether the – as yet unread – written letters as such, representing words as representations of holy matters, also played a role in the cure. We shall be looking elsewhere in Gregory's writings to find an answer to this question.

The analysis of this story shows that, for this period, it would be misleading – quite apart from the fact that it is also impossible – to treat the spoken word apart from the written one. For "reading" was then, usually, letting oneself be read to.[16] When we remember, in addition, that the glimpses that we get of daily life in this period show that people are seldom completely alone – everyone, including the most ascetic hermit, seems to have been surrounded constantly by servants, a retinue, family or friends – it becomes clear that in this period orality and written culture are related differently to each other than in our modern, individualized society, in which a person withdraws from others' company to read a book silently and (because of academic pressure) too fast: the modern situation which must have brought Ong to his view. In what follows, it will become clear that Gregory's testimony indicates that it was not the practice itself of dealing with the written word, but the ideology in which this word was embedded, that determined the manner in which it was used.[17]

In Ong's view, an oral attitude – that is: one that cannot easily reflect upon its own mental products – is also evident in a particular concept of the "sign": not as an abstract reference to a word as such, but as a meaningful, visible form or a specific message.[18] Can we detect Gregory's view of the "sign" in the story of the deacon's cure? In the Bible, the word is the central means of communication between man and God.[19] But, as such, it is not a

---

[16] Evident, for instance, in: Caesarius Arelatensis, *Sermones* 6:1–2, ed. G. Morin, *Sancti Caesarii Arelatensis Sermones* 1, Corpus Christianorum, Series Latina [CCSL] 103 (Turnhout 1953).

[17] This is also the position of B.V. Street, *Literacy in theory and in practice*, Cambridge Studies in Oral and Literate Culture 9 (Cambridge 1984), p. 8.

[18] Ong, *Orality*, pp. 75–76.

[19] On this, see: *New International Dictionary of New Testament Theology* [NIDNTT] vol. 3 (Grand Rapids 1978), pp. 1078–1146.

"sign". This term (*signum*) and that of "power" (*virtus*) are used in the New Testament for miracles:[20] manifestations of the presence of the spiritual reality.[21] In his treatise *On Christian Doctrine*, the influential Church Father and former teacher of rhetoric, Augustine (354–430) (whom Gregory does not mention anywhere, however), regards the word as such, irrespective of its content, as the central "sign (*signum*)" that transmits knowledge to men about the divine will, reality and Creation.[22] And God's acts, but also the metaphorical statements in the Bible that have a hidden meaning beside the literal one, are qualified as "metaphorical signs (*signa translata*)" or "figures of speech (*figuratae locutiones*)".[23] They are symbols of the divine reality.[24]

Gregory too not infrequently refers to miracles as "signs (*signa*)",[25] but he also uses this term for extraordinary natural phenomena announcing God's imminent acts to men.[26] Sometimes, as we shall see, he uses a term from the sphere of divination – *auspicium* (traditionally: omen) in the sense of "sign" – for accidentally overheard spoken or sung words which are translated into the listener's context and understood as a personal message from God. For biblical events, persons or objects that have a hidden meaning, Gregory uses the term "archetype (*tipus*)" or the verb "prefigure (*figurare*)".[27] For Gregory, then, a "sign" is either a concealed verbal message or a visible phenomenon which he regards as a manifestation of an invisible spiritual reality. Its essence is that of an appearance that simultaneously conceals and reveals.

In what follows, we shall be examining what Gregory tells us about the manner in which, for him and his contemporaries, the spoken and the written word functioned and interacted. And we will find that, in his stories, the secular and the religious spheres manifest completely different attitudes toward texts: respectively a distanced, critical one and a meditative,

---

[20] Discussed in: NIDNTT vol. 2 (Grand Rapids 1976), pp. 620–635.

[21] As H.C. Kee, *Miracle in the Early Christian World* (London 1983), pp. 146–241.

[22] J. Coleman, *Ancient and Medieval Memories* (Cambridge 1992), p. 84.

[23] Augustinus, *De doctrina christiana* [*Doctr.*] 2.16.23, ed. J. Martin, *Aurelii Augustini opera* 4.1, CCSL 32.4.1 (Turnhout 1962).

[24] As J.A. Mazzeo, *Renaissance and Seventeenth-Century Studies* (New York–London 1964), pp. 1–28, especially pp. 10–11.

[25] As in *Virt. Mart.* 1.*prol.*.

[26] On this, see G. de Nie, *Views from a Many-Windowed Tower*, Studies in Classical Antiquity 7 (Amsterdam 1987), pp. 27–69.

[27] Respectively in: *Hist.* 1.1 and 5.43.

participative one, but also that – somewhat surprisingly perhaps – these two attitudes can coexist in one and the same person. It will become evident that my separate treatment of "human words" and "God's Word" has to do with the same distinction as that made by Augustine between conventional human language and the interior, unspoken divine "word" through which mankind learns the truth.[28] In the last section we shall see that for Gregory, the word – however powerful – ultimately yields precedence to the non-verbal "sign".

I. Human words: "chatter", charters and tax registers

In his rapid synopsis of biblical history, Gregory has the following to say about man's attempt to build a tower that would reach into heaven:

> [...] God confounded them through their vain and empty thought and language (*vana cogitatione simul et lingua*), and dispersed them into all the countries of the wide world. The name of the city was Babel, that is confusion (*confusio*), because God had confounded their languages there.[29]

Human thought and language by itself, then, is vain, idle – in fact: "empty" – and can lead only to confusion and dispersion. Elsewhere, Gregory compares what he designates as the "invented stories (*fabularum commenta*)" of the classical Roman authors with a house built on sand that will be washed away when a storm comes.[30]

But "empty" human words – as will become evident later, the adjective is not an arbitrary one – can also do a great deal of damage. Whenever he gets an opportunity, Gregory vents his wrath on the Arian heretics who attacked the Catholic dogma of the indivisible and equal Trinity, and who could not be convinced otherwise by any verbal argument. Words alone are not sufficient; the only thing that can convince is a miracle such as the following one, that proves the truth of the Catholic position. During the mass of thanks after the lifting of the Arian Visigoths' siege of the city of Bazas, for instance, the celebrating priest saw three drops of liquid – of equal size, clearness and crystalline brightness – fall as it were from the roof above the

[28] Mazzeo, *Studies*, p. 16.
[29] *Hist.* 1.6; cf. Genesis 11:1–9.
[30] *Glor. mart. prol.*; cf. Matthew 7:26.

altar. Caught in a silver bowl, they coagulated at once and, as Gregory says, "made as it were (*quasi*) one most beautiful jewel". He continues:

> It is obvious that this happened to contradict the wicked heresy, hateful to God, that proliferated like a weed in that time. And [thereby] it proved that the holy Trinity, united in one equality of omnipotence, cannot be separated by any chatter (*nullis garrulationibus*).[31]

Here what would seem to us to be the result of a leaking roof is perceived – because of the sacred space and the critical moment – as a non-verbal, visible and divine sign that confounds human words and is itself irrefutable. As Gregory elsewhere says, with grim satisfaction, about an ordeal with the same result: "[...] and that was the end of the dispute".[32]

Nevertheless, he was able to admire the beauty of human words. Although Augustine, in his treatise on Christian doctrine, had legitimized the use of the pagan principles of rhetoric by Christian preachers,[33] Gregory's mother had chosen to let her son be educated only in Christian literature.[34] Quotations and reminiscences of classical Roman authors in Gregory's writings indicate, however, that he must have made himself acquainted with these later. We find too that he much admired others' literary qualities, for instance those of his friend and client, the originally Italian professional poet Venantius Fortunatus, whom he encouraged to collect and publish his poems.[35] A few references in the latter's work appear to indicate that Gregory tried his hand at poetry himself.[36] In the course of his writing, however, Gregory appears to have become convinced that, as he says, his succinct and less decorated language, close to that which was spoken, was more suitable for the proclamation of God's deeds to all layers of the population than the swollen rhetoric of contemporary orators.[37]

---

31 *Glor. mart.* 12.

32 *Glor. mart.* 80.

33 *Doctr.* 2.42.63.

34 *Vit. patr.* 2.2.

35 Venantius Fortunatus, *Carmina* [*Carm.*] 1. *praefatio*, ed. F. Leo, MGH Auctores Antiquissimi [AA] 4.1 (Berlin 1881).

36 *Carm.* 5.8b.1 and 8.19.2.

37 *Virt. Mart.* 2.19.

But the capable bishop of the diocese of Tours[38] certainly did not regard all human words either as idle chatter or as frivolous invention. As we saw, government in this period, especially that involving time-lags and large territories, made use of written documents that could be inspected and authenticated. How important a document, a charter for instance, could be in this society is evident in Gregory's story about the priest Anastasius.[39] Rather than hand over the deed of sale for his property and thereby leave his family in poverty, he let a greedy bishop bury him alive in a sarcophagus on top of the decomposing corpse of an old man!

And when a rebellion of the nuns in the convent of Poitiers needed to be quenched, Gregory tells us that he read to its ringleader Chrodichild preceptive letters of the foundress and of an episcopal council which had been deposited in the church archives of Tours.[40] But he also does not hide the fact that the furious former Frankish princess was unimpressed by these. For, although these letters prescribed excommunication for those disobeying the abbess or leaving the convent, she went on to seek support from her royal relatives instead. Nevertheless, although she subsequently organized robbery, murder and arson in and around the convent, this did not preclude her appreciating the *practical* value of written documents as proofs of ownership: she seized the convent's deeds of property and refused to hand them over to the ecclesiastical authorities. And when she found that the bishops' judgement on the matter was not in her favour, she withdrew permanently to a country estate given to her by her relatives. In these events we see the tensions between, on the one hand, the new forms of religious life, embedded in an administrative culture founded upon obligations recorded in written documents and, on the other, the orality of the traditional Frankish kinship system.[41]

Now and then, Gregory lets us see how the surviving administrative tradition based upon writing functioned at the Merovingian court. During his

---

[38] L. Pietri, *La ville de Tours du IVe au VIe siècle: naissance d'une cité chrétienne* (Rome 1983), pp. 246–334, gives a detailed biography of the bishop based upon the material contained in his writings.

[39] *Hist.* 4.12.

[40] *Hist.* 9.39–42. See on this and the issues involved: G. Schreibelreiter, "Königstöchter im Kloster. Radegund (ob. 587) und der Nonnenaufstand von Poitiers (589)", *Mitteilungen des Instituts für Österreichische Geschichtsforschung* [*MIÖG*] 87 (1979), pp. 1–37.

[41] See on the latter: S.F. Wemple, *Women in Frankish Society* (Philadelphia 1981), pp. 51–70, 149–58.

trial for treason at the court of King Childebert, Bishop Aegidius of Reims denied having once received an estate from the king's brother and enemy, King Chilperic; to prove this, he presented King Childebert with what appeared to be a charter from the king himself, granting him the estate.[42] When the latter denied having given this, the former *referendarius* or head of the chancery at the time of the purported charter was called in to authenticate the document. The latter looked at what appeared to be his signature and declared it to be a fake. After this, other letters were read to the assembled company: letters from Aegidius to King Chilperic containing much scurrilous talk about the King Childebert's influential mother Brunhild, as well as letters from Chilperic to the bishop with similar content. When Aegidius denied having written or received these, one of his servants was found to have a register of his outgoing and incoming correspondence in which these letters were referred to – so that no one could doubt any longer that they were authentic. After all this and other incriminating evidence, the bishop was accordingly deposed and exiled.

In a similar case, the trial for treachery of Bishop Praetextatus of Rouen, it is the king – here, Chilperic – who tampers with documents, this time: those of the Church.[43] In the collection of ecclesiastical canons which he presented the collected bishops at the crucial moment, he had (according to Gregory) slipped in one of his own invention, with which he hoped to achieve his purposes with the accused. The story does not make clear whether anyone actually dared to tell him so publicly or not. Notwithstanding Gregory's insistence that the affair should be conducted "according to the canons", he was not able to prevent the royal manipulation that finally led to the condemnation and deposition of the bishop. This story shows that the written word could be scrutinized as a source of authority, but that it could nevertheless be the current constellation of political power that decided a case.

Elsewhere, Gregory tells us how an unscrupulous but very well educated former slave manipulated written culture as well as oral social forms to his own advantage.[44] Andarchius, after he had worked his way up in royal service, tried to force his way into a marriage to a wealthy young lady in Clermont by contriving to draw up a false document of affiancement in the following, very devious, manner. While both parties were at court to be

---

[42] *Hist.* 9.19.
[43] *Hist.* 5.18.
[44] *Hist.* 4.46.

heard by the king, Andarchius placed witnesses who could only hear but not see the action near someone who had the same name as the bride's father – Ursus – swearing an oath that if he did not give his daughter to Andarchius in marriage, he would return the 16,000 solidi which Andarchius (falsely) claimed he had already given to him as a bride-price. After this ceremony, Andarchius sent his future bride's father away from court with deceitfully friendly words, before their case had been heard by the king. As soon as Ursus had gone, Andarchius used the testimony of the "witnesses" to have an official document drawn up, and presented it to the king. According to the practice customary in these times, this resulted in his receiving a royal charter ordering the young lady to be given to him in marriage or the bride price to be returned. When Ursus heard that the document had been presented to the local authorities in Clermont, he fled to another region. Andarchius was thereupon awarded all Ursus' properties as compensation for his supposed loss of the ante-nuptial payment to the family. Some time after this, however, while he lay in a drunken sleep in one of Ursus' villa's, the former owner's loyal servants set it afire, and he perished in the flames. Ursus thereupon sought asylum in a church. Through his gifts to the king – and, one suspects, through episcopal diplomacy – his properties were finally restored to him. Here, again, a document itself (fortunately in this case) does not have the last word, but – as so often in Gregory's stories – first, brute violence and, ultimately, civilised diplomacy based upon an invisible, just punishing power.

What we see, then, is that Gregory could examine written texts with a cool and sharp eye, and that he was well aware of how they could be manipulated and abused. The same is evident in his answer to the tax collectors who arrived in the city of Tours in 589, with a register containing, as they said, the taxes collected in this region under previous kings.[45] Gregory reminds them that the former King Clothar as well as his successor King Charibert had thrown the royal tax registers into the fire out of respect for St Martin, and that they had both given an oath of perpetual tax immunity to the region from that time. After this, taxes had never been collected there. The roll they showed him, then, could not possibly derive from the royal treasury, as they claimed. He would not be surprised, he says, if the roll they were holding was a copy which someone had kept in his house out of enmity against the city. Moreover, Gregory warned, the collectors should also take care not to

---

[45] *Hist.* 9.30.

act against the royal oaths. And thereupon he hits them with this other dimension; he says to the men: "God will execute his judgement upon (*Iudica[b]it enim Deus*) those who, in order to rob our citizens, bring forward this book after such a long time!" And while this was happening, he tells us, the son of one of the collectors fell ill; he died two days later. After this, Gregory sent a messenger to the king to ask for his instructions concerning the matter. The latter immediately sent an order waiving all taxes for the city out of reverence for St Martin.

Here, again, a document does not decide the case. Gregory's spirited spoken words, bringing the past into the present, carry the day. Speaking of the practical uses of history ...! The content of the spoken word, too, is more impressive than that of the written document. For the almost certainly orally executed royal oaths in the past, and Gregory's present public statement – difficult to classify but coming close to a curse – both call upon an invisible punishing power. The spoken word here prevails, however, only because it is linked to another, more powerful reality. And the latter is probably the greatest difference between Gregory's assessment of the possibilities of the word and our modern, secular one.

This difference appears unmistakably in the criteria which Gregory gives for the reliability of oral testimony to biographical, historical facts:

> I believe that [Abbot Aredius] was not mistaken about this because, at the time that he told me these things, God illumined the eyes of the blind through him, and let the lame walk, and, by the putting to flight of the demons, restored the possessed to their healthy mind. Nor can it be believed that he could be darkened by the cloud of falsehood (*eum mendacii nube obumbrari posse*), since God often in such a manner protected him from a cloud of pelting rain (*ab imbrium nube obtectum [...] protexit*) that, while his companions were drenched, he himself was not moistened by an infusion of the falling drops.[46]

Truth, then, is guaranteed by the connection with the other – invisible – reality, and the latter can "speak", just as in the Bible, in "figures" or signs: events that are visible analogies of spiritual truths.

[46] *Vit. patr.* 17. *prol.*

II. God's words: "the seeds of eternal life"

But if human words, in themselves, are "empty", how can they – in Gregory's view – connect, or become filled, with divine "reality" or "power"? The answer the bishop gives is in essence: by becoming part of God's "speaking" to mankind. The various ways in which Gregory shows God speaking are best described in two (necessarily artificial) divisions of the material: situations which appear to be wholly oral, and those in which a written text is at hand.

A. In the physical absence of a written text

When the count of Clermont arrested, without good reason, one of Bishop Quintianus' relatives, and did not respond to his requests for an audience and a release, the aged bishop let himself be carried to the count's house. There, he shook the dust of his shoes against it and said:

> "Let this house be cursed (*maledicta*), and cursed its inhabitants through the ages; let it be deserted and let there be no one living there!" And all the people said, "Amen".[47]

As soon as the bishop had left, the people in the house started becoming ill, and many died. When the count saw that he would soon have no one left, he went to the bishop, prostrated himself at the latter's feet with tears, and requested forgiveness. The request was granted, and he was given some blessed water: when this was sprinkled the walls of his house, the illness ceased.

This bishop's deed and words are modelled upon Christ's instruction to his disciples to shake the dust of their shoes against the houses that will not receive them:[48] for the count had not listened to his words and had not received him. The context indicates that Quintianus does not execute the punishment himself; but that with his words he invokes the punishing power of God. His phrasing is reminiscent of Christ's curse of the unfruitful fig tree.[49] And so what looked like a completely oral event was in fact shaped by the memory of internalized passages in the Bible.[50]

---

[47] *Vit. patr.* 4.3.
[48] Matthew 10:14.
[49] Matthew 21:19.
[50] Cf. Aune, "Magic", pp. 1551–7.

Spoken words could also effect the opposite, however: a cure. Often the central word was the holy name of Christ.[51] For the monk-priest Julian, for instance,

> it was easy to cure the possessed, illuminate the blind and repel the other diseases through the invocation of the Lord's name and the sign of the Cross. [....] I once saw him cure a possessed person in the church of the blessed martyr Julian by means of a word alone (*verbo tantum*).[52]

The latter formulation is reminiscent of the Gospel of Matthew's saying about Christ: "and he drove out the spirits with his word and cured all those who were ill".[53] Elsewhere, Gregory quotes other words of Christ which are turned into practice here: "All things that you ask in my name, believe that you will receive them and they will come to you".[54]

Similarly, Gregory tells us that his hero, the Frankish king Clovis, won the battle against the Alemanni "by calling upon the name of Christ": for "when he had said these things, the Alemanni turned around and began to flee".[55] And elsewhere, Gregory exhibits his unlimited confidence in the power of the divine names by stating that, in contrast with an Arian heretic, the Catholic faithful cannot be harmed by poison in the Eucharistic wine:

> We, however, who confess the Trinity as equal, as one in substance and omnipotence – even if we should drink deadly poison in the name of the Father, the Son and the Holy Ghost, the true and imperishable God, it would not hurt us.[56]

But calling upon the name of a holy man, too, can produce results. After his chains had already fallen off him once through the prayers of a bishop, the innocently accused priest Wiliacharius again stood fettered in front of the king:

> But through his calling upon the name (*invocato nomine*) of our oft-mentioned patron [St Martin], all the iron on him broke apart into little pieces in such a way that you would have thought it was potter's clay. [Therefore his being

---

[51] *Ibid.*, pp. 1545–9.
[52] *Hist.* 4.32.
[53] Matthew 8:16.
[54] *Glor. mart.* 6; Mark 11:24.
[55] *Hist.* 2.30.
[56] *Hist.* 3.31; cf. Mark 16:18, Romans 1:23.

chained again] in the meantime only happened so that he would not be released from chains until he had invoked that most sacred name (*quoadusque nomen illud sacratissimum invocasset*): when he had invoked it, everything dissolved.[57]

Immediately after the sounding of the name, the miracle happens. This coicidence may point to magical element in this event.[58]

But Christian liturgy, too, may have been a model. In it, of course, verbal formulae, and especially the eucharistic one, were means to a connection with spiritual reality. This is evident in Gregory's words to the assembled people when, during a ceremonial translation of relics, a sudden, blinding flash of light terrified everyone. He told them:

> "Don't be afraid! For what you see is the power (*virtus*) of the saints. Remember the book on the *Life of the blessed Martin* and recall how, when he recited the sacred words (*verba sacrata promenti*) [of the Eucharistic prayer], a sphere of fire was seen to come out of his head and rise to heaven. [59] So don't be frightened but believe that he has come to visit us together with his holy relics."[60]

The strange and terrifying fiery light, then, is "domesticized" as a visualization – or sign – of Martin's "power" or holiness, as it had once been seen to rise to heaven with or through his pronouncing "sacred words". In this situation of crisis, too, a text – this time a saint's life – is the model for a collective interpretation that removes the agitation. But it is also clear that, notwithstanding the central importance of a written text, we cannot get around the equally decisive role of the visible sign.

A request for help usually takes the form of a prayer. Gregory tells us and often lets us see that the prayers of the just – the saints – are heard and granted.[61] This is why it was useful to enlist the help of the saints as mediators between God and ordinary sinners. No doubt with Christ's saying

---

[57] *Virt. Mart.* 1.23.

[58] As Aune, "Magic", p. 1551.

[59] Sulpicius Severus, *Dialogi* 2.2.1–2, ed. C. Halm, Corpus Scriptorum Ecclesiasticorum Latinorum [CSEL] 1 (Vienna 1866).

[60] *Glor. conf.* 20.

[61] In *Hist.* 2.34, for instance.

"All that you shall ask in faith through prayer, you shall receive"[62] in mind, Gregory shows that sustained praying – and even outright pressure, for instance through a hunger strike[63] – is an effective means of being heard. Something similar happened, as Gregory tells it, when the Frankish kings besieged Saragossa. All the citizens turned with such humility to God that they wore hair shirts, fasted, and prayed; in addition, they carried the mantle of St Vincent, their patron saint, along the top of the city ramparts with psalm-singing. By this,

> the city to such an extent placed all its hope in the compassion of the Lord that one would say that the fasting of the Ninevites was [again] being celebrated there, and would presume that the only thing that could possibly happen *(nec aestimaretur aliud posse fieri*) would be that the divine compassion would be moved by their prayers.[64]

When the besiegers – after they had initially thought that the procession on the walls was "some kind of magic" – heard that it was the mantle of St Vincent that was being carried in procession, and that he had been called upon to intercede with the Lord for help, they became afraid and lifted the siege. And thus the city was saved.

Whether all this actually happened as described or not is, for our purpose here, not important. What does matter is that we know from Gregory's stories that St Vincent was also venerated in Frankish Gaul, and will thus have been regarded as "powerful".[65] Gregory here wants to show his readers how, in his view, the spiritual reality can be spurred into action: ritual penitence (effecting the purification from sins), extreme self-humiliation and sustained praying are presented more often as recognizable – and thus, for enemies, potentially fear-inspiring – ways of invoking God's help and getting it.[66]

As often happens in the Bible, however, man can also become a mouthpiece for God without knowing it. Augustine's interpreting the words of a children's song overheard at a critical moment in his life as a divine command addressed to him[67] is a well-known example of a manner of

---

[62] Matthew 21:22.
[63] *Glor. mart.* 13.
[64] *Hist.* 3.29.
[65] *Glor. mart.* 89.
[66] As, for instance, also in *Hist.* 9.21.
[67] Augustinus, *Confessiones* 8.12, ed. L. Verheijen, CCSL 27 (Turnhout 1981).

thinking that is also present in Gregory's stories. When King Clovis was on his way to south-western France to fight the Arian Visigoths, he sent a messenger ahead to the church of St Martin, saying: "Go, and perhaps you will receive a sign of victory (*victoriae auspicium*) in the holy church".[68] He added a prayer to the Lord to deign "to reveal" something upon [the envoys'] entering the church of St Martin. When the messengers entered the church and heard Psalm 18:40–1 being sung – in which enemies are put to flight – they thanked the Lord and promised gifts to St Martin. The subsequent events proved the truth of the prophecy.

We come closer to God's spoken word in the following. The beautifully formulated religious content of inspired sermons, such as those of Bishop Sidonius Apollinaris of Clermont, our author says, seemed to have been formulated by an angel, not a human being.[69] In a longer story about this bishop, however, Gregory lets God himself speak in two different ways.[70] When the bishop lay dying, and the people of Clermont, gathered around him, wept and asked who would now lead them,

> the bishop at last answered, while the Holy Spirit flowed into him (*spiritu in se sancto influente*),
>
> "Don't be afraid, O people! For behold, my brother Aprunculus lives, and he will be your bishop!"
>
> The people, however, did not understand him, and thought he said something in a trance (*eum loqui aliquid in extasi*).

For Aprunculus was then still bishop of another city, which was under the domination of the Arian Visigoths. Because he was thereafter driven into exile, he was able, as Gregory writes: "according to the word of the Lord, which he placed in the mouth of the holy Sidonius (*iuxta verbum Domini quod posuit in ore sancti Sidonii*), [to become] the eleventh bishop." Here, then, God's words appear in the speaking of a human being, and they bring consolation as well as prophecy.

Further in the same story, however, God's words kill instantly. After Sidonius' death, an unworthy priest seized the episcopal administration. During the celebratory banquet with the city's notables, however, the cupbearer told him a dream which he had had the preceding night. In it, the dead

---

[68] *Hist*. 2.37.
[69] *Hist*. 2.22.
[70] *Hist*. 2.23.

Sidonius accused the priest of his crime before the heavenly Judge, and the latter ordered the cup-bearer, being acquainted with the accused, to bring the court's summons to him. Gregory lets the cup-bearer repeat the Judge's own terrifying words:

> "'Don't be afraid, lad, but go and tell that priest: "Come to answer for yourself in your case, because Sidonius has requested you to be summoned."'
>
> So don't delay in going there, because the King ordered me to say these things with a great sanction, saying: "If you say nothing, you will die a miserable death!"'
>
> When [the cup-bearer] had said this, the priest was terrified, let the cup fall from his hand and died immediately; he was carried as a dead man from where he fell and was buried, to inhabit hell with his accomplice. Such a judgement did the Lord bring forth upon contumacious clerics in this world [...].

All this is supposed to have happened a hundred years earlier in Gregory's native city. It seems extremely unlikely that an oral tradition would preserve this story *verbatim*. Gregory is a literary artist. With this story, he wants to show how the irresistible power of God's *ipsissima verba* can reach and affect men. Here, this happens through a dream in which the manner of God's judgement and punishment of a crime would have been recognizable to Franco-Gallic society.

In a last example, Gregory shows us – not without irony – how one should *not* proceed if one wants to ask God something. The already-mentioned King Chilperic was, for his time, a well-educated man. Gregory tells us, disdainfully, that he added letters to the alphabet, and wrote not only poetry but also an eccentric treatise on the Trinity.[71] When this king wanted to know whether St Martin would permit him to have someone who had sought asylum in his church, and whom the king suspected of the murder of his son, taken out of there with violence, he sent a deacon with an actual written letter containing this question to the saint's tomb in Tours.[72] The king's letter was put upon the tomb with a blank page next to it for the saint's answer. Gregory dryly tells us what happened: "And when, after three days, he received nothing in writing (*nihil rescripti*), he returned to Chilperic." The king thereupon took other measures. One wonders whether this crafty king had believed in what was doing, or whether he had

---

[71] *Hist.* 5.44.
[72] *Hist.* 5.14.

attempted to seduce Gregory into a hoax which could then be unmasked. Gregory, who – as is evident in all his stories – took the Gospel verse "everything is possible to him who believes" literally,[73] seems to have awaited the outcome of events. Believing, as we saw, that there is writing in heaven, and that (as he tells us elsewhere) a voice can speak directly out of heaven,[74] could not a letter descend in a similar way? Bishop Caesarius of Arles (502–42), in one of his sermons to the people, had said: "... the divine Scriptures are as it were letters sent to us from our [heavenly] fatherland".[75]

The story of the hermit Patroclus, however, shows how something like this did, in fact, almost happen.[76] The latter asked God's will concerning him: should he remain among the people to serve them, or should he retire into the wilderness? To find an answer,

> he placed two pages with writing on the altar as an oracle (*pro auspicio*), and kept vigils for three nights, praying that the Lord would deign to show him most clearly what he commanded him to do. But the sublime compassion of the divine Benevolence, whose foreknowledge had decreed that he should be a hermit, commanded him to take the note that would make him hasten to the wilderness.

The random picking up of notes resembles the tossing of sticks (*sortes*), a pagan manner of divination which was still being practised in Gregory's time.[77] Viewed from the Christian tradition, however, one could regard Patroclus' deed as the written equivalent of the dream, in which an angel or a saint gives oral advice, of which Gregory gives many examples.[78] Significantly, here again, the unexpressed premise is that "truth" or the right decision should be sought *outside* everyday consciousness and the practical sphere.

B. With a text physically present

The words which Augustine heard ordered him, he thought, to open the Bible, read the first words that caught his eye, and regard these as a personal

---

[73] Mark 9:22; as in *Hist.* 2.24.
[74] *Hist.* 2.24.
[75] *Serm.* 7.2.
[76] *Vit. patr.* 9.2.
[77] *Virt. Jul.* 45.
[78] On these, see: de Nie, *Views*, pp. 251–287.

message to him from God. This is a Christian version of the older so-called Vergilian oracle.[79] Gregory castigates the consultation of soothsayers,[80] but lets us see a number of times that opening up and reading the Bible in this manner with urgent questions in mind can yield prophetic "answers" which are subsequently confirmed by events.[81]

In such a case, the biblical event, words of advice, and/or metaphors needed to be understood so as to fit the current situation in one way or another. In the New Testament, of course, we find a similar understanding of its own situation in terms of Old Testament events and prophecies. Augustine's already-mentioned treatise about Christian doctrine shows that the kind of reading that looked through the surface or literal text to deeper, figural meanings had become dominant in the late antique Church.[82] Gregory refers to this manner of reading the biblical text – which he elsewhere designates as "spiritual understanding (*spiritalis intellegentia*)"[83] – when he begins his story about the conversion of Jews in Clermont by saying that Bishop Avitus

> had already exhorted them frequently to lay off the veil (*velamen*) of the Mosaic law so that they might understand what they read spiritually (*spiritaliter lecta intellegerent*), and might contemplate Christ, the Son of the living God, promised by the prophetic and legal authority, with a most pure heart in the sacred letters (*corde purissimo in sacris litteris contemplarent*).[84]

If we take Gregory's formulation here seriously, this is a twofold process. First, one understands the words read "spiritually", that is, as metaphors or parables of divine messages or truth. Thereupon or simultaneously, one "contemplates with a most pure heart" Christ as present "in the sacred letters". It looks as though Gregory is saying that Christ is present in these not only in a metaphorical sense but also as a real, actual presence – as

---

[79] D. Harmening, *Superstitio. Überlieferungs- und theoriegeschichtliche Untersuchungen zur kirchlich-theologischen Aberglaubensliteratur des Mittelalters* (Berlin 1979), p. 193.

[80] Cf. 1 Samuel 28:3.

[81] As in *Hist.* 4.16.

[82] Cf. G.B. Ladner, "Medieval and modern understanding of symbolism: a comparison", *Speculum* 54 (1979), pp. 223–33.

[83] Gregorius Turonensis, *In psalterii tractatum commentarius. praefatio*, ed. B. Krusch, MGH SSrM 1.2 (Hannover 1885).

[84] *Hist.* 5.11.

Augustine had also believed.[85] Approaching a sacred text in this manner was thus a conscious move into a receptivity that did not distance and relativize, but opened up affectively and synthesized associatively.[86] This is also evident in Pope Gregory the Great's comparison of his own concentric, associative ruminations about the text of the book of Job to the meanderings of a river.[87]

Our Gregory also gives this state of mind a name. Because two bishops with a history of profligacy would not be able to keep up their state of penitence for very long, he says, sarcastically,

> it seemed as though they would never stop singing psalms, celebrating fasts, giving alms, working through the book of David's songs completely during the day, and spending the nights meditating upon hymns and readings (*in hymnis ac lectionibus meditando*).[88]

In the preface to his book of St Julian's miracles we seem to see something of the effect which he hoped that this meditation through singing would have. He says there:

> Somehow (*quoddammodo*), the divine Benevolence lights a large spark [of desire] in us to enter into the path of righteousness when He says: "The eyes of the Lord are upon the righteous, and his ears to their prayers".[89] This shows that whoever loves righteousness with his whole heart will be heard by the Lord when he prays.
>
> O let it happen that each one of us, when he begins to sing this [verse], at once [*statim*] spurns the scandals of the world, turns away from empty desires, leaves behind perverse ways, and tries to enter the path of righteousness quickly and unencumbered by worldly concerns![90]

What is this "somehow", this manner in which the word of God lights a spark in the heart? Elsewhere, Gregory uses another image, from the New Testament, and says:

---

[85] Coleman, *Memories*, p. 100.

[86] Cf. Ladner, "Symbolism", pp. 225, 230.

[87] Gregorius Magnus, *Moralia in Job, Epistola dedicatoria* 2, ed. R. Gillett, tr. A. de Gaudemaris, Sources chrétiennes [SC] 32bis (Paris 1975).

[88] *Hist.* 5.20.

[89] Psalm 33 (34):16.

[90] *Virt. Jul. prol.*

> Among the seeds of eternal life (*vitae perpetuae semina*) which, in the field of the uneducated mind, the heavenly Sower waters from the Fount of Divinity with his precept and causes to sprout with his teaching (*dogmate fecundavit*), is that in which He says [...]."[91]

God's word, then, is something like a husked seed which will germinate and yield its hidden eternal life when received and processed in the right manner.[92] When these words are read more happens than just the recognizing of their referent. The "holy reading (*sacra lectio*)", as Gregory also calls the Bible[93] – in the sense of the text itself, but, it seems to me, possibly also in the sense of the activity of reading it – is in some way an encounter with divine reality.

For John the apostle had reported Christ as saying the following: "The words I which I speak to you I do not speak from myself, but the Father who is in me himself does his works".[94] In Augustine's view, a development of this New Testament one, the human word became the vehicle of the divine Word through the incarnation of the latter in the God-man, Christ.[95] What Gregory says, in the prologue to *The glory of the martyrs*, about his own human words about miracles seems to be a continuation of Augustine's view:

> [...] it behooves us to seek, write and speak of those things which build up the Church and which, through holy instruction, cause barren minds to become fruitful in the knowledge of perfect faith *(quae mentes inopes ad notitiam perfectae fidei instructione sancta fecundent*). [....] *That is why* [italics added] (*Unde*) John the Evangelist began by saying "In the beginning was the Word, and the Word was with God, and God was the Word. This [Word] was in the beginning with God. All things were made by Him, and without him nothing was made". And thereafter he said: "And the Word was made flesh and lived among us, full of grace and truth, and we saw his glory, glory as that of the only Son from the Father [....]"[96] [....] He is the salvation of the world.[97]

---

[91] *Vit. patr*. 2. *prol.*

[92] Cf. Matthew 13:18– 9, 23.

[93] *Vit. patr*. 8. *prol.*

[94] John 14:10.

[95] M. Colish, *The Mirror of Language. A Study in the Medieval Theory of Knowledge*, revised edition (Lincoln–London 1983), p. 26.

[96] John 1:1–3, 14.

[97] *Glor. mart. prol.*

What Gregory appears to be saying in this elliptic passage is that the creative power of the Word – and thus also of Christ, the incarnated Word – is immanent, perhaps as a sort of seed, in his own human words about miracles. For miracles, as he elsewhere lets a holy man say, are themselves the forms and signs of Christ's continued creative power through his servants.[98] In and through these words about miracles, then, the glory of God's creative power is made visible.

As Gregory in his own way probably realised, and modern reception theory also indicates, the reader's mentally visualizing words about such miracles is an experiencing of these events as present realities or "re-enactment".[99] Seeing images of miraculous recreations, therefore, means experiencing something of this creative action in oneself. I would suggest that it is this experience, with the conviction it generates, that Gregory designates as the manner in which he thinks his words would be able to make barren minds fruitful in faith.[100] How fruitful indeed such a reading could be is evident in his reports of liturgical readings of miracle stories (not improbably sometimes his own) precipitate sudden cures among the listeners.[101] Such cures could also occur at other moments in the liturgy – perhaps (in Gregory's view) through the sounding of the "sacred words".[102]

For our author, then, words about the holy content of the faith – even when apprehended visually through written signs on a page – are definitely not something to be inspected and manipulated in a distanced manner. As carriers of the Other Reality, they are meditatively absorbed. "In the sacred letters" Christ himself, present as the creative Word, is internalized[103] or perhaps even "seen". That Gregory was not the only one to experience this is evident in an illustration in the Utrecht Psalter some centuries later. In it, we see a church gathering sitting around two opened books (the Old and the New Testaments?) that may have represented Christ as the presider of the meeting.[104]

---

[98] *Hist.* 6.6.

[99] P. Ricoeur, *Time and Narrative*, vol. 3, tr. K. Blamey and D. Pellauer (Chicago–London 1988), pp. 142–92, esp. 144.

[100] Cf. Augustinus, *In Johannis Evangelium Tractatus* 1.8–9, ed. and tr. M.-F Berrouard, Bibliothèque Augustinienne, Oeuvres de St Augustine 71 (Paris 1969).

[101] As, for instance, in *Virt. Mart.* 2.14.

[102] As in *Virt. Mart.* 3.19.

[103] Coleman, *Memories*, p. 87.

[104] Fol. 90v (reference in P. Dinzelbacher, "Die Bedeutung des Buches im Zeitalter des hl. Liudger", in: A. van Berkum *et al.* [ed.], *Liudger 742–809* [Dieren 1984] p. 53, n. 121).

C. The touching of written words

Although the spoken word and the sign of the Cross are involved in many of the cures which Gregory relates, we saw in the story of the blind deacon that making contact with a holy object could also be decisive. Gregory tells us that his father once recovered from an illness when, according to oral instructions which Gregory himself received in a dream, the name Joshua (an analogue to the name Jesus) had been written on sliver of wood and placed under his father's pillow.[105] This looks like name-magic – here through the contact with the written instead of the sounded word.[106]

Something more or less similar appears in a story about Bishop Nicetius of Lyon.[107] Gregory tells us there that, after the bishop's death, his signature functioned as a touch-oracle or ordeal – in a manner similar to saint's tombs. For a certain beggar had received a letter of recommendation from Nicetius which would help him receive alms at the houses of the faithful. After the bishop's death, the beggar was making good money through this letter, because everyone wanted to see the holy man's signature – indicating that it was already coming close to being regarded as a relic. When a certain Burgundian had robbed him in the forest of his money, however, the beggar went to the bishop to tell him what had happened, and the latter transmitted the information to the count of the city. Because the Burgundian refused to admit his guilt, he was ordered to swear to his innocence with his hand upon Nicetius' signature. As soon as he touched it, however, and before he had uttered a word, he fell over backwards, eyes closed and foaming at the mouth, and lay as though he were dead. After about two hours, he opened his eyes again and confessed to the crime. A holy man's signature, then – perhaps also because it made his holy name visible and palpable – was regarded as an object filled with his spiritual power, just as everything else which he had touched during his life.

We return now to the questions we asked in the beginning about the meaning of the expressions: "the power of the book", "the divine power that came forth out of it", and "the power of what is said". Another example of the power of a book is a story in Gregory's *Miracles of St Martin*, in which the book containing his *Life* survived a fire undamaged[108] – evidence of its being

---

[105] *Glor. conf.* 40.
[106] Cf. Harmening, *Superstitio*, p. 239.
[107] *Vit. patr.* 8.9.
[108] *Virt. Mart.* 3.42.

suffused with holiness or with holy power. For Gregory, these are two aspects of the same thing. That the touching of a holy book could effect a cure would seem to follow from this. But how and why have the written marks themselves become the vehicles of holy power? The saint himself has never touched them, and the book is not said to have been in contact with his tomb either. The explanation appears to be that, just as in the case of the written name Joshua, the written marks possess the power of that to which they refer. "The power of what is said" would then be the holy power operative in the miracles described; in Gregory's view, evidently, this power could also be transmitted by the words referring to it.

In other words, Gregory evidently regards *all spoken and written words in the religious context as participating in the realities to which they refer.* In his stories, however, we see that everything – from human thoughts up to and including the phenomena of the visible world – is power-laden; it is a view that recurs in other contemporary sources.[109] It was the notion of connecting with the divine power that effectuated a cure or its opposite, a curse. It seems to me that this notion must be connected with the meditative mode of perception described earlier. What we have seen is that these attitudes, although they have been observed to occur in contemporary oral cultures, are not necessarily limited to these. For it was even in the ostensibly restored, highly literate Roman Empire of the late fourth century that a well-educated and gifted literary artist, Sulpicius Severus, wrote the first western saint's life, replete with miracles: that of Martin of Tours.[110] A few decades later, the poet, lawyer, administrator and former imperial councillor Prudentius wrote meditative Christian hymns.[111] As adults both authors withdrew from the world into the monastic life.

III. From word to sign

We have seen that what might seem to be accidentally overheard words, but also passages "chanced upon" in the Bible and letters "accidentally" picked up, could be understood as divine "signs". And also that biblical events and

---

[109] See on this: A. Angenendt, "Die Liturgie und die Organisation des kirchlichen Lebens auf dem Lande", in: *Cristianizzazione ed organizzazione ecclesiastica delle campagne nell'alto medioevo: espansione e resistenze*, vol. 1, Settimane di Studio del Centro Italiano di Studi sull'alto Medioevo 28 (Spoleto 1982), pp. 169–226.

[110] Sulpicius Severus, *Vita sancti Martini*, ed. and tr. J. Fontaine, SC 133 (Paris 1967).

[111] Aurelius Prudentius, *Liber cathemerinon*, ed. and tr. H.J. Thomson, vol. 1, Loeb Library 387 (Cambridge, Mass. 1969), pp. 6–115.

metaphors could be interpreted as "signs" of hidden truths. In a dispute with a heretic envoy from Spain, Gregory lists the prefigurations of the Christian faith in the Old Testament.[112] They are the same ones that we meet with in early Christian art: Abraham's oak, Isaac and the ram, the stone of Jacob, and the breastplate of Aaron.[113] Such images of religious truths which could not be adequately verbalized dominate late antique Christian writing.[114] They were regarded meditatively,[115] rather than "thought", and experienced as symbols of a reality "present" in them.[116] In other words, through the meditative receptiveness of the late antique reader and observer, both verbal and visual images of religious symbols were experienced as participating in, and effectively as it were embodying, that which they represented.

Gregory's stories show too that truth was now primarily *seen*, and in a reality other than the everyday one, for instance in a dream. When a woman in Paris warned the citizens that there would be a fire, and they ridiculed her, saying that she had practised divination (*sortium praesagio diceret*), had dreamed some kind of nonsense, or that a demon had whispered it in her ear, she said: "It is not as you say. I speak the truth, for I saw in a dream [...]."[117] Likewise, for Gregory, the "truth" about the unsolved murder of King Chilperic becomes evident through dreams: one of the latter's brother King Guntram and the other of Gregory himself.[118]

Supersensory truth is most evident, however, in the visual aspect of the non-everyday *par excellence*: the miracle. Gregory lets us see that when words, even those of a cleric, cannot convince a heretic, a miracle, which is at the same time an ordeal, can decide the matter. The Catholic party says:

> "If the testimonies of our faith and of the Holy Scriptures do not move you to believe, then experience the power (*virtutem*) of the indivisible Trinity through its miracles (*miraculis*) [...]."[119]

Then, after the Catholic had invited the heretic to prove the truth of his view by picking up a ring from among glowing embers, and the man had refused,

---

[112] *Hist.* 5.43.
[113] Cf. Ladner, "Symbolism".
[114] A. Cameron, *Christianity and the Rhetoric of Empire* (Berkeley 1992), pp. 59–60.
[115] S. Spence, *Rhetorics of Reason and Desire* (Ithaca–London 1988), pp. 62, 67.
[116] Ladner, "Symbolism", p. 243.
[117] *Hist.* 8.33.
[118] *Hist.* 8.6.
[119] *Glor. conf.* 14.

the cleric did so without being burned. For "The Kingdom of God does not consist in speaking (*in sermone*), but in power (*in virtute*)":[120] Gregory does not say this, but he shows it happening.

In the prologue to his only biography of a woman,[121] which was one of the first of its kind in Gaul, Gregory makes his view of word and sign explicit:

> The extraordinary graces of the divine benefits which are granted in a heavenly manner to the human race, can neither be conceived by the consciousness, nor expressed through words, nor contained in writing (*nec sensu concipi, nec verbis effari, nec scripturis poterunt comprehendi*).

He then mentions the central facts of the coming of the Saviour and the salvation of the human race through his death and resurrection. Further graces, however, are now the dogma of the Church and the examples of the saints,

> such as now the blessed Monegund, who left her native region. Just as the prudent queen [of Sheba], who came to hear the wisdom (*audire sapientiam*) of Solomon,[122] she came to the church of the blessed Martin, so that she might gaze in wonder at his miracles (*miracula ... miraretur*), granted in daily moments [...].

It seems as though we see a transition here from *hearing sounded words of wisdom* to *gazing in wonder at miracles* – or, as Gregory often calls them, signs. For him, then, a sign is not – as in Augustine's thought – an arbitrary sound or written mark to represent the function of the word as such; it is an event or an image through which God wishes to say – or rather: show in a visible manner – something that cannot be adequately verbalized.

This view did not derive from an oral attitude brought about by a decline of written culture. Quite the contrary. Based upon a long written tradition which is, as it were, enveloped by an oral one in which meditative receptiveness is central, it is aware of the limitations of word and script in communicating the most essential dimensions in human experience.

---

120 1 Corinthians 4:20.
121 *Vit. patr.* 19. *prol.*
122 1 Kings 10:1–10.

XVI

Text, symbol and 'oral culture' in the sixth-century church: the miracle story[1]

Since a certain woman was suffering greatly through an invasion [i.e. possession] by the Enemy so that [her relatives] were scarcely able to bring the rebellious Foe to the saint, [St. Radegund] commanded the Adversary to prostrate himself with his fear on the pavement. Presently, throwing himself on the ground upon the words of the blessed lady, the one who had been feared was himself afraid. When the saint, full of faith, had trampled upon his neck, he came out [of the woman's body] by a ventral elimination.

Mulier quaedam dum inimici invasione graviter laboraret et vix ad sanctam potuissent hostem rebellem adducere, imperat adversario, ut se suo cum timore pavimento prosterneret. Mox ad beatae sermonem in terra se deiciens, qui timebatur extimuit. Cui sancta plena fide cum calcasset in cervice, fluxu ventris egressus est.[2]

The Enemy, Foe and Adversary are names for the Devil or his demons.[3] Exactly what is said to happen in this story is less clear, however. We are not told what the Devil looks like as - upon the command of St. Radegund (c.520-587) - 'he prostrated himself with his fear on the pavement': is he visible at all? Or is the body of the woman understood to be his present manifestation? When the saint 'trampled upon his neck', is a symbolical gesture made or is the woman's neck meant? Only then, as though he has been indeed still in the afflicted woman, does he 'leave' the latter in

---

1 I am grateful to the University of Utrecht for a year's leave of absence and to the Netherlands Institute for Advanced Study in Wassenaar for their hospitality to me as a member of an "Orality and literacy" research group during that year, in which the first version of this article was conceived and written.

2 Venantius Fortunatus, *Vita sanctae Radegundis* (*Vit. Rad.*) 71. Edition: B. Krusch in *Venanti Honori Clementiani Fortunati Opera pedestria*. Berlin 1885. Monumenta Germaniae Historica, Auctores antiquissimi 4, pars posterior. pp. 38-49. J.A. McNamara and J.E. Halborg have published an English translation of the Life in *Sainted Women of the Dark Ages*. Durham-London 1992. pp. 70-86. On Radegund's life see B. Brennan, 'St Radegund and the early development of her cult at Poitiers', *Journal of religious history* 13 (1983) pp. 340-354.

3 Occurring more often under these names; for instance in Fortunatus's *Vita sancti Germani* (ed. Krusch pp. 11-27) 52, 15 and 142 respectively. Cf. in general: *Santi e Demoni nell'alto medioevo occidentale*. 2 vols. (Settimane di studio del centro italiano di studi sull'alto medioevo 36) Spoleto 1989; here, especially: P. Dinzelbacher, 'Der Kampf der Heiligen mit den Dämonen', *Ibid.* vol. 1, pp. 681-682. For modern equivalents see: W. Sargant, *The Mind Possessed. A Physiology of Possession, Mysticism and Faith Healing*. Philadelphia-New York 1974.

another way and form, disguised but visible. It looks as though a series of symbolic acts have effected the cure.

Is this 'magic' - or 'religion'? Or should we step outside this misleading western dichotomy[4] and see the event from an anthropological viewpoint as a pre-verbal embodied enactment of metaphors or symbols that triggers emotional and physical transformation? If so, what is this pre-verbal ritual doing in and as a written text?

Texts: their use in society and the Church in sixth-century Gaul

The above-quoted three-sentence narrative is part of a saint's life in prose written in the second half of the sixth century by the professional poet, later priest and eventually bishop of Poitiers, Venantius Fortunatus.[5] Together with the latter's poems, his patron and friend Bishop Gregory of Tours' *Histories* and a number of letters and administrative documents, Fortunatus's and Gregory's saints' lives and miracle stories are among the relatively few written sources that survive from this troubled period in Gaul.[6]

---

4 As in D.E. Aune, 'Magic in early Christianity', in: W. Haase ed., *Aufstieg und Niedergang der römischen Welt* 2.23.2, Berlin 1980, pp. 1507-1557. In V.I.J. Flint, *The Rise of Magic in Early Medieval Europe* (Princeton 1990), most of early medieval religion is subsumed under the heading of 'magic', understood as a manipulation of unseen forces as a strategy of survival.

5 Fortunatus's prose Lives are collected in the edition of B. Krusch indicated in note 2. Besides the Lives of Radegund (from now on referred to as *Vit.Rad.*) and Germanus of Paris (*Vit.Germ.*), there are biographies of Albinus of Angers (*Vit.Alb.*)(pp. 27-33), Paternus of Avranches (*Vit.Pat.*)(pp. 33-37), Marcellus of Paris (*Vit.Marc.*)(pp. 49-54), and a Life as well as a separate list of miracles of Hilary of Poitiers (*Vit.Hil.*, *Virt.Hil.*)(pp. 1-7, 7-11).
On Fortunatus's life and career, see now J. George, *Venantius Fortunatus. A Poet in Merovingian Gaul.* Oxford 1992. pp. 4-34; further: B. Brennan, 'The career of Venantius Fortunatus', *Traditio* 41 (1985) pp. 49-78. On his Lives, R. Collins, 'Observations on the form, language and public of the prose biographies of Venantius Fortunatus in the hagiography of Merovingian Gaul', in: H.B. Clarke and M. Brennan ed., *Columbanus and Merovingian monasticism.* Oxford 1981. BAR series 114. pp. 105-131.

6 Venantius Fortunatus, *Carmina* (*Carm.*), in idem, *Opera poetica*, ed. F. Leo. Berlin 1881. Monumenta Germaniae Historica, Auctores antiquissimi 4, pars prior. The first volume of a new edition with a French translation has appeared: M. Reydellet ed., *Venance Fortunat. Poèmes*, vol. 1 (Paris 1994). Aspects of social history discernible in Fortunatus's poems are presented by George in her *Venantius Fortunatus* (see previous note).
Gregorius Turonensis, *Historiarum libri decem* (*Hist.*), ed. and transl. R. Buchner, 2 vols., Darmstadt 1967. Ausgewählte Quellen zur deutschen Geschichte des Mittelalters. Freiherr vom Stein-Gedächtnisausgabe 2, 3. Idem, *In gloria martyrum* (*Glor.mart.*), *De virtutibus sancti Juliani* (*Virt.Jul.*), *De virtutibus sancti Martini* (*Virt.Mart.*), *In gloria confessorum* (*Glor.conf.*). and *Vita patrum* (*Vit.patr.*), ed. B. Krusch, Hanno-

In 566, when Fortunatus arrived at the court of Clovis's grandson, King Sigebert, the former Roman province had been under Frankish domination for several generations. Roughly speaking, there were three strata of culture: that of the Gallo-Roman aristocracy, traditionally possessing an administrative as well as a classical literacy;[7] that of the Gallic rural population, through the former Roman government in touch with literacy but otherwise still living in primary orality;[8] and that of the Germanic newcomers from an oral society in contact with the literate late Roman one for centuries: their aristocracy and kings maintained their oral culture with its traditions while simultaneously, as Fortunatus's poems show, striving to emulate Roman culture.[9] One could add the then rapidly diminishing urban middle class population, including foreign merchants, which must have possessed varying degrees of pragmatic literacy.[10]

Even among those who could read and write, however, oral modes of conducting affairs tended to predominate:[11] Gallo-Roman aristocrats and educated Frankish ones read their (efforts at) poems aloud to each other as an important part of their practice

---

ver 1885, in: W. Arndt and B. Krusch ed., *Gregorii Turonensis opera*. Monumenta Germaniae Historica, Scriptores rerum Merovingicarum 1.2. pp. 451-820. A full biography of Gregory is found in L. Pietri, *La ville de Tours du IVe au VIe siècle*: naissance d'une cite chrétienne. Rome 1983. pp. 246-334. On the historical context see now I. Wood, *The Merovingian Kingdoms 450-751*. London-New York 1994.

7 On this subject see P. Riché, *Education et culture dans l'occident barbare*. VIe - VIIIe siècles. Paris 1962. Patristica Sorbonensia 4. pp. 220-290, and I. Wood, 'Administration, law and culture in Merovingian Gaul', in: R. McKitterick ed., *The uses of literacy in early mediaeval Europe*. Cambridge 1990. pp.63-81.

8 P. Riché, 'Croyances et pratiques populaires pendant le Haut Moyen Age', in: B. Plongeron and R. Pannet ed., *Le Christianisme populaire*. Les dossiers de l'histoire. Paris 1976. pp. 79-104, here p. 85.

9 Cf. on the Franks, generally: E. James, *The Franks*. Oxford 1988; on the up to now seriously underestimated contemporary oral culture: M. Richter, *The formation of the Medieval West. Studies in the Oral Culture of the Barbarians*. Dublin 1994. Passim. On Fortunatus and his contacts, P. Godman, *Poets and emperors*. Frankish politics and Carolingian poetry. Oxford 1987. pp. 1-37.

10 In the *explicit* of his *Passio sanctorum martyrum septem dormientium* (B. Krusch ed., in Arndt and Krusch, *Gregorius Turonensis opera, Pars* 2, pp. 848-853, Gregory says that a Syrian (merchant?) translated the Greek (?) original for him: *interpretante Iohanne Syro*. Cf. *Glor.mart*. 94.

11 Cf. H. Vollrath, 'Das Mittelalter in der Typik oralen Gesellschaft', *Historische Zeitschrift* 233 (1981) pp. 571-594, here p. 588, and especially Richter (n. 9), p. 44 and passim.
On the evidence of various uses of the spoken and written word in the writings of Gregory of Tours, see G. de Nie, 'De "kracht" van wat in het boek gezegd wordt: woord, schrift en teken in zesde-eeuws Gallië' (The 'power' of what is said in the book: word, script and sign in sixth-century Gaul), in: R.E.V. Stuip en C. Vellekoop eds., *Oraliteit en schriftcultuur* (Orality and literacy). Hilversum 1993. pp. 63-88.

of friendship;[12] written official documents were read aloud to the undersigned as a way to remember them;[13] and a personal letter could be a prefatory decoration, the real information being communicated orally by the messenger who brought it.[14] Alongside all this, written charters were a regular phenomenon, however, and could play a crucial role.[15] As for religious texts: the reading aloud at home of biblical texts was recommended by bishop Caesarius of Arles as a way of reaching the many illiterates.[16] The traditional purposely meditative individual reading of religious texts by ecclesiastical and monastic elites is also likely to have been sounded.[17] Generally, by far most of the surviving texts emanated from or were used by the Church, a perennial corporation that was solidly based on a corpus of texts, and stood to profit most from written privileges and charters over long periods of time.

The Church having no interest in preserving it - and in fact engaged in a large-scale effort to exterminate it -, we get only tantalizing glimpses of the still largely pagan sixth-century oral culture in the Frankish and rural Gallic spheres. References in Gregory of Tours' *Histories* tell us that there was at that time a Frankish oral tradition about the origin of their kingdom.[18] As is well-known, epics about what had been the Burgundian wars in the fifth century surfaced in writing only centuries later, together with what must have been oral traditions of the autochthonic Gallic population.[19] Certain motifs in Gregory's and Fortunatus's stories may derive from folklore

---

12 Evident, for instance, in Fortunatus's dedicatory letter to Gregory, who had commissioned the publication of his collected poems. *Carm.* 1.*praef.*: *aut tibi tantummodo innotescentia relegas, aut intimorum auribus tecum amicaliter, quaeso, conlatura committas.*

13 *Hist.* 9.20: *Haec nobis loquentibus, pactionem ipsam relegi rex coram adstantibus iubet.*

14 *Carm.* 8.12a: ... *causa, qua conservus meus presbyter, praesentium portitor, ad vos pro singulari praesidio confidens occurrit (sicut ipse singula poterit explicare)* ....

15 In *Hist.*4.12, Gregory tells us that a priest let himself be buried alive - on top of a decomposing corpse - rather than hand over the deed to his property to a rapacious bishop! Cf. Wood, 'Administration' (n. 6), p. 63.

16 Caesarius of Arles, *Sermo* 6.1 (32): ... *etiamsi aliquis nesciens litteras non potest legere, potest tamen legentem libenter audire.* G. Morin ed., *S. Caesarii Arelatensis Sermones.* vol. 1. editio altera. Corpus Christianorum, series Latina 103. Turnhout 1953.

17 As in *Hist.* 5.20: penitent bishops, who later relapse into their scandalous excesses, are (sarcastically) said *per diem noctesque in hymnis ac lectionibus meditando deducere.* The hymns would, of course, have been sung. Gregory also gives us a glimpse of such meditative singing when he writes: *Utinam quisque nostrum, cum haec cantare coeperit, statim spretis mundi scandalis, ... iustitiae viam ... conaretur irrepere (Virt. Jul. prol.).* On early Christian meditation, see P. Hadot, 'Antike Methodik der geistigen Übungen im Frühchristentum', *Humanistische Bildung* 4 (1981) pp. 31-62.

18 *Hist.*2.9: *Tradunt enim multi, eosdem de Pannonia fuisse degressus ... reges crinitos super se creavisse....*

19 Richter (n. 9), p. 256. Cf. A. Ebenbauer, "Heldenlied und 'historisches Lied' im

traditions.[20] Acts of church councils, but also Bishop Caesarius of Arles (502-542) in his sermons, prohibit (clerical) participation in, and thereby indicate the continuing existence of, secular mime, dance, song and music in this period.[21] In addition, traditional pagan healers surface in Gregory's miracle stories as rivals to the new-style cures by the (dead) saint. Unfortunately, his scant and contemptuous references do not tell us more than that they used lots, amulets and incantations. Their, in his view totally ineffective, rites are derisively categorized as 'magic'.[22] Archeological finds, however, indicate the existence of popular solar, fire and nature cults, as well as cults of the dead, and ritual ceremonies linked with fecundation.[23]

Saints' lives, including miracle stories, appear to be an essential part of an ecclesiastical attempt to supplant this existing oral culture of heroic and folk stories, ancestor and fertility cults, and pagan sanctuaries' healing ritual, with tales of Christian heroes and healers, presented almost as semi-divine, who had been historical individuals.[24] Just as with the oral performances of heroic lays in the co-existing tradition of a pre-Christian oral culture, in which central truths of an idealized past inhering in the present are affectively presented and shared, the recital of saints' lives and their miracles directed attention to the Christian world view, and loyalty toward the saints' shrines. But also toward the clergy and bishops, who often presented them-

Frühmittelalter - und davor", in: H. Beck ed., *Heldensage und Heldendichtung im Germanischen*, Berlin-New York 1988, p. 27.

20 For instance, a stag showing Clovis's army a ford in a river (*Hist.* 2.37), and a hawk carrying off a garment of the young saint Paternus (*Vit.Pat.* 11). On this subject see F. Graus, *Volk, Herrscher und Heiliger im Reich der Merowinger*. Studien zur Hagiographie der Merowingerzeit. Prague 1965. pp. 197-302.

21 Synodus dioecesana Autissiodorensis (561/605), canon 40: *Non licet presbytero inter epulas cantare nec saltare.* C. de Clercq ed., *Concilia Galliae*, A. 511-695. Turnhout 1963. Corpus christianorum, series latina 148a. p. 270. Caesarius Arel., *Sermo* 1.12 (10): *Quis est, qui non possit admonere, ut nullus in suo aut alieno convivio luxuriosos cantatores, lusores, vel cantatrices, castitati et honestati inimicos aut videre velit, aut venire permittat?* Cf. E.C. Dunn, *The Gallican Saint's Life and the late Roman dramatic tradition.* Washington 1989. pp. 46-72. See also: Richter (n. 9), pp. 105-122.

22 E.g. Gregory of Tours, *Virt.Jul.* 45: *Incantationes immurmurat, sortes iactat, ligaturas collo suspendit*; and *Hist.* 9.6, and 10.25. Cf. Riché, 'Croyances'(note 7); D. Harmening, *Superstitio.* Überlieferungs- und theoriegeschichtliche Untersuchungen zur kirchlich-theologischen Aberglaubensliteratur des Mittelalters. Berlin 1979. pp. 217-258; and A. Rousselle, 'Du sanctuaire au thaumaturge: la guérison en Gaule au IVe siècle', *Annales* 31 (1976) pp. 1085-1107; the same author describes the process of transition from pagan temples to saints' shrines in *Croire et guérir. La foi en Gaule dans l'Antiquité tardive* (*Croire*). Paris 1990.

23 Popular cults: E. Salin, *La civilisation mérovingienne d'apres les sepultures, les textes et le laboratoire.* vol. 4. Paris 1959. pp. 8-15, 466-469. Popular culture: Dunn, *Gallican* (n. 21), p. 76 and passim.

24 Riché, 'Croyances' (n. 7), p. 103; Salin, *Civilisation* 4, pp. 467-470; Rousselle, 'Sanctuaire' and *Croire* (all n. 22); Dunn, *Gallican* (n. 21), p. 77, 94, 101-102 and passim..

selves as the dead saints' living representatives in the world and, as such, able to wield their beneficent as well as punishing spiritual power. The latter was necessary to establish and maintain the position of the – at least in principle – unarmed Church in a strife-ridden Gallo-Frankish society in which issues tended to be settled by the recourse to armed violence. But this did not prevent the laity - much to the church's displeasure - from occasionally appropriating saints' cults for their own purposes, or from inserting saints' stories into what looks like their own traditional oral performances including, music, dance and drinking.[25]

The author of the story quoted at the beginning of this paper was educated in late imperial Ravenna, and, as far as we know, the only professional poet and writer in Gaul. His and his friend Gregory of Tours' writings indicate that in this period one individual could combine at least three kinds of literacy:[26] the hard-headed pragmatic use of written texts in the governmental sphere,[27] sophisticated seriousness as well as play with - often orally delivered - highly stylized 'literary' texts (his poems; these could be conflated in official correspondence in the governmental sphere[28]), and the production and presentation of what, I suggest, is a completely different kind of text, of which the story with which we began is an example.

For, alongside the centrality of its textual tradition, the Church had what may be called an 'oral' one. Walter Ong writes: 'The orality of the mind-set of the Bible, even

---

25 The Church and its 'arms': *quia arma nobis non sunt altera, auxiliante Christo circumsepto clericali choro necaturi pauperum, ut veniat super eum illa maledictio, quae super Iudam venit, qui, dum loculos faceret, subtrahebat pauperum alimenta; ut non solum excommunis, sed etiam anathema moriatur et coelesti gladio feriatur, qui in dispectu Dei et ecclesiae et pontificum in hac perversionem praesumit assurgere* (Concilium Turonense a. 567, canon 25, C. de Clercg ed., *Concilia Galliae*, CCSL 148a, pp. 192-193). 'Barbarian' oral performances: Richter (n. 9), pp. 88-96. Ecclesiastical strategies: P. Brown, 'Relics and social status in the Age of Gregory of Tours'. The Stenton Lecture, 1976; University of Reading, 1977. Reprinted in P. Brown, *Society and the holy in late Antiquity*. London-New York 1982. pp. 222-250, and R. van Dam, *Leadership and community in late antique Gaul* (The transformation of the classical heritage 8) Berkeley 1985. See now especially: idem, *Saints and Their Miracles in Late Antique Gaul* (*Saints*), Princeton 1993, pp. 82-115. Appropriation: A. Rousselle, 'La sage-femme et le thaumaturge dans la Gaule tardive', in: A. Pelletier ed., *La médecine en Gaule. Villes d'eaux, sanctuaires des eaux*. Paris 1985. p. 246. Insertion in oral performances: as prohibited in a *constitutio* of king Childebert I (a. 554), MGH LL, p. 1, cited by Richter (n. 9), p. 153.

26 Cf. B.V. Street, *Literacy in theory and practice*, Cambridge 1984 (Cambridge studies in oral and literate culture 9), p. 8 and passim.

27 See De Nie, 'Kracht' (n. 11), pp. 68-73.

28 As in the poem addressed to the Emperor Justin and his Empress Sophia to thank them in Radegund's name for sending a relic of the Holy Cross (*Carm. Ap.* 2). His formal letter to Bishop Martin of Braga (*Carm.* 5.1) is an elaborate example of the flowery style also used in other extant official letters of the period.

in its epistolary sections, is overwhelming'.[29] God is presented as speaking to man continually, through his prophets and through his Son as the Word.[30] But this Christian tradition of direct, oral confrontation has another dimension - one which has not yet received the attention it deserves. In the New Testament, healing miracles - over against verbal messages - tend to be regarded as visible, embodied manifestations of the presence of the Kingdom of God.[31] In the sixth century too, I shall argue, the miracle story - consciously continuing the biblical tradition - is not a text in the sense of its being primarily a written statement of a truth that is adequately expressible in words and language. Alongside, but also as a corollary of, its function as propaganda for the Church's power, it is a miniature model of the central Christian truths, not in the form of verbal statements but as the *non-logocentric, embodied truth* that predominates in oral culture,[32] and it is a verbalized *model for the regenerative enactment* of this embodied truth. Through its inscription as a text, the miracle story was preserved for institutionalized remembering in highly uncertain circumstances by a corporation basing its larger ideology as well as its practical administration on the written word.

It is, therefore, not a text in which contemporaries would have expected to find essentially new information. Intended for regular oral presentation to this community during liturgy,[33] it gives only another variation on a central truth that is brought for-

29 W. Ong, *Orality and Literacy. The Technologizing of the Word*, London-New York 1982, p. 75, referring to his own *The Presence of the Word*, New Haven-London 1967, pp. 176-191.

30 Jn 1:1-4. On Gregory of Tours' view of the human word and the divine Word, see G. de Nie, 'Die Sprache im Wunder - das Wunder in der Sprache. Menschenwort und Logos bei Gregor von Tours', *Mitteilungen des Instituts für Österreichische Geschichtsforschung* 103 (1995), pp. 1-25.

31 E.g. Lk 10:9.

32 On sixth-century miracle stories as conscious imitations and variations of biblical ones: M. van Uytfanghe, *Stylisation biblique et condition humaine dans l'hagiographie mérovingienne [600-750]*. Brussel 1987. Verhandelingen van de Koninklijke Academie voor Wetenschappen, Letteren en Schone Kunsten van België, Klasse der Letteren, Jrg. 49, nr. 120. p. 13: 'Si l'hagiographie a la prétention d'actualiser la Bible, il faut bien mesurer aussi les écarts et les détours.'
On ritual and embodied truth: R.J. Devisch, *Weaving the threads of life: the Khita gyneco-logical healing cult among the Yaka* (*Weaving*). Chicago 1993. p. 264-265: 'The body as both weave and weaving loom is the major elaborating and transformative process and force that permits the transposition of meaning, structuring, and energies between the bodily, social, and cosmological fields.' Richter, in his *Formation*, does not mention this aspect of oral culture. By contrast, R. van Dam, quoting A. Kleinman supportively, regards the cure as a reading and interpretation of an ideological concern or 'text': *Saints and their miracles in late antique Gaul*. Princeton 1993. p. 85, n. 15.

33 As is evident in *Virt.Mart.* 2.14: *cumque nos rite sacrosancta solemnia celebrantes, contestationem de sancti domni virtutibus narraremus* .... Cf. Dunn, *Gallican* (n. 21), pp. 73-101, and passim, and Richter, *Formation* (n. 11), p. 96.

ward as already known and shared by the whole church community. In what follows, I hope to show how - as in the healing ritual of an oral culture - in certain types of miraculous cures a specific symbolic ritual is enacted to articulate and resolve what must have been literally unutterable tensions, and to establish the identity of an individual and integrate him or her more firmly into the relatively new Christian group[34] and its world view.

Symbol: the 'worm'

In the sixth century, spirits were thought to be everywhere: 'Das Bemühen, den dämonischen Einfluss zu beseitigen und gute Kräfte herbeizurüfen, ist ein Grundanliegen der frühmittelalterlichen Religiosität.'[35] According to Devisch, 'the spirit idiom structures inchoate feelings':

> [o]n the one hand, they [the spirits] mirror some portion of the individual or some significant (introjected?) figure in his experience that he may refuse to recognize or accept; on the other hand, they may be a means of articulating desires that are unacceptable to someone in his position.[36]

As we have seen in the story quoted above, in sixth-century Gaul, too, uncontrollable and socially unacceptable behaviour is understood as possession by an evil spirit. According to Devisch, 'The healing drama seeks to mobilize the affects, driving them to the point of an abreaction and catharsis.'[37] In such a re-enactment of the origin of the blocking and resulting disorientation of the personality, the unutterable is articulated. Once articulated, it becomes graspable and can be manipulated. In other words, the identification of the possessing agent as the Devil, whom the benefi-

---

34 This is Devisch's view of ritual (n. 32). It will be evident that my view of miracles as enacted metaphors does not distinguish between 'magic' and 'religion', as do L. Kolmer, 'Heilige als magische Heiler', *Mediaevistik* 6 (1993) 153-175, and V.I.J. Flint, (n. 4). See also my 'Caesarius of Arles and Gregory of Tours: two sixth-century Gallic bishops and "Christian magic"', in: D. Edel ed., *Cultural Identity and Cultural Integration. Ireland and Europe in the Early Middle Ages*, Dublin 1995, pp. 170-196.

35 A. Angenendt, 'Die Liturgie und die Organisation des kirchlichen Lebens auf dem Lande', in: *Cristianizzazione ed organizzazione ecclesiastica delle campagne nell' alto Medioevo: espansione ed resistenze*. vol. 1. Spoleto 1982. Settimane di studio del Centro Italiano sull' alto Medioevo 28. pp. 169-226, here p. 189. See also: idem, *Das Frühmittelalter*. Stuttgart etc. 1990. pp. 182-190; and C.E. Stancliffe, *St Martin and His Hagiographer. History and Miracle in Sulpicius Severus*, Oxford 1983, pp. 205-227. Cf. B. Kapferer, *A Celebration of Demons. Exorcism and the Aesthetics of Healing in Sri Lanka*, 49-91.

36 V. Crapanzano, 'Introduction', p. 16, in: V. Crapanzano and V. Garrison ed., *Case studies in spirit possession*. New York 1977.

37 *Weaving* (n. 32), p. 256.

cent power of Christ is believed to be able to overcome, makes the cure conceptually possible. But '...[t]he elements within the [spirit] idiom resonate with the individual and his world; however constraining the logic or grammar of the idiom may be, the idiom provides a powerful rhetorical strategy for the definition of self and world....'[38] Thus the Devil, defined as not being part of the healthy Christian personality, can be cast out and the personality reconstituted. In addition, the cured person incurs a debt of gratitude to the healing saint which turns into a relation of dependence upon him as a figure of authority in the Christian community.[39]

In the same *Life of Radegund*, a little before the story told above, there is a very similar one. But here the possessing agent becomes visible before it is trampled underfoot:

> A certain woman named Leubila in the countryside was gravely afflicted by the Adversary. [Having heard about her], the following day the saint [came and] prayed, and through a new cure of Christ [in which] the skin in [the afflicted lady's] shoulder opened and a worm came out, she was cured publicly; and she related that she had been liberated by grinding that very worm underfoot.

> *Femina quaedam Leubila dum vexaretur in rure ab adversario graviter, sequenti die sancta orante, nova Christi curatione in scapula crepante cute et verme foras exeunte, sana est reddita publice et ipsum vermem calcans pede liberata se retulit.*[40]

The grinding underfoot of the Adversary or Devil in the form of a 'worm' is the central image in this story: after the preliminary prayer by the saint, its dynamic appears to precipitate the cure. Significantly, the treading appears to have been done, this time, not by the saint but by the patient herself.[41]

The event would not have been told as a miracle story if everyone had accepted a worm spontaneously coming out of a shoulder as a normal, unsurprising phenomenon. It must have been one that, somehow, was extremely unusual or went against common-sense experience.[42] However, although I have not found such a thing described for Europe, there are in the present-day tropics certain kinds of flies whose larves penetrate also human skin, to develop subcutaneously for days or weeks, and then emerge and drop off.[43] Does the story show us a rare case of this kind?[44] The

38 Crapanzano, 'Introduction' (n. 36), p. 19.

39 Cf. Rousselle, *Croire* (n. 22), pp. 133-154.

40 *Vit.Rad.* 67.

41 See on this my 'Saint Radegund's *mysterium*' in: A.J.A.C.M. Korte ed., *Women and Miracles* (forthcoming).

42 Cf. Stancliffe, *St. Martin* (n. 35), p. 257: 'hard-headed common sense': 'there may well have been more of this around [in the fourth century] than we customarily assume'.

43 Subcutaneous myiasis, Dermatobia hominis and Dermal myiasis: P.E.C. Manson-Bahr and D.R. Bell, *Manson's Tropical Diseases* (*Diseases*), 19th ed., London etc. 1987, pp. 911-917.

44 M. Rouche, 'Miracles, maladies et psychologie dela foi à l'époque carolingienne en

expulsion itself of the worm appears not to be regarded as effecting the cure, however. What is said to 'liberate' the woman was something that looks like symbolic, ritual action: her grinding it underfoot. Why was that so important?

Rudolf Arnheim has drawn attention to the fact that 'almost every act of perception involves subsuming a given particular phenomenon under some visual concept - an operation most typical of thinking'. The perception process, he says, is the result of

> interaction between the structure suggested by the shaping of the stimulus configuration and the components brought into play by the knowledge, expectations, wishes and fears of the observer.[45]

In this story, what are the expectations, wishes and fears around the visual concept of the 'worm'? The combination of the latter and treading underfoot leads us straight to what must be the origin of this symbolism: the story of the cursing of the serpent in the book of Genesis - the Christian story of the origin of the cosmos. There the Lord says to the serpent who had beguiled Eve: '... I will put enmity between you and the woman, and between your seed and her seed; she shall grind your head underfoot (*ipsa conteret caput tuum*), and you shall lie in wait for her heel.'[46] In the Gospel of Luke, after they tell Christ that 'even demons were overcome (*subiciuntur*) by us in your name', the disciples too are given '... the power of treading upon serpents and scorpions, and upon every power of the Enemy (*potestatem calcandi supra serpentes et scorpiones, et supra omnem virtutem inimici*)'.[47] Treading upon a serpent, then, is the dynamic image or symbolic act for the overcoming of Evil in all its guises in the cosmos. In this story, a 'worm' is evidently sufficiently like a serpent to stand for one. And it is very likely that, in the first story, in which the Enemy is also somehow trampled upon, his being imagined as a serpent-like figure went without saying.

Francie', in: *Hagiographies, cultures et sociétés IV-XII siècles*, Paris 1981, pp. 319-335, does not mention such a phenomenon; however, he does identify the fevers also mentioned in sixth-century sources as a kind of malaria (p. 322). As for the emergence of a disease-causing agent: C. Lévi-Strauss, in a memorable article, relates the story of a sceptical Kwakiutl Indian who unintentionally became a successful sorcerer and overcame his rivals through producing 'a bloody worm' (actually a piece of down mixed with blood from his tongue, bitten at the right moment) ostensibly from the patient's body (but in fact from his mouth). It seems unlikely, however, that the patient herself would do something like this. C. Lévi-Strauss, 'Le sorcier et sa magie', *Le temps modernes* 4.41 (1949) pp. 3-24, reprinted in C. Lévi-Strauss, *Anthropologie structurale*, Paris 1958, pp.183-203, here p. 192-196.

45 R. Arnheim, *Visual thinking*. Berkeley 1969. pp. 90-91.

46 Gen. 3:15.

47 Lk. 10:19.

What we see in these stories, then, is that when the central symbolic deed of trampling upon the serpent is re-enacted according to the biblical promise, in a ritual drama around and upon the body as a microcosm, the patient is restored to health. How can such a thing happen? A healing ritual, the anthropologist René Devisch writes,

> ... is a dream of health and an incarnation of values, moving through metaphor beyond language .... operative at a level that largely escapes the grasp of colloquial speech and representational thinking.... [C]ultural traditions .... come to articulation, in and through the body, with the community and the life-world.... through feeling and sensing out the meaning of the embodied interwovenness ..., the body is deeply moved, intensified, and remolded.[48]

In other words: bodily enacting a metaphor can initiate emotional and physical processes that lead to healing. This is the crux of the matter.

Discharges had been traditional in Greek, Roman and Gallic curing techniques.[49] As also in these stories, the disease-causing agent was thought to be expelled with such discharges. Devisch describes this phenomenon as 'the phatic function of skin and orifices'. For the latter, he says,

> provide for both differentiation and bridging between inner and outer, ... between mortal agony and rebirth, ... destruction and regeneration.... These poetics of transcoding at the junction and disjunction of domains or fields - otherwise kept separate by conventional thought - serve to release self-healing in the patient.[50]

Again: bodily experiencing and enacting the metaphor precipitates this healing. In the U.S., a medical authority has recently presented clinical evidence that even the visualization of appropriate images can transmit healing messages to the body's autonomous systems.[51]

What are the 'lignes de force' of the world view which the symbolism we have seen in Fortunatus's stories makes visible? It is one, evidently, that opposes the Good as high, closed, firm, erect and whole to the Evil as low, fluid, prostrate and desintegrated.[52] In other words, order through power from 'above' versus chaos from

---

48 Devisch, *Weaving* (n. 32), p. 255. Cf. M.T. Kelsey, *Healing and Christianity* (*Healing*), London 1973, p. 84: 'psychic healing ... apparently works at the level of unconscious images and attitudes'; and J.L. Singer, *Imagery and daydream methods in psychotherapy and behavior modification*. New York 1974. pp. 179-180.

49 Rousselle, 'Sanctuaire' (n. 22), p. 1094.

50 Devisch, *Weaving* (n. 32), pp. 265-266.

51 B.S. Siegel, *Love, medicine and miracles*. New York 1986. Kelsey, *Healing* (n. 48), p. 243-306, says something very similar.

52 Not surprisingly, Gregory's writings show that he shared this view; see my 'Le corps, la fluidité et l'identité personelle dans la vision du monde de Grégoire de Tours', in: M. van Uytfanghe and R. Demeulenaere ed., *Aevum inter utrumque*. Mélanges offerts à Gabriel Sanders. Steenbrugge-the Hague 1991. pp. 75-87.

'below'. It is more than tempting to see a correlation between this mental-emotional imaging and the severely hierarchical, paternalistic and formalistic social structure that - as is abundantly evident in Gregory of Tours' *Histories* - the Church wished to maintain over society. This world view is evident also in the other stories of miraculous cures that Fortunatus tells us. His most telling and succinct formulation occurs in the story of the cure of a dying little girl by saint Hilary of Poitiers:

suddenly, through the working of the word, he made the flowing fabric of her limbs firm and erect, and reformed them into their pristine state as though there had been nothing dissolved about them.

subito membrorum fluentem fabricam verbo operante subrexit et in statum pristinum tamquam si nihil fuisset solubile reformavit.[53]

Mary Douglas has connected the concern with orifices and dualistic values with anxiety about the existence of two opposing ideologies or power groups in a society.[54] And these images associated with Evil in fact recur in Fortunatus's and Gregory's references to enemies of the Church: Arians, accordingly, are involved in a 'serpentine fall', St. Hilary 'by fighting, ground the heretics' crimes underfoot (*pugnando calcavit haeretica crimina*)', and Nero's heart was invaded by 'the envy of the old serpent'.[55] In his saints' Lives Fortunatus relates stories of saints' victories over snakes and a dragon.[56] The opposition between the clerical or monastic way of life - in which celibacy was a central element - and life in 'the world' could also be expressed through a formulation opposing the spirit to the lower body, as in: 'having sloughed off the pollution of the world (*defecato mundi contagio*)'.[57] A ventral or other elimination, as especially Gregory's stories show, is another important symbol of the purgation of evil: in some cases he says explicitly that the Devil or demon came out with it or perhaps in it.[58] One way of being integrated into oneself, the group and the cosmos, then, was to enact a ritual drama in which one's 'dissolving' fluidity - visible or otherwise -, in other words, the external (invaded) cause[59] of

53 *Virt.Hil.* 8.

54 M. Douglas, *Purity and danger*. An analysis of the concepts of pollution and taboo. London 1966/1985. pp. 41, 115, 124.

55 *Vit.Hil.*26: *fraus heretica serpentino lapsu subripuit. Vit. Hil.* 52. *Hist.* 1.25: *oritur contra [ecclesiam Christi] antique serpentes invidia, et totis se imperatoris praecordiis inmittit saeva malignitas.* Cf. Rev. 12:9: *serpens antiquus qui vocatur Diabolus et Satanas.*

56 *Vit.Hil.* 35-39 and *Vit.Marc.* 40-49.

57 *Vit.Rad.* 2.

58 As in *Virt.Mart.* 2.20: *evomens purulentum nescio quid cum sanguine, daemone eiecto, purgatus est.* This view, too, was traditional in Roman and Gallic medical practice: Rousselle, 'Sanctuaire' (n. 22), p. 1103.

59 A traditional Gallic view: Rousselle, 'Sanctuaire' (n. 22), p. 1095.

one's state of non-integration with oneself or with the community or both, is expurged and trodden underfoot through power from 'above'. This is a world view that emphasizes healing through *purging* and through *ordering via the eye*, by means of *verticality* and *repressive power*. All this reflects the 'Kingdom' and 'Father' metaphors of the New Testament, but also the Church's view of the contemporary social structure in Gaul. In practice, however, this approach is almost certainly not the whole picture.

In the following cure by saint Germanus, besides the dramatic role that direct discourse could play in the enactment of the ritual, what is here made explicit is the healing power not only of certain symbolic actions - which engage the visualizing capacity - but also of direct sensation: *touch*, contact with the body of the healer. This is embodied truth in its purest form. Two centuries earlier, St. Martin of Tours, perhaps taking Elijah as his example, had revived a dead boy by body-to-body contact.[60] I saw a trace of such contact happening today during a recent visit to the oldest church of Paris, that of St. Germain-des-Prés (the same Germanus of Paris whose sixth-century cures we are now looking at). There, a woman, after praying to a statue of Peter the Apostle, laid her hand affectionately and lingeringly on his feet for a few seconds before hurriedly going her way. Fortunatus tells us about Germanus's cure of the possessed Magnofledis that

> Immediately when the the hand of the holy man was placed upon the head of the tottering girl, the hidden Foe was discovered by such a searching, and he confessed with many sighs that he had concealed himself there for a long time; he shouted that he was not able to cover up his own deceptions in the presence of the blessed man. Having therefore shown himself and come out in this way, he was overcome with great fierceness. While the bishop kept picturing the sign of the Cross with his hand, everyone saw the Enemy finally leave, bursting forth through the nose of the woman in the appearance of flies with blood.

> *Confestim ut sancti manus super caput puellae titubantis inponitur, tali investigatione occultus hostis detegitur et se diu latuisse multo gemitu confitetur nec in beati praesentiam clamat propio se posse celare praestigio. Ergo ita se proditum et egressurum gravi ardore conqueritur. Interim non cessante sacerdote manu crucem depingere, expectantibus omnibus in muscae similitudinem prorumpens, cum sanguine de naribus mulieris egressus est.*[61]

In the Roman medical tradition, 'larves' - i.e. evil spirits - were thought to leave through the mouth or nose.[62] In today's tropics, however, fly larvae can also nestle in

---

60 Sulpicius Severus, *Epistola* 2.4. Cited in Rousselle, 'Sanctuaire' (n. 22), p. 1100. Cf. 1 Kings 17:21: *et expandit se atque mensus est super puerum tribus vicibus, clamavitque ad Dominum* .... Cf. L. Bieler, 'Totenerweckung durch synanáchrosis', and O. Weinreich, 'Zum Wundertypus der synanáchrosis' ('Wundertypus'), *Archiv für Religionswissenschaft* 32 (1935), pp. 228-245, 246-264.

61 *Vit.Germ.* 78-79. Cf. ibidem 142-143 (n. 52).

62 Rousselle, 'Sanctuaire' (n. 22), 1103.

bodily cavities and perhaps emerge in such a way;[63] is this story another piece of evidence that such flies were then around in Gaul? However this may be, the dialogue and ritual event are presented as high drama, in which the presumed possessing agent interacts with the saint through the mouth of the patient. The spirit is called forth by the saint's laying his hand upon her head, and she is thereby able to articulate what she conceives to be her emotional problem in the spirit idiom and work it out. If this was in fact only a purely physical illness, the ritual would still resolve any anxieties she may have had, and enact her new security in dependence upon the saint as part of his community.

Touching is central too in the cure of a cripple with 'dissolved limbs (*membris dissolutus*)': after having poured 'sanctified oil' on the patient, 'when [the saint] touched the top layer of his skin, vigor entered into the marrow of his bones (*cum cutem summam tetigisset, vigor medullas introiit*).'[64] Elsewhere, Fortunatus says of Germanus: 'reviving this whole mass of her insides was, for the saint, the same as touching it (*totamque viscerum molem hoc fuit apud sanctum vivificare quod tangere*).'[65] Judging from these statements, touching must have played a greater role in his cures, and perhaps in those of every saint, than we are told.[66] In Fortunatus's description of Radegund's cures, however, touching - in the form of washing, cradling, embracing, and stroking - is especially prominently mentioned. As I have shown elsewhere, there may have been special reasons for this.[67] The stories appear to show that this more direct, body-to-body, communication of vital energy is, to one degree or another, always there, and that it is probably the 'horizontal', assimilative complement - not always made explicit - of the symbolic acts representing 'verticalizing' repression and purgation.

How are we to understand the many sudden cures reported in this period? It has been suggested that social and economic insecurity and political instability must have led to a great deal of anxiety and disorientation, resulting in so-called psycho-somatic illnesses which, although the symptoms are very real, may be suddenly cured through what might be termed 'de-blocking'.[68] Claude Lévi-Strauss has emphasized the crucial role of the group in the effectuation of cures as well as deaths through symbolic activities which he designates as 'magic' or sorcery (concepts which I do not find useful for my subject): 'Physical integrity cannot withstand the dissolution of the social

---

63 Manson-Bahr and Bell, *Diseases* (n. 43), p. 917. The bloody blister over someone's eye in *Vit. Alb.* 47-48 may also have been a case of this.

64 *Vit.Germ.* 106.

65 *Vit.Germ.* 127.

66 As, for instance, also in *Vit.Germ.* 158: *Ita beatissimus non solum manu sanavit quod tetigit, sed nominatus curas sparsit.* Cf. also *ibidem* 72 and 75.

67 As in: *Vit.Rad.* 68-70, 80-85. The same activities as charity, without miracles: 39, 44. But Weinreich reports intensive contact as an ancient motif: Weinreich, 'Wundertypus' (n. 60), p. 246-249. See my "St Radegund's *mysterium*" (n. 41).

68 Rousselle, 'Sanctuaire' (n. 22), p. 1104. Cf. Kelsey, *Healing* (n. 48), p. 291.

personality.'[69] These very terms - integrity and dissolution - are however the key ones, as we have seen, in Fortunatus's descriptions of the inverse kind of events: miraculous cures. They have to do with the individual's relation not only to himself, but to the Christian community in the process of being constituted. At the same time, in the Church's effort to gain control of society, the beneficent, powerful and protective person of the saint is a model of the new Christian personality that everyone should attempt to imitate to some degree.[70] The latter's ritual of enacted Christian symbolism is forcefully presented as more effective than that of the traditional pagan healers.

The Church's 'oral culture': word, mental image and body

If healing ritual effects emotional and physical transformation through the enactment of symbolic forms, how can a terse, three-sentence story merely narrated to a presumably passive audience about what appears to be a ritual in the past make any of the latter's transformational power become operative in the present?

First, as already stated, by its being embedded in church liturgy as a broader enunciation and enactment by the whole community of shared views and values concerning self, group and cosmos in which the same symbolism is central.[71] The stories of cures of individuals fit into the larger picture as particularized instances or variations of a general pattern. In this way, the larger 'ritual' context and the narration by a member of the officiating clergy, experienced as an 'authority', make the cure stories appear factual and realistic. In Clifford Geertz's terms, they become not only 'models *of*' belief reality but also 'models *for*' - producing - mental representations inducing affective experiences of such 'reality' in the worshipper.[72]

Geertz does not explain more precisely how this producing takes place: how what he calls a 'leap' from common sense to belief reality is made.[73] I suggest that at least two processes are operative in this leap. One is generic to the *narrative* as the form

69 Lévi-Strauss, 'Sorcier' (n. 44), p. 182. The context here is death through ensorcelment, but he shows in his article that the statement has a wider applicability.

70 Integration: see van Dam, *Saints* (n. 25), pp. 82-115. The saint as model: Gregory of Tours, *Vita patrum* 4.*prol.*: *Ergo ... nos ... sanctorum exemplis inlecti ... opera ad caelestia ac sempiterna sustollat.* Cf. Rousselle, 'Sanctuaire' (n. 22), pp. 1104-1105. Cf. idem, *Croire* (n. 22), pp. 109-132, 171-208.

71 As also, very briefly, Collins, 'Observations' (n. 5), p. 112.

72 C. Geertz, 'Religion as a cultural system', in: C. Geertz, *The interpretation of cultures*. New York 1973, pp. 87-125, here p. 124, 112-113, 118. On this phenomenon in a story by Gregory of Tours, see G. de Nie, "A broken lamp or the effluence of holy power? Common sense and belief reality in Gregory of Tours' own experience", *Mediaevistik* 3 (1990), pp. 269-279.

73 Ibidem, p. 122.

in which personal awareness becomes a coherent experience of identity.[74] It is that of the identification with another person's experience through recognizing its patterns of experience as similar to one's own. The second process is independent of the narrative configuration but may be reinforced by it. More direct and, as such, much more powerful, it has been termed the 'affective mimesis' of *mental images* that are evoked by the symbols acted out, mentioned or hinted at in the story. Somehow, the human subject imitates the pattern of emotional and bio-electrical energy made visible in the image or symbol when it is perceived by the senses or imaginatively evoked through verbal means: 'Every image has in itself a motor drive', and 'images and mental pictures tend to produce the physical conditions and external acts corresponding to them'.[75]

In his prose saints' lives, Fortunatus - following a convention - apologizes for the brevity and for the common or plain language he uses in order to reach the understanding of the people.[76] To come alive, his minimal stories with their inhering images must have been not simply read aloud as they stand, but used as an aid to memory for an elaborated and dramatically visualized oral improvisation on its content.[77] There being no poetic metre in these texts to be disrupted, they would not have functioned as the inflexible formulation of a word-centered truth that needed to be repeated *verbatim*. Instead, just as in the performances of the concurrent pre-Christian oral tradition, they are likely to have been the taking-off point for improvisations, adjusted to the expectations of the audience, transmitting, through their physical descriptions of bodies in the process of transformation through well-known and powerful symbols, a non-verbal, embodied truth.

The written words of the miracle story, then, cannot be understood by themselves as pure texts; *they point beyond themselves to the quality of the shared experience of an oral performance*. Dependent for its effectivity upon this experience, it is the basis of a collective affirmation of a world view as well as the germ of a model for the enactment of an individual healing ritual.[78] That Fortunatus was aware of this

---

74 P. Ricoeur, *Time and narrative*. Transl. by K. Blamey and D. Pellauer. vol. 3. Chicago 1988. p. 247: 'narrative identity'.

75 R. Assagioli, *Psychosynthesis*. New York 1965, p. 144. apparently citing Charles Baudoin, *Suggestion and autosuggestion*, London 1920, without page reference. '[A]ffective mimesis': K. F. Morrison, *History as a visual art in the twelfth-century Renaissance*. Princeton 1990. p. 47.

76 Brevity: *Vit.Hil.* 5, *Vit.Alb.* 9, *Vit.Rad.* 75; *impar lingua*: *Vit.Alb.*; *privatus sermo*: *Vit.Rad.* 2; intellibility for the people: *Vit.Alb* 8. This manner of presentation was conventional since Sulpicius Severus' *Vita Martini* (Sources chrétiennes 133).

77 I am grateful to my co-Fellow at the N.I.A.S., Professor D. Ogden, of the Department of Dramatic Art, University of California at Berkeley, for this suggestion.

78 Dunn, *Gallican* (n. 21), pp. 71-72, 85 and passim, sees the saints' and miracle plays of the high Middle Ages originating in the occasional use of music, mime and perhaps dance by *professional artists* to accompany the *liturgical readings* in certain churches in this period. There is no indication of this in the writings of Gregory and Fortunatus,

appears from the preface to his record of the deceased Hilary's miracles. He will preserve the memory of these, he says,

so that whoever apprehends these, as he should, through a faithful hearing, will both rejoice in recognizing the past miracles and be confident that similar things will be done by the power of the confessor in the future.

ut quisquis haec fideli sicut condecet auditu perceperit, et praeterita recognoscere gaudeat et similia fieri virtute confessoris in futuro confidat.[79]

Believing what one hears - that is, internalizing it -, he is saying, will make it happen again. In modern terms, the image-symbols are stored affective patterns in the memory, to be re-experienced, re-enacted if need arises.[80]

The introduction to the *Life of saint Caesarius of Arles* tells us that while the authors 'talk about him' - probably what is meant is also the reading aloud of his biography - they 'rejoice in somehow even seeing him (*nos dum de ipso loquimur, ipsum nos etiam videre quodam modo gratulemur).*'[81] This image of the saint, then, is explicitly said to be called up by the words about him. The saints' lives add a powerful human symbol to the cosmic ones given in the *Urtext* of the Bible: the figure of the saint as approachable, human intermediary between men and what has become a high and distant, majestic divinity. That which, according to Devisch, a modern non-European oral culture in practice recognizes as the regenerative power located in the embodied self,[82] Fortunatus's Lives visualize and attribute to the catalytic, model image of the saint:

---

however, and the 'entertainment' quality - in church - seems foreign to their frequent stress on awe (see below). The canons mentioned by Dunn (Syn. Aut. 561/605, c. 3 and 5), refer to the celebration of saints' vigils in private homes: *Non licet conpensus in domibus propriis nec pervigilius in festivitates sanctorum facere* (c.3); idem for the vigil of St. Martin (c. 5) (de Clercq, *Concilia*, p. 265). Canon 9 (p. 266) may point to secular theater and songs in some churches as a popular practice, but indicates clearly that it was not encouraged by church authorities: *Non licet in ecclesia chorus saecularium vel puellarum cantica exercere nec convivia in ecclesia praeparare, quia scriptum est: Domus mea domus orationis vocabitur.*

79 *Virt.Hil.* 5. Cf. *Vit.Pat.* 8.

80 On the medieval versus the modern understanding of symbols, see: G.B. Ladner, 'Medieval and modern understanding of symbolism: a comparison', *Speculum* 54 (1979) pp. 223-256.

81 *Vita sancti Caesarii episcopi* 1.1. B. Krusch ed., in: B. Krusch ed., *Passiones vitaeque sanctorum aevi merovingici.* Hannover 1896. Monumenta Germaniae Historica, Scriptores rerum Merovingicarum 3. pp. 433-501. W. Klingshirn has published a translation in the series Translated Texts for Historians 19. Liverpool 1994. pp. 9-42. Cf. idem, *Caesarius of Arles. The making of a Christian community in late antique Gaul.* Cambridge 1994.

82 '*The genuinely self-generative body praxis* is, I contend, the *very heart of the Yaka healing art.*' Devisch, *Weaving* (n. 32), p. 266.

Thus the image of the bishop was the cause of salvation for many, and like the blessed Peter, the very figure of our priest gave remedies.

Sic multis causa salutis fuit imago pontificis et ad vicem beati Petri dedit nostri sacerdotis ipsa figura remedia.[83]

This sentence occurs after a description of the saint telling prisoners in a dream-vision how they could escape. The image of liberation from bondage - the dominant one in the *Life of saint Germanus* and, of course, an analogue to Christ's liberation of man from sin and death - seems to be presented as the basic pattern of all that this saint does.[84] It is tempting to recognize a symbolic value also in the repeated references to prisons being underground:[85] that of the lower body.

But Germanus's appearance in a dream, after tearful prayers for his aid, and, as such, making the sign of the Cross over blind eyes, could also precipitate a cure. The following morning, the lady, as she had fervently desired, was able to join the people in the liturgical procession,'so that the image of the holy man thus seen in her dream had been the remedy (*ita ut sancti viri sic visa per somnium esset imago remedium*).'[86] In these cases, the saint's beneficent aid to the reintegration of self and body, and of self and group, is explicitly said to have been apprehended through seeing an image: that of the saint's physical appearance, here significantly making a gesture of power close to the patient's body; one suspects that he also touched her, but that Fortunatus or the original narrator did not think it worth mentioning. Another lady reported that when the living saint Germanus entered her home, she seemed to see the shining, horned Moses having just descended from the mountain after speaking with God. This superposed image had an emotional effect; recalling the moment, she says: 'so that I am scarcely able either to see him because of the light or to speak (*quod paene vix valeo aut intuere lumine aut sermone conferre*).'[87]

An *image* - but also a visible gesture - is thus *a visualized affective pattern, and a vector of psychic and bio-electrical energy.*[88] As such, it can initiate change and action.[89] That of the saint - perhaps an idealized image of the higher self - represents hope, confidence, and power, and could therefore be a catalyst of recovery and reintegration in uncertain and violent times.

---

83 *Vit.Germ.* 179.

84 Germanus is described as sad when there is no one to 'redeem' from captivity, and much happier when such an opportunity presents itself: *ut crederes hominem pro redimendis aliis se ipsum servitutis vinculo liberandum* (*Vit.Germ.* 194, 196).

85 As in *Vit.Germ.* 87, 182.

86 *Vit.Germ.* 98.

87 *Vit.Germ.* 23.

88 G. Epstein, *Waking dream therapy. Dream process as imagination*. New York 1981. pp. 84, 149.

89 G. de Nie, *Views from a many-windowed tower. Studies of imagination in the works of Gregory of Tours*. Amsterdam 1987. pp. 213-294, esp. 291.

The process of individual psycho-physical regeneration which can be achieved in the ritual of a present-day oral culture through the communal bodily enactment of a symbolism that does not to any significant degree surface in language, thus appears to be verbalized in sixth-century hagiographical texts. These were intended for oral presentation during liturgy as a cognitive event: that of miracle executed by - mediated - power from outside and 'above' the individual. At the same time, however, the telling is likely to have been an oral 'performance' in the sense of an affective sharing of the ideals, values and traditions of the community.

But the oral dimension of the miracle story is much deeper. Both Gregory and Fortunatus repeatedly mention bystanders', including their own, reactions to the witnessing of a miracle as a 'speechlessness' through awe, as in: 'stupefaction took hold of all (*cunctos stupor amplectitur*)'.[90] We have also seen that a confrontation with the appearance of the living saint could also 'trigger' the perception of an associated image of numinosity that induced such (near)speechlessness. This testimony, I suggest, seems to indicate that even when verbally communicated, the miracle story is intended to point to, and to some degree induce, the pre-verbal - ritual - mode of body-awareness in which touch and symbols create and shape experience. For, as anthropological parallels show, it must have been through this mode of awareness, and through touching and the enacting of such symbols, that what was regarded as the divine regenerative power effected the transformations which are recorded as 'miracles'.[91]

90 Gregory: *admiratusque silui* (*Glor.mart.*5); *Obstupefactus ego ob virtutem sancti liquoris* (*Virt.Mart.* 2.32). Fortunatus: *Stupor animus invasit praesenti miraculo .... Haec quoque veneranda praesente me gesta sunt* (*Vit.Germ.* 177), *cunctos stupor amplectitur* (*ibid.*, 109).

91 See on this also my 'Iconic alchemy: imaging miracles in late sixth-century Gaul', *Studia Patristica* vol. 30 (forthcoming), and 'History and miracle: Gregory's use of metaphor', in: I.N. Wood ed., *The World of Gregory of Tours*, Ithaca 1997 (forthcoming).

XVII

The Language in Miracle – the Miracle in Language: Words and the Word according to Gregory of Tours[1]

Tantalizing glimpses in the writings of bishop Gregory of Tours (539–594) reveal such a many-sided personality and author that it is hardly an exaggeration to say that each Gregory scholar tends to have his "own" Gregory.[2] The following interpretation of one of his prefaces is intended to highlight only one aspect of his writing: the imagery in his stories about miracles. It does not take into consideration his views on historical writing,[3] or the fact that he can be much impressed by the aesthetic qualities of the flowery language of late antique rhetoric as well as severely critical and completely businesslike in his judgement of secular documents.[4]

---

[1] I am grateful to the University of Utrecht for a leave of absence during the academic year 1991–1992, and to the Netherlands Institute for Advanced Study in the Humanities and Social Sciences for inviting me to spend that year doing research in Wassenaar, where this article was first conceived and written. In addition, the sessions of the international seminar "Word, image and reality in medieval texts", sponsored by the Erasmus Network Nederlands in Europa, has stimulated the development of the arguments focused upon in this paper. Further, I wish to thank Dr P. Fouracre of Goldsmiths' College, London, and Prof. N. Palmer of the University of Oxford for their comments and suggestions on this paper at the Fourth Conference on Interdisciplinary Approaches to Medieval Studies at Goldsmiths' College in September 1994.

This is the original English version of the paper published as "Die Sprache im Wunder – das Wunder ind der Sprache. Menschenwort und Logos bei Gregor von Tours", in: *Mitteilungen des Instituts für Österreichischen Geschichtsforschung* 103 (1995), pp. 1–25.

[2] For a survey of opinions on Gregory and his writings, see G. de Nie, *Views from a many-windowed tower. Studies of imagination in the works of Gregory of Tours*, Studies in classical antiquity 7 (Amsterdam 1987), pp. 8–22. In 1988, W. Goffart added an interpretation of Gregory's *Historiae* as satire: *Narrators of barbarian history* (Princeton 1988), pp. 112–234.

[3] See on this now: M. Heinzelmann, *Gregor von Tours (538–594), "Zehn Bücher Geschichte". Historiographie und Gesellschaftkonzept im 6. Jahrhundert* (Darmstadt 1994).

[4] As I have shown in G. de Nie, "De "kracht" van wat in het boek gezegd wordt: woord, schrift en teken in zesde-eeuws Gallië" [The "power" of what is said in the book: word, script and sign in sixth-century Gaul], in: R.E.V. Stuip and C. Vellekoop (ed.), *Oraliteit en schrift-*

The preface to what was probably his first work, *In gloria martyrum*, shows us a view of language that is completely different. There, he gives as his reason for recording miracles that they would "cause barren minds to become fruitful". In other words, that such stories would bring about a miracle: the creation of something out of nothing. What does he mean? Here is the passage in its context:

> Paul the Apostle also said: [...] "Let no evil talk come out of your mouth; but if someone is good in edifying, let him impart grace to those who hear."[5] Therefore it is fitting for us to follow, write and speak of those things which build up the Church of God and which, through holy instruction, *cause barren minds to become fruitful in the knowledge of perfect faith* [emphasis added] [...]. [I will not repeat] [...] the versions of the other stories which this author [Virgil] either mendaciously fashioned or pictured with heroic verse. But, seeing that all these are as though placed on sand and soon to be destroyed [in the approaching end of the world], let us turn to divine and evangelical miracles.[6]

---

cultuur [*Orality and Literacy*], Utrechtse Bijdragen tot de Mediëvistiek 12 (Hilversum 1993), pp. 63–88.

[5] Ephesians 4:29.

[6] *Sed et Paulus apostolus, ... Omnis sermo malus ex ore vestro non procedat; sed si quis bonus ad aedificationem, ut det gratiam audientibus. Ergo haec nos oportet sequi, scribere atque loqui quae ecclesiam Dei aedificent, et quae mentes inopes ad notitiam perfectae fidei instructione sancta fecundent....non reliquarum fabularum commenta, quae hic auctor aut finxit mendacio, aut versu depinxit heroico: sed ista omnia tanquam super arenam locata, et cito ruitura conspiciens, ad Divina et Evangelica miracula revertamur*. Gregorius Turonensis, *In gloria martyrum (Glor. mart.*), *prologus*, ed. B. Krusch, in: W. Arndt and B. Krusch (ed.), *Gregorii Turonensis opera*, Pars II: *Miracula et opera minora*, Monumenta Germaniae Historica [MGH], Scriptores rerum Merovingicarum [SSrM] 1.2 (Hannover 1885), pp. 484–561).

Georgius Florentius Gregorius was born in 539 in Clermont, became bishop of Tours in 573 and died in 594. Besides the above-mentioned, he wrote six other books of miracles and one of saints' lives (as he says in his *Histories* 10.31), collected in the above edition, 562–820: *De virtutibus S. Juliani* [*Virt. Jul.*], *De virtutibus S. Martini* [*Virt. Mart.*], *De vita patrum* [*Vit. patr.*], and *In gloria confessorum* [*Glor. conf.*]. His other works referred to in this paper are: *De cursu stellarum ratio qualiter ad officium implendum debeat observari* [*De cursu*], ed. B. Krusch, in: Arndt and Krusch, pp. 854–872; *In psalterii tractatum commentarius* [*In Psal.*], *ibid.* pp. 873–877; and finally: *Historiarum libri decem* [*Hist.*], ed. and transl. R. Buchner, 2 vols., Ausgewählte Quellen zur deutschen Geschichte des Mittelalters. Freiherr vom Stein-Gedächtnisausgabe 2 and 3 (Darmstadt 1967), based upon the edition by B. Krusch and W. Levison, MGH SSrM 1.1, editio altera (Hannover 1951).

One underlying text here, of course, is Paul's statement that "faith [comes forth] out of hearing (*fides ex auditu*)".[7] But how can a grace which "causes barren minds to become fruitful" be transmitted by the words of a miracle story? As if to explain this, Gregory goes on to say something that – as presented – does not seem to make sense or even be a coherent statement, either in itself, or as a reason for writing miracle stories:

> *That is why* [emphasis added] John the Evangelist began [his Gospel] by saying: "In the beginning was the Word, and the Word was with God, and God was the Word. This [Word] was in the beginning with God. All things were made by Him, and without Him nothing was made." And after that he said: "And the Word was made flesh and dwelled among us; and we saw His glory, the glory as of the only-begotten Son of the Father, full of grace and truth, [...]." [John 1:1–3, 14] [....] He is the salvation of the world.[8]

The manner of associative aggregation rather than abstract systematization of thoughts that we see in this passage is evident also in his reports of theological debates in the *Historiae*.[9] With the phrase "That is why", Gregory makes an unstated association which he expects his readers to be able to follow, and which supports his just-mentioned reason for writing: i.e. that, through the holy instruction of miracle stories, barren minds will become fruitful in the knowledge of perfect faith. But what is the unexpressed connection between this thought and those ostensibly unconnected quotations? One way to achieve an understanding of this elliptical – and crucial – passage is to uncover its *imagistic structure*.[10] With the latter, I mean the associative coherence or dynamic structure of the explicit and implicit imagery it contains. Upon closer examination, the passage at which we have just looked appears to consist of three implicitly associated clusters of images and notions. The first cluster is that around *the human word*: as in

---

[7] Romans 10:17.

[8] *Unde Johannis Evangelista exorsus est dicens: "In principio erat Verbum, et Verbum erat apud Deum, et Deus erat Verbum. Hoc erat in principio apud Deum. Omnia per ipsum facta sunt, et sine ipso factum est nihil." Et deinceps ait: "Et Verbum caro factum est, et habitavit in nobis; et vidimus gloriam eius, gloriam quasi Unigeniti a Patre, plenum gratia et veritate[...]" [....] Ipse est et salus mundi* (*Glor. mart. prol.*). J.H. Corbett, "Hagiography and the experience of the holy in the work of Gregory of Tours", *Florilegium* 7 (1985), pp. 40–54, also uses literary theory to interpret this preface, but in a different way.

[9] Theological discussions: *Hist.* 6.40 and 10.13; on Gregory's associative thinking in general, see de Nie, *Views*, 68–69.

[10] This phrase is P. Cox Miller's, in her: "The Blazing Body: Ascetic Desire in Jerome's Letter to Eustochium", *Journal of Early Christian Studies* 1.1 (1993), pp. 21–45, here p. 43.

Gregory's own words about miracle stories causing barren minds to become fruitful in faith; the second is structured around *God's Word as Creator*; and the third centres on the visible grace, truth and glory of *the embodied Word* and Son of God who saves the world. Equally essential, however, are the operative contexts within which these clusters occur: *hearing (or reading)* the human word, *knowing about* the divine Creator Word, and *seeing* the glory of the embodied Word.

To investigate the associations and resonances of these clusters in Gregory's writings, we need to recognize any connected images and notions in their various contexts, and to investigate their meanings, connotations and interrelations. The ones that I have spotted so far are:

- the divine Word as Creator
- creation from nothing
- the Virgin conception and birth
- words as "seeds of eternal life"
- the body of Christ as a symbol, and
- the idea of seeing Christ's glory in miraculous cures.

I shall argue that these images and notions, although remaining largely implicit, constitute a central associative network – or imagistic structure – underlying and configuring Gregory's presentation of his material.

Are Gregory's compressed thoughts about human words and the Word in this preface perhaps a reminiscence of Augustine's "Treatises on the Gospel of John", which discusses the same theme?[11] Since Gregory nowhere mentions the Church Father, one cannot prove direct knowledge, but one also cannot disprove it. In order to connect the idea of a creative dynamic in words with a notion with which we are familiar, and thus, to bring it somewhat into our "horizon of expectation",[12] I shall also place Gregory's view of words causing barren minds to become fruitful alongside two modern theories: on the one hand, modern reception theory's view of reader re-enactment (*réeffectuation*[13]) of a text, and, on the other, contemporary psychology's insight into the transformational potentialities of mental images. And, in arguing my case, I shall use not only distanced analysis and

[11] Aurelius Augustinus, *In Iohannis Evangelium Tractatus CXXIV*, 1.8–12, ed. and tr. M.-F. Berrouard, Oeuvres de St Augustin 71, 72, 73a, 73b, 74a (Paris 1993, 1987, 1988, 1989, 1993 resp.).

[12] Cf. H.R. Jauss, *Ästhetische Erfahrung und literarische Hermeneutik* I. *Versuche im Feld der ästhetischen Erfahrung*, UniTaschenbuch 692 (Munich 1977), p. 13.

[13] As P. Ricoeur, *Temps et récit* 3 (Paris 1985), p. 269.

linear argument. In order to show how Gregory's images 'work', I shall also use some of the same associative – that is: synthetic, multidimensional, concentric, analogical, participative and transformational – image-logic that appears in the writings of this late antique author.[14] For the main point that I wish to make in this paper is Gregory's recognition of what I would call, in modern terms, the dynamic of the image in the reception of a text.

Because of what will be seen to be their inseparable overlapping, I shall investigate the contents of the first two clusters, those of hearing the human word and knowing about the divine Word, together, and thereafter examine the third one, that of seeing the glory of the embodied Word.

I. The human and the divine word

A. *Church tradition: "incarnational rhetoric"*

A first way to begin to understand what Gregory is saying in the preface quoted above is to put it into its historical and literary context: the tradition of the Church on this point as it had developed up to his time. If indeed, as we saw, "faith [comes forth] out of hearing", what, more specifically, is heard? An answer to this question is found in another apostolic letter to which Gregory may be implicitly referring. Here, the Thessalonians are told:

> And we also thank God constantly for this, that when you received from us the word of God which you heard (*cum accepissetis a nobis verbum auditus Dei)*, you received it not as the word of men, but as what it really is: the word of God that works in you who have come to believe (*verbum Dei qui operatur in vobis qui credidistis*).[15]

[14] K.F. Morrison, *History as a visual art in the twelfth-century renaissance* (Princeton 1990), p. 47 and passim, has a similar approach to early medieval texts.

[15] Thessalonians 2:13. Throughout this paper, the biblical passages quoted in Latin are from the Vulgate. This viewpoint is interpreted as follows by a New Testament scholar: "... the primary and intrinsic secret to which the New Testament message directs us is that God's word has become *one* with man's word, that it has come to us and become understandable in a human word" (G. Bornkamm, "God's Word and Man's Word in the New Testament" (in his *Early Christian experience* [London 1969] pp. 4–5). The quotation occurs on p. 1113 in an overview of the meaning of the word in the classical texts, the Old and New Testaments and modern scholarly thought: 'Word, tongue, utterance' in *The New International Dictionary of New Testament Theology* 3 (Grand Rapids 1976), pp. 1078–1146. According to J. Soldati, the second-century Church Father Irenaeus understood the Logos as the 'voice' with which the Father speaks in the revelation to mankind, as did the writer of the Fourth Gospel: J.A. Soldati,

That Gregory shared this view is evident in his referring to the apostle Paul as he "in whom Christ himself, as he says, spoke (*in quo ipse, ut ait, Christus loquebatur*)".[16]

The notion of "fruitfulness" is, of course, found in Christ's parable of the Sower. Luke's Gospel reports him saying that "the seed is the word of God", and that the growth of seeds in good soil is like that in those of good heart who, having heard it, "bring forth fruit (*fructum adferunt*)".[17] Mark speaks of these as those "who hear the word and accept it and bear fruit (*qui audiunt et suscipiunt et fructificant*), thirtyfold, and sixtyfold and a hundred-fold."[18] Gregory's emphasis upon the divine Word in connection with his own words about miracles, however, points to a more developed meaning: a larger cluster of associated images and notions.

Marcia Colish has shown that Augustine, whose works dominated western Church tradition for centuries, also held the view that God's creative Word, as such, can be actively present in human words about the truths of faith. In very pregnant phrasing, she says:

> For Augustine, [...] God creates the world and man through his Word, and he takes on humanity in the Word made flesh *so that human words may take on divinity*, thereby bringing man and the world back to God [...]. *Christian eloquence becomes, both literally and figuratively, a vessel of the Spirit, bearing the Word to mankind.* [emphasis added]

She designates this as Augustine's view of "incarnational rhetoric", based upon the dynamic of words creating – as in the Annunciation – something from nothing in the hearer.[19] Discussing the passages that Gregory quotes and showing their meaning for the phenomenon of language, the Church Father may be saying more explicitly what Gregory expects the (clerical?)

'Talking like gods: new voices of authority', in: R.C. Smith and J. Lounibos (ed.), *Pagan and Christian anxiety* (Lanham 1984), pp. 184–5. See also: R.M. Grant, *The Letter and the Spirit* (London 1957), passim.

[16] *Hist.* 10.13; cf. 2 Corinthians 13.3.

[17] Luke 8:11, 15.

[18] Mark 4:20.

[19] M. Colish, *The mirror of language. A study in the medieval theory of knowledge*, Revised edition (Lincoln–London 1983), p. 26. On pagan and Christian rhetoric in the late antique period see J.J. Murphy, *Rhetoric in the Middle Ages. A history of rhetorical theory from St. Augustine to the Renaissance* (Berkeley 1974), pp. 43–77. S. Spence, *The rhetorics of reason and desire* (Ithaca–London 1988), pp. 80–90, builds upon Colish's view of Augustine's "incarnational rhetoric" and, pointing to his view of the role of language, shows how the Annunciation is a central configuring theme in his work.

reader to understand. After mentioning that ordinary words seem to disappear when their sound passes away, Augustine says:

> But there is also a word in man himself, that remains inside him, for the sound goes forth from the mouth. There is a word which is truly spoken in a spiritual way: that which you understand by hearing the sound, not the sound itself (*Est verbum et in ipso homine, quod manet intus, nam sonus procedit ex ore. Est verbum quod vere spiritualiter dicitur, illud quod intelligis de sono, non ipse sonus*).[20]

For Augustine, the rhetor, the verbal sign was therefore the necessary medium for becoming aware of things, and hence the medium of all knowing and understanding.[21]

Elsewhere in the same work, he writes that when God – through human words – speaks the Word which is the Truth to the understanding mind, [the] Truth is born there. Was Gregory thinking of this kind of fruitfulness or generation? Augustine says:

> [the Truth] speaks internally to the understanding minds; she instructs without sound, she flows through with intelligible light. The one who is able to see in her the eternity of her birth, in this manner hears her speaking, according to what the Father says to her that she should speak (*intelligentibus mentibus intus loquitur, sine sono instruit, intellegibili luce perfundit. Qui ergo potest in ea videre nativitatis eius aeternitatem, ipse illam sic audit loquentem, sicut ei dixit Pater quod loqueretur*).[22]

This truth can only be Christ, who not only is the divine Word, but, as Augustine says elsewhere, also the divine Wisdom.[23] This becomes clear in one of his sermons, when he tells his audience:

> You too are [the] members of Christ [...]. Therefore, let the members of Christ give birth in mind, as Mary, a virgin, gave birth to Him in her womb; and thus you will be mothers of Christ (*et vos membra Christi estis[...]. Ergo in mente*

---

[20] *Tract.* 1.8.

[21] As J. Coleman, *Ancient and medieval memories. Studies in the reconstruction of the past* (Cambridge 1992), p. 84.

[22] *Tract.* 54.8.

[23] *Tract.* 1.16. Cf. 1 Corinthians 1:24: *[nos autem praedicamus] Christum Dei virtutem et Dei sapientiam.*

> *pariant membra Christi, sicut Maria in ventre virgo peperit Christum; et sic eritis matres Christi*).[24]

In the receiving-through-hearing of God's word through human words, then, Christ – as the divine Word, the Truth, and Wisdom – is born in the heart. He dwells there as the interior Teacher – the Word of God as the *verbum mentis*.[25] As Janet Coleman formulates it:

> True words were none other than signs of the *verbum mentis* [...]. There is no distinct historical Christ here. Verbal signs truly mirror an eternal, unchanging truth, and it is through words that a believer is transformed in Christ to a trans-linguistic vision of God.[26]

As we shall see below, elsewhere in the *Treatises* Augustine speaks of (Christ's) miracles as God's visible words, and this impinges upon another theme that is central to Gregory's thinking. If he did not read Augustine's work, such views must have reached him through church tradition. In my recent research on sanctity and motherhood in late Antiquity, I have found the notion of spiritual generation through the divine Word, as imaged in the Annunciation and the Virgin Birth, to be a central ideal and model for life in ascetic and celibate circles.[27] The "mind fruitful through [with?] God (*mens fecunda Deo*)", as Gregory's friend Venantius Fortunatus formulated it,[28] or fruitfulness in the knowing of faith, as Gregory called it, must have been an ideal state of mind to which many aspired.

Modern reception theory, of course, says something very similar in non-religious terms. Paul Ricoeur, for instance, asserts that the reading of a narrative will induce in the reader an involuntary affective mimesis, and thus an inner re-enactment, of its dynamic affective pattern or "configuration". To integrate this new experience into his existing world view, the reader must thereupon "refigure" the latter to some degree.[29] Similarly, Sallie McFague,

---

[24] Augustinus, *Sermo* (Denis) 15.8, ed. G. Morin, *Sancti Augustini Sermones post Maurinos reperti* (Rome 1930).

[25] Augustinus, *De Magistro* 11.38 and 12.40 (PL 32.1216–17); cited in J.A. Mazzeo, *Renaissance and Seventeenth-century Studies* (New York–London 1964), p. 16.

[26] Coleman, *Memories*, pp. 87, 100.

[27] G. de Nie, "'Consciousness fecund through God': from male fighter to spiritual bride-mother in late antique female sanctity", in: Anneke B. Mulder-Bakker (ed.), *Sanctity and Motherhood* (New York 1995), p. 101.

[28] *Mens fecunda Deo*: Venantius Fortunatus, *Carmina* (*Carm.*) 8.9.1, ed. F. Leo, MGH Auctores Antiquissimi [AA] 4.1 (Berlin 1881).

[29] Cf. P. Ricoeur, *Temps et récit* III, *Le temps raconté* (Paris 1985), pp. 203–79.

a philosophically inclined theologian, has argued that a parable such as that of the seed that must die to live – but also any story or poem – can be an extended metaphor or a visualization of invisible and inexpressible experience as embodied in sensory phenomena. To understand it, the reader must not only imitate the movement of the image (e.g. that of the dying seed that bursts into new life), but also 'translate' the statement, or make the 'leap' from the visible event to the invisible experience which it symbolizes or 'figures'. In doing so, she says, he undergoes an inner transformation.[30] Karl Morrison has shown that in certain medieval texts the same effect was achieved by leaving out the crux of the matter: the reader must "leap" over the discontinuities of the silences between the words" to construct it himself – thereby mimicking and thus experiencing the movement of its configuration or affective pattern.[31] Gregory's apparently discontinuous passage about the Word of God appears to be an example of this latter kind of writing.

His succinct and often understated manner of telling miracle stories, too, seems to show that, in his own sixth-century way, he used the above-mentioned literary strategies to make his miracle stories effect similar transformations. In the preface to one of these, for instance, he tells us:

> to us, versed as we are in the doctrine of the Church, it seems that the history (*historia*) that pertains to the edification of the church should avoid wordiness (*verbositas*) and be woven with brief and simple speech (*brevi atque simplici sermone texatur*), so that it [...] brings forward (*prodat*) the power of the blessed bishop [...].[32]

What does he mean with the latter phrase: how is the saint's power "brought forward"? In Gregory's world view – just as in that of oral cultures of the present and recent past – mind, body and cosmos, divine and human, as well as visible and invisible, are essentially connected and participate in each other through analogical forms.[33] Accordingly, a spiritual reality or message

---

[30] S. McFague, *Speaking in parables. A study in metaphor and theology* (Philadelphia 1975), pp. 66–89.

[31] K.F. Morrison, *History as a Visual Art in the Twelfth-Century Renaissance* (Princeton 1990), p. 54, and idem, *I Am You. The Hermeneutics of Empathy in Western Literature, Theology and Art* (Princeton 1988), pp. 169–71.

[32] *Virt. Mart.* 2.19.

[33] Cf. R. Devisch, "The *Mbwoolu* cosmogony and healing cult among the northern Yaka of Zaire", in: A. Jacobson-Widding and W. Van Beek (ed.), *The Creative Communion. African folk models of fertility and the regeneration of life*, Uppsala studies in cultural anthropology 15

can be observed as present in a visible pattern in a natural phenomenon (a sword-like comet, for instance, to indicate imminent slaughter) or in a human event (as: epidemics and false prophets, pointing to the beginning of the Last Times before the end of the world). We shall see that Gregory uses the term "figure" or "sign" for such a pattern.[34] As for Augustine (but with a significant difference), for Gregory too, miracles – and this is central to our present concern – are such "signs" or embodied spiritual patterns.[35] In what follows, I hope to show that the pattern of the invisible sudden recreation – the "leap" of the saint's (but in fact, Christ's) creative power in effecting a cure – is what he feels that a miracle makes visible, and what he wishes to induce the listener to re-enact.

Having looked at the tradition in which Gregory stands, and at some modern views which may offer insights into this late antique way of thinking, we will now look at the images and ideas which Gregory associated with the themes of human and divine words.

B. *The Word as Creator*

To begin with the divine Word: Gregory explicitly designates Christ as the Word and as Creator. In the preface to Book 1 of the *Histories*, beginning with a confession of Catholic orthodoxy, Gregory states: "I believe Christ to be the Word (*Verbum*) of the Father through Whom all is made. This Word I believe to have been made flesh (*carne[m] factum*), through Whose suffering the world was redeemed." Chapter 1 then commences: "In the beginning the Lord formed (*furmavit* [sic]) heaven and earth in His Christ – that is, in His Son – who is the origin of all." In what is left of his *In psalterii tractatum commentarius*, Gregory says that Christ "created all the elements that we see".[36] But he also – significantly – says that he "is the highest [deepest] indweller of all (*omnis et altissimus habitator*)".[37] According to Gregory, then, the divine Word and Creator is immanent in the world, as well as transcendent. The far-reaching implications of this idea will become evident.

(Uppsala 1990), pp. 111–28. On this view in late Antiquity, see C. Stancliffe, *St Martin and his hagiographer. History and miracle in Sulpicius Severus* (Oxford 1983), pp. 215–16.

[34] A compendium of such "figures" is that of Eucherius Lugdunensis, *Formulae spiritualis intelligentiae*, ed. C. Wotke, CSEL 31 (Prague–Vienna–Leipzig 1894), pp. 1–62.

[35] As for instance, about St Martin's miracles: *Nemo ergo de anteactis virtutibus dubitet, cum praesentium signorum cernit munera dispensari* (*Virt. Mart. prol.*)

[36] *In Psal.* 73.

[37] *Ibid.* 82.

Further, Gregory says about the content of Psalm 32: "[It shows] that in Him, Who is the Word of the Father (*Verbum Patris*), the heavens and their powers are confirmed (*caeli virtutesque eorum firmati sunt*)".[38] The passage in the psalm that he must be referring to is: "Through the word of the Lord the heavens are confirmed, and through the breath of his mouth all their power (*verbo Domini caeli firmati sunt, et spiritu oris eius omnis virtus eorum*)".[39] The reference in the Psalm is to the spoken divine word of creation. Gregory's explicit purpose in his *Commentary*, however, is to show, as he says, that the Psalms "teach, pronounce and designate (*docent, pronuntia[n]t, designa[n]t*)" Christ's redemption of man and the promise of the Kingdom of Heaven as their "truth of spiritual understanding (*veritas spiritalis intellegentiae*)".[40] Not only visible phenomena, then, but also texts – and specifically those of the Old Testament – contain hidden patterns of spiritual truth. Such patterns he variously designates as "figures (*figurae*)" or "forms (*typi*)".[41] Of the crossing through the Red Sea, for instance, he says that it is a *typus* of the later Christian baptism.[42] What spiritual pattern did he see in Psalm 32? It is tempting to regard Gregory's making the singular *virtus* in the Bible quotation into the plural *virtutes* as a reference to Christ's miracles sent from heaven, about which he wrote so much and which he often designates as powerful deeds or *virtutes*.[43] If so, this is a significant move from an abstract, conceptual meaning to a visible, embodied one – a characteristic of his writing which I shall be concerned to emphasize.

C. *Creation from nothing and the Virginal conception*

Connected with the Word as Creator, the idea of creation from nothing is one of the cardinal, and most dynamic, tenets of Gregory's world view, and the fundament of his expectation of the miraculous at any and every moment. He likes to refer to it when he wishes to indicate that nothing is impossible for God: "all things are possible for he who believes (*omnia possibilia sunt credenti*)".[44] To introduce the story of a poor hermit who cooked his food in a wooden pot, for instance, Gregory says:

---

[38] *Ibid.* 32.

[39] Psalm 32:6.

[40] *In Psal. prol.*

[41] On "figurative" thinking in late antiquity see E. Auerbach, "Figura", *Archivum Romanicum* 22 (1938), pp. 436–89.

[42] *Hist.* 1.10.

[43] As in the titles of his miracle books; see note 6.

[44] *Hist.* 2.3.

> Behold the quality and number of riches that poverty in the world gathers for its adherents, so that the Redeemer – who created all things from nothing – not only gives them all that they desire, but even commands the elements to obey them.[45]

Elsewhere, after having stated that the germination of seeds and the new leaves each spring on trees are a sign of (*signat*) of the Resurrection – thus: a pattern or figure of spiritual truth made visible in sensory phenomena – Gregory continues:

> Which miracle (*miraculum*), even though here used as a parable (*similitudine*), here and now exhibits a favour to the peoples [of the world], so that man should know that he receives food from the One who created him out of nothing.[46]

Gregory here reflects the biblical view, reformulated by Augustine, that God continues his Creation in all phenomena, and that hence everything is a miracle. Some miracles, however, are more familiar than others.[47] At the Resurrection, Gregory says elsewhere, God can also restore mutilated bodies to their pristine form, because "for Him who created unborn things from nothing (*qui ex nihilo non nata creavit*), it is not difficult to restore what has been lost".[48]

But Gregory also uses the image of the Virginal Conception and birth to point to the dynamic of the creation of something material – in this case: Jesus' human body – from nothing.[49] Thus, when a previously half empty wine cask overflowed with wine after a vigil in honour of the martyr Julian, Gregory explains the event by saying: "The Lord did this to glorify the martyr, just as He filled the womb of the Virgin without seed, making her a mother while remaining chaste".[50] And when, also after a vigil, this time by destitute monks of a monastery dedicated to the Virgin, praying for food, a heap of gold coins was found the following morning on the altar of their locked church, Gregory again refers to the creation out of nothing in the Virgin's conception: "It is no wonder (*Nec mirum*) that the blessed Virgin, without any labour, produced (*sine labore ... protulit*) food for her

[45] *Glor. Conf.* 96.

[46] *De Cursu* 11.

[47] *Tract.* 24.1. See also: R.M. Grant, *Miracle and Natural Law in Graeco-Roman and Early Christian Thought* (Amsterdam 1952), pp. 217, 263.

[48] *Hist.* 10.13. Cf. 2 Maccabees 7:28.

[49] Mentioned in the author's confession of orthodox belief in *Hist.* 1. *prol.*.

[50] *Virt. Jul.* 35.

dependants, since she conceived without union with a man, and remained a virgin also after having given birth."[51]

Characteristically, Gregory here *images rather than conceptualizes* the dynamic pattern or figure that is made visible in the event narrated: the Annunciation. Golden coins were created out of nothing in the locked church just as Christ was conceived and brought forth in Mary through the spoken word that, without rupturing the body, penetrated to the heart and created something out of nothing there. Because the church and the monastery were dedicated to the Virgin, they are somehow expected to participate in her qualities. In other words: the dynamic pattern realized in her extended to those who had joined themselves, spiritually, to her. But the Annunciation, the unexpressed central image or figure in this passage, does not surface in Gregory's language. Perhaps because of what he saw as its self-evident centrality here and elsewhere, Gregory – similarly to what we have seen him do in the preface – even does not mention it explicitly anywhere in his works. Equally unsaid, but associatively evoked, is Christ's creating out of nothing as the core of miraculous action.

That Gregory indeed regarded creation out of nothing, or "causing to become fruitful", as the innermost dynamic and fundamental pattern of all beneficent miracles[52] may also be inferred from the following passage:

> But why should we wonder at [the saint's] giving back to human beings a mind that had been troubled by adversity, when he often converts sterility into fruitfulness (*Sed quid mirum, si sensum adversitate turbatum reddat hominibus, qui saepius sterilitatem in fecunditatem convertit*)?[53]

D. *Words: "seeds of eternal life"*

The abbot of the Virgin's monastery, however, had anticipated her aid. In what Gregory makes him say we see another example of the idea of participative analogy: "Let us pray, most beloved brothers, and the Lord will give us food; for *it cannot happen* [emphasis added] that wheat be lacking in the monastery of the one who brought forth from her womb the fruit of life (*frugem vitae*) for a perishing world". Here, we see again how Gregory regards biblical events as the models for interpreting contemporary ones that

[51] *Glor. Mart.* 11.

[52] It is obvious that miracles can also make visible a religious message – apprehended only by those who already believe – or intimidate by the punishment of the wicked. The "faith" that may be induced by the latter, however, is in fact fear.

[53] *Virt. Mart.* 4.11.

can be made to look analogical. The fruit (grain?) of life is, of course, Christ as the bread of the Eucharist, through which the believer receives eternal life.

But Gregory also speaks of another kind of seeds in connection with Christ and eternal life. In the preface to one of his saints' lives he tells us:

> Among the other seeds of eternal life which the heavenly Sower irrigated the field of the untilled mind from the Fount of Divinity by His precept and made fertile by His teaching, He said (*Inter reliqua vitae perpetuae semina, quae coelestis sator ex illo divinitatis fonte mentis incultae arvum vel irrigavit institutione, vel dogmate fecundavit, ait*): "Whoever does not take up his cross and follow Me, is not worthy of Me."[54]

Here, the seeds are Christ's sayings or parables: divine words in human language 'out of' which, as it were, eternal life sprouts when these 'seeds' are introduced into the untaught human mind as a barren, uncultivated field. This is the image behind Gregory's expression "barren (*inops*) mind": it is a field lying waste. Gregory has taken the biblical image of God's word as a seed and applied it to his own words relaying those of God. Although other writers in this period appeal to divine inspiration to guide their writing, as Gregory also does,[55] they do not say that Christ, as the divine Word, is immanent in their own human words, as Gregory here appears to do. I have indicated that direct or indirect Augustinian influence as a reason for this is likely, but must remain speculative.

How can Christ's saying be a "seed" and how does it sprout? Gregory suggests that the sprouting happens through the listener's meditation upon, which is internalization and interior re-enactment of, the imaged dynamic pattern presented in the text. In this case, the image is Christ's suffering and death, leading to resurrection, which is analogous to the image of the seed dying into new life which is suggested in the first part of the passage. The imitation of Christ effects disengagement from the world as a means to future rebirth into eternal life.

Elsewhere, Gregory explicitly associates the sprouting of seeds with a dynamic in words:

---

[54] *Vit. Patr.* 2. *prol.*; Matthew 10:38.

[55] Gregorius: *Virt. Mart. prol.* Cf. his friend Venantius Fortunatus, *Vita Martini. praef.* 9: *De Verbo poscite verba*, ed. F. Leo, MGH AA 4.1 (Berlin 1881).

> When seeds are sown in the earth and covered by the furrows, they rise up high with the coming of the summer, adorned with leaves and ears, nourished inside with sap and fat. This the Lord, the Sower of spiritual doctrine, turned into a parable about the advance of His words, which He scattered among the people (*de profecto verborum suorum, quae in populos iaciebat*), saying: "Thus is the word of God (*Sic est verbum Dei*): as if a man should scatter seed, and should rise night and day; [...] [Gregory omits a verse here] for the earth produces of itself, first the blade, then the ear, then the full grain in the ear".[56]

Here, Gregory appears to be quoting Mark, but he has omitted Mark's statement verbalizing the mystery as such: "[...] and the seed should sprout and grow, he knows not how".[57] It is the mystery that happens in the silence between sowing and sprouting, and also that between the hearing of Christ's words and their "producing" faith in human hearts. Mark's passage, however, does not speak of the advance of the *word* of God, but of that of "the Kingdom of God (*regnum Dei*)". Gregory himself has substituted "word" for "Kingdom". Although it is based on Mark's statement that this Kingdom is sown through the word: "The one who sows, sows the word (*Qui seminat, verbum seminat*)"[58], it is a very significant substitution indeed. For Gregory, then, words can contain a "seed" that can "advance", or produce something new.

Luke's Gospel, however, specifies: "The seed is the word of God (*Semen est verbum Dei*)".[59] The notion of the overlapping of the human and the divine word in the Gospel message must be implicit here. In addition, Gregory may have in mind a dynamic such as that mentioned in Isaiah:[60]

> Just as rain and snow fall from heaven and do not return there, but drench the earth and pour into it, and make it germinate (*sed inebriat terram et infundit eam et germinare eam facit*), giving seed to the sower and bread to the eater, thus will be My word (*verbum*) that goes forth from my mouth, and does not return to me empty.

As in the passage about Christ's teaching, the word of God, then, is also the rain that makes the field – i.e. the human mind – fruitful.

---

[56] *De Cursu* 11; Mark 4:26, 28.
[57] Mark 4:27. Luke's statement, however, is similar; see below.
[58] Mark 4:14.
[59] Luke 8:11.
[60] Isaiah 55:10–11.

Is there more specific evidence of *how* Gregory thinks that the word can – analogically – "pour into" human beings and make something "germinate" in them?

E. *The seed in the word*

An answer to this question is found in one story, in which Gregory shows us how he thinks words –with a good admixture of tears, however – can in fact 'generate' eternal life: a new bride persuading her husband to live in chastity together in order to merit Paradise. In this speech – of course wholly invented by our author – the bride looks through the worldly riches that her husband brings to the marriage to the images of the true, spiritual reality as the Church has presented it to her:

> Earthly beauties horrify me because I see (*suspicio*) the hands of the Redeemer pierced for the life of the world. Nor do I perceive (*Non cerno*) diadems flashing with precious jewels, when in my mind I gaze in wonder *(miror mente)* at the crown of thorns.[61]

She rejects her husband's vast lands "because I long for the pleasantness of Paradise. Your terraces disgust me when I see (*suspicio*) the Lord seated [on His throne] above the stars." When her husband remonstrates that their parents want heirs to their properties, she counters that this transitory life is nothing compared to the life in heaven that is not ended by death or destruction, and in which one remains "in eternal beatitude", "lives in never-setting sunlight", "enjoying the presence of the Lord Himself through contemplation, translated into the angelic state, and rejoices with indissoluble gladness."

As Gregory tells it, the bridegroom's inner re-enactment of this verbalized visualization of a rejection of this world for a total experience of radiant beauty, engendering joy and love,[62] causes him to 'refigure'[63] his world view. This is evident in what he lets the bridegroom say:

---

[61] *Hist.* 1.47.

[62] On Bede's aesthetic, Morrison, *History*, p. 64, writes: "The object was to understand images, not only as manifestations but also as revelations. In the end, that rendering, whether of verbal or of visual forms, was an affective, indeed an erotic, translation of fear into the love that casts out fear, an affective transport [...]."

[63] Ricoeur's term for the activity of the reader appropriating the 'configuration' of experience in a text, in his *Temps et récit* III, p. 270.

> "Through your sweetest discourse," he said, "eternal life shines into me like a great star (*Dulcissimis [...] eloquiis tuis aeterna mihi vita tamquam magnum iubar inluxit*), and therefore if you wish to abstain from carnal desire, I will join you in this undertaking."

This passage is the key to Gregory's view of the effects of mental images evoked by words. Through a deliberate choice of images and counter-images, he creates the new, composite mental image of the light-filled life in Paradise. Then he lets this "great star" which the bride's words have evoked in her bridegroom, precipitate the latter's new decision.

A modern psychotherapist has stated that a mental image can be a visualized pattern of feeling.[64] Roberto Assagioli, the founder of an important humanist school of psychotherapy, has said about the potentialities of mental images that symbols (such as, in this case, a star-like existence in heaven) "can be visualized and this [visualization] sets into motion unconscious psychological processes. [They] are transformers of psychic energy". And further, quoting Ch. Baudoin: "images and mental pictures tend to produce the physical conditions and external acts corresponding to them."[65] Images introduced into the mind from without, then, induce an involuntary affective mimesis whose dynamic is analogous to their symbolic form, and this experience initiates an autonomous process of mental, emotional, and physical transformation.[66]

In an important sense, then, what Gregory called "creation out of nothing" through the word can be understood to occur, as in this last story: namely, through the transforming effect of an affect-laden composite mental image, evoked by the verbal one – the pierced hands and the crown of thorns, over against the liberating light of the new, eternal life. This image is the "seed of eternal life" that "germinates" by inducing an experience of Christ's renunciation as leading to inexpressible peace and joy. Through the transforming effect of this experience, the image initiates a new mode of life: that is, it creates something out of nothing. The Annunciation must be Gregory's unexpressed model for words producing this "fruitfulness" which,

---

[64] G. Epstein, *Waking dream therapy: dream process as imagination* (New York–London 1981), p. 18: "images are the concretizations of emotions".

[65] R. Assagioli, *Psychosynthesis* (New York 1965), pp. 180 and 144 resp. Cf. also: D. Ogden, "The mimetic impulse or the Doppelgänger effect", in: R.L. Erenstein (ed.), *Theatre and television* (Amsterdam 1988), pp. 21–49.

[66] Cf. Morrison, *History*, p. 47, who speaks of "the multiplication of visual and verbal images and their translation by affective mimesis into epiphanies not open to all."

as we saw, was the late antique ideal of the knowledge or experience of "faith". The "seed" in the word, then, is likely to be an image.

II. Seeing the glory of the embodied Word

A. *The Virgin birth*

The third notional cluster – which is also a composite image –, is that of seeing the glory of the embodied Word. For the Annunciation not only shows how words can create something out of nothing; it also shows how verbal truth can become embodied truth. In the preface to his only spiritual biography of a woman, the lady Monegund, Gregory says:

> The extraordinary spiritual gifts (*charismata*) of the divine benefits which are granted in a heavenly manner to the human race, can neither be conceived by the understanding, nor expressed through words, nor contained in writing (*nec sensu concipi, nec verbis effari, nec scripturis poterunt comprehendi*): when the Saviour of the world himself in the beginning of time let himself be seen (*videri*) by the uneducated patriarchs, be announced (*annuntiari*) by the prophets, and, finally, he deigned to let himself be received by the womb (*utero suscipi*) of the ever virginal Mary; and [thus] the most powerful and immortal Creator suffered to be clothed with the covering of mortal flesh.[67]

Men "saw", i.e. mentally imaged, the Creator-Saviour, or received verbal messages about Him, but a woman "received" him in her womb: that is, was willing to serve as the instrument for his becoming embodied. Both kinds of reception, by the way, visual-auditive and physical, are presented as purely passive: the receiver does no more than provide as it were the 'soil' for the 'seed', which alone contains the generative principle. For the world view that Gregory inherited was patriarchal and monogenetic.[68] Gregory seems to be saying here – and this is a crucial point – that, with the Incarnation, this spiritual truth is no longer represented only by words: it can also be seen, and experienced in the body. At the same time, however, he says that this truth can hardly be verbalized or mentally inspected.[69] He appears to be

---

[67] *Vit. Patr.* 19. *prol.*

[68] Cf. C. Delaney, "The meaning of paternity and the virgin birth debate", *Man* (1986), pp. 494–513.

[69] Compare Venantius Fortunatus, *Vita S. Hilarii* 3, ed. B. Krusch, MGH AA 4.2: *Ut pene mihi videatur aequale tam istud posse dicere quam digito caelum tangere.*

talking about the truth in which we live and act and are empowered, but cannot adequately conceptualize – in other words: "embodied" truth.[70]

Perhaps precisely because, as we saw, the Virgin's receiving the Word in her heart had come to represent the model of the relations between God and human beings in general, Gregory here and there manifests a special reverence for motherhood and nurturing. This is evident not only in his affectionate relations with his own mother,[71] but also, for instance, in the passage on the cherished little ones, up to then tenderly protected from every danger, that died in an epidemic.[72] One of his best friends was the saintly and royal nun Radegund in nearby Poitiers, whose funeral he describes in his *In Gloria Confessorum*. A nun later described Gregory's reaction when he came in and saw her:

> as he himself later used to say, weeping and with an oath, it seemed to him as though he had seen the face of an angel in the appearance of a human being – a face that shone as a rose and a lily; the devout man, full of God, stood there, trembling and so struck with awe, [that it seemed to him] as though he were in the presence of the blessed Mother of God.[73]

Here, we see a reflection of the late antique ascetic ideal of spiritual motherhood as another associative dimension of Gregory's thinking about "fruitfulness" through receiving and conceiving the Word. What we are also seeing is the unresolved tension between a mental image and sensory perception in an overpowering experience of embodied truth.[74]

B. *Christ as embodied Truth*

What, however, was felt to be the "embodied truth" about oneself? A very prominent image of the self, individual and collective, in Gregory's work is

[70] Compare P. Bourdieu, *Le sens pratique* (Paris 1980), p. 94.

[71] Gregory mentions her in: *Hist.* 5.5; *Glor. mart.* 50, 85; *Virt. Mart.* 1. *prol.*; 3.10, 60; *Glor. conf.* 3, 40, 84; *Vit. patr.* 7.2.

[72] *Hist.* 5.34.

[73] *Cum autem venit ad locum, ubi sanctum corpus iacebat, – quod ipse postea cum sacramento lacrimans dicebat, quod in specie hominis vultum angelicum viderat, facies illius velut rosa et lilium fulgebat, – ita tremefactus est ac metu concussus, tamquam si ante praesentiam beatae genetricis Domini adstaret devotus vir, Deo plenus.* Baudonivia, *Vita sanctae Radegundis* 23, ed. B. Krusch, *Vitae sanctorum generis regii*, MGH SSrM 2 (Hannover 1888), pp. 377–393.

[74] See on this, G. de Nie, "Seeing and believing in the early middle ages: a preliminary investigation", in: M. Heusser *et al.* (ed.), *The Pictured Word* (Amsterdam 1998), pp. 67–76.

an ambiguous one: that of the wounded body.[75] One meaning of this image appears most explicitly when he says that Christ, "the immortal Creator",

> leads us, pierced by the arrowheads of our heinous crimes, and covered with wounds [inflicted by] deceitful brigands, after having poured [upon us] wine and oil, through His teaching, to the abode of the heavenly remedy, which is: the teaching of the holy Church (*nos, gravium facinoribus spiculis sauciatos, ac latronum insidiantium vulneribus affectos, infuso meri oleique liquore, ad stabulum medicinae coelestis, id est Ecclesiae sanctae, dogma perduxit*).[76]

Underneath this image of woundedness, the ideal is, of course, its opposite: the inviolate, closed body and mind as perfect receptacle for the indwelling Christ. This ideal was associated with the ascetic celibates in the Church, and it may have symbolized the analogous position of the Christian monk or of a clerical or monastic corporation that is set apart from society.[77]

In the Pauline epistles, however, the ideal of the Christian community is to recognize oneself in, and to be assimilated to, the body of Christ.[78] Gregory mentions this view in the prologue to his *Commentary on the Psalms*, speaking of "the Church, which is the body of Christ (*eclesia [sic], quae est corpus Christi*)". Assimilation to this body was the way to salvation. Gregory quotes the apostle Paul saying: "For we are buried into death with Christ through our baptism, so that, as he died and rose again, likewise we too shall walk in the newness of life".[79] Elsewhere Gregory formulates the theme somewhat differently: "Through His birth we are

---

[75] An image that is connected with closure and with pollution. On Gregory's view of the body see G. de Nie, "Le corps, la fluidité, et l'identité personelle dans la vision du monde de Grégoire de Tours", in: M. van Uytfange and R. Demeulenaere (ed.), *Aevum inter utrumque*, Instrumenta patristica 23 (Steenbrugge–the Hague 1991), pp. 75–87; on pollution: G. de Nie, "Is een vrouw een mens? Voorschrift, vooroordeel en praktijk in zesde-eeuws Gallië" [Is a woman a human being? Precept, prejudice and practice in sixth-century Gaul], in: F. de Haan *et al.* (ed.), *Het raadsel Vrouwengeschiedenis* [*The riddle of women's history*], 10e Jaarboek voor Vrouwengeschiedenis (Nijmegen 1989), pp. 56–64. On the body in Late Antiquity see P. Brown, *The Body and Society. Men, Women, and Sexual Renunciation in Early Christianity* (New York 1988).

[76] *Vit. Patr.* 19. *prol.*

[77] Cf. M. Douglas, *Purity and danger. An analysis of the concepts of pollution and taboo* (London [1966] 1984), p. 128: "[...] rituals work upon the body politic through the symbolic medium of the physical body."

[78] As for instance in Romans 12:5: *ita multi unum corpus sumus in Christo*. Cf. 1 Corinthians 12.

[79] Romans 6:4; *Hist.* 10.13.

reborn, through His baptism we are cleansed, through His wound healed (*vulnere curati*), through His resurrection raised up, and through His ascension glorified".[80] This statement combines assimilation through congruence with assimilation through inversion.[81] Clearly, the remedy for the wounded body-self was a voluntary assimilation to the suffering of Christ, an assimilation which would guarantee a new spiritual body-self in heaven. Human suffering, then, is given a *raison d'être* and is even intensified because, through the imitation of Christ, it was regarded as a purification.

It is especially in the hearts of the saints that Christ's wounded and resurrected body is constantly realized. Gregory paraphrases and quotes the apostle Paul's description of the Christian life:

> Ever enclosing the dying [on the Cross; or mortification] (*mortificatio*) of Christ in your body (*corpus*), so that the life (*vita*) of Jesus is manifested on your mortal heart (*cor*), so as to be able to say with the apostle Paul: "Not I live, but Christ lives in me."[82]

Similarly, he speaks of saints as being predestined by God "to be conformed to the image of His Son (*conformes fieri imaginis Filii sui*)".[83] "Conformation to the body of the Lord (*dominici corporis conformatio*)", as Gregory says elsewhere about the corpses of two priests – whose tombs are mysteriously rising out of the ground – is being taken up into His resurrected life.[84]

How is this assimilation to the body and life of Christ achieved during life? Gregory tells us explicitly: through meditatively dwelling upon mental images.[85] He writes:

> Through the eyes of the inner mind they were seeing the Lord of the Heavens descending to the earth [...]; they were seeing Him hanging upon the Cross [...].They were experiencing in themselves also the affixion of the nails [...].

---

[80] *Hist.* 6.5.

[81] Cf. Morrison, *History*, p. 47.

[82] *Vit. Patr.* 2. *prol.*; 2 Corinthians 4:10 ; Galatians 2:20.

[83] *Vit. Patr.* 8. *prol.*; also 20.1.

[84] *O admirabile mysterium Deitatis! quod artuum sepultorum puritatem manifestat saeculo, dum prodit e pavimento et praeparat ad resurrectionem, non vermi non morituro dandos, sed luci solis claritati aequandos, ac dominici corporis conformatione clarificandos* (*Glor. Conf.* 51).

[85] Cf. *Vit. patr.* 8.2: *ut tam antiphonis quam meditationibus diversis, ut devotio flagitabat animi, posset implere.* See also *In psal.* 42: *Quod ipse [Christus] sit in quem per splendorem me...is* [the MS is unclear here] *debeamus in matutinis meditationibus exercere.*

(*Aspiciebant enim per illos mentis internae oculos Dominum coelorum descendisse ad terras[..].aspiciebant pendentem in patibulo [...]. Habebant in se et clavorum affixionem [...]*).[86]

Through mental images, then, saints introduced Christ's experience into their own hearts and bodies: "they carried nothing unworthy of His omnipotence in the dwelling of their bodies (*nihil indignum eius omnipotentiae in corporis sui habitatione gerebant*)". And thus:

> [i]n these men shone also that extraordinary light of the Resurrection (*resurrectionis lumen*), with which the angel shone, when he rolled back the stone from the tomb [...] and with which Jesus also was resplendent when, unexpectedly, he stood in the midst of the meeting of the apostles' senate [...].[87]

The notion of mental and physical renewal or recreation through mental images recurs further on in the same preface. There Gregory says that saint Illidius merited to be made, in this life, a "temple of the Holy Spirit"[88] by placing "the words of life" (*verba vitae*) – almost certainly accompanied by images – "in the tabernacle of his heart". Elsewhere, Gregory lets the Psalmist's words about God, "He sent His word and healed them (*Misit verbum suum et sanavit eos*)", be allegorically interpreted by King Chilperic as "For these things [the psalmist] said of the people, that is reborn in Him through faith (*qui in eum per fidem renascitur*)".[89] All this shows that the three meanings of the notion of the word – that as an element of human language, also when uttered by God; that as the creating dimension of the Divinity; and that as the embodied Christ – cannot be disentangled. Literal and metaphorical sense, visible and invisible, man and God, coalesce. As we saw: Christ – the Creator and the Wisdom of God – is the inmost indweller of all.

It was only through their internal assimilation to Christ, the Creator, too, that saints could perform miracles. This is evident when, after a miraculous cure, Gregory lets the hermit Hospitius say:

---

[86] *Vit. Patr.* 2. *prol.*

[87] *Vit. Patr.* 2. *prol.* Mark 16:4–5; Luke 24:36–49.

[88] *Ibid.*, referring to 1 Corinthians 6:19.

[89] *Hist.* 6.5; Psalm 107:20.

> "Be silent! Be silent, most beloved brother! It is not I who do these things, but He Who made the world out of nothing, Who became a human being for us [...] and grants ever-flowing (*adfluens*) means of healing to all the sick".[90]

The adjectival image of ever-flowing evokes the analogical one of Christ as the generative Fount of Life (*fons vitae*), mentioned elsewhere by Gregory.[91] Evidently, creativity can operate in human beings only through the internalization of the image of Christ, the Creator.

What we see here, then, is that a miraculous cure is said to be a micro-image – or, as Gregory himself would phrase it, a "sign" – of the dynamic spiritual pattern of ongoing physical and spiritual Creation. As such, it manifests the glory of Christ as Creator and Redeemer through the human body.[92]

C. *Seeing Christ's glory in miraculous cures*

Augustine writes: "For, just as human custom talks by means of words, Divine Power does so through facts (*nam sicut humana consuetudo verbis ita divina potentia etiam factis loquitur*)".[93] Miracles are "like visible words, one might say, signifying something (*quasi verba, si dici potest, visibilia et aliquid significantia*)",[94] "so that we may admire the invisible God through visible things (*ut invisibilem Deum per visibilia opera miraremur*)".[95] He continues:

> But it is not enough only to look at these things in Christ's miracles. We ask these miracles what they tell us about Christ; for if they are understood, they have their own language. For since Christ himself is the Word of God, even a deed of the Word is a word to us (*Nec tamen sufficit haec intueri in miraculis Christi. Interrogamus ipsa miracula, quid nobis loquantur de Christo; habent*

---

[90] *Hist.* 6.6.

[91] *In Psal.* 35.

[92] Cf. Eugen Drewermann, *Tiefenpsychologie und Exegese* 2 (Olten 1985), p. 209.

[93] Augustinus, *Epistola* 102.33: *Aurelii Augustini Epistolae*, ed. Al. Goldbacher, Corpus Scriptorum Ecclesiasticorum Latinorum [CSEL] 34 (Prague etc. 1885). Compare Gregory: *Quid longis sermocinationum intentionibus fatigamur? factis rei veritas approbetur* (*Glor. mart.* 80) – an ordeal by boiling water decides the case.

[94] *Sermo* 77.5.7, PL 38 (Paris 1845), col. 486.

[95] *Tract.* 24.1.

> *enim si intelligantur, linguam suam. Nam quia ipse Christus Verbum Dei est, etiam factum Verbi, verbum nobis est*).[96]

As such, then, a miracle may present the verbal teaching of the Christian Church in visible, embodied form.

Gregory says something similar. For him, however, the miracle is not, primarily, a verbal message, but an image of embodied experience that can, in its turn, effect transformation. This becomes clear in the following passage, in which he tells us that besides his teaching and his Church, Christ also gives our wounded body-selves two other – non-verbal – 'remedies': the examples of the lives of the saints, and their miracles, predominantly cures. And, therefore,

> [j]ust as the prudent queen [of Sheba], who came to hear the wisdom (*audire sapientiam*) of Solomon, [the blessed lady Monegund] came to the church of blessed Martin, so that she might gaze in wonder at his miracles (*miracula [...] miraretur*), granted in daily moments, and so that she might drink from the priestly fount (*fons*) that which could open [for her] the gate of the grove of Paradise.[97]

Contemplating in awe the embodied, enacted glory of Christ as the Truth of Creation is receiving the teaching of the Word in a perceptual image, without words. The seeing of this image itself, Gregory evidently believes, can bring about the generative activity in the mind or heart that produces – and, as generativity, perhaps itself *is* – what Gregory designated as the experience of the 'knowledge' of perfect faith.

Phrases occurring in stories of cures such as "born anew (*denuo renatum*)" and "to be born anew in this world (*renasci denuo ... in mundum*)"[98] show that (re)creation, implicitly associated with the Resurrection, is a central image in Gregory's thinking about them. At the same time, however, the image of the spring (associated, of course, with Christ as the Fount of Life) is superimposed upon the saint's miraculous activity.[99] For through his

---

[96] *Tract.* 24.2.

[97] *Vit. Patr.* 19.*prol.*

[98] Respectively *Virt. Mart.* 1.40 and 2.13.

[99] This image recurs in Gregory's miracle stories as that of perpetually burning lamps: see G. de Nie, "A broken lamp or the effluence of holy power? Common sense and belief reality in Gregory of Tours' own experience", *Mediävistik* 3 (1990), pp. 269–279. It may be a God-symbol: cf. A.O. Lovejoy, *The Great Chain of Being. A Study in the History of an Idea* (New York 1936; 1960), p. 49, speaking of the late antique notion of the Divinity as "Self-

saints, as we saw, it is Christ the Creator who heals. What Gregory is saying, then, is that witnessing a miraculous cure is internalizing an image or visible pattern of the continuous Creation which brings about – generates – a subsequent re-creation in the viewer. In modern psychological terms: the affective mimesis of the perceived dynamic pattern – that is: the creative "leap" at the moment of healing – in the visible event, replicates the latter experience in the viewer.

The image evoked by words heard about eternal life, then, can induce an experience of eternal life, and thus access it; and the non-verbal experience of seeing a miraculous cure itself can cause this micro-Creation to be replicated in the viewer, thereby also accessing the continuous recreation that is eternal life. To return now to Gregory's reason for writing: what about *stories* of such miraculous cures?

III. Re-creation through the word

Gregory shows us – and this must also be implied in his preface to the *In gloria martyrum* – that the hearing of stories about such miraculous cures can effect the same: another miracle. The healing of man's wounded body is one of the main themes of his work as a whole. Elsewhere, I have investigated the models and dynamics of cures in some detail.[100] Here, I will consider briefly how, as Gregory tells it, physical cures could be precipitated by a story told in a liturgical context. In the following report, the story of one of Martin's miracles read during the liturgy could well have been one of Gregory's own:

> Neither will I keep silent about what our patron [St Martin] did on his feast day. A certain girl from the court, who had been struck with a humour of paralysis, was reduced to being unable to walk, so that through the contracted nerves in her knees, she held her heels against her thighs. Her father brought her to Tours and devoutly placed her before the feet (*ante pedes*) of the blessed Martin; there she lay for three months, and begged alms from passers-by.
>
> On the day of the distinguished ceremony of the blessed man [St Martin], it happened however that, while we were saying mass, she was faithfully praying in the place we mentioned earlier. When we, celebrating the sacrosanct

Transcending Fecundity". The spring of eternal life is mentioned in John 4:14. Christ is referred to as the Spring in Eucherius, *Formulae* 7.

[100] De Nie, *Views*, pp. 227–251.

solemnities in the ordinary manner, were telling a story about the testimony of the miracles of our holy lord (*contestationem de sancti domni virtutibus narraremus*), she suddenly began to shout and wail, showing that she was being tortured. And when, after the testimony had been completed and all the people proclaimed the *Sanctus* in praise of the Lord, her bound nerves were at once loosed, and she stood up on her feet, while all the people were watching. And thus, through the favour of the Lord (*propitiante Domino*), she came on her own two feet without leaning on anyone to the holy altar to receive communion. Up to this day she has remained well.[101]

Gregory's "telling a story" of an earlier miracle (did he use his tersely written ones as notes for oral, on-the-spot improvisations?[102]) here coincided with the sudden onset of the crisis that often precedes a miraculous cure.[103] The community's "proclamation" of the Sanctus – in which the whole earth is said to be full of the glory of the Lord – coincided with the girl's definitive liberation from her constriction, so that she could go unaided to participate in the Eucharist. The latter, as Peter Brown has pointed out, is a reintegration into the community, and, as such, a powerful motive for re-achieving health.[104] In a contemporary African oral culture, healing is similarly experienced as a renewed integration with oneself, the group and the cosmos.[105] One story of Gregory's tells us that a cure took place just after the Eucharist – one may assume that it began to happen during that rite.[106] Being able to join in the community's recitation of the Lord's Prayer may have been a similar incentive for a mute woman who found her voice precisely at that moment.[107] Gregory records that in three cases a cure coincided with the celebration of mass.[108]

In one case, the description is more specific: "And when (*cumque*) the clergy began to sing the praise of David's song, a sweet odour came into the

---

[101] *Virt. Mart.* 2.14.

[102] I owe this suggestion to my co-Fellow at the N.I.A.S., Professor D. Ogden of the Department of Dramatic Art, University of California at Berkeley.

[103] De Nie, *Views*, pp. 250–251.

[104] P. Brown, *The cult of the saints. Its rise and function in Latin Christianity*, Haskell Lectures on the History of Religions, N.S. 2 (Chicago 1981), p. 112.

[105] Special thanks are due to my co-Fellow at the N.I.A.S., Professor R. Devisch of the University of Louvain, for permission to read there a draft of the final chapter of his *Weaving the Threads of Life. The Khita Gyn-Eco-Logical Healing Cult Among the Yaka* (Chicago 1993).

[106] *Virt. Mart.* 2.25.

[107] *Virt. Mart.* 2.30.

[108] *Virt. Mart.* 2.13, 4.18 and *Glor. Conf.* 93.

church of the saint, and the man was raised up healthy by the straightening of his legs".[109] In two other cases, Gregory tells us that cures took place upon hearing the words in St Martin's *Life*: "When (*Cum*) the reader, ... having picked up the book, had begun to read (*coepisset legere*) the *Life* of the holy confessor", and "while (*dum*) miracles (*virtutes*) from his *Life* were being read (*legerentur*)".[110] And in one, last, case, Gregory reports the cure "after mass", "at the moment that (*cum*) ... the people began to receive the sacrosanct body of the Redeemer".[111] It then being the feast day of the saint, however, this service must have included readings or stories about the saint's deeds and miracles.[112]

What we see in these stories about stories, is words about a miracle (or about the unlimited power of God) producing a miracle. Words – or rather, as I hope to have shown: what is likely to have been the images evoked by the words – transform not only minds but also bodies. Such events have not stopped happening today. In Clifford Geertz's concept of religion as a cultural system, the reciting of a myth – a story – by an authority in a ritual context (when mental distancing and critical inspection would be put aside) presents the worshipper with not only a model *of* the "really real", but also a model *for* what he calls "producing" this reality in the perception of the listener.[113] In a different sphere, the practical evidence of psychotherapy shows that certain visualizations can help make serious illnesses disappear, sometimes in an exceedingly short time.[114] In contemporary oral cultures, the same happens through the acting out in ritual of metaphors of transgressive situations such as death and rebirth, which are experienced as potent spiritual realities by the participants: the images effect not only mental but also physical transformation – cures.[115] All this is exactly what we see happening in the last-mentioned stories of Gregory's.

He himself, however, might have worded it as follows. Not only is Christ's body itself the model for human renewal, but in the miracles of the Gospel, the Word as Creator, having taken on a human body, re-created human soul-bodies into wholeness or new life. Christ continues this re-

[109] *Glor. Conf.* 94.

[110] *Virt. Mart.* 2.49 and 2.29 respectively.

[111] *Virt. Mart.* 2.47.

[112] As indicated in *Virt. Mart.* 2.14 above.

[113] C. Geertz, "Religion as a cultural system", in: idem, *The Interpretation of Cultures* (New York 1973), pp. 93, 103–118, 112.

[114] B.S. Siegel, *Love, medicine and miracles. Lessons learned about self-healing from a surgeon's experience with exceptional patients* (New York 1986), passim.

[115] See Devisch, "Mbwoolu cosmogony".

creation after his Resurrection through the miracles done by his saints. When such experiences are re-presented – made present again – through the verbal language of imaged narratives, Christ, as the Creating Word, is present in these words. Those who, through these words, receive him into their hearts in the image of the visible miracle – which makes the dynamic moment of the Creation visible – are recreated by and in this very experience.

I do not think it is going too far to attribute such thinking to our sixth-century bishop. As a priest, he would be familiar with the notion that words spoken in a liturgical context – such as the consecration of the bread and wine – can bring divine presence into a material object and so into the believer's heart. In addition, he shows us elsewhere how the touching of the written letters of an as yet unread miracle story cured a deacon's physical blindness.[116] Here again, we see that Gregory regards representations – words as well as images, and even written letters themselves – as participating in that to which they point. In other words, for Gregory, the divine creative dynamic is literally immanent in the very words – spoken and written – which are used to communicate it. The Creator, who is also the divine Word, dwells in all of creation, including human words about spiritual realities, as its inmost inhabitant.

Conclusion: the image in the word

To conclude: I have tried to show that Gregory regards his verbal configuration, or icon, of a miracle not only as representing, but also as participating in, the divine creativity which it makes visible. Translated into modern terms: when a visualized pattern of emotional energy in which the body is essentially implicated is introduced into the mind through the stimulus of a text, it induces an analogously patterned interior experience. This experience can bring about emotional change such as a conversion or a "rebirth in faith", but also – as appears from reports of cures taking place after the liturgical reading of miracle stories – physical change that is analogous to the event's symbolic form.

Divine Truth being invisible, it can be represented only indirectly through the description of transformations in sensory phenomena. A divine dynamic pattern becomes accessible to human cognition through being embodied and

[116] *Vit. Patr.* 8.12.

enacted in a story. And it becomes accessible to human experience by its being re-enacted in the reader or listener. For in the latter, the imagistic dynamics in the verbal language of the story can induce an analogous transforming experience – or miracle.

For Gregory, then, the miracle in the language about miracle is the transforming image of the dynamic pattern of Creation.

INDEX

of Subjects, *Persons* and **Authors**